THE WAR MINISTRY OF WINSTON CHURCHILL

The War Ministry of WINSTON CHURCHILL

MAXWELL PHILIP SCHOENFELD

The Iowa State University Press / Ames, Iowa

MAXWELL PHILIP SCHOENFELD is Associate Professor of History at the University of Wisconsin, Eau Claire. He earned the B.A. degree at Allegheny College and the M.A. and Ph.D. degrees at Cornell University. His special interest is modern British history; he has written on topics in politics, administration, and military affairs.

Library of Congress Cataloging in Publication Data
Schoenfeld, Maxwell Philip, 1936–
The war ministry of Winston Churchill.
Bibliography: p.
1. Churchill, Sir Winston Leonard Spencer, 1874–1965. 2. World War, 1939–1945—Gt. Brit. 3. Gt. Brit.—Foreign relations—1936–1945. I. Title. DA566.9.C5S36 942.084
72–153159 ISBN 0–8138–0260–1

Maps on pages xvi–xix are from With Prejudice *by Lord Tedder, © Cassell and Company Ltd., London, and are used with permission.*

Composed and printed by
The Iowa State University Press

First edition, 1972

THIS BOOK IS FOR MY STUDENTS WHO ASKED FOR IT
AND IS DEDICATED TO A GREAT TEACHER

FREDERICK GEORGE MARCHAM

WHO TAUGHT ME THE WISDOM OF JOHN COLET'S LINE:
"Teche that thou hast lern'd lovyngly"

LIVERPOOL POLYTECHNIC LIBRARY
3 1111 00078 5913
SCHOENFELD, M.P
WAR MINISTRY OF WINSTON CHURCHILL
T M 942.084 CHU 1972

CONTENTS

PREFACE

THIS BOOK grew out of a senior honors seminar on Sir Winston Churchill in which I discovered that a man who was a living person to me was almost entirely a historical figure to my students. Further, I discovered that they held some views of Churchill's career that perhaps sprang more from American popular political lore than from historical study and a careful examination of the records of the Churchillian era. I thought it desirable, therefore, to provide an essay on Churchill's war ministry which might serve as an introduction for the beginning student and as a suggested interpretation of that ministry which the more advanced university student could test against his study of the record of the period.

This is not a biography of Winston Churchill during the period 1940–45. That task belongs to the appropriate volumes of the official biography as they appear. I have omitted much from his career in this period and have pulled to the fore those events and decisions to which I wish to direct attention. This book is not in any way a substitute for the great riches that await the student in the six volumes of Churchill's memoirs of World War II.

I hope I have been as fair in the judgment of men and opinions in this account as Sir Winston was in his own. The decisions made and the actions taken in the Second World War retain today much of the heat of controversy they acquired when they were forged amid the stresses of those strenuous years. It is my theme that the men—political and military, British and American—who led the Western Alliance in that time, for all their failings and differences and difficulties, ordered their conduct by a high standard of conviction and personal integrity. If, in describing their differences, stating the issues which from time to time divided them, and presenting the arguments their particular postwar advocates have put forward, I have seemed unfair, I hope this defect will be laid against my deficient craftsmanship rather than attributed to an intentional bias. I have not attempted to mask my own views. The era is too storm-tossed, its events too significant in their impact upon our own time and too close to us in human perspective, for me to claim a position of historical dispassion which I do not occupy. The reader, therefore, is urged to bring his own critical facilities to the evaluation of this work. There is now available a substantial literature of official histories, written particularly on the British side by historians of great experience and eminence, and of personal accounts, written by those men who bore the burden of decisions, to supply the critical reader with evidence for his own conclusions.

The reader should bear in mind that behind the official histories, themselves not yet complete, stand the vast records of government archives extensive beyond the mastery of any one man. The United Kingdom archives for this period are only now becoming available for examination by independent scholars. We may hope and anticipate that there will soon begin to appear the first generation of monographic studies which will both deepen and in some respects correct our understanding of the period. The reader should also understand that the official histories do not imply a government interpretation of the events of the era. The judgments offered and conclusions reached are those of the individual scholars, who are responsible for them according to the generally recognized standards of scholarly integrity as understood in Western societies.

Certain problems will remain. We are not likely to learn much more than we have from the Soviet government. The deaths in harness of Franklin D. Roosevelt, Sir John Dill, and Sir Dudley Pound—to cite only the most obvious cases—leave us with permanent gaps in our knowledge, particularly of motives and reasons for decisions which the official papers only record. Yet for all these deficiencies, the record of what happened is now sufficiently well established that it is not likely to undergo major revision. Our interpretations of that basic account, however, are likely to remain a battleground of conflicting ideological viewpoints, of divergent national attitudes, of fond desires butting against unpleasant realities, and of honest differences of thoughtful men struggling to understand the world they have inherited.

I wish to thank Dr. Lester W. Hunt for the encouragement and support he gave me in the writing of this book. Mrs. Mary Jane Curran struggled ably to translate my illegible hand into intelligible notes. Mrs. Mary Lou Albrecht, Mrs. Cecilia Bilbrey, and Mrs. Sheri Jackson patiently and skillfully produced the typescript of this account. I am particularly indebted to my good friend and gifted colleague Dr. Robert S. Fraser for a meticulous reading of the entire manuscript, his careful criticism, and his wise advice. The dedication of this book is properly his too, for we began our academic careers together as teaching assistants at Cornell University under the guidance of Frederick George Marcham.

M.P.S.

EAU CLAIRE, WISCONSIN
December, 1970

CODE NAMES

OPERATIONS

TORCH	Invasion of French Northwest Africa in November 1942
OVERLORD	Invasion of France at Normandy in June 1944
DRAGOON	Invasion of southern France in August 1944 (originally named Anvil)
BUCCANEER	Planned capture of the Andaman Islands in the Bay of Bengal

CONFERENCES

ARCADIA	Washington, December 1941
TRIDENT	Washington, May 1943
QUADRANT	Quebec, August 1943
OCTAGON	Quebec, September 1944

CHRONOLOGY

1939

AUGUST 23	Molotov-Ribbentrop pact
SEPTEMBER 1	Germany invades Poland

1940

APRIL 9	Germany invades Denmark and Norway
MAY 10	Churchill becomes Prime Minister; Germany attacks in West
MAY 23–JUNE 4	BEF evacuated from Dunkirk
JUNE 22	France and Germany conclude armistice
SEPTEMBER 15	Battle of Britain ends in RAF victory
NOVEMBER 5	Roosevelt elected to third term

1941

MARCH 4–MAY 1	Unsuccessful British expedition to Greece
MAY 6–7	Commons debates war; sustains government, 477–3
MAY 20–27	Germany captures Crete
MAY 24	*Bismarck* sinks *Hood,* is sunk in turn three days later
JUNE 22	Germany invades Russia
JULY 1	Auchinleck replaces Wavell in Middle East Command
AUGUST 9–12	Atlantic Charter meeting
DECEMBER 7–8	Japan attacks US and UK in Pacific
DECEMBER 22–JANUARY 16, 1942	Washington (Arcadia) Conference
DECEMBER 25	Brooke becomes CIGS

1942

JANUARY 27–29	Commons debates war; sustains government, 464–1
FEBRUARY 15	Singapore surrenders
FEBRUARY 19–24	Major War Cabinet reorganization
FEBRUARY 22	Harris appointed to Bomber Command
JUNE 4–7	US naval victory at Midway
JUNE 19–25	Churchill in US; allied strategy debated
JUNE 21	Rommel captures Tobruk
JULY 1–2	Commons debate; vote of no confidence defeated, 475–25
AUGUST 4–10	Churchill and Brooke in Cairo, replace Auchinleck with Alexander-Montgomery team
AUGUST 12–15	Churchill in Moscow; second-front issue discussed
OCTOBER 23–NOVEMBER 4	Montgomery defeats Rommel in battle of El Alamein
NOVEMBER 8	Allied landings in French Northwest Africa (Torch)

1943

JANUARY 14–25	Casablanca Conference
JANUARY 31	Battle of Stalingrad ends in Russian victory
MAY 12	Last Axis forces in North Africa surrender in Tunisia
MAY 12–25	Washington (Trident) Conference
JULY 10	Allies invade Sicily
AUGUST 14–24	Quebec (Quadrant) Conference
AUGUST 25	SEAC set up; Mountbatten named commander
SEPTEMBER 8	Italian government surrenders
SEPTEMBER 9	Salerno and Rhodes landings
SEPTEMBER 12	British evacuate Rhodes
OCTOBER 14	USAAF losses heavy in Schweinfurt raid
NOVEMBER 22–DECEMBER 7	Cairo and Teheran conferences; Buccaneer canceled

1944

JANUARY 22	Anzio landing
JUNE 4	Allies enter Rome
JUNE 6	Normandy landings (Overlord)

August 1–October 3	Warsaw rising
August 15	Allied landings in southern France (Dragoon)
August 19–25	Paris liberated
September 11–19	Quebec (Octagon) Conference
September 25–26	Attack at Arnhem fails; western front stalls
October 9–17	Churchill in Moscow; postwar Europe discussed
December 7–8	Commons debates intervention in Greece; sustains government, 281–32
December 16–January 16, 1945	Battle of the Bulge
December 25–28	Churchill in Athens

1945

February 4–11	Yalta Conference
February 13–14	Dresden bombed heavily
April 12	Roosevelt dies; Truman becomes President
May 8	Germany surrenders
May 23	Coalition ends; Churchill forms caretaker government
July 17–August 2	Potsdam Conference
July 26	Churchill's war ministry ends; Attlee becomes Prime Minister
August 6	US drops A-bomb on Hiroshima
August 14	Japan surrenders

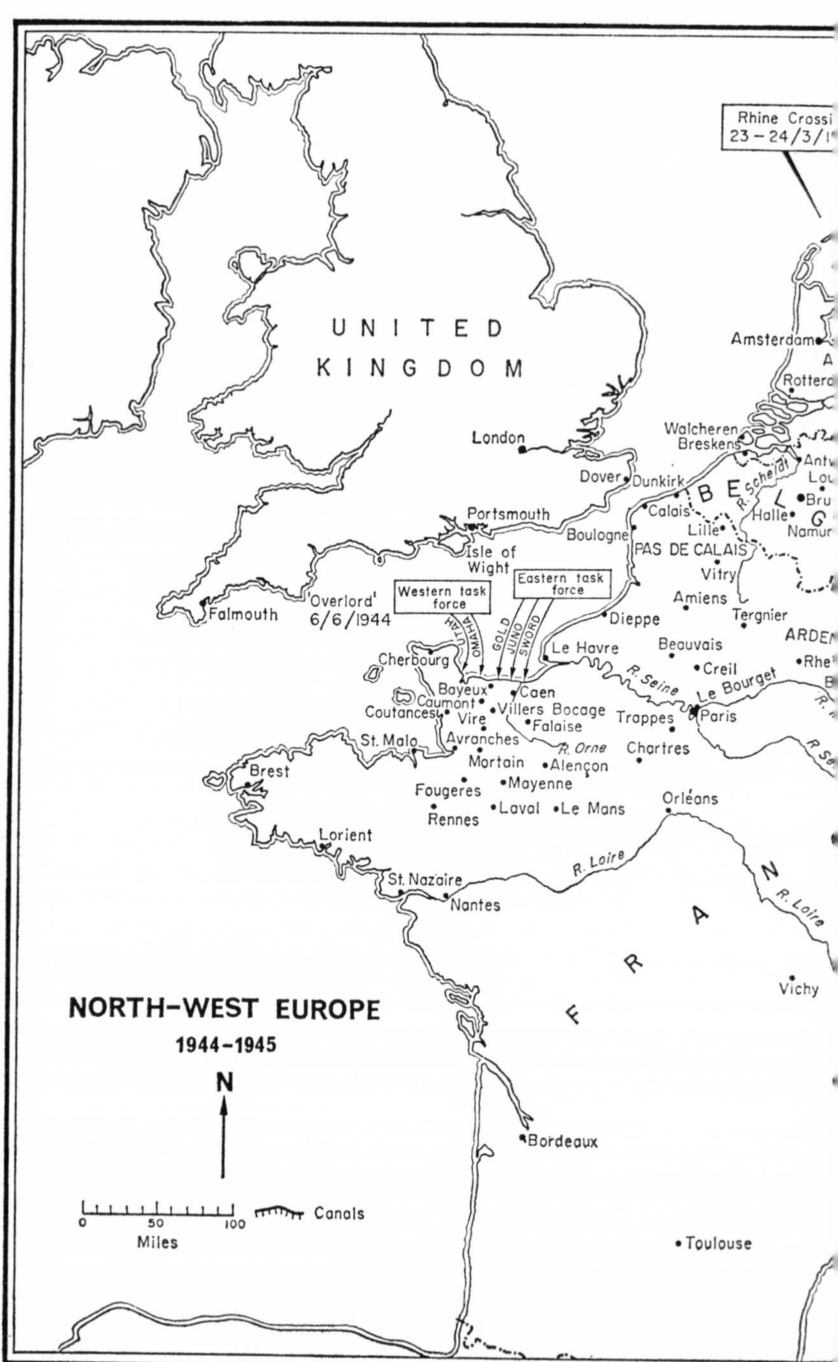
NORTH-WEST EUROPE
1944-1945
N
0
50
100
Miles
Canals
UNITED KINGDOM
London
Dover
Portsmouth
Isle of Wight
Falmouth
'Overlord' 6/6/1944
Western task force
Eastern task force
UTAH
OMAHA
GOLD
JUNO
SWORD
Cherbourg
Bayeux
Caen
Caumont
Coutances
Vire
Villers Bocage
Falaise
St. Malo
Avranches
R. Orne
Mortain
Alençon
Brest
Fougeres
Mayenne
Rennes
Laval
Le Mans
Lorient
St. Nazaire
Nantes
R. Loire
Bordeaux
Toulouse
Vichy
Orléans
Chartres
Trappes
Paris
Le Bourget
R. Seine
Creil
Beauvais
Le Havre
Dieppe
Amiens
Tergnier
Vitry
PAS DE CALAIS
Boulogne
Calais
Dunkirk
Lille
Halle
Namur
R. Scheldt
Walcheren
Breskens
Amsterdam
Rhine Crossi
23-24/3/1
F R A N

POLAND
Keil
Lübeck
Hamburg
R. Elbe
Berlin
R. Weser
Stendal
Mittelland
Brunswick
Wittenberg
Weser-Ems
Hanover
Magdeburg
SILESIA
Dortmund-Ems
Munster
Paderborn
Halle
Leipzig
Dresden
R. Elbe
Hamm
R. Weser
Wesel
Dortmund
Kessel
Erfurt
R. Lippe
Essen
Duisberg
R. Elbe
Dusseldorf
Karlsbad
Prague
Cologne
R. Weser
GERMANY
Bonn
CZECHOSLOVAKIA
Pilsen
Stadtkyll
EIFEL
Coblenz
Frankfurt
Prum
Bitburg
Trier
Vienna
Luxembourg
Regensburg
R. Rhine
R. Saar
Linz
Wiener Neustadt
AUSTRIA
HUNGARY
Metz
THE VOSGES
Munich
Strasbourg
Nancy
R. Moselle
Epinal
Colmar
Mulhausen
R. Rhine
SWITZERLAND
St. Vith
R. Rhône
YUGOSLAVIA
Trieste
Venice
Milan
Reggio
ITALY
Leghorn
Nice
Cannes
St. Raphael
St. Tropez
'Dragoon'
15/8/1944
Toulon
C. Bénat
CORSICA

SICILY
Bizerta
CAP BON
Tebourba
Tunis
M.el Bab
PANTELLARIA
Enfidaville
MALTA
Sousse(Susa)
LAMPEDUSA
Tebessa
Thelepte
Sfax
WADI AKARIT
M E D I T E R
Gafsa
El Hamma
Gabes
Mareth
Medenine
Kasr Rhilane
Tripoli
T U N I S I A
Buerat
Sirte
T R I P O L I T A N I A
NORTH AFRICA
L I B
0 50 100 150 200 250 MILES

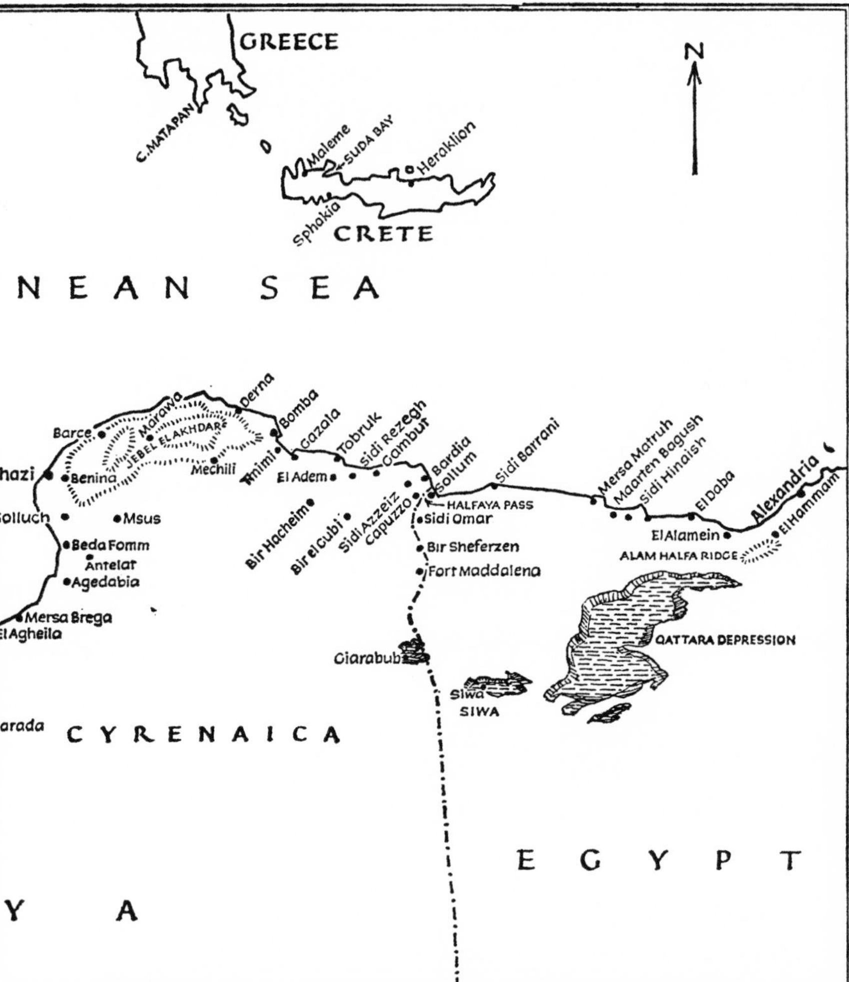

GREECE
N
C.MATAPAN
Maleme
SUDA BAY
Heraklion
Sphakia
CRETE
NEAN SEA
Derna
Bomba
Gazala
Tobruk
Sidi Rezegh
Gambut
Bardia
Sollum
Sidi Barrani
Mersa Matruh
Maaten Bagush
Sidi Hinaish
El Daba
Alexandria
El Hammam
Barce
Marawa
JEBEL EL AKHDAR
Mechili
Tmimi
El Adem
hazi
Benina
Solluch
Msus
Beda Fomm
Antelat
Agedabia
Mersa Brega
El Agheila
Bir Hacheim
Bir el Gubi
Sidi Azzeiz
Capuzzo
HALFAYA PASS
Sidi Omar
Bir Sheferzen
Fort Maddalena
El Alamein
ALAM HALFA RIDGE
QATTARA DEPRESSION
Giarabub
Siwa
SIWA
arada
CYRENAICA
EGYPT
Y A

THE WAR MINISTRY OF WINSTON CHURCHILL

1 / THE MAKING OF THE PRIME MINISTER

WHEN WAR CAME to Great Britain in the early days of September 1939, it brought the return to public office of Winston Churchill. His return was in effect a pledge that the Chamberlain government would prosecute the war against Hitler vigorously, for Churchill was no ordinary man and no ordinary civilian minister. He was well read in military history and had seen active military service in his youth and again during World War I. Except for the Foreign Office he had held all the great civil offices concerned with the waging of war—President of the Board of Trade, Home Secretary, First Lord of the Admiralty, Secretary of State for War and Air, Colonial Secretary, and Chancellor of the Exchequer.

At the outbreak of World War II Churchill was approaching his sixty-fifth birthday and his personality, character, and habits were already fully formed. He presented every possible plan in oral discussion, to clear his own thinking and to test the minds of his advisers. But his final judgments were usually the result of careful study and long thought. P. J. Grigg, who had worked for Churchill in the 1920s, has described his dislike of giving snap decisions on cases stated orally. After oral discussion Churchill preferred to commit his ideas to paper, to exchange those ideas with his advisers, and then to reach an agreed decision.[1]

In his personal character Churchill was brave and steadfast. He had demonstrated extraordinary physical bravery in his youth, and his moral courage was even greater. He valued honor perhaps more than many politicians.[2] Fundamentally straightforward and simple in his outlook, he believed in the basic dignity and decency of man. On the outbreak of war he said, "We are fighting to save the whole world . . . and in defence of all that is most sacred to man."[3] Lord Beaverbrook, one of the few who knew Churchill well from the days of World War I, said of him, "He was always truthful. He could keep a secret."[4] This was not a paradox but a fact. When Churchill spoke in Parliament on the death of Lloyd George, he described the former Prime Minister as having seized the main power in the state. Some members of the House were disturbed, but Churchill did not retract his statement. But he was also discreet. In describing his first meeting with General Montgomery, he said only that the weather had been lovely and he enjoyed his outing thoroughly. But Churchill's minutes reveal that he immediately issued orders to carry out suggestions he had gained from his conversation with Montgomery.[5]

Beaverbrook once wrote of Churchill:

> He was in every sense a professional politician, having trained himself for his vocation. Impetuous in action, he was determined when resisting opposition. . . . He lived well, and ate everything. He exaggerated his drinking habits by his own remarks in praise of wine and brandy. He appeared to smoke cigars incessantly. Not at all. He smoked very little, although relighting a cigar frequently. His use of matches outstripped his consumption of cigars.[6]

Above all, Churchill lived the life of a completely public man in his interests.[7] He could resent attacks on his public policy as if they were attacks on his private life. He did not particularly possess what we could call a sense of humor; he was too much the man of affairs for that. At the end of a long political life which many might envy, Churchill expressed regret at having finally to lay down the burden of office.[8] His emotions were strong and ran deep, although they also sprang swiftly to the surface. He could weep openly in public and did so on many notable occasions. He could be swept up by his emotions and by the power of his own rhetoric, but in the end he usually acted on the basis of cold facts with shrewd political judgment.[9]

He was a man of many moods. Beaverbrook once said, "What a creature of strange moods he is—always at the top of the wheel of confidence or at the bottom of an intense depression."[10] But Beaverbrook also warned, "Churchill on top of the wave has in him the stuff of which tyrants are made." And perhaps he did. Beaverbrook also admitted that Churchill was without malice and was never treacherous.[11] John Colville, who served Churchill as Assistant Private Secretary during the war, agreed with Beaverbrook: "Once his affection was given it lasted, but his animosity was transitory and it was not in his nature to bear a grudge."[12] Churchill in power was notably kind to both Stanley Baldwin and Neville Chamberlain, neither of whom had treated him particularly well in the 1930s (the fault in Baldwin's case was not all on one side). If Churchill had a characteristic weakness, it was to rush into action too soon, although at times that could be a strength. Churchill wrote of President Beneš of Czechoslovakia, "Where he failed—and it cost him and his country much—was in not taking violent decisions at the supreme moment. He was too experienced a diplomatist, too astute a year-to-year politician, to realise the moment and to stake all on victory or death."[13]

When Churchill returned to the Admiralty, he bombarded Chamberlain with messages concerning every aspect of the war; in September 1939 Churchill was not only ready to fight but in fact armed to the teeth. He wrote,

I had enough information to convince me that Hitler recognised me as a foe. My former Scotland Yard detective, Inspector Thompson, was in retirement. I told him to come along and bring his pistol with him. I got out my own weapons, which were good. While one slept, the other watched. Thus, nobody would have had a walk over. In these hours I knew that if war came—and who could doubt its coming?—a major burden would fall upon me.[14]

Churchill brought with him into office a strong sense of history, particularly his own experiences in World War I. He had never forgotten the failure of Gallipoli or the bitter political experience that befell him after that when he lost his cabinet post. He wrote that his memories of World War I caused him to underestimate the force of the German tank attack in World War II.[15] His early experience led him to look upon the core of Germany as Prussia. He said that Nazi tyranny and Prussian militarism were the two main elements in German life which must be destroyed.[16] Both aptitude and experience pointed Churchill toward taking a broad strategic view on most military issues. His own experience was vast, and he did not hesitate to draw on that of others. With a certain amount of irony he wrote that he knew nothing about science but knew something of scientists and had much practice in handling things he did not understand.[17] His character was that of a man of courage, conviction, ability, and vigor.

From 1929 until 1939 and the outbreak of war, Churchill was out of office and faced the animosity of Tories and Labour alike. This long, lonely decade left its mark. When P. J. Grigg returned from India in March 1939, he visited Churchill at Chartwell (his country home in Kent) and found him gloomy over the German occupation of Prague but not as upset as he had expected. Churchill explained, "One cannot break one's heart more than once."[18]

The 1930s found Churchill with only a few friends, some of whom were important for the war years ahead. One of these was Frederick Lindemann, who would later be made Lord Cherwell. Lindemann was professor of experimental philosophy at Oxford University and by general agreement one of the best scientific minds of his time. Churchill would come to depend heavily on him for scientific advice. Another friend and adviser, a brave soldier from World War I, was Major Desmond Morton.[19]

Churchill had been out of step with the spirit of the 1930s, particularly the last half. As he began to warn of the future and the danger of the European dictators, British opinion showed little sympathy for his views. Public opinion rejected Churchill's warnings and preferred to ignore the threat building on the Continent; yet it was officially recognized that no adequate preparation for war could be made until there was a general recognition of the danger facing the country, popular support of the government, and a government strong enough and decisive enough to make use of that support.[20] Although Churchill was decisive, he was not popular—one reason he was omitted from the government. The war planning that did take place following the summer of 1937 continued to prepare for what was called a war of limited liability. This was unrealistic—particularly after Munich—and at the time of Prague in March 1939 the government began to recognize how great the danger facing it truly was. Churchill came to believe late in the 1930s, and retained his belief throughout the 1940s, that World War II could have been prevented. He called it the unnecessary war.[21]

Churchill's declared readiness to use force to defy tyranny made him unpopular in a pacific period. Early in 1931 he had broken with the official Conservative party over the policy of dealing with India. His break with the Tories, the second in his long political career, left him with few friends among the parliamentary majority and few on the other side of the House. He had always opposed Socialism and even, it seemed, the working classes themselves at the time of the general strike in 1926. He did not favor popular left-wing causes. In the Spanish Civil War, his position was neutral. In the late 1930s he assumed the role of chief parliamentary critic of the Chamberlain government, declaring it grossly negligent in preparing the country for war.[22]

But Churchill's break with the government was less than complete. In 1935 he was invited by the government to sit on the Air Defence Research Committee. This he undertook to do, provided Professor Lindemann would sit on the technical subcommittee. Churchill thus knew a great deal about the most important developments affecting modern warfare, including a knowledge of radar. Unfortunately, Lindemann was a difficult scientific colleague, and his professional quarrels and Churchill's insistence on his aid did nothing to make affairs move more smoothly. In spite of these difficulties, the fact remains that Churchill was one of the few politicians in Britain when war came who was equipped to make intelligent decisions based on a knowledge of the most recent scientific developments.[23]

Churchill's link with the government remained fragile. When Hitler remilitarized the Rhineland early in 1936, Churchill hoped to be recalled to office to head defense matters, but he was passed over in favor of Sir Thomas Inskip. That Churchill was hurt is revealed by his memoirs; he wrote that Inskip was "an able lawyer, who had the advantages of being little known himself and knowing nothing about military subjects."[24] Worse was to follow. When Anthony Eden resigned from the government in February 1938 in a protest over its Italian policy, Churchill reported that sleep deserted him and that from midnight until dawn, he lay in his bed, "consumed by emotions of sorrow and fear."[25] Even the oldest of Churchill's friends were prepared to turn against him at this time—including Beaverbrook. It seemed by early winter of 1938–39 that his parliamentary seat itself was in danger. He was sustained in his constituency meeting with a vote of confidence by the margin of only three to two. Those members of Parliament who distrusted or feared the government's policy did not rally around Churchill but rather around a man like Eden; so on the eve of war Churchill's position in Parliament was unique and lonely. He had served there nearly forty years and as a government minister for nearly twenty. His experience was unrivaled; his loneliness unequaled. Had he retired from public life on the eve of his sixty-fifth birthday, he may well have been written off as a spectacular failure; yet for Churchill a great career was only beginning.[26]

At the outbreak of the war, Hitler held the initiative. His pact with Russia had rendered it impossible for Britain and France to provide direct aid to Poland which was overrun and divided up in a matter of weeks. There then followed a period of relative calm while people waited and wondered where Hitler would strike next. While they waited, members of Parliament showed increasing dissatisfaction with Chamberlain's leadership. Harold Nicolson scathingly recorded in his diary, "The Prime Minister has no gift for inspiring anybody, and he might have been the Secretary of a firm of undertakers reading the minutes of the last meeting."[27] Nicolson described a friend of his reporting on the attitude of Chamberlain's front bench: "Everyone kept exclaiming, 'I wish I were twenty. I cannot bear this responsibility.' What they really mean is, 'I wish I did not know how bad things are.' "[28] One person these parliamentary critics excepted from their general dissatisfaction was Winston Churchill. Indeed they felt Churchill had been silenced by Chamberlain's inclusion of him in the government. The first secret session of the House of Commons held on December 13, 1939, revealed that parliamentary dissatisfaction was very broad. The government seemed to lack energy. Chamberlain himself did not really believe military victory possible; the best he hoped for was stalemate. The winter of 1939–40 seemed to give some substance to Chamberlain's hopes, for there was little military action except at sea.[29]

There were also problems inside Chamberlain's government, which was in some ways a combination of Chamberlain and his old critics—notably Churchill and Eden. Particularly difficult was the problem of just where Churchill fit in. His great energy, his eloquence, and his independence of mind made Churchill a difficult subordinate. He seemed to be cast on a scale which belonged in the first place and fit badly into any other. Could such an arrangement last indefinitely?

Discontent outside the government and difficulties within were pushed to a crisis by Hitler's daring attack on Norway in the spring of 1940. The official naval historian has argued convincingly that in the circumstances prevailing at the time, an expedition had to be sent by Britain to Norway in an effort to counter the German landing; but he has also sharply criticized the serious lack of coordination the government showed in the Norwegian operations. Hitler's attack on Norway produced widespread anger among the British public. After all, Britain was thought to control the seas, even if she could not face Germany on land. Worst of all for those members of Parliament who looked upon Churchill as the only man who could furnish the government with sufficient energy to carry

Britain through to victory, it was he as civilian chief of the Navy who was most vulnerable to criticism. A long debate on Norway on April 11, 1940, failed to remove discontent in the House of Commons. Friends of Churchill feared the effect on his position.[30]

By mid-April there were at least two groups functioning unofficially in the House of Commons: a group of unhappy Conservatives guided by Lord Salisbury and an all-party group chaired by the Liberal, Clement Davies. There were other groups, but these two were the most important. By early May, as it became apparent that the Norwegian effort was ending in failure, there was feeling in these groups that the time had come to try to bring down the government. Clement Attlee, the Labour leader, was asked if he would put down a vote of want of confidence. Wisely, Attlee declined, pointing out that such a vote would tend to rally Conservatives to the government, and their majority in the House of Commons was then much larger than its natural support in the country. It was decided, therefore, to oppose the government's motion for a summer adjournment, and the debate was set for May 7 and 8. On the first day two heavy blows were struck against the government. Admiral of the Fleet Sir Roger Keyes delivered the best speech of his career. The old seaman troubled the House deeply as he suggested there was serious lack of military cooperation. A very restless House then was subjected to the greatest speech of the debate, delivered by the old Conservative, Leo Amery. A man of substantial ability and a powerful debater, Amery rained blow after blow upon Chamberlain's lack of leadership. He concluded, quoting Oliver Cromwell, by telling the government that it must go.[31]

By the night of May 7 two separate but connected issues were forming. The survival of the government with sufficient support in the House of Commons now seemed very doubtful. But the second point was serious too. Could Churchill be saved from the general collapse of the government? This would be particularly difficult since it was Churchill who would deliver the final speech summing up the government's case. Churchill's position was extremely vulnerable, and it was typical of his courage and loyalty that he had accepted the difficult and dangerous task.

On May 8 Herbert Morrison announced for the opposition that the motion to adjourn would be pressed to a division. This was understood to be for all practical purposes a vote of censure. Chamberlain's reply was weak as he suggested the vote should be a party issue. Members of Parliament felt this was no time to place party above patriotism. The harshest speech of the second day was delivered by former Prime Minister David Lloyd George. He was particularly effective in separating Churchill from the rest of the front bench, but the remainder of his speech was bitter—perhaps too bitter. Duff Cooper, a former minister who also made a strong attack on the government, acted to protect Churchill. Finally, late in the evening, Churchill rose to sum up and defend the government. He forcefully delivered a powerful speech, making it clear that the prime problem the services had encountered in Norway was inability to dominate in the air. Since no man in the 1930s had warned more often of Britain's need to rearm adequately in the air than had Churchill, this weakness could not properly be blamed on him. He was repeatedly interrupted, a process he took with his usual good spirit. He concluded by calling for unity against the common enemy. The House then divided. The government was sustained by a vote of 281 to 200. Thus the majority for the government shrank to about 80 from a normal figure of about 240. Clearly a war could not be prosecuted on such a base, particularly when public opinion polls revealed that only a minority of the British public was satisfied with the conduct of the war. The questions now were, How would the government be rebuilt? Would there be a new Prime Minister? If so, who?[32]

The crisis through the night of May 8 had been a public affair. The members of Parliament had done their duty; they had broken the back of the government. But the reconstructive surgery would take place in private, and those who supported Churchill feared that what had been won in open debate on the floor of the Commons would be lost in the private rooms of Number 10 Downing Street. The Labour party leadership made it clear that they would not enter a government under Chamberlain. Another Prime Minister must be found. The two leading contenders were Churchill and Lord Halifax, the Foreign Secretary. In the afternoon of May 9, Churchill met with Halifax and Chamberlain. Chamberlain hoped that Halifax would succeed him, as did some of the Labour leadership. Halifax was preferred by King George VI also. For the Chamberlain supporters all depended on whether Churchill would cooperate with this arrangement. Chamberlain indicated to Halifax and Churchill that one of them should follow him. Churchill had received good advice before the meeting. He sat silent. In those few minutes of silence the hopes of his rivals vanished like morning mists before the burning sun. Halifax broke the silence. He admitted that his seat in the House of Lords would make his position as Prime Minister difficult. Churchill had won. But the next morning Hitler attacked in the west, and Chamberlain briefly thought he could stay on. This time a close Conservative friend in the government told him he must go. There was no sign of Labour or Liberal support for Chamberlain. That afternoon the verdict of the previous day was ratified, and at six in the evening Churchill was summoned to Buckingham Palace. With newspapers full of the crisis on the Continent, few people realized that the crisis in London had reached its conclusion. On the evening of May 10, 1940, King George VI charged Winston Churchill with the formation of a government.[33] As the Germanic storm breaking on the Continent reached hurricane force, the wheel of the British ship of state was grasped by a man equal to the intensity of events. The war ministry of Winston Churchill had begun.

Churchill's own account is revealing for its sense of constitutional and political proprieties. Churchill wrote that if he had found it impossible to come to terms with Labour and Liberals, he would have been willing to form a government along any lines that could command a majority in the House of Commons; but such a step was not necessary. Churchill met with the Labour leadership that night and arranged that Labour should occupy about one-third of the offices in the new government. This was somewhat more than their strength in the House of Commons. Churchill also recognized the importance of conciliating the Chamberlain Conservatives who made up a clear majority of the House. He needed their support as much as he needed the support of the opposition parties. The formation of the government required great political skill. It would have to incorporate men who had only shortly before exchanged the harshest of words. That Churchill was successful in his cabinet building is a testimony to his ability, the crisis of the moment, and the standard of public service which prevailed among British politicians.[34]

Chamberlain was magnanimous. He agreed to serve under Churchill and became Lord President of the Council, but not Leader of the House of Commons as Churchill had wished, for Labour objected to this. Lord Halifax remained Foreign Secretary. These two, Churchill, and the two Labour leaders—Clement Attlee as Lord Privy Seal and Arthur Greenwood as Minister without Portfolio—made up the War Cabinet. The three service ministers were A. V. Alexander, a Labour former First Lord who now returned to the Admiralty; Archibald Sinclair, the Liberal leader who became Secretary of State for Air; and Anthony Eden, Conservative, who became Secretary of State for War. A broadly based national coalition government was thus achieved by Churchill.[35]

When the House of Commons assembled again on May 13, Chamberlain was more loudly cheered than Churchill. Churchill would have to prove his right to occupy the first place. The first of his great wartime speeches delivered that day was a strong beginning.[36]

The political crisis of early May 1940 remains one of the triumphant moments of parliamentary democracy. The system by which Britain was governed proved capable of finding a leader equal to the gravest of challenges. The crisis had been particularly a parliamentary one, not brought on by any great or violent public protest. The general dissatisfaction felt by the public was not intensely focused. The political crisis had been brought on by members of Parliament who were convinced that the situation could not be allowed to continue unchanged. The old arrangements had been terminated entirely in a parliamentary manner. The crisis was a triumph of political democracy as much as a triumph of parliamentary institutions, for the new government (and in particular Churchill's right to command the first place) had depended ultimately on Churchill's position with the British people. This was why his silence on May 9 had been so significant. Had he stood out against a reconstructed government, that government would have faced the British people only at great peril. The same qualities which had made Churchill so unacceptable to the public in the 1930s made him the public choice in May of 1940. Thus the most critical political episode of World War II—unlike the government reconstructions of World War I—took place with a minimum of political intrigue and in accordance with the highest standards of parliamentary democracy. The institutions of political freedom had justified their right to be defended by summoning as their leader a man fit to wrestle victory out of adversity.

2 / THE POLITICIAN

During the summer battle for France, Charles de Gaulle met Churchill for the first time. He found a man "equal to the rudest task, provided it had also grandeur." De Gaulle described the new British Prime Minister as "well tried in politics," and he felt that Churchill possessed "a mastery . . . of the terrible game in which he was engaged."[1] De Gaulle's instinct was accurate. Churchill was first of all a politician and indeed equal to the terrible game. How terrible quickly became evident. Before Churchill was Prime Minister a month, the British Expeditionary Force had been thrown off the Continent, the back of the French army broken, and the French will to resist smashed. By autumn of 1940 the regular bombing of British cities, particularly London, had begun. The British Communists were quick to solicit signatures to peace petitions. Peace on what terms was not made clear. Only an optimist could see a way to victory or even a way to survive. Almost the only bright moment was provided by the escape of the British army at Dunkirk. That had been, to be sure, something less than a victory; but it was also something more than a defeat.[2]

Churchill described the conditions of the people he had to view every day as he went about his tasks in London: Large areas were deprived by bombing damage of gas or electricity or both; sometimes there was no water; often railways were cut; whole districts, particularly working-class areas, were destroyed by fire. In these circumstances Churchill chose the wisest course. He proposed to follow the advice he had given to the government at the time of Munich—to tell the people the truth.[3] And Churchill told the truth to a people who needed at least the certainty that they knew the worst; for in a fight for existence itself, uncertainty was the most terrible of all enemy weapons. The British people, by and large, responded with a courage equal to Churchill's own, and Churchill announced from the beginning that victory would come—however long and hard the struggle—in time.[4] So Britain prepared to face the threat of invasion and the punishment of nightly bombings, secured by the presence of the men who had returned from the beaches of Dunkirk, defended by the Royal Air Force (RAF) fighting over their heads, and sustained by the strong words of their chosen leader who told them they would not yield until they had achieved victory.

Every speech of Churchill's that autumn was a great one. He had begun on May 13, telling the House that he had nothing to offer them but "blood, toil, tears and sweat," and he went on to proclaim that the aim of the government was victory. He said he took up his task "with buoyancy and hope. I feel sure that our cause will not be suffered to fail among men."[5] Six days later, in case anyone had failed to grasp how far-reaching the change was in British leadership, Churchill announced, "The interests of property, the hours of labour, are nothing compared with the struggle for life and honour, for right and freedom, to which we have vowed ourselves."[6] After Dunkirk on June 4, he proclaimed,

> We shall go on to the end, we shall fight in France, we shall fight on the seas and oceans, we shall fight with growing confidence and growing strength in the air, we shall defend our island, whatever the cost may be, we shall fight on the beaches, we shall fight on the landing-grounds, we shall fight in the fields and in the streets, we shall fight in the hills; we shall never surrender, and even if, which I do not for a moment believe, this island or a large part of it were subjugated and starving, then our Empire beyond the seas, armed and guarded by the British Fleet, would carry on the struggle, until, in God's good time, the New World, with all its power and might, steps forth to the rescue and the liberation of the Old.[7]

The almost Elizabethan cadence of Churchill's language and the power of his resolve sustained courage amid the evidences of military ruin. On June 18 he called the British people to "their finest hour"[8]; on July 14 he declared this war a war of unknown warriors, a war of every person, and he called on them to strive "without failing in faith or in duty."[9] His resolution was infectious. It recalled to Harold Nicolson the lines of Horace's Ode: "If the whole world were to crack and collapse about him, its ruins would find him unafraid."[10] On October 21 Churchill broadcast to the French people then under German domination: "We are waiting for the long promised invasion. So are the fishes."[11] His concluding words offered a ray of light amid darkness, "Good night then: sleep to gather strength for the morning. For the morning will come. Brightly will it shine on the brave and true, kindly upon all who suffer for the cause, glorious upon the tombs of heroes. Thus will shine the dawn."[12]

Churchill drew upon the grim events themselves for inspiration. Lord Ismay tells us that Churchill found the phrase "Never in the field of human conflict has so much been owed by so many to so few" while he was viewing the air battle at an RAF headquarters.[13] But the larger inspiration lay within the man himself, for the virtues he stressed in his speeches were his own virtues or those to which he aspired and, more successfully than most men, achieved. Harold Nicolson listed the most important: tenderness; humor; a sense of language; a sense of fitness;

great-heartedness; pertinacity; courage; and the capacity to love, hate, and forgive.[14] In May 1942, when Churchill had completed two years as Prime Minister, he expressed the opinion that his speeches of 1940 had been only the expression of a national resolve. Perhaps so, but that resolve had slumbered until Churchill gave voice to it. Even a professional soldier like Arthur Tedder could be stirred by the promise of Churchill's words.[15] As the most eloquent of politicians, Churchill could provide a generous supply of words; as a statesman, he realized that words alone would not be enough.

Churchill made a point of moving about London so that those people who were suffering the most could see him. Tears came honestly and often to his eyes. Ismay describes him in tears one day saying, "Poor people. They trust me, and I can give them nothing but disaster for quite a long time."[16] When Americans visited Churchill, he took them to see the bombing damage, thus exposing the American observers to the courage of the British under fire and reassuring President Roosevelt that any investment in Britain would not go down the drain of defeat. At the same time Churchill could show the American visitors to the British people and offer them the hope that they would not always be alone. Harry Hopkins, investigating for Roosevelt, reported to the American President that Churchill quite dominated the British scene: "He is the directing force behind the strategy and the conduct of the war in all its essentials. He has an amazing hold on the British people of all classes and groups."[17]

So Churchill gave the British people a diet of defiant speeches and the spectacle of a few stray American observers. What else could he offer them? One dramatic event revealed to all the determination of the new government to risk everything for ultimate victory. The fall of France in the summer of 1940 had ended in an armistice which left the main units of the French navy outside the reach of Hitler but also beyond association with the British. French naval units in British bases were secured under varying terms, but important units were at Oran in North Africa. If they ever came to German hands, they could perhaps overthrow the narrow balance on the seas that existed in Britain's favor. What then was to be done about these ships at Oran? On the night of July 2 the issue was debated by, among others, Churchill and the respected First Sea Lord, Admiral of the Fleet Sir Dudley Pound. The First Sea Lord was firm. If British terms were rejected, the French ships must be fired on. Churchill agreed. Lord Beaverbrook tells us that at 2:00 A.M. Churchill went into the garden of Number 10 Downing Street where he declared to his old friend that there was no other decision possible. Then he wept. Perhaps Churchill even signed the orders on this occasion because he did not wish the professional navy men to have to bear the burden. On July 3, compromise failing, the French ships at Oran were fired on by a British force. There was anger in Vichy, but the message was unmistakable to all. No sentiment would be allowed to stand in the way of the ruthless prosecution of the war until victory was secured. On July 4 Churchill, once more in tears, defended his action to the House of Commons. The House sustained him with a great ovation.[18]

Churchill's words nourished the British public and their support sustained his government. He wrote after the war that he was well aware of the strength of his position with the people for the share he had in their survival.[19] His public strength enabled him to reject unwisdom. As he opposed the Communist peace petitions before June 1941, so he opposed Communist cries for a second front after that date. When such persons urged a premature invasion of the Continent, he replied, "We should not in a matter of this kind take advice from British Communists, because we know that they stood aside and cared nothing for our fortunes in our time of mortal peril."[20] Churchill's political sense usually warned him of public unrest. When Hitler's new weapons, the V-1 and V-2, began to fall on Britain in 1944, he again met the challenge by urging the public to associate themselves with their fighting men on the fronts and thus to share in the soldiers' dangers. Being a politician and sensitive to the often bitter experiences of World War I, Churchill paid acute attention to the press and public information.

His speeches became both less frequent and less popular as the war went on and weariness set in.[21] Finally the bitter day came. Harold Nicolson recorded it in his diary for February 7, 1944. Visiting an RAF station, Nicolson found scrawled in a lavatory, "Winston Churchill is a bastard." The shocked Nicolson was informed by an officer that the message was found everywhere. When Nicolson protested, he was informed that "the men hate politicians." This produced from Nicolson the exclamation, "Winston a politician! Good God!"[22] As the British public turned from the energy of Lloyd George in 1922, so they would turn from Churchill in 1945. But in the summer and autumn of 1940, his great ministry was just beginning.

CHILD OF THE HOUSE

To Churchill the politician, politics meant Parliament and Parliament meant the House of Commons. He never wished to leave it.[23] This attitude was born of equal parts of sentiment and practical sense—sentiment toward the House which he had come to know so well and a practical sense born of the reality that power had transferred itself fully to the Commons by the end of World War I. In four decades of service in the House of Commons, Churchill had trained himself in a deep knowledge of its customs and workings, and during his war ministry he was to acquire an ascendency rare in English history.

Fortunately for posterity, there also sat in the Parliament of 1935–45 a man who managed to record for us the character and color of Churchill in the House. This man, Churchill's parliamentary Boswell, was Harold Nicolson. Nicolson had given up a promising diplomatic career for love of his wife, had taken to writing professionally, and had been elected to the 1935 House as a National Labour candidate. He shared Churchill's deep affection for the House of Commons and recorded in 1945, "I have loved my ten years at Westminster, and have found there that combination of genial surroundings with useful activity which is the basis of all human happiness."[24] In November of 1940 Nicolson recorded in his diary a graphic description of Churchill:

> He seems better in health than he has ever seemed. That pale and globular look about his cheeks has gone. He is more solid about the face and thinner. But there is something odd about his eyes. The lids are not in the least weary, nor are there any pouches or black lines. But the eyes themselves are glaucous, vigilant, angry, combative, visionary and tragic. In a way they are the eyes of a man who is much preoccupied and is unable to rivet his attention on minor things (such as me). But in another sense they are the eyes of a man faced by an ordeal or tragedy, and combining vision, truculence, resolution and great unhappiness.[25]

Churchill's affection for the House extended to most of its members, and during the war he expressed the desire that a list of all members who gave their lives should be placed in the new House as an example to future generations of the service rendered.[26] He could deal with winning sympathy toward his critics. On one noted occasion Churchill told Emanuel Shinwell that he had been a vigilant and severe critic, but as a real opposition figure he had failed because he could never conceal his satisfaction when the government was successful.[27] The House was pleased and so was Shinwell. When Churchill was one day short of his seventieth birthday, Nicolson captured him speaking in the House on the subject of political controversy, " 'I am not afraid of it in this country,' he said, and then he took off his glasses and grinned round at the Conservative benches. 'We are a decent lot,' he said, beaming upon them. Then he swung around and leant forward over the box right into the faces of the Labour people: 'All of us,' he added, 'the whole nation.' "[28] Nicolson called it a perfect illustration of the parliamentary art, and this it was. But it was an art born of conviction.

Churchill always took his responsibilities in the House seriously; if the press of running the government did not permit him to attend all debates, he was meticulous in reading them before he attempted to speak to a particular issue.[29] He was respectful of the customs of the House. On one occasion, Churchill asked the House of Commons to consider permitting broadcasts. This would have eased his burden since he often had to deliver a speech there and repeat it for broadcast later. The House was of divided mind, and Churchill indicated he did not intend to press his request. When one member was more persistent, Churchill was final, saying, "I think we have had enough of it."[30] Churchill did his share at question time, answering questions (in Nicolson's phrase) "dutifully, carefully, subserviently." Nicolson concluded with reason that he "elevates the whole standard of our public life."[31]

Churchill insisted on the principle that the representation of the people was the highest service to the state in wartime. He was willing to defend this point even against Ernest Bevin with whom he rarely differed. But on December 10, 1941, Bevin received a message from Churchill marked Action This Day, an imperative sign that Churchill would tolerate no challenge. The message read, "I see it reported that you say Members of Parliament are liable to be called up equally with others. The rule I have made, which was followed in the last war and must be followed in this, was that service in the House of Commons ranks with the highest service in the State." Churchill insisted that members of Parliament must be free to determine as individuals their form of service.[32]

Churchill, always the sensitive politician, recognized that the strength of the government rested in good measure upon the vitality of parliamentary life.[33] He encouraged debate on broad and general issues which would capture the public imagination.[34] In the summer of 1943 Churchill thanked the House for the "extraordinary kindness" which he felt it had extended him.[35] He believed that the ultimate test of government responsibility belonged in the House of Commons. When it was proposed that Defence Regulation 18B (which granted broad state power over the freedom of the individual in wartime) be transferred from the authority of the Home Secretary to a tribunal, Churchill objected, arguing that the best defense of civil liberties was in the political power of the House of Commons to bring the government to answer for its conduct.[36] In late 1944 Churchill summed up his feelings about Parliament when he called it "almost the only successful instance of a legislative body with plenary powers, elected on universal suffrage, which is capable of discharging, with restraint and with resolution, all the functions of peace and of war."[37] Churchill's basic approach to the House of Commons was conservative; he opposed changing the traditional procedure[38] of which he was himself a master.[39] He insisted that the government not use wartime conditions to impede unnecessarily the freedom of debate in Parliament and that members of the government respond as customary at question time.[40] On at least one occasion, however, Churchill carried the niceties of procedure perhaps too far. When the Education Bill of 1944 lost a clause in a light House, he insisted on making the issue a vote of confidence. This technicality was not well understood by all members, much less by the public, and perhaps was unnecessary, although Baldwin had done the same in a similar case in April 1936.[41]

The House of Commons itself was destroyed by wartime bombing, and the membership moved eventually to the House of Lords for the duration of the war. In discussing the rebuilding of the old House, Churchill insisted that it retain its oblong shape and not be semicircular and that it be only big enough to hold about two-thirds of its members. He believed the oblong shape with benches opposing encouraged a two-party system which in turn encouraged stable government and unified opposition. He felt that conversational style and facility for quick, informal interruptions and interchanges were important for good House of Commons speaking; this required a fairly small space, and there should be on major occasions a sense of crowd and urgency to emphasize the significance of the debate.[42] Churchill had his way; indeed, the House widely supported him.

The shape and size of the House had dictated how young Churchill had learned his speaking skills, but over the years he had educated himself diligently in the craft of speaking in all circumstances. His mastery of that craft amounted to genius. On one occasion he said, "What an ineffectual method of conveying human thought correspondence is—even when it is telegraphed with all the rapidity and all the facilities of modern intercommunication. They are simply dead blank walls compared to personal contacts."[43] Personal contact and public speech were the tools with which Churchill the politician lived. He was usually anxious and worried before every major speech he gave and took all his speeches seriously.[44] The preparation of a major Churchill speech was always a matter of wringing order out of chaos. When Hitler attacked Russia, John Colville was awakened at 4:00 A.M. Colville did not wake Churchill until 8:00 A.M. and was informed by the Prime Minister that he would broadcast to the nation at 9:00 that evening. There followed a frantic day, but the speech was ready on time.[45] Even speeches scheduled well in advance tended to go through the same last-minute stages of development, for Churchill had a tendency to postpone the ordeal of preparation as long as possible. Since Churchill was insistent on the accuracy of his statements, his various staffs were worked hard on the eve of his major addresses. Ismay recalls that the Prime Minister's demands were always met but there were some "hairbreadth escapes."[46] Even the Chief of the Imperial General Staff (CIGS) with all his burdens was not spared responsibilities in checking Churchill's preparations to speak.[47] It was well that Churchill possessed such a mastery of language for, as Sir John Kennedy observed, he often had to skate over thin ice when dealing with failures and errors.[48] Charles de Gaulle, no rude journeyman at language himself, testified to Churchill's eloquence: "Whatever his audience—crowd, assembly, council, even a single interlocuter, whether he was before a microphone, on the floor of the House, at table or behind a desk, the original, poetic, stirring flow of his ideas, arguments and feelings brought him an almost infallible ascendency in the tragic atmosphere in which the poor world was gasping."[49]

The meticulous care with which Churchill prepared his speeches, particularly to the House, was only the beginning of his parliamentary craft. He used every advantage within the House itself. Members occupying the front bench had the advantage that they could place notes on the dispatch box before them. A tall man might have to bend over to read his notes. Churchill once told Eden that this should never be done; it was better to flaunt notes rather than to pretend not to use them. Eden suspected Churchill was not beyond reading his notes with special spectacles designed to blow up the print. Eden observed, "A master of his craft as an orator, he was never ashamed to learn the tricks."[50]

In the House, Churchill used his colorful personality to the full. Nicolson described him when still First Lord as sitting hunched on the front bench "looking like the Chinese god of plenty suffering from acute indigestion."[51] That was on a bad day. On a better day, Nicolson described Churchill rubbing "the palm of his hand with five fingers extended up and down the front of his coat, searching for the right phrase, indicating cautious selection, conveying almost medicinal poise."[52] Churchill's rhetoric was rich, perhaps too rich for present-day tastes, and he could be moved by his own oratory to the point where he had to pause to recover himself.[53] Nicolson wrote his two sons a classic description of Churchill speaking. "His most characteristic gesture is strange, indeed. You know the movement that a man makes when he taps his trouser pockets to see whether he has got his latch-key? Well, Winston pats both trouser pockets and then passes his hands up and down from groin to tummy. It is very strange." On the same occasion Nicolson described Churchill having difficulty explaining the terms of the Italian surrender. After having made heavy weather of his explanations, he leaned across to the opposition benches and asked in a conversational tone, "That all right?" Nicolson reported that they grinned back affectionately.[54] Churchill's skill in going from the oratorical to the conversational was a technique which always worked in the House.

He was capable of making a bad speech occasionally, which could be very bad indeed. The famous debate on Norway on April 11, 1940, was such an occasion. He kept getting the wrong words, fumbling with his spectacles, seemed distracted, and left the House "in a mood of grave anxiety."[55] Members of the House tended to be infected by his moods; when he was depressed, they were too.[56]

Despondency was not Churchill's normal character in the House; his wit there was quick. On one occasion a member called upon him to denounce Laval. Churchill replied, "I am afraid I have rather exhausted the possibilities of the English language."[57] When, in January 1944, one member was so carried away as to call upon all to drink the toast "Death to all Dictators and Long Life to All Liberators, among whom the Prime Minister is first," Churchill replied, "It is very early in the morning."[58] Asked if he would consider selecting a member of the government to speak for the government, Churchill replied: "If the worst came to the worst, I might have a shot at it myself."[59] On one occasion while Churchill was paying tribute to the British army, he described a meeting in the field, saying that the spit and polish of the troops was "as if they had just left Wellington Barracks." Noticing a restlessness of the Labour benches, Churchill quickly added, "Never have I seen so smart an army since I reviewed the Guard of Honour which greeted me at the Moscow airport." This reduced the Socialists to laughter.[60]

Churchill was at his best on these occasions, and the House was at its best with him. But when the House was recalcitrant, Churchill could be difficult. He was not beyond threatening them, sometimes not very subtly. In 1943 when he was under considerable pressure to embark on a more imaginative social policy, he was particularly short with the House. The desirability of secret sessions was another topic which could produce a wrathful Winston. In October of 1943 an obviously irritated Churchill lectured the House, pointing out that parliamentary democracy proceeds not only by debate but by debate and division. He observed that the majority can dismiss an administration at any time, unless of course the administration obtains a dissolution from the Crown and finds itself sustained by the people.[61] This was Churchill's ultimate threat to a difficult House. The Parliament of 1935 had extended its life in the war emergency and had existed long past its normal constitutional age by the autumn of 1943, and Churchill repeatedly declared, "I certainly could not take the responsibility of making far-reaching, controversial changes which I am not convinced are directly needed for the war effort, without a Parliament refreshed by contact with the electorate."[62] Few members were particularly anxious to face an election.

Churchill—by oratory, by skillful preparation, by painstaking care, by sheer power of personality, by quick and ready wit, by warm sympathy with friend and often with foe in the House, and even if necessary by threat—exercised a mastery over the House of Commons which in the opinion of Sir Llewellyn Woodward had not been seen since the days of Gladstone. Nicolson wrote, "When he feels that he has the whole House with him, he finds it difficult to conceal his enjoyment of his speech, and that, in fact, is part of his amazing charm. He thrusts both his hands deep into his trouser pockets, and turns his tummy now to the right, now to the left, in evident enjoyment of his mastery of the position."[63]

FIRST MINISTER

THE REMARKABLE political power which Churchill exercised as wartime Prime Minister was built upon his service to the nation at a moment of grave crisis, by his power to capture the public imagination and fortify the people and by his evident mastery over the House of Commons, the center of parliamentary democracy. However, this was not the full extent of his political power and skill; as he dominated the House of Commons, so too he dominated his own government.

Lord Beaverbrook once described the front bench: "There Attlee and Greenwood, a sparrow and a jackdaw, are perched on either side of the glittering bird of Paradise."[64] It was an apt description. Churchill had learned, however, by hard experience to distinguish between the glittering attributes of political power and its reality. Basic to the reality of power in the House of Commons was the fact that membership was based along lines of political allegiance, however much those lines might be blurred by the necessity of wartime coalition government. So it was that when on November 9, 1940, death removed Chamberlain from the leadership of the Conservative party, Churchill did not hesitate to grasp the leadership for himself. His argument was politically convincing—the Conservative party possessed a very large majority in the House of Commons over all other parties combined, and thus the leader of that majority would be the true possessor of political power.[65] Churchill had every intention of exercising the real political power himself. Nor did he deplore political parties, although he had had his share of difficulties over the years. On one occasion he said, "A variety of attacks are made upon the composition of the Government. It is said that it is formed on a party and political basis. But so is the House of Commons."[66] He recognized the reality of political parties, and his government was indeed a coalition of parties. The Labour leader, Attlee, was the only man other than Churchill who sat in the War Cabinet from the first day of the government to the last.[67] Churchill was prepared to make compromises to secure an all-party coalition. Thus he retracted his offer to Chamberlain to be Leader of the House when it was clear that Labour would not be comfortable under this arrangement. The only solution to this problem was for Churchill to carry the added responsibility of Leader of the House himself, which he continued to do from May 1940 until February 1942. During this period, Attlee acted as Churchill's deputy in the House in the conduct of its daily work.[68]

From the outset of his administration Churchill was Prime Minister and Leader of the House of Commons, and to that position he soon added leadership of the Conservative party. He also took the office of Minister of Defence without defining exactly the powers and scope of that office. He once told the Commons that there was nothing he did as Minister of Defence which he could not do as Prime Minister, and that was true. But the point was that by taking the title, Churchill announced from the beginning that he would in effect direct the strategy of the war.[69] Thus Churchill exercised a range or extent of power almost unique in British constitutional history, a power that could be wielded occasionally with a firmness which approached ruthlessness. When Lord Hankey spoke critically of Churchill's conduct of high affairs during the political crisis of early 1942, he soon found himself out of the government. The ultimate political weapon Churchill possessed was the right to dissolve Parliament. He described it as almost the only constitutional privilege a British Prime Minister possesses, but, as he noted, it was also a fairly solid foundation of power.[70]

As Prime Minister in time of peril, with a people and Parliament disposed to allow him a wide range of activity, the power actually in Churchill's hands was great, indeed vast. But Churchill had been reared for four decades in the House of Commons and always thought of the exercise of his position and power as operating through the cabinet system of government. He insisted that the government stand united as a corporate body and was prepared to protect its more vulnerable members from attack. In the political crisis of early 1942, he took "fullest personal responsibility."[71] The Cabinet he constructed, and in 1942 extensively reconstructed, was a monument to his skill as political leader and executive. Probably the burning memory of the aftermath of Gallipoli left him sensitive about defending members of the government. When Ernest Bevin was new to Parliament and still feeling his way there, Churchill was strong and steadfast in his defense.[72] P. J. Grigg, a former civil servant who became a nonparty member of the government, believed that Churchill was more than scrupulously fair in holding the scales even between Conservatives and Labour members of the government.[73] Churchill defended the men of Munich as steadfastly as he defended his Minister of Labour. He said of his government, "Its members are going to stand together, and, subject to the authority of the House of Commons, we are going to govern the country and fight the war."[74] Churchill's defense of the collective responsibility of the government produced its own reward when, toward the end of the coalition, the Labour membership of the House became restless. The Labour members by and large remained loyal to Churchill as he had to them in the early years of the war.[75] On the whole, Churchill showed no small skill in constructing and, when necessary, reconstructing a government which involved nearly seventy ministers from three parties.[76]

The fact that Churchill's government was a coalition of three parties (and in the case of Conservatives and Labour the differences on some points were wide) created a clear need for a defined principle which would offer guidance to the members. Churchill laid down that principle in the following terms:

> What holds us together is the conduct of the war, the prosecution of the war. No Socialist, or Liberal, or Labour man has been in any way asked to give up his convictions. That would be indecent and improper. We are held together by something outside, which rivets all our attention. The principle we work on is: "Everything for the war, whether controversial or not, and nothing controversial that is not *bona fide* needed for the war."[77]

This was more easily said than done, particularly in the last eighteen months of the coalition when on occasion Churchill had some difficulty reconciling the statements of Conservative and Labour members.[78]

On the whole, the unity was remarkable; however, a few particular issues always gave trouble. One of these was the management of the Royal Ordnance Factories (ROF). To Socialists the ROF were proof of the effectiveness of nationalization; therefore, they did not want private management.[79] Far more volatile an issue involved coal mining and distribution. There was no more difficult political issue in Britain, and its antecedents stretched back to the beginning of the century. Churchill and some of his Labour associates were in a good position to remember that trouble in the coal mines had led to the general strike of 1926, during which Churchill's controversial role did so much to damage his subsequent reputation with the British left. Not surprisingly, therefore, Churchill stayed a good distance from the issue of coal for as long as he could. It fell to Ernest Bevin and Gwilym Lloyd George to struggle with that problem. But when the situation showed signs of blowing up in October 1943, the Prime Minister intervened swiftly. It was on this occasion that he produced his principle "everything for the war. . . ."[80] In the end the mines were left to be managed by appointed group production directors, responsible to regional controllers, who would ensure that government policy was effectively executed.[81] That there was no coal nationalization was probably inevitable in the face of the large Conservative majority in the House, but there can be no doubt that the Labour membership did not take this well. A far less serious issue than coal was the matter of land compensation in a town and country planning bill in late 1944. Again Churchill had to intervene to reach a compromise—in this case, the deletion of a troublesome clause.[82] In spite of such political difficulties, Churchill had good cause to refer to his ministry as "the most capable government England has had or is likely to have."[83]

At the center of the government was the War Cabinet. As announced on May 11, 1940, it consisted of five men: Churchill, Chamberlain, Attlee, Halifax, and Greenwood. The membership of the War Cabinet revealed that the principle of choice had been primarily politics. To call it a strong Cabinet would be difficult, but to say it was merely the rubber stamp of Churchill himself is not fair. Certainly in the early days Churchill powered and even sustained his colleagues. It appears that even the topic of negotiations with Hitler was raised briefly by Halifax on May 27, 1940. This possibility was firmly repudiated and evidently not raised again.[84]

Churchill believed that members of the War Cabinet should combine overseeing the whole war effort with responsibility for certain executive departments. In a political sense he hoped that this would keep his most able colleagues fully occupied, but sound administrative reasons also existed.[85] The War Cabinet reconstruction of February 1942 produced a stronger group. Attlee was now officially recognized as Deputy Prime Minister and took over the Dominions Office, thus soothing dissatisfactions—particularly in Australia—with the small voice Dominions had in shaping imperial war policy. Anthony Eden as Foreign Secretary managed an important department, as did Ernest Bevin as Minister of Labour and National Service. Bevin had entered the War Cabinet in October 1940 and Eden in December of that year when he had given up the War Office for the Foreign Ministry. Sir Stafford Cripps, who entered the War Cabinet in the 1942 reconstruction as Lord Privy Seal, took over Churchill's burdens as Leader of the House of Commons. This last arrangement did not prove successful. Sir John Anderson, Lord President of the Council and War Cabinet member since October 1940, presided over what was almost a separate cabinet concerned only with domestic affairs. Finally, Oliver Lyttelton returned to England as

Minister of Production. He had been a member of the War Cabinet since July 1941 in his capacity as Minister of State resident in the Middle East. Sir Kingsley Wood, Chancellor of the Exchequer, left the cabinet in February 1942. With the exception of Cripps, who despite his great ability fit awkwardly not only with the Prime Minister but with his former Labour associates, this made up a powerful team.[86]

At the time he made these changes, Churchill defended his War Cabinet and compared it favorably with that of World War I. He rightly pointed out there had been criticism of the war leadership at that time just as criticism was again apparent in early 1942. On February 24, 1942, he said that members of the War Cabinet were collectively and individually responsible for the whole policy of the country and they alone were accountable for the conduct of the war. However, they also had particular duties.[87] The War Cabinet also remained an imperial one, more by lip service than in reality.[88] The Cabinet underwent few changes during the remainder of the war. Cripps left in November 1942 and Herbert Morrison, the Home Secretary, came in. Sir Richard Casey, who succeeded Lyttelton in the Middle East, was a member from March 1942 until December 1943. Lord Woolton as Minister of Reconstruction entered the Cabinet in November 1943.

The War Cabinet could and did restrain Churchill from time to time. For example, at one time Churchill was prepared to bring force to bear to secure the use of the Azores. The War Cabinet blocked the Prime Minister's desire, although it had to absorb a stinging rebuke and be described as pursuing a policy which would "paralyse action."[89] By that time the members were surely well accustomed to strong language from the Prime Minister. Eden, as a Foreign Secretary of considerable experience and temperamentally inclined to prudence and realism and personally close to Churchill, was in a good position to exercise his influence. If that influence was not greater, perhaps the fault was Eden's and not Churchill's. Ernest Bevin was much more independent. Churchill fully recognized his own weakness in the area of labor and never attempted to meddle in Bevin's domain.[90] In return, Churchill received loyalty and great service from Bevin. Given its range of political personalities and views, the War Cabinet operated with remarkable efficiency. When Churchill met Roosevelt to draw up the Atlantic Charter, he was in regular consultation with the War Cabinet in London which had to approve the drafts of the charter. The Americans were very much impressed by Churchill's responsibility to the Cabinet and by the efficiency with which communication between the *Prince of Wales* and London was achieved.[91]

The Cabinet had problems of personality as well as problems born of political differences. Churchill's sheer power, the energy with which he put forward his positions, his formidable skill in argumentation, his explosive temperament—all could make him a difficult master. He went on all day every day amid constant conversation, cigar smoke, and unfinished whiskeys. This was certainly hard for more austere colleagues like Cripps. Lord Beaverbrook's various tenures of office were always filled with storm and controversy. Beaverbrook's most strenuous encounters took place with Ernest Bevin who viewed Beaverbrook with deep suspicion. The relations between Production under Beaverbrook and Labour were never smooth until the general reshuffle of early 1942 and the arrival of Oliver Lyttelton as Minister of Production.[92] Beaverbrook had a genius for stirring animosities, and he clashed with Sir Archibald Sinclair when in charge of Aircraft Production, although not as seriously as in his quarrels with Bevin.[93]

If the Cabinet had its weaknesses born of political differences and clashes of personality, it also had great strengths. Attlee was steadfast and cooperative in a difficult position. Perhaps the greatest triumph of the Cabinet was the inclusion of Ernest Bevin, with no previous parliamentary experience, who came directly from his leadership of the Transport and General Workers' Union. He apparently entered the Cabinet upon Churchill's personal initiative.[94] In many aspects of their personalities Bevin and Churchill were opposites, but they shared in common great determination, courage, and perseverance when the going was roughest.[95] Churchill clearly respected Bevin, although their differences precluded much experience in common. They were equally determined to prosecute the war to a victorious conclusion.[96]

Another successful aspect of Churchill's wartime government was the inclusion of nonparty men whose background was that of civil servants. Sir John Anderson was the most notable example—a man of great efficiency, undisturbed by the pressure of events, and dealing with manifold and complex issues with an ease and organization remarkable in contrast to the rather chaotic conditions prevailing in the defense side of the government where Churchill manned the helm. Sir James Grigg, who became Secretary of State for War but not a member of the Cabinet, rose to that position from the Permanent Undersecretaryship, causing some political comment. This appears to have been something of a constitutional innovation on Churchill's part and, although successful, perhaps in the long run a dubious one.[97]

The true power of the War Cabinet is perhaps best indicated by the fact that it contained at one time or another five of the six men who may have been considered potential candidates for the position of Prime Minister. Churchill's handling of his six potential rivals is a good measure of his political capacity. With perhaps one notable exception Churchill judged each man rightly and dealt with each man according to his judgment. The first of these rivals was of course Lord Halifax. Churchill had secured the premiership only narrowly from his grasp. The temperament of Halifax was also in sharp contrast to that of Churchill. They did not mix well. When Lord Lothian, the Ambassador in Washington, died on December 12, 1940, Churchill promptly sent Halifax to America. Lady Halifax fought this decision harder than Halifax himself, but in the end Churchill prevailed. The Cabinet was stronger for Halifax's absence. He was a man not temperamentally suited to executive strains and stresses, and in the ambassadorship to the United States Halifax found a career in which he was able to do valuable service.[98]

Halifax had not been Churchill's first consideration for the American appointment. That man had been Churchill's former World War I master, David Lloyd George. It may seem exaggeration to suggest that Lloyd George in old age and still surrounded by the storms and tempests he had stirred in his earlier career could have been a serious rival to Churchill. But in fact there was always reserved for Lloyd George one potential role to play, that of the British Pétain, and in 1940 he indicated that he might be prepared for it. By the middle of 1941 circumstances made this most improbable, and Lloyd George's continually failing health removed him more and more from the center of the scene. Nonetheless, early in his ministry Churchill correctly appraised the potential danger which Lloyd George constituted. Churchill was bound to Lloyd George by memories of the past, some of which encouraged affection; but other memories warned caution.[99] Surely it was political wisdom always to deal carefully with David Lloyd George.

Anthony Eden was the third potential rival and throughout most of the war remained probably the most popular member of the Cabinet with the British people as a whole. The particular role Eden played contributed to this; he was not directly involved in decisions which could be uncomfortable to the public. Eden thus possessed a popular base which could have become significant if Churchill had experienced sustained adversity. Churchill surely recognized this, but he weighed the political power of Eden correctly and never treated him seriously as a rival. Rather he viewed the younger Eden as his political heir, but the inheritance Churchill cheerfully regarded as distant. He could jokingly remind Eden that Gladstone formed his last ministry at the age of eighty-three.

The fourth possible rival was Sir Stafford Cripps, and he gave Churchill the most difficulty. He was a remarkable man. Before the war he had achieved distinction at the bar and had taken up a political position so far to the left that he had been expelled from the parliamentary Labour party. His radical Marxism was combined with a deep Christian faith, and his standards of personal morality often appeared oppressive. He had been sent to Russia, and during the winter of 1941–42 when the prestige of the British government was low and Russia had become most popular, there was a strong movement of emotion in the country toward Cripps. In fact, Cripps had not been a good ambassador to Russia. The Russian government had no love for a radical Marxist, a point perhaps not sufficiently appreciated in the West. Furthermore, there was in Cripps's personality a streak of confidence in the rightness of his own judgment which rendered him an unreliable agent for the conduct of foreign policy. Churchill brought him into the government in the reshuffle of February 1942; however, he was not particularly successful. At the end of nine months he had exhausted the patience of the House of Commons by his attitudes, and it was necessary to replace him with Eden as Leader of the House. Once the crisis of 1942 was over, Cripps's popularity faded sharply. While Churchill was plagued from time to time with him, Cripps never again posed a serious threat to Churchill's power. He took over the Ministry of Aircraft Production which kept him fully occupied for the remainder of the war.[100]

Ernest Bevin must also be considered as a possible rival. Bevin's strength with the working people was formidable but his political experience was brief; in any case, Bevin was steadfastly loyal. Churchill recognized that this loyalty was his safeguard, and there was no real political rivalry between the two men.

The most unusual rival to Churchill was one of his oldest political associates, Lord Beaverbrook. Their friendship was extended and strong, although it had known various times of trouble and had appeared on the point of rupture in the late 1930s. When Churchill became Prime Minister, he summoned Beaverbrook to the Ministry of Aircraft Production to meet the challenge of supplying the RAF with sufficient aircraft to win the Battle of Britain. By methods fair and foul, Beaverbrook met the challenge, but he did so at the high price of creating many antagonisms and was sustained in 1941 only by the loyalty of Churchill. Beaverbrook's health was never strong and suffered as much from emotional as physical exhaustion. At the end of April 1941 he left Aircraft Production, spent a brief time as Minister of State, and took on the duties of Minister of Supply, in which position his running fight with Ernest Bevin was soon renewed.[101]

Beaverbrook's friendship with Churchill and his long career as a power broker behind the scenes in politics won him few friends and many enemies. He was described as possessing a mesmeric influence on Churchill.[102] Beaverbrook's executive capacity was great, just as his political abilities could run deep. Harold Macmillan, no mean judge of these matters, has given a favorable portrait of him.[103] But Macmillan is almost unique in this. The critical moment in the long relationship between Churchill and Beaverbrook came at the height of the political crisis in February 1942. Beaverbrook left the War Cabinet then and departed to the United States. Churchill's contemporary messages to Harry Hopkins and President Roosevelt make clear that the friendship between the two men was undiminished at this point. Once in the United States, however, Beaverbrook launched a vigorous campaign in behalf of a stronger measure of assistance to Russia in the war. He went so far as to advocate the opening of a second front in western Europe and made assertions which could hardly be reconciled comfortably to the realities of British military power at that point. Aid to Russia was a popular theme, and it received considerable publicity in both America and Britain.

Beaverbrook returned to Britain on May 5, 1942. Churchill by this point seems to have been seriously considering Beaverbrook for appointment as ambassador to Washington. A question immediately arises regarding Churchill's motives, which probably cannot be unraveled until we can judge better what Beaverbrook's goals were. These are not easy to discover. As late as May 21 Beaverbrook was describing in a private letter the position of the Prime Minister as unchallenged. This hardly is the tone of a man about to attempt to seize the first place in the government. Yet shortly thereafter Beaverbrook attempted to open a palace intrigue with Bevin to throw out Churchill. In retrospect this appears sheer madness considering Bevin's barely disguised feelings toward Beaverbrook. On this occasion Bevin was to say of Churchill's relationship with Beaverbrook, "He's like a man who's married a whore: he knows she's a whore but he loves her just the same." Not surprisingly, nothing came of the attempt, but any man who remembered Beaverbrook's political accomplishments at the time of World War I would have had to take the attempt seriously. Churchill's confidence in Beaverbrook evidently remained unshaken, and he returned to the government in September 1943. Beaverbrook always remained one of those men who maintained ready access to Churchill. His challenge to Churchill's leadership, if challenge it was, remains a strange episode in the career of a man who has baffled evaluation and left behind conflicting memories.[104]

Another man who dealt largely behind the scenes in politics and always remained close to Churchill was Brendan Bracken. He was Churchill's most loyal parliamentary follower in the 1930s—perhaps his only one in the latter part of that decade. Bracken had been successful in business, had a remarkable range of associations, and covered his own career with a certain element of mystery. He was one of the men whom Harry Hopkins described as making up the nocturnal cabinet—those men who met in Churchill's home on weekends but seemed to have limited influence upon the course of events. He emerges from World War II as a figure of considerable sympathy, lifting many burdens from Churchill's shoulders and advising him on the selection of individuals suitable to the wide range of positions Churchill was called upon to fill.[105]

All the serious challenges to Churchill's preeminent place in British political life came from established places within the political parties, with the possible exceptions of Cripps and Beaverbrook. However, by the late 1930s, the position of David Lloyd George had become perhaps more honorary than real. Only the challenge of Cripps ever came close to gaining public status. The most serious struggles were fought out in the dark. But Churchill the politician also had to face an organized opposition. Indeed, the very effectiveness of the parliamentary process demanded the existence of an opposition, formal if not real. Accordingly, it was arranged that the official opposition would be composed of the elder statesmen of the Labour party who served this function for the purpose of carrying on the business of the House. In more or less official opposition, there were also the four members of the Independent Labour party and a single Communist (later, two).

There soon sprang up in the House, however, an unofficial opposition. The first of its leaders seems to have been Emanuel Shinwell, who was able but perhaps placed too high a premium on his ability. He was caustic in debate, which did not win him friends, and too sweeping in his criticism, which lost support for his more well-merited points. He was joined in opposition by the father of the House, Lord Winterton. The opposition of Winterton, although hard to take seriously, clearly touched a raw spot in Churchill. Churchill was proud of his long service to the House and bitterly regretted the two-year break which denied his claim to the position of father of the House. There was always therefore a certain antagonism in exchanges between Churchill and Winterton which did not appear between Churchill and Shinwell. As late as March 1945 a certain sharpness persisted between Winterton and Churchill. When a technical discussion occurred on the procedure regarding appointment to select committees, Winterton became the object of some of Churchill's sharpest commentary of his entire ministry. Churchill concluded his remarks by warning Winterton "that he will run a very grave risk of falling into senility before he is over-taken by old age."[106]

Another opposition figure was Leslie Hore-Belisha, who had been Secretary of State for War under Chamberlain. A long controversy ensued between him and Churchill regarding the fitness of British tanks, a subject upon which Hore-Belisha viewed himself an expert and upon which he also probably had expert advice. One of the most violent of Churchill's critics was the young and volatile Labourite Aneurin Bevan from Wales. Bevan could sufficiently inflame Churchill to describe his assaults as diatribes born of "bitter animosity."[107] An opponent of strikingly different political complexion was Sir John Wardlaw-Milne, a deep-dyed Conservative who was the leader in a motion of no confidence in the government in July 1942. The unwisdom of Wardlaw-Milne's proposals, however, did much to defeat his attempt to criticize the government. He was not much of a sustained opponent. Clement Davies was a useful if somewhat long-winded critic. The rather eccentric Dick Stokes was more persistent than able. The Communist William Gallacher was often more of a foil for Churchill's barbs than an effective opponent.[108] The most dangerous element of opposition to Churchill in the House of Commons never came from his unofficial critics, for they were too few to unseat him and too unsuited temperamentally for responsible leadership to afford a really serious challenge. The unspoken potential for challenge to Churchill's leadership of the House was always the threat of a rupture within the coalition itself. In fact, on only one occasion did a substantial proportion of the membership break with the leadership of the House, and that came from the revolt of the Labour back-benchers on a domestic issue.

Churchill had learned in the hard school of experience the importance of the press in politics. He was not likely ever to forget his World War I experiences at the hands of Fleet Street. He was not, in fact, easily accessible to interviews during World War II, and his communications with the press seem to have run largely through the hands of Brendan Bracken and Lord Beaverbrook. Once in March 1942 when affairs were at their worst, Churchill appears to have lost his temper and threatened to ban the critical *Daily Mirror.* The press was often difficult, particularly in the last stages of the war, but on the whole Churchill's relations with the press were remarkably harmonious, certainly in striking contrast to the role the press played in the politics of World War I. It appears too that Churchill could on occasion make use of the press. Certainly the Americans from time to time were convinced that various criticisms did not occur in the British press simply by chance. It must be said of Churchill the politician that, in spite of all difficulties, his relations with the press remained relatively satisfactory throughout World War II.[109]

One last political relationship remains to be described, and it was more constitutional than political in nature. This was Churchill's relationship to the Crown, specifically with King George VI. The King would have preferred to have had Halifax in May 1940, but he seems to have reconciled himself quickly to Churchill. Certainly Churchill on his part always treated monarchy with what we would judge today to be exaggerated respect. He was meticulous in respecting the prerogatives remaining to the constitutional sovereign. When he resigned on May 25, 1945, Churchill insisted on an interval between his time of resignation and his time of resuming office. This was done to make clear that the Crown had the right to decide for whom it should send as Prime Minister, a constitutional nicety characteristic of Churchill. He venerated the Crown and believed it played an important role in the stability of government.[110] It was not, however, a critical political relationship, and certainly there was nothing between Churchill and King George VI similar to the difficulties which had beset Lloyd George in his relations with King George V during World War I. George VI's advice does not seem to have been significant with Churchill, although the monarch may have influenced the decision to appoint General Wavell as Viceroy of India in 1943.

The desperate circumstances under which Churchill took up his premiership did much to set the tone of politics during his ministry. His skill and astuteness as a politician did much to maintain a strong united government which served as a stable platform from which to face the challenge presented by world affairs.

PARLIAMENTARIAN

CHURCHILL'S POLITICAL POWER rested on the foundations of broad-based public support; a large coalition in the House of Commons; and a strong, well-organized, well-run government. Churchill needed these powerful political advantages, for the war he was prosecuting was certain to produce a long string of military setbacks before there could be any reasonable hope of turning the tide. In the early years of the war Churchill's political fortunes depended in large measure upon the course of military affairs. He fought out the political consequences of military misfortune in the House of Commons, which was constitutionally proper and also politically advantageous, for Churchill was strongest in the House of Commons.

The first challenge to Churchill's position appeared over the abortive adventure against Dakar. The combined British–Free French operation to seize this crucial port had revealed a lack of coordination all too similar to that in Norway. Churchill made his defense of the operation to the House of Commons on October 8, 1940. His central points were that events had taken place which could not have been anticipated, thus making a successful operation doubtful, and that no "infirmity of purpose" existed on the part of the government.[111] This was sufficient, and the House was reassured. Even if it was a failure, the Dakar operation was at least an offensive operation.

The political scene remained relatively serene until late spring of 1941. Again military events precipitated political crisis. A British expeditionary force sent to the aid of Greece was rudely ejected from the Continent by overwhelming German force. This was followed by a spectacular airborne assault upon the island of Crete. Not only did Crete fall but the process of evacuation, first from Greece and then from Crete, took a heavy toll of the Royal Navy. This time public uneasiness was far more serious and widespread. On May 7, 1941, David Lloyd George delivered a somber speech. He warned that the whole truth must be told and spoke about "dark chasms." His general theme implied that Britain was losing the war and there was little hope that Britain could win. In the afternoon Churchill counterattacked vigorously. He concentrated perhaps rather too much on scoring political points, but the House was convinced of Churchill's determination to prosecute the war and delivered a vote of confidence by a margin of 447 to 3. Perhaps an even better indicator was a spontaneous burst of cheering when Churchill left the House.[112]

The most serious crisis began in early December 1941, even though virtually at that moment the entry of the United States into the war brought final relief and assurance of ultimate victory. Ironically, even as victory was assured to Churchill, the short-term run of events conspired to create a serious challenge to his war ministry. From December 1941 until July 1942, one military disaster followed another, beginning with the sinking of the *Prince of Wales* and the *Repulse.* The loss of these two great warships to Japanese aircraft left British forces in the Far East extremely vulnerable. A gloomy Far Eastern campaign culminated in the unexpected surrender of the great British naval base of Singapore on February 15, 1942. This catastrophe was followed by the brazen stroke of the *Scharnhorst* and the *Gneisenau* sailing up the Channel despite

British efforts to sink them, and this rude shock was in turn followed by the attack of Rommel in the desert, culminating on June 21, 1942, in the fall of Tobruk. These successive misfortunes constituted repeated blows to Churchill's political position. Beaverbrook called the loss of the two British warships Churchill's darkest hour and described Churchill as "oppressed with grief and woe."[113] Churchill himself described his reaction to the sinking of the *Prince of Wales* and the *Repulse* as heavy and painful. A frank speech to the House on December 11, 1941, seems to have held critics for the moment.[114]

But as January followed December that bitter winter, Churchill's critics began to gather strength. His occupation of the offices of both Prime Minister and Minister of Defence was a particular point of criticism. At the end of January a three-day debate began. Churchill boldly asked to be sustained by a vote of confidence, making clear that he insisted upon not merely a debate but a vote. This was politically wise. It was after all easy to criticize, but it was much more serious to bring the government down. Churchill followed up his political play by making strong substantive points. He reminded the House that Britain no longer stood alone in the war but had twenty-six allies comprising more than three-fourths of the world population, and he closed the debate by paying tribute to the vitality of British political institutions that allowed so free a discussion of the conduct of the war. He then called upon the House of Commons to sustain the government in "the enormous tasks and trials which it has to endure." His basic military defense was that Britain had not the resources to be strong both in the Near East and the Far East. Priority had to be given to the active campaigns being fought around the Mediterranean Sea and the situation in the Far East left to fate. To brighten the Far Eastern picture he could offer American entry into the war. In January of 1942 that was merely a flickering light after the American naval disaster at Pearl Harbor. He was able to skate over the loss of the *Prince of Wales* and the *Repulse* by attacking a false accusation and thus saving himself from an embarrassing explanation of the exposed position of these two ships. He concluded strongly, calling on each member to act in accordance with his duty and conscience. The vote of confidence was carried by 464 to 1.[115]

Even as the House was sustaining Churchill, disaster pursued him. Rommel continued forward in the desert and criticism continued in Britain. When the episode of the *Scharnhorst* and the *Gneisenau* was discussed in the House of February 17, 1942, Churchill became irritable. The House was uneasy. Criticism mounted. Beaverbrook believed that Churchill was deliberately fanning the flames of political controversy to distract attention from military affairs and to rally support around a beleaguered government.[116] Churchill seized the political initiative on February 19 and reconstructed the War Cabinet. Greenwood, Beaverbrook, and Sir Kingsley Wood went out and Cripps came in. Beaverbrook departed on his own initiative for reasons which remain controversial. This was only a preparatory gesture.[117] On February 22 Churchill again defended his government, his conduct of the war, and the changes he had just carried out. He again appealed to memories of World War I and pointed out the criticisms which had beset the War Cabinet at that time. He refused to pass judgment on the defense of Singapore. He quoted his own words of World War I, recalling hope of triumph in time of adversity, and reiterated his intention to retain his full powers of war direction.[118] Churchill seemed satisfied with this effort to meet complaints, but his critics did not. On May 20 Nicolson described the House as in a bad mood and the debate as one long stab and dig at Winston. Nicolson did not think Churchill's position was strong.[119] With the fall of Tobruk Churchill reached the same conclusion. He decided a vote of confidence was again necessary. His critics moved first, however, and on June 25 a motion was laid down of no confidence in the central direction of the war. How precarious Churchill's position appeared to some is indicated by the fact that Lord Beaverbrook was seeking out military advisers to teach him something about the business of war, perhaps in expectation that he would be summoned to Churchill's place.[120]

But in fact the motion of censure was a political mismove. The great majority of the members of Parliament were hardly prepared to vote out the government. They would, after all, have had to repudiate their entire political leadership across the spectrum. The political crisis of June 1942 also raised starkly—perhaps for the first time—the question of who would replace Churchill as Prime Minister if he were turned out. This was a question no one had seriously asked before. No one had taken Churchill's tenure for granted, but after two years, he had gained an ascendency so great that when any potential candidate was measured against him, strong men blanched at contemplating any change.[121] Private efforts to turn out Churchill were no more successful than the public one in Parliament. Beaverbrook launched his intrigue with Bevin at this point and met an absolute rebuff. Bevin had turned away the assassin's dagger. It remained now only for Churchill to "war down" his more straightforward opponents across the floor of the House. A debate held on July 1–2 was concluded by Churchill.[122] As was his custom, Churchill took the offensive. Flaying his opponents in strong language, he vigorously supported his commanders in the field. Churchill's opponents had made his task almost easy. Sir John Wardlaw-Milne had proposed that a separate Minister of Defence be created—a sort of Chief of the Chiefs of Staff—and recommended that the Duke of Gloucester be appointed Commander-in-Chief of the British Army. This sort of proposal gave Churchill his opening. He firmly rejected having any superchief to deal with. He hammered away at the solid realities of the military situation. By contrast, the proposals of his opponents appeared insignificent. The House also received a veiled threat. Discussing the hard news from the battlefront and from Britain, which he had heard while visiting the United States, Churchill observed, "Only my unshakable confidence in the ties which bind me to the mass of the British people upheld me through those days of trial." It was a reminder of where the ultimate court of political appeal lay. Churchill then made clear he must be upheld in his fullness of power or he would resign. This was sufficient, and he was sustained by a vote of 476 to 25.[123]

At the time, when Britain had faced a long series of military reverses, the debate seemed serious enough. In retrospect it acquires a certain air of unreality. The proposals of the parliamentary critics seemed ineffective, and any real alternative to the existing arrangements of government was difficult to visualize. Churchill's victory earned a quick message from President Roosevelt, "Good for you." Sir John Kennedy summed up the most mature judgments when he said, "I do believe that, on balance, it is best that he should continue as Prime Minister. . . ."[124] It is possible at this point to say Churchill had secured tenure for the duration of the war. This was the last political crisis produced by consistent adversity in the field; the next political crisis would be the product of victory.

Not surprisingly, the political problems which came with the period of Allied success were more difficult than those Churchill had faced during the time of British defeats. Victorious powers could perhaps again enjoy the luxury of political disagreement. The issues under discussion also changed. Prior to the middle of 1942 the political crises were born of military matters; in the last half of the war, political and social issues predominated. Ultimately, military affairs could be put to the test and an irreversible verdict rendered on the field of battle. Political and social theories seldom yielded to such neat proofs. The situation was not improved by the fact that Churchill pursued the conduct of the war with an intensity which left only marginal energies for some issues, particularly social problems, which were of growing importance to a significant segment of the House of Commons and the population.

The first troublesome political consequence of military victory came at the conclusion of the Allied invasion of North Africa in November 1942. The joint British-American expeditionary force which landed in French Northwest Africa had found a political situation (in the words of the expedition commander, General Eisenhower) totally unlike anything they had been prepared to expect. In the confused days following the landings, Eisenhower acted with simple military common sense in reaching an agreement with the French Admiral Darlan. This ended French resistance to the Allied landings and even secured a measure of cooperation, enabling the Allies to push rapidly toward the Tunisian frontier. The political consequences of what came to be called the Darlan Deal, however, were violent in the extreme. In the United States, and even more violently in Great Britain, a loud cry arose—particularly from the press—opposing any dealings with Admiral Darlan. To most Englishmen, Darlan had been too closely associated with the policy of Vichy; to deal with him now was viewed as a compromise of the principles for which the war was being fought. Churchill at first seemed inclined to ride out the political storm and rejected initial proposals from Foreign Minister Eden that the issue be met head on in Parliament. Attlee and Eden together finally convinced Churchill that discussion was essential. A debate was held in secret session and Churchill defended Eisenhower's judgment. Again Churchill was in a politically strong position. Events in the field as interpreted by an Allied general had brought about the arrangement. It was really very hard to attack the British government for that. The controversy diminished by the middle of December and only a certain undercurrent of disquiet lingered on.[125]

The most violent upheaval, however, was developing even as Churchill dealt with the Darlan crisis. Early in December 1942 the Beveridge Report on Social Insurance was published, which was sweeping beyond anything the government had anticipated. It was not merely a technical report on social insurance but a new declaration of human rights which set out a comprehensive scheme of social insurance against sickness, poverty, and unemployment. It contained proposals for a national health service, family allowances, and the maintenance of full employment. Alan Bullock has written of it, "No official report has ever aroused greater popular interest or enthusiasm. . . . Here at last was a programme, more than that, a manifesto, on which people could fasten."[126] The government greeted the report with dismay. Churchill is reported to have taken such strong exception to it that he refused to meet Beveridge and tried to bar his entry into any government department. Churchill's unhappiness issued from the fact that the Beveridge Report struck directly at what held the national government together—the tacit agreement that controversial social issues would not be debated during the war. The report also went against the Conservative grain of the Prime Minister. Churchill was far from optimistic regarding the condition of Britain after the end of the war.[127] He expressed his political attitude in a memorandum on February 14: "We cannot, however, initiate the legislation now or commit ourselves to the expenditure involved. That can only be done by a responsible government and a House of Commons refreshed by contact with the people."[128] Therefore, when the Beveridge Report was presented to the House of Commons, it was not accompanied by any government proposal for implementation. The Labour back-benchers went into open revolt. The debate appears to have been badly handled by the government. The crisis came on February 18 when, in spite of a powerful speech by Herbert Morrison warning of the serious issues a back-bench revolt could create, a division was forced. The vote sustained the government 338 to 121. This constituted the most serious breach of coalition discipline during the entire ministry of Churchill. Fortunately, calmer counsels now intervened, and the Labour membership did not require their leaders to leave the coalition.

Churchill acted as if there had never been a division or a report.[129] In a broadcast in March 1943, Churchill warned strongly against mortgaging the uncertain future and announced he did not need to go about making promises in order to win political support to continue in office.[130]

The issue of the Beveridge Report was raised again in the House on June 24, 1943. Churchill observed tartly on that occasion, "I do not think there is any public anxiety on this subject."[131] In October 1943 Churchill announced that he proposed to draw upon the experiences that followed World War I to make the next transition from war to peace more orderly and disciplined.[132] The implication was clear. Churchill had no intention of implementing the report until there had been a postwar general election. This was in keeping with the terms under which members had signed on to the coalition government team for the duration. However, Churchill had badly misread the public mood. This whole subject had always been an area in which Churchill was not strong. The attitude he adopted toward the Beveridge Report certainly did him political damage. At least it may be said that Churchill's failing was the uncommon one in politicians of making too few promises.

The political scene remained calm until a brief flurry in September 1944 over a military mishap at Arnhem, involving heavy British casualties and the surrender of some men. Churchill managed the matter easily in the House, however.[133] In December 1944 and the following January the last major political crisis of Churchill's war administration occurred. It was also in many respects his most superb performance. The approaching end of the war had led to a German withdrawal of forces from Greece. Into the vacuum thus created, the Greek political parties and associated groupings were not prepared to move with unity. Greek political life was deeply fragmented over the issue of the role to be allotted the Crown. However, the Greek Communist party was prepared to move and, supported by well-armed guerilla groups, aimed at the speedy seizure of power, using ruthless means if necessary. One other person, however, was also prepared to move—the seventy-year-old British Prime Minister. From the beginning of December 1944 Churchill took direct control of the critical Greek situation. British troops were sent into Athens to restore order and ensure that democratic processes were allowed to determine the nature of any Greek government. This was not, however, the general view of Churchill's actions in either Britain or the United States. British intervention in Athens was viewed widely as power politics played by that old master imperialist Winston S. Churchill. The most influential of the British press led the attack on the Prime Minister. The American government went even further and expressed open disapproval of British conduct. Amid these storms Churchill emerged at his best, certain of the rightness of his position and determined to persevere regardless of the pressure.[134] On December 8, 1944, Churchill delivered one of the most magnificent of all his parliamentary performances. His critics had moved an amendment regretting British intervention in Greece and other parts of liberated Europe. This was their first mistake, for they had broadened the issue beyond Greece to all of liberated Europe, and Churchill seized at once upon their tactical error. He could recite an impressive record of reestablishing political processes behind the progressing Allied armies. Having taken the initiative, Churchill pushed forward, insisting that any true democracy had at its foundation a secret ballot vote conducted in conditions free from oppression. This part of his speech was interrupted frequently, which brought forth yet stronger language. He denounced "a swindle democracy, a democracy which calls itself democracy because it is Left Wing." When the Communist member Gallacher was particularly difficult, Churchill told him, "Democracy is no harlot to be picked up in the street by a man with a tommy gun." Churchill then skillfully established that the amendment of the critics constituted a broad and general attack on the whole policy of the government, making clear to the House how basic the issue was. He followed with a long and masterful survey of British conduct in liberated Europe. Churchill concluded by laying down a clear challenge: Support him and understand that he would continue his policy in Greece or dismiss him. The House supported Churchill by a vote of 279 to 30.[135]

The Greek situation staggered on until Churchill decided to give up Christmas with his family and fly to Athens in an effort to find a solution. His courage was rewarded, and a regency was established which opened the road to an eventual armistice and pacification. Churchill's critics, however, continued their drumfire, and the issue of Greece was debated again on January 18 and 19, 1945. This time Churchill led off the debate. He did not equal his performance of December, but he stated his principles: "Government of the people, by the people, for the people, set up on a basis of election by free and universal suffrage, with secrecy of the ballot and no intimidation." He followed with a description of conditions in Greece from firsthand witnesses. This was impressive. He then proceeded to give his American ally a lesson in politics. Across the Atlantic Churchill had been flayed as practicing power politics. Churchill took up the phrase and asked the question, What are power politics? Was having a navy twice as big as any other navy in the world power politics? Was having the largest air force in the world with bases in every part of the world power politics? Was having all the gold in the world power politics? If so, Churchill said the British were not guilty of these offenses; "They are luxuries that have passed away from us." He then reminded his overseas audience, "We have sacrificed everything in this war. We shall emerge from it, for the time being, more stricken and impoverished than any other victorious country." He concluded by repudiating the charge that Britain was power hungry or pursuing a policy of colonial expansion: "I repulse these aspersions, whether they come from our best friends or our worst foes."[136]

The Prime Minister had stood firmly against all abuse and criticism;

he was right and he prevailed. What more can one ask of a democratic politician? Churchill's defense of his Greek policy was to be his last great political victory. The mood of the country seemed to be steadily moving against him, and nothing in the last year of the war reversed that tide. Party politics marched to the fore as the danger of battle receded. Already hovering in the wings was the question of how much longer Churchill's coalition government would last. By January 1945 the Parliament was in its tenth year; it had been a memorable Parliament, but its time was running out. Elections were long overdue.

Within the first six months that Churchill occupied the premiership, he had already indicated his intention of resigning and retiring at the end of the war; but the closer the war's end drew, the more his inclination to retire flagged.[137] Clement Attlee speculated that by 1943 Churchill had decided he would go to the people at the end of the war and attempt to secure a mandate for carrying on a program of Conservative social reform.[138] Churchill's own remarks give some support to this speculation. In November 1943 Churchill said he viewed it as part of the duty and responsibility of his national government to have its plans perfected for a postwar program of food, work, and homes for all.[139] But by late 1944 he was reluctant to break up his government and was determined to keep it at least through the conclusion of the war against Germany.[140] Recalling memories of 1918, he also announced that there would be no snap election and that time would be provided for soldiers serving overseas to cast their ballots.[141] By 1945 it was clear to Churchill that a general election must be held as soon as the war ended.[142] He described himself as distressed at the prospect of sinking from the position of a national leader to a party leader. How deeply Churchill felt on this issue is revealed in his memoirs.

> At this time I was very tired and physically so feeble that I had to be carried upstairs in a chair by the Marines from the Cabinet meetings under the Annexe. Still, I had the world position as a whole in my mind, and I deemed myself to possess knowledge, influence, and even authority, which might be of service. I therefore saw it as my duty to try, and at the same time as my right. I could not believe this would be denied me.[143]

But it was. Labour would not continue the coalition. In late May 1945 Churchill terminated the national government and formed a predominantly Conservative caretaker government to hold office during the period of political campaigning.

The campaign of 1945 was relatively sharp considering that the chief partisans had only a few days earlier been government colleagues. Churchill was bitter about having to terminate his coalition government and was generally sharp in his speeches. He did permit himself one light note. The Prime Minister, who had celebrated his seventieth birthday in November 1944, sent a brief message to Ralph Assheton, who was managing the Conservative campaign, on March 19, 1945: "I notice in the newspapers that the Central Office or Party Chiefs have issued instructions that no one over seventy should be tolerated as a candidate at the forthcoming election. I naturally wish to know at the earliest moment whether this ban applies to me."[144]

A series of radio addresses by the three party leaders made up an important part of the campaign. Churchill led off with a violent attack on his former colleagues in the national government and left himself open to Attlee's skillful counteraction. The Labour leader observed, "The voice was the voice of Churchill, but the mind the mind of Beaverbrook." Churchill's great skill with language seemed to desert him, and his speeches tended to be vague, wordy, and unconstructive. They suffered particularly in comparison to the Labour program.[145]

The tension of the election was unique; the ballots were not counted until those of the overseas troops arrived in Great Britain. Not until the Potsdam Conference was actually in session—on July 25, 1945—was the count taken. It revealed a sweeping Labour victory. Even years afterward writing his memoirs, Churchill could not quite conceal his bitterness over the people's verdict. He said it "had been so overwhelmingly expressed that I did not wish to remain even for an hour responsible for their affairs."[146] In retrospect it does not appear so surprising as it did then to both Churchill and the American press. In Britain itself the signs were abundant that the people were prepared to cheer Churchill as he campaigned and then vote for the Labour program. In truth, Churchill was better cast in the role of a national leader than in the role of a party leader.

CONSTITUTIONALIST

As CHURCHILL LEFT office in July 1945 after a service of more than five years, he left behind a substantial political and constitutional heritage. Harry Hopkins once joked in a speech at Teheran that "the provisions of the British Constitution and the powers of the War Cabinet are just whatever Winston Churchill wants them to be at any given moment."[147] There was both truth and exaggeration in this statement. Throughout his war ministry Churchill had demanded from Parliament and the people a full and unlimited authority. Without question he contributed to the expansion of the Prime Minister's already great powers. In the midst of the most severe political crisis of his administration, Churchill made a forceful case that Parliament had the right to dismiss him but not to ask him to bear responsibilities without the power of effective action.[148] He sang this song throughout the war: Trust me or sack me. But while he demanded power, it was always responsible power. He always understood that the government answered to the House and the House ultimately to the people. Discussing statutory rules and orders, Churchill said, "The Minister is always responsible ultimately, and the Government are always responsible collectively. If the Minister has not himself seen or signed an Order, as certainly sometimes necessarily occurs, he, nevertheless, is responsible, and can be brought to book in this House. There is the great remedy."[149] To Churchill, political power was never conceived as arbitrary. He insisted that the customs of question time be scrupulously observed, that ministers come to the House and answer to the membership themselves. Nor did he ever forget that politicians exist to serve the people. He was careful during the war that if anything should happen to him, the king was advised to send for Anthony Eden. This was reasonable considering the large Conservative majority in the House. During his caretaker government, Churchill took Clement Attlee with him to Potsdam so that, whatever the results of the 1945 elections, there would be full knowledge of the government's position available to the newly elected Prime Minister.[150] He argued for the opportunity to carry on his coalition government, which he described skillfully in the following terms: "In fact, I may say—and I will indeed be quite candid on this point—that having served for 42 years in this House, I have never seen any Government to which I have been able to give a more loyal, confident and consistent support." Yet he was prepared to override even these strong feelings to serve the more important principle, "The foundation of all democracy is that the people have the right to vote. To deprive them of that right is to make a mockery of all the high sounding phrases which are so often used."[151]

Just as Churchill respected the political rights of the people as a whole, he respected the civil liberties of individuals. In late 1943, while Churchill was attending the Cairo and Teheran conferences, the Home Secretary, Herbert Morrison, was informed of the declining health of Sir Oswald Mosley. Mosley had been the leader of the British Union of Fascists in the 1930s and had been arrested by the government at the outbreak of the war. In Churchill's absence the Cabinet debated whether Mosley should be released. Churchill, consulted by the Cabinet, was firm in believing that Mosley and his wife should be released, even if the government had to face considerable protest. Morrison appears also to have come to the conclusion that this was the right course, although the Cabinet as a whole was slow to reach this decision. There was indeed considerable agitation, and Mosley was a convenient center for public hostility. Morrison released Mosley and his wife, and the political storm passed quickly, producing Churchill's comment, "People who are not prepared to do unpopular things and to defy clamour are not fit to be Ministers in times of stress."[152]

Churchill was always respectful of the political convictions of others and did not attempt to push his Labour colleagues further than they could go. Indeed, he provided the Labour Party a substantial service. Clement Attlee has testified to how different he found his task of organizing a government in 1945 compared to the problems which had faced Ramsay MacDonald in 1924 and 1929. In 1924 MacDonald had hardly any experienced ministers, and his position was not much improved in

1929. Attlee, on the other hand, was able to begin his ministry with a team of thoroughly experienced ministers. Their long training in the Churchill government prepared the way for the great Labour administration of 1945–51.[153]

Perhaps the war could not have been won without the fully national government achieved by Churchill as Prime Minister. He maintained that government with a sense of fairness which seldom faltered, and the response of the ministers to his leadership was striking. Perhaps the best comment on this political contribution came from that careful observer, Charles de Gaulle: "But there was in each of them a devotion to the public service, and between all of them a community of aims, which bound them together. The whole gave the impression of a cohesion among those in authority which I very often envied and admired."[154] The circumstances of the war and the traditions of British political life and public service certainly contributed to this. But the quality of a government is established at the top. The accomplishments of David Lloyd George were gigantic and will sustain his name in history, but it is hard to deny that in his government during and perhaps more particularly after World War I there was a serious erosion of political integrity which left deep scars. Churchill's record is striking in comparison. He did indeed, in Harold Nicolson's words, elevate the whole standard of British public life.

3 / THE ADMINISTRATOR

THE MAN WHO BECAME Prime Minister on May 10, 1940, was not only one of the most experienced British politicians but also one of the most experienced political administrators. Churchill's government service dated to 1905; between that date and 1929 he was out of office only for a time in the middle of World War I and again from 1922 to 1925. He had added another eight months of service between the outbreak of World War II and his ascendency to the premiership, bringing his total to nearly twenty years. That service had involved the civilian leadership of all three armed forces, including two tours of duty as First Lord of the Admiralty. During his first tenure there he had revealed an appreciation for the need of overall strategic war direction.[1] Few men were so well equipped to provide just that.

Churchill's long experience could serve at times as a handicap. He was fond of the men of World War I and was tempted to employ them again in World War II. Such a case was Admiral of the Fleet Keyes, who for all his fire in 1940 was perhaps too much past his prime and never fully sensitive to developments in the strategic direction of warfare.[2] But on the whole, Churchill's previous government experience was valuable in leading the administration during World War II. In particular, his World War I experience taught him what worked administratively and—perhaps more important—what did not. He understood from the outset that war could be prosecuted successfully only with a strong central direction and a clear assignment of priorities if the entire complex military and civilian administration were to coordinate its efforts to sustain the nation in its greatest crisis.[3]

Churchill brought not only his experience as a government administrator to Whitehall in late spring of 1940 but also his reputation. That reputation bore only superficial relationship to his actual administrative effectiveness. Whitehall had heard of the spectacular Churchill of sweeping visions and precipitate action, the restless Churchill who probed constantly at the frontiers of administrative procedure, the high-handed Churchill who ignored administrative boundaries. The specter of this

Churchill—a veritable monster by their standards—arriving at Number 10 Downing Street was sufficient to send a "cold chill" down the spines of all responsible civil servants.[4] But what appeared all too glaringly as Churchill's administrative weaknesses were in fact elements of strength when he was placed in the right position. That, however, had to be the first in the government—the only place large enough to give scope to Churchill's sweeping views. The truth is that Churchill looked at issues too broadly to be confined to one department.

The Norwegian campaign which preceded Churchill's arrival as Prime Minister had tended to reveal only the weaknesses.[5] But during his second tenure as First Lord, Churchill had also shown signs of the badly needed strengths which he brought to the central direction of the war. He had pointed out to the Cabinet how slow the mobilization of British labor and resources had been in the early months of the war.[6] This impelling sense of administrative urgency, this burning energy to motivate and move the whole system, was perhaps Churchill's supreme gift as an administrator in a time of crisis. Any administrative system creates its own impediments, and the more complex and sophisticated a society, the more ancient and highly developed its government, the more vast the responsibilities which that government attempts to discharge, the more the administrative machinery tends to go dead of its own weight. Certainly the impelling necessity in May 1940 was for a powerful and driving force, which Churchill unquestionably was. Grigg, who had served him in 1925–29, vividly recalled Churchill's capacity to provoke his disciplined civil servants into most untypical outbursts.[7] Churchill's wide-ranging concern for all matters might have prompted a constitutional historian to describe him as a secretary of state for all departments. Certainly no department of state was safe from the new Prime Minister's intervention.[8] But linked to the energy and sweep of his mind was also the most important of administrative virtues—diligence. His capacity for sustained labor played an important role in his own ultimate success and set a standard which he expected from all others. He believed that high office was the achievement of long and sustained effort.[9]

Churchill possessed the further administrative virtue of communicating on paper.[10] The unwary person who encountered him was impressed by his flow of language, with all its richness and capacity to range seemingly without order over the most varied topics. The verbal Churchill was thinking, sorting, sifting, winnowing; but Churchill committed to paper was demanding, directing, ordering. On paper he could be a master of administrative cogency.

On September 11, 1939, newly arrived at the Admiralty, Churchill dispatched a minute to the Prime Minister regarding the need for a Ministry of Shipping. His summary was direct and masterful.

> The functions are threefold: (a) To secure the maximum fertility and economy of freights in accordance with the war policy of the Cabinet and the pressure

of events. (b) To provide and organise the very large shipbuilding programme necessary as a safeguard against the heavy losses of tonnage. . . . (c) The care, comfort, and encouragement of the merchant seaman who will have to go to sea repeatedly after having been torpedoed and saved. These merchant seamen are a most important and potentially formidable factor in this kind of war.[11]

Churchill never wasted words in his administrative memoranda, and he was quick to demand careful justification for departmental claims.[12] He was intolerant of the bureaucratic answer that something could not be done. He claimed it was always right to probe.[13] This critical capacity was important to the leadership of a complex governmental system.

Churchill possessed also an administrative virtue too often misunderstood. He understood the exercise of power; indeed, enjoyed it. There is a difference between the use and abuse of power, and perhaps too often Churchill's evident enjoyment in his mastery over the whole scene was misunderstood by the man of small and conventional mind and limited vision and capacity as constituting the conduct of the tyrant. Churchill was not a tyrant, however demanding an administrative leader he was. He simply understood that great events demand strong men. Strength he possessed in abundance, and this more than anything else was required in May 1940. Captain Roskill has compared Churchill to Pitt the Elder by quoting the words Isaac Barré spoke of that earlier war leader, "No man ever went in to [his] closet who did not feel himself, if possible, braver at his return than when he went in."[14]

PROBLEMS

In its broadest sense, the question Churchill faced upon becoming Prime Minister was how a parliamentary democracy should efficiently conduct a war. This problem had been left over from World War I, still imperfectly resolved despite David Lloyd George's imaginative but wayward genius. The central agency concerned with the higher conduct of war was the Committee of Imperial Defence (CID). It was assumed in the interwar period that because the Prime Minister was the ex officio chairman of the CID, the complete coordination of the administration for purposes of military necessity was assured. It was the responsibility of the Chiefs of Staff (COS) sitting on the CID to advise the Prime Minister on defense policy as a whole. This had been established in 1924.[15] In July 1938 the Cabinet and the CID acquired separate secretaries. By good fortune the two men selected—Sir Edward Bridges as head of the Combined Office and Secretary of the Cabinet and Sir Hastings Ismay as Secretary of the CID—were civil servants of the highest order, one a civilian and one a soldier.[16] When war broke out in September 1939, these two secretariats were combined again, with Bridges exercising senior authority.[17] Therefore, an efficient and experienced secretariat already existed which could provide the Prime Minister and Cabinet with a central point of administrative authority.

The problem in the Chamberlain period of the war lay more within the Cabinet itself than within the secretariat which served it. Chamberlain knew virtually nothing of war and was not particularly successful in functioning as a coordinator of the various departments responsible for its conduct, especially the three service departments. To achieve this a Military Coordination Committee was set up with Lord Chatfield as chairman. This was not successful, and Chatfield resigned. Ismay believed in retrospect that his position was impossible. The Minister for Coordination of Defence was responsible to Parliament and the public for the whole field of defense, but within the administration he had no executive authority whatever. He did not control a department, nor could he exercise control over all departments; only the Prime Minister could do that. When Lord Chatfield resigned on April 3, 1940, the idea of an independent Minister of Defence passed away with him. The new chairman of the Military Coordination Committee was in fact the First Lord, the senior Service Minister—Winston Churchill.

But Churchill found the position so difficult that he called in Chamberlain in the hope of getting badly needed decisions. If the Prime Minister had to preside over the Military Coordination Committee, there was little if anything to be said for a separate defense minister. The logical thing to do was to combine the offices of Prime Minister and Minister of Defence. But this posed the problem of the aptitudes of the man who occupied the office of Prime Minister. Chamberlain seemed to recognize by the end of April 1940 that he was not well suited for the task he was being forced to assume, so he attempted another arrangement. Churchill would be responsible on behalf of the Committee for giving guidance to the COS and would have his own central staff under a senior officer. This arrangement threatened to turn confusion into chaos.

While these unhappy experiments were being attempted, Hitler was in the process of seizing Norway in an operation which revealed all too painfully the lack of coordination in the British war effort. This in turn precipitated the political crisis of early May which finally resolved the administrative difficulties.[18] This confusion at the very center of the direction of the war tended to cast the administrative capacity of the British government in a far worse light than it deserved. The administrative standards of the higher British civil service may properly be viewed as the envy of the world. The capacity, judgment, and dedication of these men were outstanding—virtues which were immediately apparent to the Americans as they were drawn into contact with the British on the eve of war.[19] The central problem was essentially one of leadership, not of staff, and it was subject to immediate solution upon Churchill's entry into the office of Prime Minister.

The same was not true of what appeared to be the more immediate problems facing the new Prime Minister as he took office. Could Britain survive the immediate military crisis of the summer? If so, should the government attempt to plan for a long war or a short war? To run on short-term priorities might mean surviving an immediate crisis only to fail at a later date through improper coordination of resources. On the other hand, to plan for a long war might mean having inadequate forces available in the early stages when the enemy was ascendant and perhaps could carry his effort to victory before long-term plans on the British side could reach fruition. The question of length also involved whether Great Britain could in fact prosecute any war. The situation was so desperate that every resource of the United Kingdom would have to be mobilized; there was no room for mistakes. Most difficult of all for the new Prime Minister, he did not have control over all the factors which went into making intelligent administrative decisions. The military initiative rested with Hitler. In a sense, Churchill had to plan his war effort in partnership with his enemy, for misjudgment of German plans or military potential or both could also produce fatal British mistakes. The mobilization of Britain for an all-out war effort also depended in large measure on the attitude of neutral powers, for the measure of economic resources which Britain could draw from abroad would substantially determine both the size and length of the war effort. The critical country in this consideration was the United States, and the critical problem in the United States in the summer of 1940 was dollars.[20]

Even before the German assault in the West, these problems had been looming on the horizon. The success of the German army on the Continent only brought them swiftly to critical proportions. When Churchill became Prime Minister, the British government had yet to face these questions directly, for they were still unanswered after eight months of war. The questions seemed so unyielding of solution that simply to state them was sufficient to turn any but the strongest of men away from attempting to resolve them. Thus the overall administrative problem of the prosecution of the war demanded the strongest of men in the summer of 1940.

POLICIES

Sir Keith Hancock has suggested that adequate treatment of the constitutional history of Britain requires combining the themes of liberty and efficiency. This is never more true than at the outset of a great national crisis of war.[21] In the summer of 1940, efficiency had priority. Strong arguments were advanced in the press in favor of a war cabinet of a few members who would jointly determine the general direction of the war unhampered by departmental duties. Churchill took a quite different position. He believed that the establishment of policy and the executive authority to see that policy carried into action should be combined. He warned that without this unity of policy and action "words and arguments are interminable, and meanwhile the torrent of war takes its headlong course."[22] There were also practical political considerations. He did not like having "unharnessed ministers" around him; he preferred to deal with men responsible for actions rather than simply responsible for their own advice. He believed this promoted harmony and reduced rivalry. He was determined from the beginning that leadership would be centralized for purposes of efficiency and at the center would stand the Prime Minister. By immediately assuming the title Minister of Defence along with his constitutional position, Churchill was able to underline the point that he would direct the prosecution of the war. When Harry Hopkins visited London in January 1941, he swiftly reported the Prime Minister's success to Roosevelt: "*Churchill* is the gov't in every sense of the word—he controls the grand strategy and often the details. . . . I cannot emphasize too strongly that he is the one and only person over here with whom you need to have a full meeting of minds."[23]

Churchill not only stood at the center but threw out constant barbs and directives and spurs to action. He told a secret session of the House of Commons on June 25, 1941,

> As to complacency, let me say this. Do not let anyone suppose that inside this enormous government we are a mutual-admiration society. I do not think, and my colleagues will bear me witness, any expression of scorn or severity which I have heard used by our critics has come anywhere near the language I have been myself accustomed to use, not only orally, but in a continued stream of written minutes. In fact, I wonder that a great many of my colleagues are on speaking terms with me. They would not be if I had not complained of and criticized all evenly and alike.[24]

By the time he made this statement, Churchill's ruthless energy had fired the entire administrative structure of the government and had burned a few of its members, but whatever wounds Churchill may have inflicted upon his colleagues were certainly less harsh than the fate they might have expected from a German occupation. The situation demanded complete efficiency—indeed extreme effort.

Two decisions in May 1940 stressed the approach of the new Prime Minister. The very life of Britain as a nation was its economy. Commerce and finance had sustained Britain in its greatness from the seventeenth century through the beginning of the twentieth. When Napoleon sought terms of abuse to hurl at his British foes, he called them a nation of shopkeepers. This was actually too narrow a description unless one thought of the term as meaning shopkeepers to the world. By 1940 there was thus deeply intrenched in British public life the concept of the importance of financial matters. But the arithmetic of finance as it appears in national budgets and is measured by the various statistics produced from the Bank of England and Treasury is only the humanly calculated measure of the resources of a nation, not the basic economic strength of the nation itself. In May 1940 financial bookkeeping was reduced to second place, and the basic components of the nation's resources were pulled forward into the war effort.[25] This was a revolutionary change of viewpoint for the government. It meant that a certain basic assumption about World War II had been faced: that national survival and the protection of the liberties traditional to the British people would have to be purchased at the cost of the nearly total exhaustion of Britain's national resources. This was a cruel decision, but it is hard to see that any other was possible in the summer of 1940. To abandon financial arithmetic as the government's basic approach to the prosecution of the war was perhaps psychologically necessary, for any figures secured in this way were going to show terrifying deficits. It was best to measure the capabilities of the national effort in more direct forms, particularly manpower, and to hope that the human potential would be sufficient.

The second important decision that summer was of more immediate significance. The British army had been thrown off the Continent. Britain's French ally had been subdued. The power of the German army was unrivaled at the moment. But Germany did not control the English Channel, and Britain still possessed its resources of sea and air power to make any attempt at crossing the Channel an operation of the gravest risk. The German navy had suffered serious losses in the Norwegian campaign and was ill-prepared to attempt to take on the vast resources of British naval power. The instrument Hitler possessed by which he hoped to secure domination of the Channel was the *Luftwaffe*. It was essential that the Royal Air Force (RAF) have sufficient aircraft available to meet the German challenge, for Britain would live or die by its capacity to meet Hitler's air power.

Churchill at once decided that this critical situation called for a certain disregard of the niceties of production schedules and organizational tables, and he summoned to head a separate Ministry of Aircraft Production an old friend whose extraordinary capacity to achieve decisive results under pressure was already well known to Churchill. On May 14, 1940, Lord Beaverbrook accepted Churchill's call to head the new ministry. This decision was vindicated by results. The delivery of new fighters rose from 256 in April to 467 in September. By the end of the Battle of Britain, the problem was no longer insufficient aircraft but insufficient air crews.[26]

Beaverbrook's methods were hardly conventional. The Prime Minister had to intervene often to soothe disputes. The Minister of Aircraft Production would not be bound by overriding general priorities. His methods elicited violent criticism, the most serious being that he employed the threats of force and fear to achieve his ends and that in achieving a short-term triumph of production, he heavily mortgaged the technical developments of the future. Perhaps the positive results could have been achieved without quite so high a price, but the luxury of debating these possibilities was not available in the summer of 1940. Churchill knew a man who could get the results he needed. Neither can it be said that the government of Britain became an instrument of methods of force and fear, nor was long-range technical development critically hurt.[27] The short-term crisis had been met, and as the winter storms began to sweep up the Channel, the British government acquired a breathing space in which to evaluate the future of the war.

With the question of Britain's survival answered positively at least until late spring of 1941, it was now necessary to turn to the question of how the total resources of Britain were to be mobilized for what was assumed to be a long struggle. The most significant contribution to developing this long-range program was the emergence of the manpower budget.[28] Lord Bridges has written that Churchill always gave this his closest personal attention and that the allocation of manpower and resources laid the foundation for much of the war effort. This excites less interest than successful campaigns, but it is something which should not be lost sight of in any assessment of Churchill's wartime premiership.[29] The first manpower budget was not designed to spread great encouragement in Whitehall. When the total male population from ages twenty to forty-one had been surveyed, it was found that the margin available to the government consisted of 200,000 men who had been allowed to defer service and about 800,000 more who were available to be called to various services—military or auxiliary. A manpower margin of 1 million for the prosecution of total war was not comforting and must have been frightening indeed to anyone who recalled the casualty figures of World War I.[30] The most exhausting demands on manpower came from the army, and it was its size which Churchill attacked with vigor. He insisted that there must be an absolute ceiling on the manpower available to the army. This figure was ultimately set at more than 2 million men late in 1941 and later in the war reached more than 2.25 million. This was a critical decision. Until the army was brought within reasonable bounds, manpower planning for all other aspects of the war could not take place.[31] Sir James Grigg has testified that he can never remember the War Cabinet allotting to the army more than half the number of men it felt it needed.[32]

The situation also meant that Churchill would be insistent, even demanding, that available manpower be used to best efficiency; army officials would soon become accustomed to an unending stream of minutes from Churchill asking why the size of the army as a whole produced such a limited number of men fighting on the front line. Considering the narrow margins with which he worked, Churchill's demand is understandable. By December 1942 it was even clearer that the manpower budget would have to be carefully balanced between fighting strength and the number of persons required to work at home. By then departmental requests exceeded available manpower by more than a million. Every possible method was employed to close the gap. Women were used to an extent hardly even considered in 1939. There were limits to the British war effort which in no way could be surpassed, and by the end of 1944 Great Britain clearly would have reached the total capacity of its manpower supply. By spring of 1945, the British war effort would have passed its absolute peak.[33] These facts did much to dictate the direction and character of the British war effort.

It was recognized early that manpower was more critical in many senses than the material resources available to Britain. To use available manpower which had fixed ceilings most advantageously dictated a policy of drawing resources to support the war from outside Britain—from the Empire and particularly from the vast productive capacity of the United States. This would become a central theme of Churchill's war diplomacy: gaining the maximum possible support for Britain from the United States. The ideal would be American entry into the war.

With the perspective of time, it is possible to debate both the short-term and long-term decisions which Churchill and his War Cabinet reached. At least they were ratified by success. It falls upon Churchill's critics to make a case that affairs could have been managed better. These were decisions reached under heavy pressures with no cushion of resources—human or material—for error.

STRUCTURE

Military Side

FROM THE OUTSET Churchill concerned himself more with the military side of administration than with the civil side. By making himself Minister of Defence, he clearly established his authority to provide strategic direction of the war.[34] He instituted two defense committees, one for operations and one for supply. These were made up of ministers whose functions were relevant to the activities of the committees. The keynote was flexibility. The Prime Minister was chairman of both defense committees, and the COS customarily were present at meetings. The committees were serviced by the War Cabinet secretariat, and the COS attending committee meetings had available to them the full structure of military planning and intelligence staffs. It swiftly became clear that the truly important members of the defense committees were not the ministers (other than the Prime Minister) but in fact the COS. Churchill said this of the arrangement:

> I do not think there has ever been a system in which the professional heads of the Fighting Services have had a freer hand or a greater or more direct influence, or have received more constant and harmonious support from the Prime Minister and the Cabinet under which they serve. It is my practice to leave the Chiefs of Staff alone to do their own work, subject to my general supervision, suggestion and guidance.[35]

Perhaps Churchill should have placed more emphasis on his general supervision, for it was substantial.

Clearly then, the people who really counted were Churchill and the COS. If anything, the influence of the COS grew at the expense of War

Cabinet and defense committee ministers as the war proceeded. This was particularly true after the United States entered the war, for the Constitution of that country provided the President with the specific powers of commander-in-chief of the armed forces. President Roosevelt thus was in a position of direct constitutional authority over the military forces of his country without any civilian intermediaries other than his own Cabinet appointments, the Secretary of War and the Secretary of the Navy. It seems likely that the American constitutional arrangements impressed Churchill. Simple cooperation between the two countries would dictate parallel organization. At the first meeting following American entry the two countries established a Combined Chiefs of Staff (CCOS) for unified strategic planning. This functioned best when arrangements between the respective heads of government and their service advisers were similar. Certainly those contacts were of great immediacy in both countries, although the British side appears more orderly in nature than was characteristic of the pattern existing in Washington.[36]

The constitutional relationship between the Prime Minister and the COS was roughly that the government could overrule them on political grounds. Further, the government could remove them, or they could resign. These were obviously alternatives of desperation. For successful operation, resolution of difficulties by discussion was clearly desirable and indeed about the only way.[37] The pattern of relations between the government and its military advisers in World War I was not a happy precedent. Certainly Churchill and his military advisers had in their minds the experience of the earlier period as a model to be avoided at all costs.

In these arrangements the War Cabinet appeared to lose considerable authority. By January 1944 the COS could plan the Anzio operation with the Prime Minister without even proposing to tell the War Cabinet the date. The War Cabinet members had their own responsibilities—Churchill had seen to that—and did not seem to be particularly anxious to exercise a general supervisory role over military operations. On one occasion Ernest Bevin flatly stated this to Churchill, who was somewhat embarrassed since he was attempting to use the War Cabinet as a lever to pressure his own policies on the COS. Also reduced in scope by these working arrangements were the functions of the three civilian heads of the service departments. They became more and more merely efficient administrators as the war proceeded, and their decision-making capacity was limited to departmental duties. How far this process was carried was revealed by the appointment of Sir James Grigg, the Permanent Undersecretary for War, to the position of Secretary of State. This was not well received in all quarters but in fact proved effective. The other two civilian service heads lasted the duration of the coalition government. Sir Archibald Sinclair, the Liberal leader and formerly Churchill's battalion second-in-command on the western front in World War I, was Secretary of State for Air. The First Lord of the Admiralty was A. V.

Alexander, who had held that office under Ramsay MacDonald. Neither man emerged in a strong role during World War II. This seems to be as Churchill wished.[38]

The central direction of the war in Britain clearly lay neither in the War Cabinet nor in the service departments. Even the defense committees became less influential for directing the war as time passed. Again, the decisive break in this pattern seems to be the entry of the United States into the war. In 1941 the Defence Committee (Operations) had 76 meetings and 41 memoranda; in 1942, 20 meetings and 33 memoranda; and in 1944, 10 meetings and 13 memoranda. The Defence Committee (Supply) held 15 meetings in 1941 and circulated 157 memoranda; in 1942, 7 meetings and 106 memoranda; and in 1944, 8 meetings and 38 memoranda. Obviously the Prime Minister and the COS on the British side and the President (although to a lesser degree than the Prime Minister) and the Joint Chiefs of Staff (JCS) on the American side constituted the central direction of the Western Alliance.[39]

The actual process of directing the British war effort on the military side started with the Prime Minister and radiated outward through the Cabinet secretariat, particularly General Ismay and Sir Edward Bridges. Ismay received strictly military matters and Bridges served to inform proper government departments and ministers when they were involved. Churchill laid down a valuable administrative principle in a memorandum to Ismay, Bridges, and the Chief of the Imperial General Staff (CIGS) on July 19, 1940:

> Let it be very clearly understood that all directions emanating from me are made in writing, or should be immediately afterwards confirmed in writing, and that I do not accept any responsibility for matters relating to national defence on which I am alleged to have given decisions, unless they are recorded in writing.

This record-keeping of decision-making was extremely important, particularly in dealing with a man who had the habit of firing off his thoughts and directives at all times of the day and to all sorts of persons. Without Churchill's habit of putting all these matters in writing, it would have been difficult to coordinate and relate them into a coherent pattern.

Churchill has described his way of doing business. He was in the habit of awaking about 8:00 A.M. and reading the flow of material that had built up for him overnight. He would then dictate (often from his bed) minutes and directives to the COS and to departments. When the COS met at 10:30, they usually had a full agenda to work through. By late afternoon the simpler matters were coordinated and the necessary orders dispatched. The responsibility for getting Churchill's orders on their way fell upon his small secretariat and particularly upon Sir Hastings Ismay. He and his civilian double, Bridges, brought order and direction to the desires of the Prime Minister. Their functions have been summed up in John Colville's felicitous expression, "They soothed the exasperated and they prodded the indolent."[40] Ismay and Bridges along with Colonel Jacob and Colonel Hollis, Ismay's assistants, not only coordinated the outflow from Churchill (which could be of very substantial proportions) but also organized the responses to Churchill's inquiries and directives. Fortunately, all four men worked easily together, and Churchill was very well served by his secretariat throughout the war.[41]

Prior to Churchill's becoming Prime Minister, the last reshuffling of defense direction by Chamberlain had left Churchill in a position to lean heavily upon his own personal staff. It was General Ismay who convinced Churchill of the wisdom of using the Cabinet secretariat rather than his own staff. Ismay's success in this was perhaps his greatest contribution to the war. It helped substantially to avoid the sort of difficulties which grew out of Lloyd George's "garden suburb" during World War I. At the same time Churchill still retained the advice of his personal staff, but they were kept to the side of the actual structure of government. Since some of these advisers were not particularly sensitive to administrative procedure, this was probably a fortunate arrangement. Ismay's second great service was the skill and tact with which he conducted relations between Churchill and the COS, softening the abrasions which could spring up so easily between a man of Churchill's temperament and his experienced military advisers who could become rather quickly irritated at his proddings and procedures. Ismay accomplished this difficult task, preserving his integrity throughout, but at times even his extraordinary goodwill was strained. Late in the war, by the time of the second conference at Quebec (Octagon), Ismay had reached the point of writing a letter of resignation.[42]

One matter which might have given trouble between Churchill and the COS was the issue of the Joint Planning Staff, which was responsible for drawing up reports to the COS with regard to operations. The Joint Planning Staff swiftly incurred the wrath of the Prime Minister who saw in them only "the dead weight of inertia and delay." He therefore directed that the joint planners should henceforth work directly under him. This contained the danger, of course, that in time Prime Minister and joint planners would direct strategic operations rather than Prime Minister and COS, the official military heads of the services. Not surprisingly, the CIGS (at that time Sir John Dill) was concerned. In fact, the planners continued to work through the COS. Churchill throughout his ministry tended occasionally to bypass the COS, particularly when he expected difficulties from them. However, the loyalty of the Cabinet secretariat and the good judgment of planners and field commanders alike, along with the tolerance of the COS, prevented any harm coming of this. When the United States entered the war, a joint staff mission in Washington contained British as well as American planners. Their administrative position then tended to become fixed, since Roosevelt never showed much inclination for planning operations himself and Churchill could hardly hope to direct the combined staff planners as he might attempt to direct only the British.[43]

Another aspect of Churchill's central direction of the war was his determination that war production would be directed essentially by decisions made by the Defence Committee (Supply). This led to certain problems in efficiently organizing the entire British war production. A production executive was attempted early in Churchill's ministry but seems to have had a limited existence of its own, being caught between policy determined in the Defence Committee (Supply) expressing the wishes of the Prime Minister on the one hand and the control over labor which was the territory of Ernest Bevin. The Cabinet reorganization in early 1942 provided a more efficient solution to this problem, which was largely one of administrative neatness. In fact, production was well coordinated on the whole from the very beginning; probably it was essential that the main lines of policy be determined by the Defence Committee.[44]

If the Defence Committee was to exercise so extensive a sway, it was essential that it possess the necessary information for making intelligent decisions. This led in turn to what was known as the statistical section. Churchill was one of the earliest politicians to recognize the importance of science and statistics for the effective direction of government. When still a lonely figure in April 1939, Churchill had told the House of Commons that the information and intelligence operations of the British government were not being coordinated effectively for the critical information to reach ministers. When he entered the government in September 1939, he moved at once to make sure that he would be served adequately in this regard. He called on his old associate Professor Lindemann (later Lord Cherwell) to organize a statistical branch of the Admiralty. When Churchill became Prime Minister, this group became the Prime Minister's statistical section and tended to work in effect under the Defence Committee (Supply). Its membership was about twenty persons—several economists, at least one scientist, at least one civil servant to make sure that the amateurs' work flowed into the proper administrative channels, a variety of clerks and typists, and six mathematicians. This section was not always popular with departments, but its importance to the Prime Minister and to the central direction of the war should not be underestimated because of the collection of critical comments which has grown up around it. In a large and sophisticated administration, every department possesses the capacity of producing that sort of evidence most suitable to its own arguments. If the Prime Minister and the central direction of the war were to be more than simply the captives of departmental decisions, a separate statistical section which could command data and analyze information critically was absolutely essential.[45] Churchill used this statistical department to deal with crucial problems such as the Battle of the Atlantic, to follow critical developments, and to find adequate solutions.

Cherwell was important to Churchill further because he could clarify complex scientific arguments and conclusions for the Prime Minister, whose mind was set in a historical rather than a quantitative frame of reference. Cherwell was more than merely head of the statistical section; he also was the Prime Minister's personal scientific adviser, and his work covered a wide range of subjects. His personality made him a controversial figure, and his scientific advice produced its critics, but his record seems more adequate than that of those who criticized. This is not to deny that Cherwell could be something of an administrative problem, for he had a tendency to assume rather sweeping powers of inquiry for himself. Ismay described him as seeming "to try to give the impression of wanting to quarrel with everybody, and of preferring everyone's room to their company. . . ."[46] These are extraordinarily hard words from the tolerant Ismay. But someone had to talk scientific sense to Churchill, who was wise enough to recognize this, and Cherwell undeniably was a master of his field. While Churchill could undervalue good but silent men, he usually picked able men to serve him. There were no empty-headed sycophants assembled for weekends at Chequers. The men who gathered there, unlike those at some tables in the 1930s, were not all of one mind. Churchill respected the integrity of the men who served him.

Another administrative device employed by Churchill was the ad hoc commitee. These committees would come into being when there was a particular difficulty in establishing agreement on the criteria necessary for intelligent war decisions, an obvious case being the evaluation of enemy potential. This could be very difficult; in at least one case—in a controversy between the Air Ministry and the Ministry of Economic Warfare with regard to the strength of the German air force—it was necessary to bring in a Justice as an arbiter. Ad hoc committees were also used to deal with particularly critical matters over which the Prime Minister wished to preside himself, pulling together those persons particularly concerned—for example, the Battle of the Atlantic Committee set up in March 1941 when sinkings in the North Atlantic were approaching the catastrophic level. Certain great operations could also result in an ad hoc committee as existed briefly before Overlord.[47]

A final example of the flexibility with which Churchill administered the war effort was his employment of Resident Ministers in military theaters of operations. These men were politicians who bore the responsibility of carrying out government policy in theater areas, thus relieving the military authorities of the worry of political implications. They were appointed by the Prime Minister and were responsible to him, but they also had the responsibility of assisting and advising the theater commanders to whom they were attached. By reporting directly to the Prime Minister, they threatened to circumvent the traditional structure of the Foreign Office. Churchill had not at first embraced the idea of Resident Ministers when they were proposed by the overworked Wavell in 1940. There was a certain delicacy then to these positions, and that they functioned extremely well is perhaps chiefly attributable to the men appointed. Oliver Lyttelton went to the Middle East in June 1941 as Resident Minister. At the time of the Darlan crisis in North Africa, Harold Macmillan was sent to provide political guidance; he later serviced much of the Mediterranean basin. These were outstanding men of great intelligence and judgment, and on the whole the use of Resident Ministers proved to be a successful arrangement.[48]

There emerges from Churchill's conduct of military affairs some picture of the relationships that existed among Cabinet government, effective strategic direction, and the character of the Prime Minister; these were the three central elements which had to be harmonized into a working arrangement. Its operation was sketched by Churchill to the House of Commons in an important statement in July 1941. He explained that in his capacity as Minister of Defence he prepared a general scheme for the War Cabinet, bringing together the whole of munition production and the import program and prescribing the highest reasonable target based upon service recommendations. The general scheme or War Supply Budget for the year then received final approval of the War Cabinet and thereafter became mandatory on all departments. Within that general framework, revision and adjustment under the pressure of events were continuous.[49]

In seeking harmony among the constitutional aspect of Cabinet government, the military aspect of effective strategic direction, and the personality of the Prime Minister himself, it must be said that the administrative structure was adjusted at its center to meet the demands and the characteristics of the Prime Minister. On the whole this worked well. Lord Ismay has testified that there was a remarkable intensification of effort in every field resulting from Churchill's personal exercise of the wide powers given to him by the War Cabinet; because of his astonishing drive, firm decisions could be reached and translated into action far more quickly than before. "For the first time in their history, the Chiefs of Staff were in direct and continuous contact with the Head of the Government, . . . as had always been contemplated."[50] The most pressing danger in this arrangement was likely to be autocracy because of the powerful personality of the Prime Minister; in fact some aspects of autocracy were not entirely averted at the administrative level. But ultimately the constitutional position of Cabinet government composed of ministers jointly responsible to Parliament was preserved. Churchill's own beliefs as much as anything else determined this.

Civil Side

While Churchill stood directly at the center of the military side of his administration, his relationship with the civilian side was more distant. From the beginning he assigned civil affairs particularly to those members of his Cabinet most experienced and best suited to work with the problems of domestic society. At the outset this meant primarily Attlee and Greenwood, if we exclude Chamberlain's brief service before he died. The civil side like the military needed tighter coordination in the summer of 1940, and Greenwood and Attlee centered attention on the Lord President's Committee. The influence of this body steadily increased throughout the war. Its original responsibility was handling on behalf of the War Cabinet all questions of domestic policy not specifically assigned to some other committee. It also had to coordinate all civil committees and keep a general watch over all domestic problems, particularly economic development. As the power of this committee grew, the position of the Lord President grew with it until he became recognized as the senior minister on the civilian side. While his power never approached that of the Minister of Defence on the military side, the primacy of the Lord President in his proper sphere was recognized when, in September 1943, Clement Attlee became Lord President, Deputy Prime Minister, and chairman of the War Cabinet when the Prime Minister was out of the country. The Lord President's Committee proved to be the most important development on the civil side of the government reorganization of the summer of 1940. By the middle of 1941 its range of activity covered such items as prices and wages, compensation, consumption, rationing, concentration of industry, mobilization of manpower, and critical supplies (coal, rubber, and petroleum). By early 1942 food policy had generally been absorbed into the functions of the Lord President's Committee through the agency of the Lord President himself.[51]

Between the brief tenure of the ill Chamberlain and the long service of Clement Attlee, the Lord President was Sir John Anderson. Anderson had risen in civil service to a recognized position of one of the most gifted servants of the state. He had been working with problems related to home defense from as early as 1924. Anderson knew Whitehall's workings intimately, and he was a man of dispassionate judgment whose strengths were those of coordination and careful decision. The Lord President's Committee was strengthened by the presence of Ernest Bevin who was responsible for labor and national service. Bevin's contribution to the committee was notable too, and from January 1941 until the end of the coalition in 1945, Bevin attended 272 of the committee's 299 meetings. His presence ensured coordination of the most vital element in the war effort, that of manpower, with all the programs which passed under the review of the Lord President's Committee. The manpower budget, so important to the entire war effort, became the personal responsibility of Anderson; even when he left the position of Lord President, he retained his responsibility in the difficult task of drawing up the manpower budget for the remainder of the war. The manpower budget was developed on the civilian side, approved by the Lord President's Committee, and then passed from that committee over to the military side where decisions for the prosecution of the war could be made on the basis of a clear understanding of what resources were available.[52]

While the Lord President's Committee achieved a permanent and important place in the prosecution of the war effort, the same could not be said of a variety of executives through which Churchill hoped to manage the always intractable problem of war production and a variety of other difficulties particularly relating to imports. Early in January 1941 an import executive was formed to determine priorities in terms of domestic consumption and materials necessary for war production and then how best to secure the needed goods. The most pressing problem was maintaining supply through the British home ports. So critical was this that it acquired the unofficial title of the Battle of the Ports; had this battle been lost, it is likely that the war also would have been lost.

The very difficult problems of port organization and merchant shipping called for a high level of expert knowledge, and in 1941 the number of people trained to grapple with these highly specialized problems, even in so mercantile a nation as Britain, was distinctly limited. From about October 1940 it became increasingly clear that there was a crisis. Complaints poured in on the government from every direction that the clearing of cargoes in the ports simply was inadequate and was reaching proportions which threatened to jam the operation of the ports entirely. This extraordinary dislocation in a nation, which above all others would be expected to cope with such mercantile matters, resulted from the ability of the *Luftwaffe* to command the approaches to the ports along the east and south coasts of Britain, particularly London and the Thames estuary. Some shipping of a coastal sort was maintained, but the ports of the west—particularly Glasgow and Liverpool and to a lesser extent Bristol—had to assume a traffic which they were not immediately prepared to handle. The collapse of the front in France had also dislocated a good deal of merchant activity. The problems were of every sort: misloaded cargoes, cranes inadequate to move particular types of cargoes, consequent inefficient unloading involving frequent movement of ships from dock to dock, an inadequate supply of specialty railway cars to carry particular materials, and outdated labor practices in the port areas. The enemy contributed some occasional bombs to the general disorder.[53]

The Battle of the Ports was particularly hard to prosecute from the administrative side because it was difficult for the government to get adequate statistical information for intelligent decision making. By December 1940 it was concluded that the original concept of emergency committees in the ports had failed. In late December the Prime Minister himself intervened. He recognized the critical nature of the situation in the Mersey and the Clyde and called the situation "the most dangerous part of our whole front." This was no exaggeration. He asked the Economic Policy Committee to supply him with "A. The facts. B. What you are doing. C. How you can be helped." This was Churchill at his administrative best. He recognized the seriousness of a problem that could have been underestimated, or at least not given the sort of priority it required for successful solution. He also recognized that the problem involved matters of such a technical character that he did not propose to try to invent a solution. He relied on the experts in the area to provide a solution and promised them that he would use his powers to expedite their recommendations.

This new energy fueled administrative action already in gear, and by December 30, 1940, a subcommittee on port clearance had decided that a type of local authority—a regional port director—would be needed. Two were required immediately, one for the Mersey and one for the Clyde. Later a third was appointed for the Bristol Channel. Bevin insisted that these port directors assume responsibility over the direction of port labor as well as all the shipping problems. Of all the ministers who sat on the port clearance subcommittee, only Bevin had personal experience with dock labor, or indeed any real knowledge of the workings of a port. Again it appears the right men were in the right place and the right decisions were made. The new port organization began to bring improved results by late spring of 1941, at about the same time that enemy bombing of the western ports began to increase significantly. Had intensive German bombing occurred at the same time as the administrative crisis, the difficulties could have become immense.[54]

This increased bombing emphasized another decision directly related to the working of the ports which required Churchill's personal intervention—the question of whether goods unloaded from ships should be immediately stored in the dock areas and then transported to their ultimate destinations or should be transported from the docks directly to inland sorting depots. The inland depots, it was argued, would reduce the dangers of congestion in the port itself and of bombing losses. On the other hand, would these depots—their construction and the railway equipment they would require—be more of a drain on the nation's resources than a help? Churchill opted for the inland sorting depots, and in March 1941 their construction was decided upon. By this date, administrative judgment was largely in their favor.

Churchill's attention to this whole problem is a good example of his intervention on the civilian side of the war effort with highly satisfactory consequences.[55] Related to this was the decision in May 1941 to combine the Ministries of Shipping and Transport into the Ministry of War Transport under the direction of Lord Leathers. Shipping and ports thus came under the same overall ministerial direction. This largely completed the rearrangements with regard to supplying Britain for the war.[56] Shipping would remain a critical problem for Britain throughout the war, largely because of its relationship to the military aspect, particularly during the Battle of the Atlantic and later in the conduct of the great Allied amphibious operations. However great those strains would be, shipping ultimately was always found; but while shipping proved adequate to the prosecution of the war, it did impose its own limits on what could be undertaken. The important point is that by May 1941 the government, spurred at moments by the Prime Minister, had found its way to an effective organization of the shipping and port situation. Without this foundation, shipping in all its aspects would have been a far more grievous problem, perhaps an insoluble one.

A less happy story is the fate that befell war production prior to the reforms of early 1942. Main production plans had been substantially determined in the Defence Committee (Supply), but there were three supply departments (one for each service), and there was constant public demand for a Minister of Production to coordinate them. For a long time Churchill remained hostile to this proposal. In 1941 a production executive was attempted, but this apparently never took charge of the main production plans and its function was never very clear; perhaps it was designed more for political purposes than for administrative ones. However, at least it functioned with what appears in retrospect to be a relatively substantial measure of efficiency. The factor which apparently changed Churchill's mind with regard to a single Minister of Production was his experience in the United States in December 1941 where he found the President inclined toward a single chairman of a War Production Board. Churchill thought it wise that this man have a British counterpart. Churchill's decision for a production minister was generally in accord with widespread opinion at the time. It was his choice for the job that created difficulties.

The Prime Minister had decided he wanted Lord Beaverbrook to direct war production. There was immediate opposition, particularly from Ernest Bevin whose conflicts with Beaverbrook were already substantial and of long standing. The two ministers clashed immediately over jurisdiction, Beaverbrook calling for ever wider powers and Bevin demanding that his authority with regard to manpower be specifically protected in any arrangements reached. Bevin won the guarantees he insisted upon. Churchill defended the arrangement in Parliament on February 10, 1942, in a speech in which he announced, "The Minister of Production and the Minister of Labour will work in the closest co-operation." All those who knew the two personalities concerned could hardly accept this statement as much more than a pious hope. Nine days later, it was all over. Beaverbrook resigned and was soon replaced by Oliver Lyttelton, an experienced businessman. On March 25, 1942, the new Minister of Production told the House that he and the Minister of Labour could "work in harmony." This proved true. By this stage of the war, the primary problems facing the Minister of Production were not so much those connected with achieving the greatest expansion of production as those associated with shaping programs and coordinating them with the efforts of the United States and Russia. It had taken rather long to get a workable arrangement, and Churchill had not been at his best in this episode.[57]

Churchill once described to Parliament the basic components of the civilian side of the war effort as finance, labor, and food; and Churchill's government dealt with all three. When he took office in May 1940, no government authority was yet prepared to face the labor problem head on. Churchill was determined to do so, and this led to the selection of the outstanding trade unionist in the British Isles as the Minister of Labour. In spite of the fact that Ernest Bevin had no previous parliamentary experience, he proceeded with shrewdness and good judgment. A national arbitration tribunal was set up to provide binding settlements in disputes, and the government made strikes and walkouts illegal under most conditions. The basic principles upon which the government proceeded in labor matters were reliance on the responsibility of the trade unions and recognition that union demands could be held in reasonable bounds only if the cost of living was also controlled. When Japan attacked, more stringent controls of manpower were deemed necessary; a national service bill was passed which instituted a system amounting to universal and compulsory service for men and women for civilian and military duties. Control of the cost of living meant particularly the cost of food. This was achieved largely through government subsidies to agriculture and was largely successful, although the government was somewhat slow to recognize that the subsidies would have to be more than a temporary expedient. Controlling food costs, however, does not control the entire cost of living. Rising costs of fuel and clothing led to a steady though limited inflation. On the whole, however, the government's record for the control of inflation was very good.

Another aspect of the food problem was the necessity of importing food and raw materials. Since the amount which could be imported was limited, some basic principles were needed to determine how much food and raw materials would be imported. The Prime Minister had to make this decision, and he established the principle that it was important to keep up a food supply sufficient to maintain the staying power of the people, even at the expense of a somewhat slower development in the military program. Some ruthless belt-tightening and the development of more resources than were originally thought available within the country prevented any crisis in food supply. The Prime Minister's judgments in striking the right balance seem to have been very close to the mark.

Finance was also important to Churchill. He was determined to preserve the value of the pound both for Britain's prestige and well-being in the world community and to protect the interests of the people. Direct taxation was ruthless but unquestionably preferable to a devastating inflation.[58] It may be said in general of the Prime Minister's contribution to the civil side of the administration that while his interventions were infrequent, the basic principles were generally his and stood the test of war. Had people gone hungry, had inflation devastated the nation, had labor unrest been widespread and violent, there can be no doubt that the blame would have been laid at Churchill's door. In reverse proportion, he deserves a measure of credit that none of these things occurred.

PRINCIPLES AND PRACTICES

CERTAIN CLEAR PRINCIPLES emerge from Churchill's approach to and conduct of his administration. The first was that his administration derived its ultimate sanction from Parliament as was constitutionally proper. In defending his government in February 1942, he stated, "I am satisfied that it is the best that can be devised to meet the extraordinary difficulties and dangers through which we are passing. There is absolutely no question of making any change in it of a serious or fundamental character as long as I retain the confidence of the House and of the country."[59] The administration was always seen by Churchill as operating in the traditional constitutional pattern of Cabinet government answerable to Parliament, even though the War Cabinet itself played a less important role than the many committees and bodies which sprang up under it. In spite of this operational arrangement, Churchill was always firm that the ministers determine the government's policy and be responsible for the conduct of affairs. Churchill made this clear in the House of Commons early in 1944 when a member suggested there should be an annual report to Parliament directly from the Committee of Imperial Defence, setting out the country's military responsibilities and the weapons programs required. Churchill replied that the Committee of Imperial Defence had no fixed constitutional membership but consisted of those persons, political and military, who were invited by the Prime Minister to take part in its deliberations. Churchill opposed a system in which naval, military, or air force officers could be invited to pronounce against the current government, which would conflict with the whole foundation of the parliamentary system.[60] Whatever the technicalities and structure of the administration, in Churchill's mind it was the government collectively which assumed responsibility for the total actions of the administration and was responsible for all actions to Parliament.[61]

A second principle of administration (to Churchill of equal importance with the first) was that the ultimate responsibility for coordinating the many and varied aspects of military policy in a time of war rested squarely upon the shoulders of the Prime Minister. There was much to be said for the argument that he alone occupied the position which enabled him to exercise a complete influence and to take a broad view of the total war effort. Churchill said on becoming Prime Minister that the post which had fallen to him was the one he liked best. He firmly believed that his failure at Gallipoli had occurred because he was not in a sufficiently high position to carry through a great operation successfully. He was therefore determined that his conduct of affairs in World War II would never be subject to the sort of hampering forces he felt in World War I.[62] Accordingly he defended with tenacity his position as Minister of Defence, and by the summer of 1942 he had won his point. His occupation of that office was never seriously challenged after that date. He had thrown down a challenge to the House which no one was prepared to pick up when he said that he would not have remained Prime Minister for an hour had he been deprived of the office of Minister of Defence. His reasoning was that "it is not possible in a major war to divide military from political affairs. At the summit they are one." That the Prime Minister and Minister of Defence was to constitute the pinnacle of the war government could not be in doubt. John Ehrman has testified that to attempt to survey the course of the war and the development of strategy from the papers of the COS alone or from the papers of the War Cabinet alone is impossible. Ehrman went on to say, "The Prime Minister's records, in contrast, provide at once a clear and a balanced picture—necessarily incomplete, but authoritative and remarkably comprehensive. . . . Here, as nowhere else, the pattern emerges; here is the core of power, the unchallenged centre of affairs."[63]

The third of Churchill's administrative principles was his insistence on the unity of supervisory and executive functions. In 1938 he had told the House that men must be answerable in their particular departments for what they do and say, and that "it is simply darkening counsel to mix up deliberative and advisory committees."[64] In practice this meant that members of Churchill's administration, particularly some of the ministers in the War Cabinet, had to carry very heavy administrative duties. Since some of these men served on many committees, there was always the danger of a certain amount of administrative confusion. Yet on the whole the record is good, and Churchill retained sufficient flexibility of organization that he could shift ministers and create committees to deal with specific problems without disrupting the basic departmental structure of the government and at the same time retaining an overall ministerial responsibility to Parliament.[65] There is nothing sacred about Churchill's unity of deliberative and executive functions in the same men. Lloyd George used a different approach in World War I, but his problems of government were different from those which confronted Churchill. Both administratively and constitutionally there is much to be said for Churchill's arrangement. It assured that someone was responsible for the entire conduct of affairs—a principle which flowed naturally from Churchill's first one.

Closely associated with this position was Churchill's fourth administrative principle—that the administrative structure must be clear and precise. He said there must be a division of functions and proper responsibility assigned to the departmental chiefs, who must have the power and authority to do their work, be able to take a proper pride when it was done, and be held accountable if it were not done. Proper and clear administrative procedures were something of a fetish to Churchill—remarkable when one considers how eccentric he could be at times about the conduct of affairs. He carried his insistence upon administrative clarity to the point of directing a memorandum early in his administration to Sir Edward Bridges and General Ismay. He wished private secretaries and others to desist from addressing each other by their first names in interdepartmental correspondence. He disliked administrative casualness and sloppiness. In late summer 1940 Churchill sent around a memorandum calling for tightening up administrative paper work. He then proceeded to lay out a series of points on how to write an administrative paper; the chief virtues stressed were brevity, clarity, and forcefulness of expression. Certainly on this point Churchill led the government. His own memos were customarily concise, certainly clear, and occasionally forceful to the point of painfulness to their recipients.[66] But ordinarily Churchill was not unreasonable. When Harold Macmillan received a blistering message from Churchill as the result of an unfortunate slip in the process of working out an Italian settlement which led to the King of Italy being referred to as King of Albania and Emperor of Ethiopia, Macmillan protested. Churchill did not challenge the protest.[67]

To Churchill, an efficient administration meant the effective use of written memoranda. This should be seen at its full value. The written word is a discipline and creates a responsibility. Churchill talked all day and most of the night, and much has been said about things Churchill may have spoken. The verbal Churchill was often Churchill the artist or Churchill at work, feeling out through expression the essentials of a decision which he faced. But when the decision was to be made, that decision and its reasons went down on paper. For Churchill the administrator, the written record was the one that counted.[68] He always believed that clarity and cogency of argument were helped by brevity. This extended to small points. He told the First Lord in 1942 that he doubted it was necessary for the Admiralty always to refer to the German battleship *Tirpitz* as the *Admiral von Tirpitz.* He concluded the memo with his usual felicity of expression, "Surely *Tirpitz* is good enough for the beast."[69] Occasionally even the master slipped. When considering the design of special offshore piers for the landing of supplies in the Normandy operation, Churchill dispatched a memorandum stating that these piers "must float up and down with the tide." The point did not escape Captain Roskill.[70]

A further principle with Churchill was his firm conviction in the right of every man to achieve according to his merits. He said, "Human beings are endowed with infinitely varying qualities and dispositions, and each one is different from the others. We cannot make them all the same. It would be a pretty dull world if we did. It is in our power, however, to secure equal opportunities for all." He had practiced this principle during his own first tenure at the Admiralty, and in March 1939 he urged the then First Lord to provide greater opportunity for promotion from the lower deck.[71] When he became First Lord for his second tenure, he acted vigorously in this matter. He wished to know what branches of the enlisted ranks were barred from the opportunity of promotion from the lower deck. He was not satisfied with the response, and his secretaries received the following blistering message:

Will you kindly explain to me the reasons which debar individuals in certain branches from rising by merit to commissioned rank? If a cook may rise, or a steward, why not an electrical artificer or an ordnance rating or a shipwright? If a telegraphist may rise, why not a painter? Apparently there is no difficulty about painters rising in Germany![72]

In April 1940, while still First Lord and enmeshed in the crisis of the Norwegian operation, Churchill found time to deal with the futures of three young men. The Admiralty Board had rejected the three candidates for cadetship although they had ranked fifth, eighth, and seventeenth in the educational competitive examination. They had been rejected nevertheless, one having what Churchill described as "a slight cockney accent," the other two being sons of a Chief Petty Officer and an engineer in merchant service respectively. Churchill told the Board, "But the whole intention of competitive examination is to open the career to ability, irrespective of class or fortune." Churchill had actually taken the time to see the three rejected candidates, all this in the midst of the heaviest sort of administrative and political burdens at a time of grave crisis. Not only was he outraged with regard to the violation of opportunity open to talent, but he also objected to the decision of the Board on constitutional grounds, calling it "wholly contrary to the principles approved by Parliament." Churchill then told the committee that "cadetships are to be given in the three cases I have mentioned." Nor did Churchill stop merely with redressing a personal wrong. He further observed,

> I am sure if the Committee, when they had these boys before them, had known that they were among the cleverest in the whole list, they would not have taken so severe a view and ruled them out altogether on a personal interview. It seems to me that in the future the Committee ought to conduct the interview *after* the examination, and with the results of it before them. Furthermore, it is wrong that a boy should be allowed to sit for examination, with all the stress and anxiety attached to it, when it has already been settled that, even if he is first on the list, he has already been ruled out.

Admiral Gretton traced the careers of the three men given cadetships and found they had all served with distinction. Gretton concluded that it was clear that the First Lord was right and the Board wrong.[73] The episode reveals Churchill at his administrative best. He was not too busy, in spite of incredible pressures, to deal personally with a case he considered unjust.

Churchill's shortcomings as an administrator are well known. His exhortations could become harangues, and his determination to proceed with optimism in the dark days of the war could turn into excuses for postponing facing hard realities. Harry Hopkins, who greatly admired the Prime Minister, had to tell him one time that he needed to take back to the President something more substantial than a speech.[74] Churchill's written encouragements, while designed to produce redoubled effort, could also create resentment. This was particularly true in the reaction of those first exposed to Churchill's way of doing business. Sir John

Kennedy, however, testifies that in time it was accepted as a matter of course that ringing charges of defeatism would be hurled at staffs by the Prime Minister and one simply toiled on.[75] There could be a lack of neatness to Churchill's administrative direction. He was inclined to overrely on his memory; remarkable though that memory was, it was occasionally erratic.[76] This was understandably the case when Churchill's memory contained so vast a store and when he was inclined to pursue so many matters, great and small, simultaneously. He sometimes pursued his projects to a point of unwisdom. He could become so enraptured that he lacked the dispassionate judgment to set them in their proper place.[77]

Occasionally he carried over into administration too much that was political. Government staffs were bombarded with minutes which originated from House of Commons complaints or smoking-room gossip, rumors from Fleet Street, and suggestions from friends and unofficial advisers.[78] At times a concern for detail became a mania for the trivial. In March 1944 the Minister of Supply received the following minute from the Prime Minister:

Just off the main road between Amersham and Uxbridge, at a place called Chalfont St. Giles, there is a rubbish heap or salvage dump where for the last three years work has been going on. I pass it every time I go to Chequers. Are tins and metal objects being recovered from what was a dump in past years, or are they being thrown down there together with other rubbish? Is it being sifted or extended? It is impossible to see as one passes. The one thing that is evident is that the work is endless, and apparently makes no progress.[79]

For all his enthusiasm in grappling with a wide range of matters, there were some which did not fire Churchill's enthusiasm. These he often postponed to his weekends when, in John Colville's elegant phrase, he would assault them "with an air of martyrdom and an effort of conscious willpower."[80] Among those matters most uncongenial to Churchill during the war were considerations of economics and social reform, partly because he recognized how inflammable these issues could become to a coalition government.[81]

Just the opposite sort of administrative shortcoming was Churchill's capacity to be carried away by the contemplation of a long-planned action to the point that he wished to be on the scene himself. It required the intervention of the monarch to keep Churchill off the beaches at Normandy. Although frustrated in this ambition, Churchill wanted to be as close as possible, and his special train bearing many associates descended to a point near Portsmouth. The results of this sort of activity are best summarized by Anthony Eden's account:

This was an imaginative but uncomfortable exercise on Mr. Churchill's part. The accommodation was limited and there was only one bath, adjoining his own compartment, and one telephone. Mr. Churchill seemed to be always in the bath and General Ismay always on the telephone. So that, though we were physically nearer the battle, it was almost impossible to conduct any business.[82]

Churchill's most commented upon administrative weakness was the hours he kept. His habit of conducting work in bed in the morning and of taking an early afternoon nap left him with renewed vigor in the late evening. This arrangement, followed since his first tenure at the Admiralty, seemed perfectly designed to extract the greatest possible energy and fullest hours of work from the Prime Minister. But it could be devastating to those people who followed a more ordinary routine of rising early in the morning and working throughout the day. When they were summoned to the Prime Minister's side in the watches of the night, their energies understandably flagged. Since these men were often official advisers with heavy responsibilities and were on these nocturnal occasions bombarded with proposals by the Prime Minister who was at the peak of his energies, the strain was very great. The postwar account from Brooke's diary has revealed how heavily he felt the burden. His American counterpart, General Marshall, certainly shared his feelings on those few occasions when the American officer was exposed to Brooke's regular evening fare. Brooke summed up his feelings after two months as CIGS, commenting that it felt like ten years.[83]

In the dark days of 1941 when it appeared that Britain alone would not be able to survive the steady advance of German forces and Churchill's pressure upon his military advisers for results was most heavy, there was some fear that the COS were being driven too hard. The immediate pressure of Churchill's conduct of business was probably too much for Sir John Dill, Brooke's predecessor at this time.[84] Certainly on some of these occasions the Prime Minister was a difficult master. The COS had to endure prime ministerial references to "the dead hand of inanition" and stinging comments like "I have to wage modern war with ancient weapons."[85] Further, his professional advisers often had to face suggestions which rose from unofficial advisers, who were not always well grounded in the principles of warfare and perhaps not always wise in their advice. Sir John Kennedy spoke for most of Churchill's critics on this point when he said there were few who did not sometimes doubt whether Churchill's great qualities were adequate compensation for his methods of handling the war machine and the immense additional effort they imposed upon the service staffs.[86]

Yet this approach of Churchill's deserves to be seen from another point of view. He was critically dependent for advice in making his decisions, and the decisions he had to make were of such a nature that if they were wrong, they carried with them a high penalty including a penalty in human life. Understandably, Churchill wanted to be provided with the best possible advice. He probed his advisers hard and sought all possible alternatives. This process was undeniably demanding on those involved in it, but it may have been the result of cruel necessity.

Rather less justifiable was Churchill's habit of imposing upon his official advisers the same range of interests he himself possessed. The COS particularly found themselves deliberating on matters ranging from the most important strategic programs to evaluation of weather reports and some matters not strictly military.[87]

Much commentary has appeared in postwar memoirs regarding the shortcomings of Churchill. Perhaps there has been too much of a tendency for the strains in Churchill's machinery of war direction to be brought to the fore. Some wise advice to those who seek to evaluate Churchill's conduct was offered by Lord Ismay (who was well placed to make such a judgment) when he said that he could testify that the War Cabinet was closely united and the relations between Churchill and his official advisers, both civil and military, were characterized by mutual understanding and regard.[88] Churchill was an administrative colossus. This had its strengths, and inevitably the strengths themselves also involved weaknesses. John Ehrman summed up this aspect of Churchill:

> . . . the defects were particularly those of the virtues. Thus, confidence could become dogmatism, resolution obstinacy, and exhortation—despite all protestations to the contrary—interference. . . . But that there was genius no one could doubt, or that the flaws occurred in a glass of exceptional strength and brilliance. In the last analysis, the achievement is tremendous.[89]

It is well to summarize the overriding impressions of Churchill's role as an administrator. He was too much an individualist to ever be a tidy administrator. But above all, he was the man who furnished the force that drove the administration through times of crisis. His driving energy and sustained optimism in the blackest days were gratefully received by the administration and the government as a whole. His courage inspired those around him; we have the testimony of Harry Hopkins who saw Churchill at close hand in these dark days and realized immediately the importance of Churchill's courage to the entire British war effort.[90] However hard Churchill drove the administration, he drove himself harder. When approaching his seventieth birthday he was in the throes of a serious bout of pneumonia, but he insisted on carrying on his full workload as usual. Ismay was so worried that he called on Brendan Bracken to intervene. Bracken responded magnificently, marching into Churchill's bedroom and asking the Prime Minister if he had informed the King that it might be necessary to send for someone to form a new government. Churchill retorted with vehemence, "Why should I? I am not going to die." Whereupon Bracken replied, "That is exactly where you are wrong. If you go on playing the fool like this, you are certain to die." Ismay concludes that this kept Churchill quiet for a while but not for long.[91]

Churchill's untidiness as an administrator sometimes sprang from conscious policy and not simply from impetuous personality. He valued the importance of free discussion without formality and without a record being kept.[92] His capacity to display insensitivity to those who worked around him is well recorded. Less often noted perhaps was his capacity to smooth and harmonize the affairs of the government, but such occasions also occurred.[93] Harold Macmillan, himself one of the most skillful political managers of men, observed, "Actually, if one stands up to him in argument I do not think he resents it. . . . He misses very little, although he does not always appear to listen."[94] Churchill's insensitivity was not born of deliberate callousness. His basic quality in human relationships was one of decency. John Colville wrote that Churchill pretended to a ruthlessness which was entirely foreign to his nature and that he could not disguise his humanity and sympathy for those in distress. Churchill told Colville that he abhorred a manhunt. Certainly anyone with memories of World War I politics might well feel that way. When as First Lord early in the war he had to report to Parliament the loss of the battleship *Royal Oak,* sunk embarrassingly by a German submarine in the middle of Scapa Flow (Britain's greatest naval base), Churchill made clear that he did not intend to embark on a judicial inquiry with a view to assigning blame to individuals.[95]

Sir Leslie Rowan recounts an episode which pays tribute to Churchill. When at the end of his ministry Churchill had just returned from the monarch after resigning, he told Rowan, "You must not think of me any more; your duty is now to serve Attlee, if he wishes you to do so. You must therefore go to him, for you must think also of your future."[96] Churchill's respect for the integrity of the civil service is one of his great qualities as an administrator just as his respect for Parliament and constitutional institutions stands at the center of his greatness as a politician.

Ismay tells the story of the Prime Minister visiting Ramsgate and observing the aged proprietress of a bombed-out tea shop dissolved in tears as she faced the destruction of her livelihood. Churchill told Ismay that something must be done to enable such people to start again in business. By October 1940 Churchill was able to bring to the House of Commons an insurance program for protection against damage to property from enemy attack. Churchill always remembered that his efforts were to preserve the people by preserving the state against its enemies and not to harness the people to the needs of the state.[97] For him the state existed to serve its citizens, and justice was an important principle of government. When, as First Lord, he intervened to prevent dismissal of a Petty Officer when charges were vague and evidence slight, Churchill observed,

> Such processes cannot be allowed. If it is thought worthwhile to pursue these not very serious though annoying leakages into the sphere of penal action, the man must plainly be charged with some definite offence known to the Naval Discipline Act and brought before a court martial which can alone pronounce upon his guilt or innocence.[98]

For Churchill the responsibility of the state to its citizens extended beyond justice alone. It assumed a certain decency of living, and Churchill was early concerned with the food supply and the quality of diet available to the population. He deplored a basal diet consisting primarily of bread, oatmeal, fats, and potatoes; he insisted that every possible effort be made to supply the people with a decent and palatable diet.[99]

A final comment may be made on the record of Churchill the administrator. His administrative record was vindicated by events. The forces unleashed by war which swept the world from 1939 to 1945, and which in a larger sense were part of a violent storm imposed by a larger and greater sweep of events, were far beyond the power of any man or men to master or direct. No man or nation could plan or act with the confidence that it could shape events without consideration of forces beyond its control. For all this, man has never ceased to endeavor to order the condition of his life. Giant among men was Churchill, and gigantic was his accomplishment. How much of the accomplishment belongs particularly to him may always defy agreement, but the overwhelming testimony of those in the British government, civil service, and military who were best placed to know is a testimony to a great servant of the state and of the British people.[100]

4 / THE WARRIOR

WHEN CHURCHILL RECORDED in his memoirs the royal intervention which blocked his participation in the Normandy landings, he set out his views on the proper place of the political-military leader in operational matters:

> A man who has to play an effective part in taking, with the highest responsibility, grave and terrible decisions of war may need the refreshment of adventure. . . . His field of personal interest, and consequently his forces of action, are stimulated by direct contact with the event. As a result of what I saw and learned in the First World War, I was convinced that generals and other high commanders should try from time to time to see the conditions and aspect of the battle-scene themselves. I had seen many grievous errors made through the silly theory that valuable lives should not be endangered.[1]

Both these themes ran throughout Churchill's conduct of military affairs in World War II. His personal desire to be refreshed by contact with events remained constant from his early flights into France in the dark days of the summer of 1940 to his desire to be present when Allied forces crossed the Rhine into western Germany at the end of the war. Summing up years later his attitudes toward the cross-Channel invasion of France, he recorded that he knew it would be a heavy and hazardous adventure and that the fearful price paid in human life and blood for the great offensives of World War I was graven in his mind. Memories of the Somme and Passchendaele and many lesser frontal attacks on the Germans were not to be blotted out by time or reflection.[2] When the Germans were showing unusual powers of resistance in Tunisia in 1943, Churchill was moved to compare this stubbornness with the long German resistance in the west in the earlier war, followed by their sudden collapse. He did caution, however, against having undue expectations of such an event. He enjoyed sharing memories and experiences of the earlier war. This was one of the reasons for his intimacy with Lord Beaverbrook, and may be part of the reason Churchill was rather slow to grasp methods of modern warfare. He tended to see the forces of the 1940s in terms no longer representative of the technological improvements which had occurred in the interwar period.[3]

Perhaps the most critical moment testing Churchill's capacity to separate memories of the first war from the realities of the second occurred almost immediately upon his becoming Prime Minister. German armored units had broken the united front in the west by mid-May 1940 and were in the process of driving those forces north of the break—including most of the British Expeditionary Force (BEF)—back toward the Channel, having severed their line of withdrawal to Paris and communications in the south of France. World War I experiences had time and again stressed the absolute importance of maintaining an unbroken front at any cost. Churchill responded to the crisis in keeping with this principle. General Ironside, then Chief of the Imperial General Staff (CIGS), seemed to share Churchill's view. There were others, however, who warned about the danger of trying to command the BEF from London. When Ironside reached BEF headquarters on May 20, he saw that the view from London was unrealistic in terms of the field situation on the Continent. Nonetheless, the Cabinet was dissatisfied with his report, and a brief attempt was made by the BEF to carry out the intentions of the government. Not surprisingly, this effort had very limited success and had to be called off. Churchill did not insist too hard or too long that the BEF attempt to do the impossible. As early as May 17 he had suggested to the Lord President that he examine problems which would arise if it were necessary to take the BEF out of France through the Channel ports. Churchill later testified in his memoirs that he had been slow to grasp the smashing power of modern armored forces. This may seem surprising in light of the fate that had befallen Poland and seems best explained by the strong grip World War I memories were always to exercise on Churchill's mind.[4]

Another World War I experience central to Churchill's character was his firm conviction of the importance of willpower to success in war. In a secret-session speech to the Commons, Churchill pointed out that the enemy had his own difficulties, that some were obvious, that there might be others which were not, and that all the great struggles of history had been won by superior willpower in the face of unfavorable odds or by narrow margins.[5] The power of Churchill's will has been marked with sufficient testimony that it need not be emphasized. Nevertheless, his will and determination ultimately yielded to the reality of any situation. Lord Alanbrooke (Sir Alan Brooke's postwar title) has testified that in spite of strenuous struggles on Churchill's part to obtain a quite impossible program, if the CIGS held his ground, Churchill would eventually come around to accepting a situation he could not change by sheer exercise of his will.[6] This could be strenuous for those facing the task of dissuading the Prime Minister from unwise courses, but it also had its positive side. Eden records in his memoirs that when misfortunes were at their greatest in the summer of 1940, he and Portal confessed to each other that they felt despair. Eden told this to Churchill in December 1940 and recorded that the Prime Minister replied that he too in those days awoke with dread in his heart. But Churchill never showed these inner thoughts. His indomitable will and his determination to win provided the strength for everyone else.[7]

Throughout World War II, apparently as a carryover from the Gallipoli affair, the Straits exercised a magnetic attraction to Churchill, and time and again he returned to the theme of bringing Turkey into the war. Time and again this ambition was frustrated, and Churchill recognized that it could not be accomplished. This situation shows Churchill both at his worst and at his best. He expended an amount of energy and attention on getting Turkey into the war that is hard to justify. On the other hand, his efforts to do so never passed beyond the ultimate boundaries of reasonableness except perhaps in the Rhodes affair late in the war.[8]

Linked to Churchill's powerful will was a strong element of daring and audacity. When visiting North Africa in late spring of 1943, Churchill expressed a desire to fly to Malta, a very dangerous procedure. Arrangements were made and then canceled when General Montgomery discovered that Churchill had expressed only a wish and not a command to see Malta. Churchill was still regretting this unaccomplished trip after the war.[9] He was always inclined to military action, and he took a dim view toward the absence of such action, once referring to prolonged preparations for an offensive in the desert in terms of "costly interludes." His determination to secure successful action and his frustration when the required forces seemed slow in coming into play could produce, his wife recalls, more than anxiety—even anger.[10]

Determination, a sense of audacity, and a strong memory of his World War I experiences were the specifics of larger and more general elements which existed in Churchill; the power of emotion was expressed in every aspect of his personality. His emotions sustained him as they sustained others and were a strong influence on the decisions he made. These emotions and his strong sense of history flowed together on great occasions. When Churchill met President Roosevelt to draw up the Atlantic Charter, the leaders of the two nations gathered in joint Sunday services. Churchill chose the hymns for that occasion, and they are notable: "For Those in Peril on the Sea," and "Onward, Christian Soldiers." Churchill recorded, "We ended with 'Oh God, Our Help in Ages Past,' which Macaulay reminds us the Ironsides had chanted as they bore John Hampden's body to the grave. Every word seemed to stir the heart. It was a great hour to live. Nearly half those who sang were soon to die."[11]

CENTRAL DIRECTION OF THE WAR

The central direction of World War II for Great Britain was essentially the business of the Prime Minister and Chiefs of Staff Committee (COS). After American entry into the war, these men and their American counterparts, the President and the Joint Chiefs of Staff (JCS), operated together to provide united direction of the Allied strategy. Churchill brought a background of history and experience to his relations with the three armed forces. He knew the Admiralty most intimately, and his attitude toward that branch was generally one of close association and considerable respect. The Air Ministry was newer than the other two services and occupied second place in Churchill's ranking. Churchill had been one of the earliest civilian ministers associated with the Air Ministry and by World War II was generally of an open mind toward it, although occasionally unhappy when it was not as responsive and flexible as he desired. The War Office brought up last place in Churchill's historical affections. He had difficulties with the War Office which dated back to the nineteenth century, and four decades of experience in the twentieth century had done little to mellow his belief that it was hidebound, devoid of imagination, extravagant of manpower, and tenaciously engaged in fighting the previous war. The three service chiefs who worked with Churchill inherited to some extent these preconceptions which Churchill brought to the conference table.[12]

An early innovation of Churchill's upon becoming Prime Minister was to add to the COS a director (later chief) of Combined Operations. This man was not a regular member of the COS but sat in on those meetings where his specialty was of concern. Churchill appointed as first Director of Combined Operations the aged Admiral of the Fleet Sir Roger Keyes, who had achieved distinction for bravery in World War I and had remained one of the few outspoken men who never wavered in his faith that the Gallipoli affair could have been successful. The experiences of World War II would prove decisively the wisdom of having a director who specialized in combined operations. Less sure was the wisdom of appointing an elderly man who for all his great personal bravery did not possess a mind with the strong powers of analysis and organization the difficult new job demanded. In 1941 Admiral Keyes was succeeded by Captain Lord Louis Mountbatten, a man of strong personality and original views. When Mountbatten was sent to command the Southeast Asia Theater, he was replaced by General Robert Laycock. The success of Allied overseas operations undoubtedly owes much to the early start Churchill gave the combined operations organization. A directly associated problem—that of adequate transport—was never handled as successfully as the actual landing operations themselves, perhaps because transport depended on what America could produce, particularly as the war progressed. This was an aspect of operations that escaped adequate British control.[13]

The COS organization for the duration of the war consisted of the three service chiefs, the Director of Combined Operations sitting in when required, and General Ismay, Churchill's personal representative. Ismay scrupulously limited himself to representing Churchill and aiding in the resolution of differing points of view between the COS and the Prime Minister. It was the three service chiefs whose role was central and decisive in the formulation of British military policy. Churchill's long and close association with these men in times of constant stress was a relationship which Churchill viewed as one of intimacy and even affection. Late in 1944 he told the House of Commons that in World War II there were none of those differences between the professional and political elements so evident in the former war. "We have worked together in perfect harmony." There is no doubt that Churchill meant this. To him the strains and turmoil, the controversy and conflict which preceded the achievement of harmony, were secondary. This was, however, not a view uniformly shared by the service chiefs who labored with Churchill.[14] Yet ultimately the harmony achieved was more important than all the storms that preceded the final victory.

Of all the members of the COS, those who suffered most from the storms were the successive holders of the office of CIGS. General Edmund Ironside briefly occupied this position when Churchill came to office. After the evacuation of the BEF he was replaced by General Sir John Dill, a man of great intelligence and competence and generally viewed in the army as the proper choice for the position. Unfortunately, the appointment did not work out well. Dill was as sensitive as he was able, and his careful mind and unwillingness to entertain the seemingly impossible placed him under a heavy strain in attempting to face the imaginative Prime Minister's proposals. Dill was also bearing great personal stress at this time, which meant that he knew little relief from tension. Churchill in debate could use harsh language that he never intended in spirit, and it must have been difficult for Dill to bear accusations of being "the dead hand of inanition." By late 1941 Dill's patience had been pushed to the point where his discussions with the Prime Minister degenerated too swiftly into acrimony. It was unfortunate, but the point remained that the Prime Minister with all his faults was more essential to the conduct of the war than the CIGS with all his virtues. A new army chief would have to be found. Fortunately the career of Dill was to have a happy ending, and his ultimate contribution to the Allied war effort was to rank among the very highest. During the earlier unhappy time, Sir James Grigg paid testimony to Dill's courage, intelligence, and good judgment: "He never clutched at straws, he never allowed others, however exalted, to clutch at straws, and yet he kept his own courage and helped others to keep theirs." It was typical of Dill's fairness of judgment that he told Sir John Kennedy if he ever wrote his memoirs, he would describe Churchill as the greatest leader Britain could possibly have had, but certainly not the greatest strategist.[15]

In November 1941 Churchill asked Sir Alan Brooke to take up the burden of CIGS. Brooke, like his good friend Dill, had commanded a corps in France in 1940. He had gone back to France after Dunkirk to command British forces in the south and had been instrumental in the second evacuation just as he had been in the first. When Dill became CIGS, Brooke took command of the home forces. It was his responsibility to be prepared to repel the invasion which seemed so likely in late summer of 1940. When it became clear that Dill could no longer sustain the pressures of his office, Churchill turned to Brooke, who set down in his diary the experience of that November 16, 1941. When Churchill asked him to take the position, Brooke was silent for some time. The concerned Prime Minister asked Brooke if he thought he would not be able to work with him. Brooke was fully aware of how difficult the task would be but recorded, "I have the greatest respect and real affection for him, so that I may hope I may be able to stand the storms of abuse which I may well have to bear frequently." Brooke was all too right. Churchill offered him the very best of luck, and thus began a notable working relationship, one which certainly had its times of storm and stress, but which survived to triumph.

Brooke's burdens were increased on March 5, 1942, when the Prime Minister determined that Brooke would replace Admiral Pound as chairman of the COS. Brooke's dominating place in the determination of British strategy was thus acknowledged.[16] Later in the war Brooke was moved to say of the Teheran Conference that "one thing is quite clear; the more politicians you put together to settle the prosecution of the war, the longer you postpone its conclusion!"[17] Sir John Kennedy relates once finding Brooke ruthlessly crossing out nine-tenths of the draft of a minute to be sent to the Prime Minister, remarking as he did so, "The more you tell that man about the war, the more you hinder the winning of it."[18] Brooke, like many military officers, had only limited contact and experience with the world of politics and the burdens and problems which faced politicians. He was not accustomed to the constant give and take of political debate which so regularly involved the hurling of phrases across the Commons' floor or a committee table. Debate was second nature to the Prime Minister, and with his great capacity for language he was indeed a master, but it fell rudely upon Brooke's ears and his emotions. His high-strung temperament and the anguish and strain in this arrangement were expressed by the CIGS as he poured the record of bruised feelings into a diary. But at the same time Brooke the professional soldier proceeded efficiently about his business. No important decision in the military direction of the war seems to have been made without Churchill and Brooke having first come to agreement on how to proceed. Perhaps Grigg, who as Secretary of State was well placed to observe, phrased it best when he said that "on essential points these two argued themselves into agreement before final action was taken."[19]

Brooke could also influence Churchill on less central affairs, as he did in discouraging the Prime Minister from intervening too often with advice and directives to field commanders who bore their share of his impatience and pressure.[20] Churchill throughout the war had the habit of communicating directly with his field commanders, sometimes without consultation with the CIGS. Late in the war he was particularly accustomed to dealing directly with the American commander Eisenhower. This did not become a problem since the field commanders were respectful of the lines of military organization.

Sir Archibald Wavell, another splendid soldier who had frequently felt the Prime Minister's forceful personality, was on one occasion so distressed that he proposed to Brooke that since Winston had lost confidence in him, he had better resign. In advising Wavell, Brooke stated that if he were to take offense when abused and given to understand that Churchill had no confidence in him, then he would have to resign at least once every day. Brooke recalled, "But I never felt that any such resignations were likely to have the least effect in reforming Winston's wicked ways!"[21] This seemed to mollify Wavell.

Just as Brooke felt the pressure of the relationship, apparently Churchill also had occasional doubts and at least once considered finding a new CIGS. Yet as the war progressed, the politician and the soldier, however different their personalities and ways of working, found themselves in accord on their attitudes toward strategic planning. What was to Churchill often an innate preference for indirect methods was to the CIGS desirable military strategy. This basic strategic agreement, although springing from different reasons, tended to tie the two men together, particularly when both were in disagreement with the approach of their American allies.[22] Brooke's sensitive temperament tended throughout the war to respond like a barometer to the Prime Minister's personality. When he was in favor with the Prime Minister, he could set down in his diary such words as "This forged one more link between him and me. He is the most difficult man I have ever served, but thank God for having given me the opportunity of trying to serve such a man in a crisis such as the one this country is going through."[23] When times were bad, Brooke responded in these terms: "Not for one moment did he realise what this meant to me. He offered no sympathy, no regrets at having had to change his mind, and dealt with the matter as if it were one of minor importance. . . ."[24] However, Brooke's temperament should not be allowed to obscure his accomplishment. Ismay said that in his eighteen years of service in Whitehall he saw the work of eight different Chiefs and stated unhesitatingly that Brooke was the best of them all.[25] Churchill's views are also on record. In his memoirs he said, "These volumes will record occasional differences between us, but also an overwhelming measure of agreement, and will witness to a friendship which I cherish."[26] That friendship was inevitably damaged when Brooke's diaries were published later; yet the war record remains. Churchill chose a man well suited to restrain his own shortcomings and to provide strength in areas where he was likely to be weak. It is to the Prime Minister's credit that he did not seek out a man prepared to yield to his will and that he did not disregard and override the military advice he received. Brooke similarly deserves credit for persevering in a position which clearly was a great strain to him. The results of the relationship endure as proof of its significance.

The First Sea Lord and Chief of the Naval Staff whom Churchill inherited when he went to the Admiralty in September 1939 was Sir Dudley Pound. Pound had earlier commanded the fleet in the Mediterranean and had been the subject of some criticism from Churchill in the House of Commons. But from the beginning of their working relationship when Churchill became First Lord, the two men joined in a close association. Churchill clearly respected his great professional and personal qualities. Pound stepped down from the chairmanship of the COS with a particular graciousness which Brooke appreciated, but this was characteristic of the man. Pound, however, was already sixty-four when he became First Sea Lord in the spring of 1939, and his age and an illness not immediately recognized placed a great burden on him. He was inclined to doze through the dull periods of meetings, although all present testified to his alertness where naval matters were concerned. He was also the only member of the COS who exercised operational control, and this additional burden must have been very heavy indeed. Inevitably, suggestions were made to Churchill that Pound be retired. The measure of Churchill's respect for him is exemplified by the tenacity with which he refused the idea. The end of their relationship came in September 1943 when Pound reported that he had sustained a stroke and could no longer carry on his work. Churchill was deeply distressed.[27] On many naval matters it had been the Prime Minister's custom to deal directly with Pound. His reluctance to part with the splendid old man is understandable. Nonetheless, the unpleasant question must be asked. Should Churchill have retained Pound when it was clear that he was failing? Admiral Gretton has suggested that mistakes were made which could be explained only by the decline in the faculties of the First Sea Lord, but perhaps in the long run more that was positive was gained from the successful relationship between the two men than was lost through such errors.[28] Pound died on October 21, 1943. As Churchill appropriately noted, it was Trafalgar Day.

Churchill's earliest instinct was to offer the position of First Sea Lord to Sir Bruce Fraser who then commanded the Home Fleet. Fraser declined, pointing out that the obvious choice was Sir Andrew Cunningham who had acquired an outstanding reputation for his courageous direction of the Royal Navy in the Mediterranean. Churchill offered the appointment to Cunningham somewhat reluctantly, probably because he and Cunningham had exchanged some sharply differing points of view during Cunningham's long tenure in the Mediterranean. Churchill perhaps feared that bringing Cunningham to London would recreate the sort of unfortunate situation between Churchill and Admiral Sir John Fisher which had ended in so catastrophic a manner in 1915. Whatever Churchill's reasons, their association tended to fall into the same pattern as Churchill's relationship with Brooke—that of the enthusiastic and driving Prime Minister on the one hand and the highly skilled professional who resented amateur strategists on the other. Certainly there were many occasions when Cunningham was reduced to speechless rage by the Prime Minister; yet the relationship was one which worked well in spite of the differences of personality involved.[29]

The longest tenure on the COS was that of Sir Charles Portal who became Chief of the Air Staff in October 1940 at the age of forty-seven and occupied that position until the conclusion of the war. Educated at Winchester and Oxford, Portal possessed the best academic and scientific training on the COS. Far more sensitive to matters of personality and with perhaps a broader and deeper capacity for human understanding than his elder colleagues, Portal was the most successful in dealing with the Prime Minister and the Americans.[30] The overriding impression Portal gives is that of a man of great intelligence and careful judgment. Churchill is reputed to have said of him, "Portal has everything."[31] His position was not an easy one, since he was significantly younger than his colleagues just as the Royal Air Force (RAF) was significantly junior to the other two services. The whole story of the strategic air offensive against Germany is a difficult and tortured tale which constantly presented Portal with problems of materiel, morale, politics, and personality. The two senior services needed education in the proper use of air power as often as or perhaps more than the Prime Minister. Portal argued with Churchill skillfully and well in this, and his relations with members of the older services were also successful. He supported his most gifted subordinate, Tedder, with fortunate results. Throughout the war he was faced with the need for difficult and painful compromises. His contribution to the successful functioning of the RAF, the COS, and the Combined Chiefs of Staff (CCOS) was very great indeed.[32]

These were the men who directed Britain's war effort. Various postwar accounts have tended to emphasize the strains in their working relationships. Perhaps the best advice given on this subject was that of Sir John Kennedy to Lord Hankey in May 1942 when Kennedy observed that nothing would be gained by appointing a professional chairman over Brooke's head even if a suitable one could be found, which was unlikely, and that it would be futile to appoint a politician as chairman of the COS with the object of exercising some control over Churchill since such a person did not exist.[33] Each chief exercised professional executive control over his own service. Together their influence and power were very great.[34] This did not mean that the chiefs were free from the Prime Minister's remarkable powers of oratory, invective, and persuasion; but he would not overrule their professional judgment, and he supported and defended them with great tenacity. Nor did he attempt to misrepresent them to the War Cabinet, although on occasion he would attempt to enlist the Cabinet's support for his position against theirs, a process which was never successful.[35] The professional direction of the war was with the COS and not Churchill. The Prime Minister's memory of the difficulties that had occurred in World War I was so acute that he wished always to be able to say truthfully that no military policy was executed which did not have the convinced support of the COS. Yet it was also right and proper that the highest level of policy should be political. The war was fought to defend constitutional principles and political freedoms, and military policy was the servant of higher goals. If anything, the professional chiefs were more insensitive to political matters than the Prime Minister was to military matters. His patience and forbearance deserve some measure of acknowledgment.

When discussions reached the point of strain, Churchill was capable of introducing a relieving humor. Struggling with the problem of inadequate supplies on one occasion, Churchill exclaimed, "There are too many little pigs and not enough teats on the old sow!"[36] Churchill's audacity could result in better solutions than the caution of the COS. His early preparedness to run risks at home in order to send substantial reinforcements to the Middle East was fully justified by events.[37] Even in the worst crisis between Churchill and his professional advisers a satisfactory solution was achieved. Near the end of the war a long and violent debate ensued between Churchill and the COS on strategy in the Far East. This became so strenuous that Ismay had to intervene in an effort to remove the discussion from the level of military affairs. Yet again, helped by the rush of events, the view of the COS prevailed.[38]

On the strictly professional military level there can be no doubt that the professional service chiefs, not Churchill, ran the war.[39] But while he respected their rightful place, Churchill never opened a broad public role to the COS. Brooke once complained that the public never understood what the COS had been doing in running the war and felt that the Prime Minister had never enlightened the people much.[40] Surely Churchill was wise in this. He and his ministerial colleagues, not the soldiers, were ultimately answerable to the people for Britain's success or failure. Churchill wanted no public military rivals to the government. That there were no poisoned conflicts in World War II is testimony both to the sense of their proper role on the part of the professional soldiers and to the determined political instincts of the Prime Minister, who believed that in a parliamentary democracy, even in wartime, the military serve the government which is electorally vested with the support of the people. Churchill protected this principle throughout his ministry.

What was the nature of the strains to which Brooke and Cunningham have given such eloquent testimony and which proved too much for Dill to endure? It is possible to create a whole category of operations which exercised a Siren influence on the Prime Minister's Odysseus. Well indeed might the COS wish to strap their master to the mast and hold the ship steady on its course in spite of his outcries. Churchill's extraordinary courage and initiative could flow quickly into the impulsive and the headstrong.[41] While First Lord, he encouraged an enterprise for sending specially prepared battleships into the Baltic. Considering the strength of German airpower, it seems fortunate that this plan did not reach fruition. One does not have to search far for its origin. Such a plan had been advocated by Sir John Fisher in World War I.[42] Out of this concept developed a desire to aid Finland in its struggle against Russia early in the World War II period. The deep-seated public rage over the Nazi-Soviet Pact which had stripped Poland and seemed to those in the West to have done so much to open the way to war was a strong spur for support to Finland. All the traditional hostility of free men toward the Russian denial of human freedoms and the sheer emotion of seeing a courageous small nation defend itself against its greater neighbor called out for aid to Finland. Only the cruel realities of war said no, and reality ultimately prevailed.[43] An emotion of outraged sense of justice, admittedly somewhat one-sided, also spurred Churchill to consider at times coercing Eire by blockade and perhaps more.[44]

Throughout the war, Churchill sought an expedition into Norway. Having been rudely ejected from that country while First Lord, Churchill never forgot the insult. The same sort of recollection drove Churchill toward Turkey. Somewhat differently, the Prime Minister's desires to seize the Portuguese Islands in the Atlantic and the Italian-held island of Pantelleria in the Mediterranean sprang from a wish on his part to take the initiative and forestall the Germans. In the case of the Atlantic islands, military action was not required. In the case of Pantelleria, a desirable operation was not technically feasible until the island fell as part of the spoils of a greater victory. The last of the Prime Minister's great ambitions was his desire for an operation against Sumatra, even though his professional chiefs believed that its military significance did not justify the effort. Sumatra was a stepping stone to the recapture of Singapore, and clearly that city constituted a wound on the Prime Minister's emotions as sharp and sore as his ejection from Norway and the misfortune of Gallipoli.[45] All of these proposed operations sprang from Churchill's impulse to action, fueled from deep emotional feelings relating to earlier reverses in most cases. All these operations demanded military resources which outstripped Churchill's strategic capabilities, or at least the resources they required would have denied them to other actions considered more valuable by Churchill's professional advisers. Finally, however tenaciously he held to them and however deeply he was emotionally involved, Churchill yielded to his professional advisers in every single instance. This fact perhaps constitutes their greatest significance.

THE SERVICES

The Royal Navy

LATE IN 1918, a member of the Lloyd George government said in a speech, "Nothing, nothing in the world, nothing that you may think of, or dream of, or anyone else may tell you; no arguments however seductive, must lead you to abandon that naval supremacy on which the life of our country depends."[46] British sea power was thus a first principle with Churchill; he knew the navy best of all the services and held a deep attachment for the Admiralty over which he had presided in the early days of both World Wars. He, more than any other man, was responsible for the preparation and readiness of the British fleet at the outbreak of World War I, and in the late 1930s he had carefully followed technological development as it affected the Royal Navy. In 1939 when he returned to the Admiralty, Churchill was already sensitive to the potentialities of radar which would become so greatly developed during World War II. Intimately familiar with the danger that the U-boat had posed to British security in the last part of World War I, he had followed developments in antisubmarine warfare with great interest. In the late 1930s the most significant development appeared to be Asdic (known to Americans as Sonar). The result of Churchill's interest in Asdic, which he saw in an early training performance, was unfortunate. The operation he viewed was so successful that he thought such conditions would obtain under all circumstances.[47] Churchill admitted in his memoirs that he had overrated what Asdic alone could do and said he forgot for a moment how broad the seas were. This was not, technically speaking, Asdic's limitation and suggests that Churchill never quite understood the conditions of atmosphere, weather, temperature, and current which could interfere with adequate Asdic reception, particularly in far northern waters. But Asdic was a significant tool, and Churchill fairly said of it, "The Asdics did not conquer the U-boat; but without the Asdics the U-boat would not have been conquered."[48]

Churchill possessed the love of ships one finds among true seamen, and he looked upon their development with the same enthusiasm that Lord Howard had shown on the eve of the Armada when he told Walsingham that he would be prepared to sail to the River Plate in any of the queen's vessels. Churchill's vessels were to gain distinction off that same estuary.

Upon becoming First Lord in 1939, Churchill immediately discovered an inadequate production of destroyers. He saw that these most useful of all ships must be increased in number and expedited in construction. He recommended more small vessels which could be delivered faster and suggested limiting the number of fleet destroyers to a minimum. Churchill's first point was entirely correct, and indeed the escort problem was eventually aided by the development of a whole series of small ships such as the corvette. But there was also to be a heavy demand for fleet-type destroyers. Churchill objected to the length of time required (twenty-one months) to build a destroyer. He tended to blame their size and increasing complexity for this delay, but perhaps the greater blame rested with outmoded construction methodology. Certainly the Americans were able to build more complex destroyers more rapidly.

Churchill also suggested that the effort to produce the fleet-type destroyers required to escort capital ships was another strike against the whole concept of the battleship.[49] This statement from Churchill is interesting, for it reveals an openness of mind which one might reasonably expect not to exist in a person who had lavished such great energies on the construction of World War I battleships and who tended to view these ships (ten of which were still in commission in 1939) as being particularly his own children. Prior to the war he had also conducted considerable discussion with responsible officials regarding the construction of the new *King George V* class which would constitute the backbone of Britain's battleship line in World War II. He was particularly outraged at the suggestion that this class of ship should bear a 14-inch gun rather than continuing with the 16-inch guns of the *Nelson* and the *Rodney*. Churchill's argument for a ship mounting nine 16-inch guns in 3 turrets was convincing. The *King George V*'s were built to mount ten 14-inch guns in 2 four-gun turrets and 1 two-gun turret. Both Japan and the United States went for nine 16-inch guns in 3 turrets. Since it took five years to build each vessel, Churchill's complaint that they might well have carried heavier gunpower seems justified.[50] Churchill was also instrumental in arguing for retaining in commission the old *Royal Sovereign* class of battleship. These World War I ships were badly outdated by the standards of modern warfare, but Churchill rightly observed before the outbreak of World War II that they could perform valuable service on convoy routes.

As he struggled to preserve that which was still useful of the old, Churchill also was interested in modern developments in the navy. While still out of office he had supported the Admiralty case that the Fleet Air Arm should be under their control and not that of the Air Ministry. Accordingly it was returned to the Admiralty shortly before the outbreak of war, although not soon enough to enable that all-important branch of the navy to achieve the level of proficiency the Japanese and Americans had.[51] Even after Churchill had left the Admiralty for broader responsibility, he followed naval developments closely. The First Lord and First Sea Lord were the rueful recipients of a memo in March 1941 bearing that most feared of Churchill's tabs, Action This Day. At issue was the fact that the battleship *Malaya* had been torpedoed while escorting a slow convoy home from Sierra Leone. The battleship and convoy were without destroyer screen since the destroyers were unable to carry enough fuel for the long route involved. Churchill told the responsible officials that when he was at the Admiralty, he repeatedly asked that more attention be paid to the development of refueling at sea. German battlecruisers seemed able to refuel at sea, why not the British? The reply of the officials did nothing to mollify Churchill, for they received a further memorandum observing that since the *Malaya* was escorting an 8-knot convoy, he did not see why the danger of her oiling a destroyer at 12 knots should be stressed. He observed that with an adequate destroyer screen there would be little danger to the battleship and the destroyer being refueled during that critical time.[52] Churchill had a reasonable point. Refueling at sea would be carried to an extraordinary point of development before World War II ended.

Another new facet of naval warfare to which Churchill was sensitive was the use of the fleet train. This was a particularly novel concept for the British. Her vast empire and great number of naval bases around the world had tended to place Britain in a position where little thought was given to the development of a fleet train to supply warships; accordingly, it was not until late in World War II that the Admiralty faced this problem. By this time the American navy was keeping ships on station or close to their area of operations for extraordinary lengths of time by having developed a fleet train which could supply and sustain them. Minor repairs could also be carried out without losing active service time while a ship returned to what was likely to be a distant port. The Americans had insisted that if a British fleet were to join them in the Pacific, it would have to show a similar capability. Churchill thus ruled in 1944 that after a first priority of the importation of 24 million tons of goods was secured, surplus shipping would go into the fleet train. Its size would in turn determine the size of the fighting fleet, which could not be greater than could be sustained by the fleet train. This was a remarkable decision for a tradition-minded Briton to make, but it was also a correct one dictated by the advancing technology and changing character of sea warfare. It indicates that Churchill retained an open-mindedness toward the problems of sea warfare.[53]

Just as Churchill labored over the technology of naval warfare, so too he brought substantial enthusiasm to its strategy and tactics. The story is told of Admiral Beatty badly trouncing Winston in a naval exercise on the eve of World War I. Churchill's difficulty on that occasion apparently was his tendency to maneuver battleships as if they were a regiment of cavalry. Certainly the offensive spirit was the very character of Churchill's approach to naval operations, an enthusiasm not always shared by admirals. Churchill once told Colonel Knox, the American Secretary of the Navy, that it was dangerous to meddle with admirals when they say they cannot do things, because they always have the weather or fuel or something to argue about.[54] The admirals were not always right. On the eve of the German assault on Norway, the responsible Admiralty officers had dismissed as impracticable a German seaborne attack. This sort of incident occurred just often enough in Churchill's career that he always carried a lingering suspicion that the responsible officers were not being sufficiently offensive minded, and Churchill was inclined to make up for that deficiency out of his own energies, which could carry him to the opposite extreme.[55]

Churchill's readiness to act boldly at sea resulted in at least one early coup. In February 1940, while Norway was still neutral, the German ship *Altmark* was using the security of Norwegian coastal waters to return to Germany carrying, it was believed, British prisoners. A British destroyer flotilla had shadowed the German ship, but the British captain felt he could not, on his own, violate Norwegian neutrality. A cursory Norwegian inspection of the *Altmark* had found no British prisoners. This did not satisfy either the British captain or, when he was radioed,

Churchill. Churchill ordered the British captain to board the *Altmark* since the Norwegians were failing to maintain a fair neutrality. Captain Vian took HMS *Cossack* alongside the *Altmark* and after a brief skirmish liberated the British prisoners aboard. This offensive action was greeted with enthusiasm in a Britain which at that time had little cheering war news.[56]

On another occasion just after Churchill had become Prime Minister, France had fallen, and the whole of the French fleet was lost to the service of the Allies (now reduced to Britain, its Empire, and a collection of exile governments), there was consideration in London to withdraw the British fleet from the eastern end of the Mediterranean Sea lest it become trapped. Churchill was among those who determined that the fleet was to remain, which was in keeping with the wishes of its commander Admiral Cunningham. The course of affairs in the Mediterranean would fully justify this policy.[57]

However, Churchill's offensive spirit was to create problems in the area of convoy and antisubmarine warfare. Churchill was fully cognizant of the critical importance of convoy to the adequate protection of merchant vessels against the U-boat. In March 1939 he had paid generous tribute to Admiral Henderson, one of the men responsible for bringing about the timely institution of convoys late in World War I. But it seems that Churchill (because he was overrating the effectiveness of Asdic) had come to the quite unsupportable conclusion that Britain would be forced in any war that might occur to reinstitute the convoy system, not so much against the submarine as against enemy cruisers.[58] Immediately upon becoming First Lord, Churchill vigorously pushed the production of escort vessels, but he used their shortage as an argument against immediately organizing convoys over all routes. This did not work, and after the sinking of the *Athenia*, convoy in the North Atlantic was adopted. In addition to pressing a vast program of construction of escort ships and the conversion of such vessels as trawlers for antisubmarine warfare, he also ordered the move of the Western Approaches Command headquarters from Plymouth to Liverpool. The Admiralty was reluctant to do this, but Churchill insisted that the headquarters be located closer to the most critical points of operations.[59]

Once it became clear just how critical the U-boat problem was, Churchill marshaled every energy in facing the challenge. In February 1941 he formed a special committee, over which he himself presided, to fight the Battle of the Atlantic. This body was reorganized in October 1942 and titled the Anti-U-Boat Warfare Committee. He supported, if perhaps somewhat tardily, the assignment of long-range aircraft from Bomber Command to Coastal Command, a badly needed step to close the midocean gap where submarines could operate without fear of air interference. Churchill also concluded on the basis of a series of experiments that all except the very fastest of vessels would have to sail in convoy. His impatience at restraining vessels capable of 13–15 knots to the pace of slower vessels had led him to press for independent sailings, resulting in a rate of sinkings significantly higher than that in the slower convoys. By late 1942 the correct decisions had been made and in time would bear fruit,[60] but this was, to say the least, rather late in the war. Churchill must bear a measure of the blame for this. From the very beginning he had been dissatisfied with a policy of convoy and blockade and had wished to exercise sea power more positively, producing a comment from the long-suffering Pound: "It is only politicians who imagine that ships are not earning their keep unless they are rushing madly about the ocean."[61] Churchill wanted to use ships designed for convoy escort to sweep about the ocean seeking out U-boats. It is hard to conceive a policy better designed to produce inadequate results for the effort expended. Admiral Gretton has written that the best place to find U-boats was around the convoys which they must attack if they were to succeed. There they could be destroyed, if possible before they attacked but if necessary afterwards. The diversion of the precious escorts to offensive sweeps left the convoys dangerously weak—some were escorted by one destroyer or even by one trawler—and this failed to sink U-boats.[62] It is only fair to add that not only Churchill but also a segment of the professional staff of the Admiralty responsible for antisubmarine warfare held these views in the early part of the war.[63] Churchill would rarely impose a policy which did not have professional support, but if professional opinion were divided on a subject, he would certainly choose the opinion most in line with his own. On this point he remained unregenerate. Of the improved escort position late in the war, Churchill could write in his memoirs, "We were now strong enough to form independent flotilla groups to act like cavalry divisions, apart from all escort duties. This I had long desired to see." By then such deployment was justified and, with air search and sound scientific and statistical methodology applied to the U-boat hunting process, brought some good returns. It seems likely that the evidence presented by the Blackett Committee proving the efficacy of the convoy system was decisive for Churchill, however unhappy he may have been about it.[64] While Churchill's offensive proclivities must bear part of the responsibility for prolonging the time before the U-boat was mastered, on the other hand, he recognized the peril the U-boat posed, mobilized the resources of the government to meet the challenge, and ultimately made the right decisions when presented with convincing evidence. It is worth contrasting Churchill's behavior with the reluctance of Germany's leader to accept facts contradicting his preconceptions, and with the Japanese, also an island people, who might have been expected to be all-sensitive to the significance of mercantile shipping but dismally failed to deal with the attack of American submarines upon their lifelines.[65]

In June 1940, with a German invasion threatening, the Admiralty brought cruiser and destroyer forces down from Scapa Flow north of Scotland to cover the east coast. The Commander in Chief of the Home Fleet at Scapa argued that this was a mistake. Events supported his position, for the detached cruisers and destroyers achieved little success, while Atlantic convoys suffered heavy losses. Churchill accepted this Admiralty arrangement, although it was directly contrary to the view he had held as First Lord in the earlier war when he insisted that the fleet must remain intact at Scapa.[66]

A somewhat similar case developed in 1941 over the correct use of the Mediterranean fleet. The issue at this point rested on the fact that by April 1941 the German General Rommel was outside Tobruk, and the British position in the western desert was precarious. Rommel's main port of supply was Tripoli, and Churchill and his advisers in London determined that an assault of major proportions should be carried out against Tripoli by the Mediterranean fleet. The commander in the Mediterranean, Andrew Cunningham, had already risked four destroyers by sending them to Malta in an effort to interdict the German supply route across the Mediterranean. However, the Admiralty had decided the crisis was so acute that a battleship should be sent to block the port of Tripoli. This of course constituted a direct intervention on the part of the London authorities into the conduct of the struggle in the Middle Eastern Theater. Not surprisingly, Cunningham decided to question the order, pointing out that blockade of the harbor at the expense of a battleship was a dubious sacrifice; that the success of the operation was questionable; that even if successful, it would not prevent unloading by lighters; and that the sacrifice of the battleship would be interpreted by the enemy as an act of desperation and thus encourage him to yet greater offensive efforts.

At this point Churchill intervened and wired Cunningham a strong message supporting the London position. In the meantime the destroyers which Cunningham had based on Malta had carried off a successful attack on an enemy supply convoy. Cunningham then informed the Admiralty that he was prepared to bombard Tripoli as the lesser evil to sacrificing a battleship, even though it involved unreasonable risks to his fleet. On April 21, 1941, Cunningham carried out a successful bombardment of Tripoli and returned to Alexandria without damage, but he viewed his successful operation more as a measure of Italian incapacity than justification of the risks run. He argued that the job could have been done better by heavy bomber squadrons. Clearly irritated by what he considered an unreasonable interference from London in his handling of the Mediterranean fleet, Cunningham allowed himself a rather wide range of commentary on planning there. The Air Ministry in particular came in for some unkind words from the fighting admiral. Not surprisingly, Cunningham immediately received a very full message from the Prime Minister. Churchill disagreed with Cunningham's conclusion that the successful operation against Tripoli was essentially a fluke and argued that it was wrong to overestimate the enemy capabilities. "I suppose there is no doubt that the blocking plan would, in these circumstances, have come off." Churchill also easily refuted Cunningham's proposition about the bombers, pointing out that it would have required, depending on range and type of plane used, from 10.5 to 30 weeks of bombing to achieve the same weight of explosives thrown into Tripoli by the fleet in 42 minutes. He followed this with a survey of the naval war as seen as a whole from London and concluded that he had taken pains to give Cunningham a full account "out of my admiration for the successes you have achieved, your many cares, my sympathy for you in the many risks your fleet has to run, and because of the commanding importance of the duty you have to discharge." Certainly Churchill was rather quick to become involved in dictating tactical operations to a responsible commander on the scene, but neither does Cunningham emerge from the episode with virtue intact. Tedder, who was on the scene with the air force, was of the opinion that Cunningham's position was wrong. Furthermore, the operation pressed upon Cunningham by London was totally successful. The entire episode is typical of Churchill's interventions into the realm of tactics during the war. Basically it was not a wise policy, yet it had successes as well as failures, and professional opinion was by no means united in opposition to Churchill's judgments.[67]

On one occasion, and evidently only one, did Churchill overrule all naval opinion in dictating a strategic deployment of naval power. By late 1941 it seemed increasingly clear that Japan was about to undertake even more positive offensive actions than previously. Churchill thought it important, therefore, to have a naval force at Singapore, which he argued would have a deterrent effect on further Japanese aggression. Admiral Pound argued that Japanese naval power was so great that to place a few powerful units in as forward a position as Singapore would not deter the Japanese if they were serious and also would risk the loss of the ships. Pound believed that Britain could not operate farther forward than Ceylon and should occupy itself with a defensive program protecting Indian Ocean routes. Churchill continued to press the political importance of dispatching a few vessels to Singapore, and in mid-October 1941 he invited the Admiralty to send a modern battleship and an aircraft carrier to join the battle cruiser *Repulse* at Singapore. Again Pound argued against this proposal. Nevertheless, the *Prince of Wales* was sent to Capetown with the understanding that her final destination would be decided after she arrived there. In fact, the *Prince of Wales* went to Capetown on the understanding that she would continue on to Singapore unless otherwise ordered. She went to Singapore. No carrier, however, joined the two warships there, for the only one available had been put out of action by an accidental grounding. Accordingly, when the Japanese launched their offensive in the Pacific with such devastating effectiveness in their attack on Pearl Harbor (a truly frightening display of the high development and extensive capabilities of Japanese naval air power) the British had two very vulnerable trophies sitting at Singapore. Churchill's response to the disaster of Pearl Harbor was that the British ships must go to sea and vanish among the innumerable islands. By then it was too late. The British admiral at Singapore had acted otherwise.[68] Churchill later wrote that he had believed the placement of these ships at Singapore would create a kind of vague menace to Japanese naval calculations; yet he should have known better. Before this time the German battleship *Bismarck* had been found in the Atlantic by Fleet Air Arm planes and had been slowed by their attack until it was destroyed by heavy British naval units. And the operations of German aircraft in the Norwegian campaign and again in the desperate evacuations from Greece and Crete should have served notice of the folly of permitting warships to operate without adequate air cover. On the morning of December 10, 1941, Pound informed Churchill that the *Prince of Wales* and the *Repulse* had both been sunk by Japanese aircraft. Churchill recorded that when he put down the telephone, "I was thankful to be alone. In all the war I never received a more direct shock." He had only himself to blame.[69] While First Lord, Churchill had established as his usual working relationship with his professional advisers that he would submit his working papers to his naval staff for consideration, criticism, and correction and hope to receive proposals for action in the direction he desired.[70] He would prod and urge and push proposals for action, but he remained open to professional advice. It is unfortunate that on this one occasion he violated his own working rule.

Churchill's offensive spirit could produce striking successes, as in the *Altmark* affair. On the other hand it also brought misfortune, as in the convoy situation. While Churchill was First Lord, some aircraft carriers were being used essentially for U-boat searches. Engaged in this process off the coast of Ireland, the fleet carrier *Courageous* was sunk by a U-boat in spite of being screened by four destroyers. Churchill wrote of this loss that it was a risk which was necessary to run.[71] It is hard to agree with this judgment. Of all the units available to the Royal Navy, its fleet carriers were perhaps the most critical. To use them on U-boat searches, desperate though the problem was, was a questionable employment of these most valuable ships. Later in the war a variety of smaller carrier types were so used, and rightly so, but it is hard to defend the loss of the *Courageous*. Certainly the constant use of escort craft on offensive sweeps contributed to the problems of the Royal Navy. The official naval historian has concluded that a high price was paid for this offensive mindedness at too early a date.[72] To the end of the war it appears that Churchill had trouble recognizing the capabilities and limitations of escorts in antisubmarine warfare.

Churchill also seems to have underrated the danger of air power to naval forces. In the early years of the war there were many professional naval officers who denied the efficacy of air power against powerful naval units, in spite of early graphic evidence of the risks this involved. In April 1940 the cruiser HMS *Suffolk* bombarded Stavanger airfield in Norway with her 8-inch guns. The price paid for this was a continual bombardment from the air for seven hours while the *Suffolk* withdrew. The cruiser reached Scapa Flow with her quarterdeck awash. In May Churchill told the House of Commons that German air power over Norway was such that regular naval patrols could not be maintained in close proximity. He said, "We have to face a fact like that." He himself would have done well to recall that fact in 1941.[73] Why did he choose to ignore it? The explanation seems to be his incurable desire for offensive action combined with the belief that taking risks was sometimes justified by possible successes. Because Churchill knew the navy best of all three services, he took greater liberties in interposing himself into professional matters. The mistakes he made in playing this role should not be exaggerated, but neither should they be ignored or excused.

The Royal Air Force

Churchill did not possess the same assuredness in matters of air policy that he brought to questions of naval action. However, he has written that when he became Prime Minister, he had the advantage of a layman's insight into the problems of air warfare resulting from four years of study and thought based on official and technical information.[74] Immediately upon assuming his new responsibility as Prime Minister, Churchill was faced with the necessity of making the most critical of decisions regarding deployment of air power.

The French in desperation called in mid-May for the assignment of more British fighter aircraft to the battle on the Continent. Head of the Fighter Command, Sir Hugh Dowding, informed the War Cabinet that the limit of safety to Britain's security had been reached; no more fighter planes could be spared for the Continent. Powerfully moved by the French crisis, intensely loyal to the Allies, and determined to make every effort, Churchill balked at Dowding's resistance. The matter was argued out before the War Cabinet with Dowding present. He made clear that he could not accept professional responsibility for the Fighter Command unless the War Cabinet supported the minimal force he believed essential for Britain's security. The War Cabinet yielded to Dowding's professional advice. Its decision of May 15, which gave to the battle in France the equivalent of four more squadrons of fighters, was borne by Churchill to his meeting with the French leadership the next day. Once the Prime Minister was swept up in the conflict and presented with the emotional appeals of the desperate French, he decided to ask the War Cabinet for six more squadrons and received a favorable reply by 11:30 in the evening of May 16. But while the War Cabinet agreed to the participation of the additional squadrons in the battle for France, they had wisely provided, at the insistence of Chief of the Air Staff (CAS) Sir Cyril Newall, that the squadrons be based in Kent but use French fields to refuel and rearm. Churchill had to be content with this.

The Prime Minister had strained very hard against the advice of the professional airmen, but in the end he had yielded. The significance of this is best summed up in Basil Collier's words: "Whereas Dowding and Park proved capable of standing up to men who wanted them to do the wrong things, their German counterparts proved incapable of standing up to Goering."[75] Dowding passed from the scene in late November 1940, apparently partly because his defensive strategy had offended some of the air marshals. This is not to say that it had not also offended Churchill.[76] In retrospect, Churchill's behavior toward Dowding seems rather lacking in the magnanimity which was Churchill's usual characteristic. Dowding and Wavell seemed to be unfortunate exceptions to Churchill's usual generosity toward men with whom he disagreed.

After Dowding's departure, Sir Charles Portal assumed the position of CAS and quickly achieved a rapport with Churchill which enabled him to provide the Prime Minister with guidance on the proper use of air power. In the latter part of 1941 the run of defeats in the western desert had led to acrimony between the services concerning the proper use of the RAF. This ultimately resulted in Churchill as Minister of Defence issuing on September 5, 1941, a full statement on what would become doctrine for the use of air power in theater operations. Some points of this important document are worth citing. Churchill wrote that ground troops could not expect, as a matter of course, to be protected against air attack by aircraft, and that the idea of keeping regular air patrols over moving columns would be abandoned. Churchill then laid out standards of cooperation between army and air commanders but said further that while the army would determine its requirements, the Air Officer Commanding in Chief should use his maximum force in the most effective manner. Churchill concluded by noting that enemy air power would obviously claim the first attention of the RAF.[77] It is hard to believe that this important memorandum sprang from Churchill's head fully armored like Minerva without the skillful sowing of some seeds by the CAS. Churchill himself had limited background concerning the establishment of tactical doctrine, although he was versed in various technical developments and familiar with strategic arguments. The memorandum represents the achievement of an important professional ascendancy on the part of Portal—one which he retained throughout the war—and was not the least of his contributions. If Portal's position was challenged at all during the war, it was by one of his own subordinates, Sir Arthur Harris, and involved Strategic Air Offensive policy which attracted controversy that has shown no sign of declining with time.

World War I had ended before air forces had developed to the point where it was possible to test their capabilities against strategic doctrine for their employment. The interwar period saw the advocacy of air power develop significantly. In Britain the most important figure in this was Lord Trenchard. He preached—and most important figures in the RAF accepted—the doctrine that the bomber would always get through. If this were true, then the potential of one's enemy to wage war could be attacked directly. Not only armies of the enemy but his industries and total civilian population lay vulnerable to direct attack. What slender evidence could be adduced to sustain these theories in the interwar period seemed to support the most extreme advocates of the bomber. Native villages in underdeveloped areas had been terrorized from the air, and the use of German air power in the Spanish Civil War had again seemed to prove the direst predictions of the fate awaiting civilian populations under air attack. What few statistics could be developed from brief World War I bombings of Britain suggested terrible casualty rates, which World War II would demonstrate bore no relation to reality. But this was of minor importance in the early years of air power.

It was nearly impossible to evaluate accurately and critically what bombers could do, so the theories grew. The best method of bomber evaluation, although many could be employed, was photographic reconnaissance; yet there was a startling reluctance on the part of the RAF Bomber Command to seek out the critical evaluation of the doctrine upon which its very existence rested. When World War II began, there was no developed military organization for carrying out photographic reconnaissance and evaluation. Only a private firm in Britain had developed the technology to measure with considerable accuracy the evidence supplied by photographs, and the Air Ministry showed no particular interest in acquiring its services. Churchill, while still First Lord of the Admiralty, told the Air Ministry that either they should take over the company as a unit or he would have the Admiralty do so. This finally pushed the Air Ministry to action.[78]

Churchill had been among the most air-minded of government ministers and had perhaps been the first ever to fly in an airplane. As early as 1917, while Minister of Munitions, he had laid down (in what the historians of the Strategic Air Offensive have described as "a great state paper") the principle that "the indispensable preliminary to all results in the air, as in every other sphere of war, is to defeat the armed forces of the enemy." This view did not quite square with the thinking of men like Trenchard and the doctrine that the bomber would always get through. Indeed, it implied that the bomber could be met and perhaps mastered in the air. Nor did Churchill stop there in raising questions about official doctrine as it was developing. He went on to express his doubt that a civilian population could be terrorized into surrender by bombing alone. He continued to believe that armies would decide the issues of war and that an air force could make its best contribution by bombing the bases and communications of the enemy after it had destroyed the enemy's air power.[79]

When Churchill became Prime Minister in the spring of 1940, he seems to have placed his earlier thoughts on air power in reserve. By that summer Churchill had to ask himself how he could win the war. The British army had been rudely ejected from the Continent. It was perfectly clear it would not soon return there; indeed it might never return. The

Royal Navy was stretched to the limit. The British blockade of Germany was unreal, considering the vast resources of the conquered Continent available to Germany in addition to the fullest cooperation then being given by Russia. The question at sea was not whether Germany could be blockaded and starved but whether the Royal Navy could master the U-boat before Britain was starved. Understandably then, seeking for a way through, Churchill turned to the air force. In a memorandum on September 3, 1940, Churchill wrote:

> The Navy can lose us the war, but only the Air Force can win it. Therefore, our supreme effort must be to gain overwhelming mastery in the air. The Fighters are our salvation, but the Bombers alone provide the means of victory. We must, therefore, develop the power to carry an ever-increasing volume of explosives to Germany, so as to pulverise the entire industry and scientific structure on which the war effort and economic life of the enemy depend, while holding him at arm's length from our island.[80]

As early as July he had called for absolute air mastery. The German bombings of British cities also gave rise, if not to a spirit of revenge on the part of many, at least to a determination to employ against Germany the same means Germany was employing against them. Churchill told Harry Hopkins in January 1941 that he looked forward, with American help, to mastery in the air and speculated that then Germany and all her armies would be finished. Hopkins wrote of that meeting, "He believes that this war will never see great forces massed against one another."[81]

It seems then that Churchill had partly set aside the principles of his 1917 memorandum without entirely rejecting them. The German attack on Britain had demonstrated that indeed the bombers got through, but not all of them, and the price could be made prohibitive to the attacking force. This fact obviously forced a readjustment in the theory of the followers of Trenchard, rephrased to read: The night bomber will always get through since the fighter will not be able to find it. This in turn raised the question, While the fighter may not be able to find the night bomber, can the night bomber find its target? Surprisingly, in the early part of the war there was no great urgency in the Air Ministry to supply a definitive answer.

No one was particularly anxious to examine closely the fact that the RAF Bomber Command was capable of doing almost nothing in the early part of the war. In July 1940 Churchill was already querying the Secretary of State for Air on heavy losses to Bomber Command in return for very questionable results. He wished to save aircraft and personnel as much as possible while keeping up a steady attack.[82] In fact, this was not possible. By May 1941 the capabilities of Bomber Command were recognized to be so limited that the principles laid down for the selection of targets made clear just how slight they were. A memorandum prepared for the CAS observed that Bomber Command was capable of dropping only 200 tons of bombs on Germany in a given night and admitted that, owing to the proved difficulty of finding and hitting precise targets on dark nights, many targets should be selected so that the misses and near-misses would be of value. The next paragraph of the memorandum referred to attacks that will "strike at the enemy's morale." By November 1941 a gradual process of grappling with the reality of British capabilities had brought about the definition of a bombing policy of less precise aims which had finally arrived at the position of general area attack on whole towns.[83]

The failure of Bomber Command to successfully carry out precision attacks against German oil facilities had forced the recognition of the lack of British capability without probing the underlying concepts of the bombing principle as finally defined. The discovery of just how unsuccessful these attacks were had arisen in large measure from the Prime Minister's statistical department. Lord Cherwell had raised doubts early about the accuracy of the bombing program, and Churchill had authorized an investigation which revealed that two-thirds of the air crews failed to get within five miles of the assigned target. This had led Churchill to revert to some of his earlier thoughts, and he observed to the CAS that he thought it doubtful or at least disputable whether bombing by itself would be a decisive factor in World War II. Portal seems to have interpreted these remarks as challenging the whole role assigned to the bomber in the British war effort. But Churchill responded that he had not intended to push his position that far, and he reaffirmed that the bomber remained Britain's primary offensive weapon. On October 7, 1941, he argued with the CAS that a different picture would be presented if the German air force were so far reduced as to enable heavy, accurate daylight bombing of factories to take place. Since this could not be done outside the radius of fighter protection, what bombing could accomplish remained unknown. Churchill concluded, "The only plan is to persevere."[84]

By late 1941 the Prime Minister clearly had substantial reservations about how much the Bomber Command could contribute to winning the war. It would seem desirable to have determined the proper role for the bomber and the amount of resources allotted to the bomber effort, but this apparently was not done. Sir John Kennedy testified that the bombing policy of the Air Staff was settled almost entirely by the Prime Minister in consultation with Portal and was not controlled by the COS. This was quite different from Churchill's attitude toward the employment of tactical air forces, where he insisted on cooperation with the army. Postwar evidence suggests that not much more than two percent of the German war economy was affected by strategic bombing through the latter part of 1941, but Bomber Command that year lost one plane for every ten tons of bombs dropped. It is hard to escape A. J. P. Taylor's conclusion "that the offensive did more damage to Great Britain than to Germany."[85]

In February 1942 Air Chief Marshal Sir Arthur Harris, the supreme

British advocate of strategic bombing in World War II, became head of Bomber Command. A man of determination and passion, Harris was convinced that what was needed was a more complete, total effort on Britain's part, which in turn meant allocation of an even greater proportion of her war effort to the bombing offensive. Harris showed little interest in the niceties of precision bombing, and his early targets like Lübeck and Rostock seem selected more because they would burn well than because their destruction would significantly contribute toward impairing the German capacity to wage war. An impressive demonstration of the Harris approach was achieved on May 30, 1942, when he launched a 1,000-plane raid against Cologne. Churchill applauded these efforts. Indeed, Harris was quick to establish a close personal contact with the Prime Minister; from early 1942 until early 1945 he was to exercise a strong influence on Churchill's thinking with regard to air power. Churchill supported Harris's call for a greater Bomber Command, but he did not embrace with similar enthusiasm Harris's certainty that strategic bombing carried out on a grand enough scale would alone win the war. Harris could get much from Churchill, but he could not get the unconditional priority in production and allocation of resources that he viewed as essential to securing the great strategic air victory of which he never ceased to dream.[86]

As it was, many were prepared to argue that Harris had too great a scope within which to exercise his authority. When he carried out a raid against a factory which constructed engines for submarines at Augsburg, an expensive operation, he immediately drew the fire of the Ministry of Economic Warfare, which pointed out to the Prime Minister that Harris had ignored the perfectly sound information of the ministry marking the target as unworthy of the effort. The Ministry of Economic Warfare received from Churchill a minute strongly indicating that he and Harris worked out these things between them and that interference of lesser authorities was not welcome. The Prime Minister was coming perilously close to allowing the Air Chief Marshal to wage a private war. The bitter hatred which Churchill's closer adviser Lord Cherwell nourished toward the Nazis led him also to press Churchill hard for a vast bombing effort. To the passionate advocacy of Harris and Cherwell was added the more carefully measured but no less enthusiastic support of Portal and Sinclair.[87]

At the same time that Harris was initiating his raids on German cities, British commanders in the Middle East and Far East were scratching for an adequate number of fighters (a particularly acute problem in the Far East and India) not to mention bombers. The theater commanders were distant from the Prime Minister; Harris and his associates were close. Further, as Churchill observed, "There must be a design and theme for bringing the war to a victorious end in a reasonable period." The bombing offensive had gained a life of its own—indeed, a second birth and renewed life by 1942. New technical developments increased what the bombing effort could achieve. But there were those even at this point who feared that the lack of long-range aircraft in the Atlantic struggle against the U-boat would lead to Britain's losing the war on the ocean before it could win the war on the Continent. The bitter exchanges which passed between Admiralty and Air Staff in early 1942 resulted in the diversion of some aircraft to the naval effort, but the priority of the strategic bombing effort remained.[88]

By the end of 1942 it appeared that Sir Arthur Harris had won at least a position of critical influence, if not a commanding one, in advising the Prime Minister on the proper direction of the war effort. Churchill, however, had never fully yielded to Harris's argument for massing the totality of British resources in the strategic air offensive. Early in 1943 Harris was indeed to lose forever any hope of securing his ultimate aim—to the most unlikely of opponents, the army. For as the Allies gathered as Casablanca to plan the offensive period of World War II, they had an army once again. By the time of Casablanca the British Eighth Army in the desert had secured its greatest victory and was moving steadily westward, and from the west a joint American-British army had entered North Africa. The vast manpower of the United States made a military reentry onto the European continent a feasible operation. From that point on it was possible for Churchill to return again to the principle of his 1917 memorandum. This was, furthermore, a view shared by the CAS if not by the Chief of Bomber Command. Portal observed at Casablanca that it was necessary to exert maximum pressure on Germany by land operations, and he judged that air bombardment alone was not sufficient.

Yet Casablanca also determined that a major reentry onto the Continent would be most unlikely until 1944. The operations of 1943 might reach the Continent but, if so, by the Mediterranean back door. This left a large role for Bomber Command to play in 1943. Further, Harris now had the support of the American bombing advocates, and these were even more zealous than he was. They had not turned to night bombing to avoid the superiority of the fighter in daylight but instead argued that they could arm their bombers so heavily that they would be able to fight their way through to carry out precision daylight raids. While Harris and Portal were happy to have the support of the American bombing advocates, neither man showed much enthusiasm for the American tactical doctrine. As a result, Casablanca failed to establish a truly unified combined bombing offensive. The two bomber forces were given instead a broad directive: "Your primary object will be the progressive destruction and dislocation of the German military, industrial, and economic system, and the undermining of the morale of the German people to a point where their capacity for armed resistance is fatally weakened." In a directive known as "Point-Blank" issued on June 10, 1943, the Casablanca decision was amended to give priority to attack on the German fighter forces and aircraft industry. The meaning of this is clear. The German fighter was proving more than a match for the American daylight bomber. At least part of the strategic air offensive was in serious trouble.[89]

On October 14, 1943, catastrophe overtook the daylight operations. The Americans had sent bombers against ball bearing factories at Schweinfurt, and German fighters had torn their formations to shreds. The daylight offensive was at a standstill. The painful question was how to salvage something out of the ruins of that part of the strategic bombing offensive. The American air chiefs seemed to believe that a long pause followed by a yet greater effort would do the job. The British had strong doubts. Sir Charles Portal wondered if even at this late date conversion to night bombing was not required. Churchill, far more presciently, was inclined to stress the development of the long-range fighter. Neither American nor British air chiefs were enthusiastic about this, and Sir Charles Portal spoke for them all when he predicted that fighter escort into Germany would prove impracticable.[90] But Churchill was right, and in the case of the long-range fighter, the civilians came to the rescue of the military. High-placed civilians in the American War Department pressed for development of the P-51 as the long-range fighter which ultimately proved to be the solution to the problem and verified the Prime Minister's views.

In the spring of 1944 the combined bomber offensive was ready to go forward once again. It immediately faced a new demand. Plans for Overlord, the return to the Continent in force, were now rapidly developing, and a tentative date in early summer of 1944 looked increasingly firm. The demand seemed imminent that bomber operations on the Continent be subordinated to the direction of the Supreme Allied Commander for Overlord.

Even as this question was shaping, another struggle was taking place within the RAF on the capabilities of the planes to carry out assigned missions. Sir Arthur Harris retained his position of little faith in precision bombing, but the Air Staff increasingly believed that there should be closer coordination of British and American bombing efforts. This issue was not clearly resolved when the renewed bombing offensive began in the last week of February 1944.[91] The reason for the internal struggle between Harris and the Air Staff was easy to find. Available evidence continued to show that the German war effort was not being crippled or in any sense seriously impaired by the bombing effort. By the end of 1943 the ability to cause a collapse of the German war effort seemed to be quite beyond the capacity of the combined British and American bombing forces. It could even be said that the combined offensive had cost the two Allies far more than it had cost Germany. Faced with this not very encouraging evidence, the Air Staff inevitably would demand more selective and more precise bombing, particularly as they felt that the capabilities of Bomber Command had improved to the point where these proposals were feasible. Sir Arthur Harris adamantly opposed such suggestions.

The resolution of this issue was postponed by the intervention of the immediate problem, which could not be put off: How were the strategic bombing forces to be directed toward assisting the reentry of

Allied Armies onto French soil? Supreme Allied Commander General Eisenhower had insisted that he have overall direction of these forces, a request opposed by both Harris and his American counterpart, General Spaatz. Fortunately, Eisenhower had as his Deputy Supreme Commander Sir Arthur Tedder, a man of such substantial talents and achievements that he was able to take on even the formidable Harris. By late March the Prime Minister himself was prepared to resolve the conflict between the Supreme Allied Commander and the Bomber Commanders. Portal, however, intervened, and Churchill allowed him to convene a meeting on March 25, 1944, at which all the important parties were present, including Eisenhower, Tedder, Harris, and Spaatz as well as substantial staffs and experts. The outcome of this crucial meeting was a victory for Eisenhower and Tedder. Central in their plan was an effort to destroy the transport system of France and Belgium with the object of making it impossible for the Germans to reenforce their front line faster than the Allies could bring forces ashore to support their landing. Harris had objected vigorously to this because of his disbelief in the sort of precision bombing the so-called Transportation Plan would require. On March 27, after some further brief scuffling which was resolved generally in Eisenhower's favor (although it had required the intervention of the American Joint Chiefs of Staff), Tedder took over direct control of the Transportation Plan. Structurally the arrangement was awkward, but given the character of the men involved, it was perhaps the only arrangement which held the possibility of success. Fortunately Tedder was a man equal to this difficult task.[92]

Hardly had the Overlord authorities seemed to have won from the Bomber Command the sort of program they believed essential to a successful reentry to the Continent than they had to face a new struggle with the Prime Minister. The Transportation Plan involved the bombing of certain high-density population areas in the vicinity of railroad yards. This almost certainly meant high French civilian casualties. The Prime Minister was very concerned. He told Eisenhower that both he and the entire War Cabinet had doubts about the wisdom of the Transportation Plan and feared the impact that civilian casualties might have on French attitudes. Churchill did not wish to send troops into France to find an embittered population. The initial estimates of casualties to French and Belgian civilians ranged from 80,000 to 160,000, of which it was estimated a quarter would be fatal. Several adjustments and restrictions upon the Transportation Plan followed, which by mid-April 1944 led to a vastly reduced estimate of something more than 10,000 likely to be killed and more than 5,000 seriously injured. Churchill continued his vigorous opposition to the operation. He again told Eisenhower that he deplored the killing of 10,000–15,000 French civilians and said further that experience in Italy had suggested it was difficult to stop traffic by bombing railroad marshaling yards. The issue was finally referred to President Roosevelt, who informed Churchill on May 11 that, however regrettable the attendant loss of civilian lives, he was not prepared to impose any restriction on Eisenhower that might militate against the success of Overlord or cause additional loss of life to the invasion forces. Five days later Churchill informed Eisenhower that the War Cabinet would not press their objections further.[93] The accuracy of the bombing was in fact better than anticipated, and the casualties sustained fell in the low range of estimates.

The very accuracy with which the Transportation Plan was carried out strengthened the hand of the Air Staff in their prolonged argument with Sir Arthur Harris on the capabilities of Bomber Command. When direction of the strategic bombers returned from the Supreme Allied Commander to the normal arrangement, the old argument between Harris and the Air Staff flared once more. By November 1944 the conflict had reached a deadlock. The Air Staff wanted Harris to embark on a bombing program that would stress the destruction of German oil and transport facilities. Harris all but told Sir Charles Portal that he would not carry out such a directive. This placed Portal in an impossible position. His subordinate was openly defying him, yet Harris's position was unique. He had gained an ascendancy in the minds of his air crews which earned him almost absolute obedience, and he also had very strong support from the Prime Minister. The historians of the strategic air offensive, always careful in their language, have written, "Never, indeed, in British history had such an important Commander-in-Chief been so continuously close to the centre of government power as Sir Arthur Harris was to Mr. Churchill."[94] The deadlock between Harris and the CAS was avoided rather than resolved. Oil and communications would be given priority whenever this seemed reasonable, but only within a general-area offensive. The position the Prime Minister had allowed Sir Arthur Harris to achieve in his councils was to bear a high price.

The continued emphasis on area bombing in the last days of the war in Europe blended with a variety of other threads, culminating in one of the most controversial of episodes, the bombing of Dresden. Throughout the war there was a general propensity toward area bombing of large targets. A second theme in some quarters suggested that there might be political value in demonstrating to the Russians the measure to which Western strategic bombing could assist them in their advance in the east. This led to an emphasis on attacks on such cities as Berlin, Leipzig, and Dresden. As Churchill departed for Yalta, he evidently favored this approach and urged the Secretary of State for Air, Sir Archibald Sinclair, to pursue such a program. When Sinclair returned a cautious answer which stressed the desirability of more precisely attacking German oil and transportation, the Prime Minister was not satisfied. On January 26, 1945, Churchill dispatched to Sinclair a peremptory minute.

I did not ask you last night about plans for harrying the German retreat from Breslau. On the contrary, I asked whether Berlin, and no doubt other large cities in East Germany, should not now be considered especially attractive targets. I am glad that this is "under examination." Pray report to me to-morrow what is going to be done.[95]

This pressing minute elicited an assurance from Sinclair that Churchill at Yalta would be supported in his dealings with the Russians by an adequate bombing offensive against East German cities.

At Yalta the Russians showed only moderate enthusiasm toward the assistance the Allies offered but did indicate that bombing of such centers as Leipzig and Dresden would be acceptable assistance to them. No particular effort was made to single out Dresden; it was simply one of several convenient targets which met a series of predetermined requirements. The city contained a prewar population in excess of 600,000, and that figure probably had been swelled by the influx of refugees before the advancing Russian armies. On the night of February 13, 1945, Bomber Command dispatched 800 aircraft to Dresden, where one of the most devastating attacks of the war was carried out. In daylight on the following day more than 400 American bombers took up the assault. On February 15 another 200 American bombers continued the attack. A final daylight strike involving 400 American aircraft took place on March 2. The bombings of the night of the 14th and day of the 15th were particularly devastating. Estimates of those who died in the attacks ranged from about 60,000 to a quarter of a million.

Dresden now began to acquire that haunting position it has retained to the present day in the story of Churchill's war ministry. There was nothing particularly unique about the attack; it was part of the general strategic air offensive that Britain and the United States had waged throughout the war. However, there had always been people who were unhappy about an air offensive which they viewed as a wanton assault on civilians and outside the proper morality by which civilized nations should conduct their wars (if it may be said that war has a proper morality). Nor had the British government been entirely forthright in explaining the character of the bombing offensive. Certainly it seems that some highly placed figures, religious and otherwise, had been given an impression of a greater measure of care and precision in bombing than the facts would warrant. The attack on Dresden, coming late in the war when it appeared that German resistance was collapsing, was thus particularly offensive to those who had always been uneasy about bombing policy.[96]

These pressures, including some from abroad, reached the Prime Minister by the middle of March 1945; and on March 28 Churchill communicated to Ismay, for reference to the COS and the CAS directly, what the official historians of the strategic air offensive have termed "among the least felicitous of the Prime Minister's long series of war-time minutes." Churchill wrote:

It seems to me that the moment has come when the question of bombing German cities simply for the sake of increasing the terror, though under other pretexts, should be reviewed. Otherwise we shall come into control of an utterly ruined land. . . . The destruction of Dresden remains a serious query against the conduct of Allied bombing. I am of the opinion that military objectives must henceforward be more strictly studied in our own interests rather than that of the enemy.[97]

In view of Churchill's own emphasis prior to his departure for Yalta, this minute does indeed appear unfortunate; not surprisingly Sir Charles Portal refused to accept it. Churchill agreed to substitute a modified statement, deleting any reference specifically to Dresden, which was issued on April 1, 1945. By this date the issue was largely academic. For all practical purposes the war in Europe was over.[98]

John Colville has recorded that he was surprised by the apparent equanimity with which Churchill received an account of what befell Dresden. Colville immediately follows this by saying that the Prime Minister steadfastly refused to be swayed by the demands for revenge with which he was greeted when he visited the still smoking ruins of British cities, nor did he ever listen to Lord Cherwell's violent anti-German proposals with anything but polite tolerance.[99] Churchill's own reference to Dresden in his war memoirs falls briefly inside a single sentence. Sir Arthur Harris fell entirely from view. He was not mentioned in Churchill's dispatch at the end of the war, nor did he receive a peerage like so many of Britain's other successful war leaders.[100]

The controversy over Dresden was in fact only a single episode in a whole strategic concept which was itself the object of controversy. The strategic air offensive has been indicted as an "obsession" and as the "main cause of British misfortunes in the second world war." The shortage of fighter planes in the Far East has been blamed on the allotment of priority of supplies to Bomber Command. The strategic air offensive has been further indicted as doing more damage to the Allies than to Germany; it demanded about one-fourth of Britain's war production and about 15 percent of America's, but the damage done to Germany's war production "was at most nine percent." Loss of life was heavy too. Churchill himself wrote that in early 1944 more British and American air crews were killed than there were losses in the landing at Normandy.[101] Soldiers felt throughout the war that if bombers had been available more widely in other theaters, their usefulness would have been greater in contributing to the total war effort. Naval authorities have similarly indicted the air offensive which devoured long-range aircraft. Since losses in convoy were rare when both sea and air escorts were present and shortages in shipping placed limits on Allied strategic capabilities throughout the war, the naval case was a strong one.[102]

Thus had Topsy grown. It grew it seems because the bombers were there and the doctrine was there and there was no other way of attacking Germany in the summer and autumn of 1940. Churchill's attitude swayed to and fro. In October 1940 he had told the House of Commons that when he visited bombed cities he was greeted with cries that the British could take it, but that he also heard cries of "Give it back to them." He said he did not wish to get into "a sterile controversy as to what are and what are not reprisals. Our object must be to inflict the maximum harm on the enemy's war-making capacity. That is the only object that we shall pursue."[103] One cannot help feeling that Churchill wished to have the best of both arguments. In a broadcast of May 10, 1942, he apparently had come to view the bombing effort as a form of special justice: "Though the mills of God grind slowly, yet they grind exceedingly small. And for my part, I hail it as an example of sublime and poetic justice that those who have loosed these horrors upon mankind will now in their homes and persons feel the shattering strokes of just retribution."[104] When Churchill spoke to the House of Commons in September 1943, however, he seemed to assign a lower priority to bombing as only one amid a variety of forces designed to bring down Hitler.[105] Yet he would not fetter this method of war. He told the House of Commons on February 22, 1944, that the proper course for German civilians and non-combatants was to quit the centers of munition production and take refuge in the countryside. "We intend to make war production in its widest sense impossible in all German cities, towns, and factory centres."[106] One can only wonder if Churchill was convinced by his own argument. In the same speech he said,

> This air power was the weapon which both the marauding States selected as their main tool of conquest. This was the sphere in which they were to triumph. This was the method by which the nations were to be subjugated to their rule. I shall not moralise further than to say that there is a strange, stern justice in the long swing of events.[107]

Perhaps Churchill was convinced of the moral justice of the strategic air offensive. He had other reasons for it, however. When he went to Moscow with empty hands in the autumn of 1942 to tell Stalin there would be no second front in 1943, one of the arguments deployed to soothe him was the capacity of the Western powers to bomb Germany. The American observer Averell Harriman reported back to Washington that Stalin and Churchill between them had swiftly destroyed most of Germany's important industrial centers.[108] Perhaps circumstances and necessity fell in with a stern code of justice to propel the Prime Minister's support of the strategic air offensive. Yet perhaps in Churchill's mind the ultimate feeling was regret. When he wrote his war memoirs, he observed that the "hideous process of bombarding open cities" started by the Germans was repaid many times over by the Allies and found its culmination in Hiroshima and Nagasaki.[109] He further recalled a bombed-out crowd calling to him to give it back to the Germans, and he wrote, "I undertook forthwith to see that their wishes were carried out; and this promise was certainly kept. . . . Certainly the enemy got it all back in good measure, pressed down and running over. Alas for poor humanity!"[110] A. J. P. Taylor has written that "Churchill at least had the redeeming quality of disliking what he was compelled to do. Though he, too, waged war ruthlessly, he remained a humane man."[111]

The Army

When British forces left the Continent in the summer of 1940, direct contact between the opponents ceased. The struggle in Western Europe became a struggle of sea and air power and would remain so for several years. But a much different and more complicated arrangement existed in the Mediterranean basin, particularly at its eastern end in that general area the British lumped under the heading of the Middle East Command. To Britain this area was of critical importance; one of the lifelines of the British Empire ran through the Mediterranean. There was of course the alternate route around Africa, but the vastly greater distance clearly was undesirable. To keep the Mediterranean open as long as possible was an important principle of British war policy. Britain had anchors at either end of the Mediterranean—Gibraltar on the west and the naval base at Alexandria on the east. Between these two bases there existed only the island of Malta, dangerously isolated in the central Mediterranean, in what was virtually an Italian sea. Sicily was not far to the north of Malta, and to the south stretched Italian-occupied Africa. To the west was French Africa, then maintaining a neutrality which leaned toward Berlin. Farther to the east in Africa the Italians occupied Ethiopia and had a strong position in that area. It was estimated in 1940 that there were over 200,000 Italian troops based in Ethiopia and more than another 200,000 in Libya. Sandwiched between these two Italian positions lay the territory that was the responsibility of the British Commander in Chief in the Middle East. His command also included the Balkans (with particular importance on Greece) plus Turkey, Iraq, Aden, and East Africa. When Italy declared war in June 1940, the British had about 36,000 troops in Egypt, 9,000 in the Sudan, over 5,000 in Kenya, over 27,000 in Palestine, and a few smaller detachments elsewhere.

The position was clearly precarious as well as of great strategic importance; accordingly, the man chosen to command the Middle East had been one of the brightest stars of the British army, Sir Archibald Wavell. Wavell was a remarkable man who combined in his character the qualities of the soldier's soldier and soldier-scholar. The air commander in the area was Sir Arthur Longmore, who also was responsible for Malta, and the naval commander was Sir Andrew Cunningham. It was fortunate that Wavell was a man of formidable abilities, for the situation required a military giant. In his favor Wavell had good reasons to suspect that the quality of the Italian forces opposing him was far short of the standards of their German allies and indeed of their British opponents. Events would prove this supposition correct. Yet the Italians had a strongly prepared position and a vast superiority in manpower. Wavell furthermore had to serve as a sort of center in the Middle East for all political and organizational matters as well as military, and in the summer of 1940 it was necessary to start almost from scratch to build the sort of elaborate administrative base needed to operate modern armies.

Few resources existed in the Middle East to provide the sort of technology modern warfare required. Most of these necessities had to come from Britain. One of the boldest of Churchill's decisions was to rush reinforcements to Wavell at the very time there were grave doubts that Britain herself could resist a German invasion. This was an invaluable aid. But as early as June 1940 Wavell had raised the issue of the coordination of strategy which was to plague relations between him and the Prime Minister for the following year. The central direction of the entire war effort was located in London and was operated primarily by the Prime Minister acting as Minister of Defence and by the COS. Wavell had suggested early that the Middle East would require a large measure of autonomy to meet the rapidly shifting demands of a theater which could produce many battlefields simultaneously. Although Churchill created a special committee in July to oversee problems in the Middle East, retention of war direction was kept firmly in London.[112]

The early exchange of views between Wavell and Churchill was not satisfactory to the Prime Minister, and he urged that Wavell come to London so that he might have the opportunity to thrash out matters with his theater commander face to face. Wavell was a man of great reputation, part of which were his famous silences. He was always taciturn, and unfortunately this was a characteristic to which the Prime Minister did not respond. To make a mark with Churchill, it was best to be highly articulate. While Wavell was a master of the written word, he had little facility at oral expression. Wavell further combined in his personality the strong-minded soldier prepared to take risks and endure reverses with a much more sensitive aspect of spirit, and he was quick to feel he did not command Churchill's full support. In mid-August 1940 Wavell met for several days with Churchill and the London authorities, but the meetings did not go particularly well. Churchill tended to take the position that there were really quite a few men available to Wavell in the Middle East; Wavell had to point out that in modern warfare, equipment was as important as men and under certain conditions far more so. Churchill was unimpressed and told Eden that Wavell was a good average colonel. Churchill later wrote of this occasion that he was not in full agreement with Wavell's use of the resources at his disposal but thought it best to leave him in command because so many people had confidence in him.[113]

Almost at once an issue arose to make an already weak relationship more difficult. Wavell had proposed not to defend British Somaliland on the ground that the position was indefensible with the few men available. It would be hard to fault this judgment, but Churchill insisted that Somaliland should at least be fought for. Wavell agreed to do this. The total British casualties were 260 in the campaign which ended in a British evacuation. Churchill was displeased and felt this showed that little fight had been offered. But the Italians admitted the loss of 1,800 men in gaining British Somaliland, which presented quite a different prospect of the intensity of the fighting. Wavell had defended the conduct of his field commander and had concluded his observations to Churchill with the remark that "a big butcher's bill is not necessarily evidence of good tactics." General Dill in London observed that this sentence fired Churchill to a greater anger than he had ever seen before.[114] It was an unhappy beginning. Since Churchill lacked confidence in Wavell, he tended to pour onto his head an endless stream of directives which only further intensified Wavell's sensitive knowledge that the Prime Minister did not trust him. In particular, Churchill wanted action. On the other hand, Wavell, fearing Churchill's intervention, did not wish to reveal his plans to the Prime Minister. The unhappy Churchill in turn sent Anthony Eden, then Secretary of State for War, to see Wavell in October. It should be noted that Churchill was also dispatching forces as fast as he could, and by late September the Middle East was receiving the first supply of infantry tanks which were to be so useful shortly thereafter.

By this time Italy had attacked Greece, an operation which had brought the Italians little glory and a good many hard knocks. But it had also led the British to provide aid to Greece, at first in the form of antiaircraft batteries and then some aircraft. It also was the beginning of an operation which was to become one of the most controversial of the war.

Eden returned to London on November 8, 1940, bearing with him the secret knowledge imparted by Wavell that an offensive was being planned in the Libyan Desert. Churchill responded positively to this news. On November 14 Churchill told Wavell that the general political situation made it very desirable that he undertake his proposed operation in the western desert.[115] Less than a fortnight later Churchill was still urging Wavell on: "As we told you the other day, we shall stand by you and Wilson in any well-conceived action irrespective of result, because no one can guarantee success in war, but only deserve it."[116] Churchill's point was valid. Germany possessed the potential to disrupt the precarious balance between Italian ineffectiveness and lack of British resources that existed in the eastern Mediterranean basin—a point to which Wavell himself was sensitive. He had been planning an operation in the desert for some time and had postponed it when it was necessary to divert part of his small air force to aid the Greeks against Italian attack. But early in December the army in the western desert, commanded by Richard O'Conner, set out on an operation of tactical brilliance which was rewarded by sweeping success. By January 22, 1941, O'Conner was in possession of the very important port of Tobruk, and by early February he held the bulge of Libya and the port of Benghazi. The two months' campaign in the western desert had netted 130,000 prisoners at a cost of 500 British killed and fewer than 1,500 wounded and missing. Churchill was thoroughly delighted.[117]

The desert victory was important to Churchill the politician, giving some positive demonstration that Britain could still win military actions, and it encouraged fence-sitters to withhold any decisions in favor of the Axis. This was critically important in the case of Spain and the government of Vichy France and also induced the United States to support Britain more boldly. Churchill used Wavell's success as the basis for a powerful broadcast to the Italian people. The Prime Minister was well aware that there was substantial unhappiness in Italy over the war and was determined to do whatever he could to prod Italy out of her alliance with Hitler.

The United States was sufficiently encouraged by these events that in early January 1941 the close adviser of President Roosevelt, Harry Hopkins, was sent to London to survey the overall situation. Hopkins's report to the President indicated that Churchill had decided to reinforce the Greeks at the expense of weakening the army in Africa after its desert victory. There are elements of the report which are puzzling, for Hopkins said of the Prime Minister, "He thinks Greece is lost. . . . He knows this will be a blow to British prestige and is obviously considering ways and means of preparing the British public for it. . . . This debacle in Greece will be overcome in part by what he considers to be the sure defeat of the Italians in Africa."[118] If this did constitute Churchill's mind at the moment, it was surely unwise to strip away the forces that had been successful in Africa to pursue a lost cause in Greece and thus risk also losing what had been secured in the desert.

Churchill was also telling his commanders in the Middle East that nothing must hamper the capture of Tobruk, but thereafter all operations in Libya were subordinate to aiding Greece. "We expect and require prompt and active compliance with our decisions, for which we bear full responsibility." Whether it is ever wise to send so categorical an order to perfectly competent theater commanders is an open question. Certainly Wavell's reply made clear his own feelings when he said the messages pouring out from London filled him with dismay. He was opposed to dispersing his forces over the entire Middle East, believed that the new pressure against Greece was only a German bluff, and concluded, "Nothing we can do from here is likely to be in time to stop German advance if really intended, it will lead to most dangerous dispersion of force and is playing enemy's game. . . ."[119] London was right that the German threat was more than a bluff, but the theater commander's view that there was little militarily to be gained and much to be lost by attempting to support Greece against a determined German assault was clearly military wisdom.

Politics, however, overruled military considerations. There was a feeling in London that Greece could not be abandoned, that what happened there might have a decisive effect upon the position of neutral Turkey, and that world opinion in general required that Britain support its commitment to the Greeks. Accordingly, in mid-January Wavell flew to Athens for discussions with Greek military leaders. The American government received a report from one of its traveling officers at this time, suggesting that British ambitions in Greece extended to the point of hoping to create an entire Balkan coalition against a German advance. Attitudes in Yugoslavia were deeply divided over the wisdom of cooperating with Germany or resisting Hitler. Wavell's meetings with the Greeks were not particularly encouraging. They were not immediately anxious for British land forces to come to their support. The situation in the Mediterranean was shifting dangerously against the British with the arrival of German air forces, a much more serious matter than having to cope with the Italians. Accordingly, on January 21, 1941, the COS in London began to shift away from the Greek adventure. Wavell was told to establish a secure desert flank at Benghazi. He was to make a renewed offer of military assistance to Greece. To assist him in measuring the problems, the government was sending to the Middle East Anthony Eden, now Foreign Secretary, and the CIGS Sir John Dill.[120] Indeed, at this time London seemed filled with tergiversation. At one point Greece was to be supported to the end, at the next moment there were doubts on the wisdom of this policy.

By February 12 Churchill seems to have settled down to supporting Greece. Dill by no means shared Churchill's point of view and believed that the troops in the Middle East were fully employed and there simply were none available for Greece. This evidently produced a violent outburst from the Prime Minister on the subject of how desirable firing squads were to spur generals to action. But when Dill reached the scene, his views changed and he became converted to the view that Britain must help Greece and that this was the only chance of preventing the Balkans from being devoured piecemeal by Germany. He was also satisfied that there was a reasonable military chance of successfully holding a line in northern Greece. Eden agreed. Now the Prime Minister wavered. On February 21 he told the men on the scene, "Do not consider yourselves obligated to a Greek enterprise if in your hearts you feel it will only be another Norwegian fiasco. If no good plan can be made please say so. But of course you know how valuable success would be." There is no doubt that the Prime Minister longed for success and that his enthusiasm was always on the side of bold risks. But he certainly emphasized that he wished the men on the scene to give him their true and fair estimate of what could be done.[121]

During this time the COS were reporting their views to Churchill. It seemed to them that while the potential military advantages of a successful defense in Greece were great, the achievement was doubtful and the risks of failure serious. But they concluded that leaving Greece to her fate was perhaps more serious in the long run than the failure of an honorable attempt to help. By this time Wavell too had become convinced that the operation in Greece was militarily justifiable. He thought that a Balkan operation would be a strain even for Germany, and in particular he believed on the basis of his intelligence reports that his western flank in the desert was secure. He summed up his views saying that while the choice was difficult, he believed the British were more likely to be playing the enemy game by remaining inactive than by taking action in the Balkans. In short, by the end of February Churchill and his military advisers had exactly reversed their positions. The Prime Minister now was doubtful of success, and the soldiers were urging action.[122]

When the British leaders returned to Athens on March 2, they found the Greeks in a depressed mood. Neither Turkey nor Yugoslavia had been particularly receptive to suggestions of military cooperation. Further, the Greek generals were going to attempt defense of an unreasonably long front far beyond what the joint Greek-British military resources could possibly justify. Eden and Dill still seemed hopeful, but London was gloomier. The Prime Minister warned Eden that grave imperial issues could be raised if British commanders committed Australian and New Zealand troops to an increasingly hazardous operation. Churchill certainly had not forgotten Gallipoli and Anzac Beach. He warned Eden that the Cabinet would most likely decide to call off the whole Greek affair. Churchill further noted that he had asked repeatedly for a precise military evaluation from his commanders on the scene and that nothing more than general opinions had been forthcoming. This was a fair comment. Churchill concluded that it was not right for the British to take upon themselves the responsibility of persuading the Greeks to fight a hopeless battle against their better judgment.

On March 6 Eden replied that he had reexamined the whole question with Dill, Wavell, and others and that there was unanimous agreement that it was right to support the Greeks. On March 7 a further telegram arrived from Eden stating that the Greeks were determined to fight, whatever the odds, and that while British prestige would suffer if their forces were ignominiously ejected as they had been at Dunkirk, he believed it would be even more damaging to leave Greece to her fate. Field Marshal Smuts, Churchill's old South African foe and later friend whose wisdom he so much respected, had arrived on the scene and added his support to the views of Eden and Dill. Churchill then replied that he was deeply impressed with the steadfast attitude of Eden, Dill, Wavell, and others, including the Australian and New Zealand commanders, Generals Blamey and Freyberg. Churchill took these views to the Cabinet and the decision was made to go ahead. Churchill recorded that the Cabinet was short and its decision final; one rather wishes it had been a longer one. Churchill perhaps should not have been satisfied with his failure to get a full outline of the actual military situation, but the fact remains that everyone on the scene (and it was a most impressive array of talent—Eden, Smuts, Dill, Wavell, Wilson, Blamey, Freyberg) advised the Cabinet that it was right to proceed. In short, for a second time London authorities had doubted the wisdom of the Greek operation and for a second time they had been advised by the men on the scene that the risks were worth taking.[123]

But the forces of disaster were already beginning to gather over the

Greek adventure. As early as mid-February Germany was beginning to send forces into Africa. These were placed under the command of General Erwin Rommel, a commander of thrusting activity and high tactical competence. By late March 1941 Rommel decided that the British position in the desert was ripe for attack. He was quite right, and Rommel's offensive caught the British ill prepared. Further, the British commanders in the desert lost control of their forces, and in the chaos that followed, several high officers were captured. By April 11 the British were back on the Egyptian frontier except for a garrison left invested in Tobruk. Little of the British armor in the desert was left intact. Nor were things going any better in Greece. The landing of British forces was being carried out under the direct observation of German agents; by the end of March Britain had over 30,000 men in Greece who looked increasingly like hostages to fortune. On April 6, 1941, Field Marshal List unleashed his assault on Greece and Yugoslavia. In short order the British had two first-class crises on their hands in the Middle East. Well might Wavell have told Dill as the latter departed for London, "Jack, I hope when this action is reviewed you will be elected to sit on my court martial."[124]

But this was not the Prime Minister's mood at all. As usual when the situation was worst, the Prime Minister was at his best. On April 10 Wavell received an encouraging message from Churchill endorsing the decision to hold Tobruk even if isolated and telling Wavell that London would do "all in our power to bring you aid." On April 7 it was decided to send out six complete squadrons of Hurricane fighter planes to support the Middle East, and on April 21 the Prime Minister decided to risk sending a fast merchant convoy directly through the Mediterranean in order to rush tanks to Wavell with all speed and at any cost. This courageous decision was fully justified when the convoy reached Egypt on May 12 after losing only one ship, and that to a mine. It brought 43 badly needed Hurricanes and 238 desperately needed tanks.[125]

In the interval before these reinforcements could reach Wavell, it was necessary to determine priorities in the face of adversity. The overwhelming extent of German power in the Balkans made clear that resistance in Greece would be short; indeed the Greek generals suggested by April 16 that the British would do well to think about withdrawal. The island of Crete was to be held, and many of the forces evacuated from Greece went there. The Greek evacuation itself was a second Dunkirk and worse, for there was not the same control of the air over the Greek beaches that had obtained over Dunkirk. On April 18 Churchill set these priorities: victory in the western desert first, evacuation of troops from Greece second, and everything else would follow. The situation, however, was extremely desperate. It is an enduring testimony to the courage of the Royal Navy that they faced constant, severe German air attack to get the men out of Greece. The great bulk of the British troops were evacuated, but all equipment was lost.[126]

The constant adversity in the Middle East coupled with a serious crisis in the Atlantic was obviously placing its strains upon the government. On April 19, 1941, Wavell and Wilson were the recipients of a testy message from Churchill complaining that he was not getting clear reports from them on the progress of the fighting in Greece. He observed, "This is not the way H. M. Government should be treated. It is also detrimental to the service as many decisions have to be taken here and we are in constant relations with the Dominions and with foreign countries. I wish you to make sure that this state of things ends at once. . . ."[127] Even Churchill seemed to be feeling the strain of constant misfortune.

On the night of April 27, 1941, one of the most violent scenes in Churchill's entire wartime ministry took place at Chequers, the Prime Minister's weekend residence. A fairly large company was gathered there including General Ismay, General Kennedy, General Brooke, and Lord Cherwell. Discussion not surprisingly turned to the Middle East. Kennedy suggested that the situation was so critical that it might not be possible to hold even Egypt. At this the Prime Minister lost his temper, suggested that he would have firing squads to shoot the generals (a customary reference of Churchill's, not to be taken too seriously), and went on to accuse Kennedy of defeatism. Defending himself, Kennedy observed that the commanders in the Middle East had a plan for withdrawal from Egypt if that should prove necessary. At this revelation, the Prime Minister's anger reached titanic proportions. He evidently announced to the badly shaken Director of Military Operations, "This comes as a flash of lightning to me. I never heard such ideas. War is a contest of wills. It is pure defeatism to speak as you have done." Efforts to avoid the subject failed. Throughout the evening Churchill returned to the theme in a towering rage. References were made to the fate of Admiral Byng. Praising Rommel, Churchill called his advance in the western desert the "quintessence of generalship. It is generalship we need in Egypt."[128]

The pressure on Churchill at this juncture was extreme. The Greek army had surrendered on April 24, ending all hopes for a Balkan coalition. New problems emerged at once. German successes led to an uprising in Iraq which threatened to overrun the small British position there. Wavell was directed to send assistance, and he replied that this was impossible. It required virtually a direct order to get him to dispatch a small force across the desert to Iraq. Hardly was this done when it became clear that German aircraft were using bases in Syria, which was governed by Vichy France. The Free French in the area urged Wavell to help them intervene swiftly in Syria before Germany took over. For a time Wavell was able to resist this Free French proposal; his hands were so full in the western desert, in Iraq, and in trying to strengthen the garrison on Crete that he could bear few more burdens. The operation in Iraq at least was successful, and by the end of May the British position there had been reestablished. To the London authorities the success in

Iraq appeared to justify their decision to order Wavell to intervene there against his judgment and suggested that Wavell was becoming a tired man.[129] The wonder was that Wavell had not passed the point of absolute exhaustion, for in late May he had to sustain a yet more staggering blow.

Crete was within range of German and Italian aircraft but beyond that of British fighters based in Egypt. This simple fact was to seal the island's doom. Heavy German pressure drove the few RAF planes off the island, for adequate ground protection could not be provided to the airfields. This was followed on May 20 by the arrival of German paratroops in one of the most spectacular actions of the war. After several days of the most violent fighting, it became increasingly clear that the Germans were going to secure the island. On May 24 Wavell judged that there was still some hope; accordingly on the following day the COS and Prime Minister sent a strong signal urging that every effort be made to keep the island and every risk be run by the fleet and RAF in supporting the effort there. The pressures of the situation were so great that Admiral Cunningham all but offered the government his resignation from command, a gesture which Wavell had already made. Both offers were ignored.

By May 27 the struggle for Crete was lost, and Wavell so informed the government. By the night of May 31 the Royal Navy had completed yet another evacuation, carried out in spite of the heaviest of casualties. Of the 32,000 men on the island, the navy took off some 18,000 at the price of the loss of three cruisers and six destroyers and serious damage to two battleships and an aircraft carrier. Following the already heavy losses sustained in the evacuation from Greece, it was a wonder that the Royal Navy had accomplished what it had. Indeed, one wonders if any navy with less than three centuries of unbroken tradition could have maintained its morale in the face of such adversity.

The overall picture was bleak indeed. In exchange for having secured a messy situation in Iraq, Britain had to face serious setbacks in Libya, an ignominious evacuation from Greece, and a spectacular defeat on Crete in addition to an increasing German presence in Syria.[130] Again priorities had to be reviewed, and Churchill's conclusion was that every effort had to be made to defeat Rommel. He believed that if this could be done, the position in the Middle East could still be secured and that the reinforcements which he had sent at such great risk directly through the Mediterranean in the face of German and Italian air power would be adequate to permit Wavell to undertake a new offensive in the desert. This was surely too optimistic and tended to leave out of consideration the disorganization and shattering effects to morale of the sustained misfortunes in the Middle East. Wavell further reported that the condition of the newly arrived tanks would not permit an immediate new offensive in the western desert. London pressed hard for action, and in mid-June Wavell perhaps unwisely complied. The attack never came closer than fifty miles to the surrounded garrison at Tobruk. The failure in the desert struck Churchill very hard. He records that reports of the misfortune reached him at his home at Chartwell and "I wandered about the valley disconsolately for some hours." On June 21, 1941, Churchill relieved Wavell of his command and appointed General Sir Claude Auchinleck in his place.[131]

Much could be assessed to Wavell's credit as he left his command. He had all but completely cleared the Italian position in and around Ethiopia by the time he departed and had accomplished this with far inferior numbers. He had gained a victory of similarly great proportions in the western desert, and throughout he had sustained the British position in the Middle East in the face of overwhelming odds and at great peril. But London had sound reason by June 1941 to doubt the freshness of Wavell's judgment. His intelligence had served him badly on the German forces in Africa, and a serious setback had thus been suffered in the desert. In particular, the necessity of London to overrule him in supporting Iraq had been considered a point against the general's judgment. The failure of the new operation in the desert was perhaps unfairly viewed as the final strike against Wavell.

Churchill was always unhappy with what seemed to be a disproportionate number of men in the Middle East Theater (which the Prime Minister placed at 530,000) compared to the total number available for fighting. Wavell had pointed out that in desert war, vehicles were of crucial importance, and he had lost nearly 9,000 in Greece and Crete. Further, of the total number of men available to him, over 130,000 were native Africans who could be used successfully only in their own regions, and armed forces in the Middle East had to perform many administrative functions normally carried out by others in Britain and similar highly developed regions. London believed, however, that many of the administrative problems of the Middle East could be blamed on the men on the scene, and certainly Tedder believed that Wavell was badly served by his staffs. For better or worse, Churchill had lost confidence in his commander and had replaced him.[132]

The Greek venture has been as controversial in retrospect as it was difficult at the time and has produced both staunch defenders and acid critics. In its favor it has been argued that it significantly delayed the German attack on Russia and that this later date greatly aided the Russian resistance by shortening the time between the beginning of the German offensive and the arrival of winter. In fact, the German high command had already determined upon a postponement of the attack on Russia until June 22. The Greek action to some extent weakened and dislocated the forces placed on the southern flank of Russia, but it was Yugoslav resistance to German proposals that led the German high command to delay the offensive against Russia.[133] Similarly, it has been argued that the defense of Crete, which left the Germans without any organized paratroop forces because of their high casualties in the operation, did much to save the island of Malta from capture. It appears that the German high command already had grave doubts about an airborne attack on Malta which had far better prepared defenses than Crete. However, it seems clear that the concentration of German air effort in the eastern end of the Mediterranean followed by the switch to the Russian front contributed to the British ability to sustain their garrison at Malta and to hold that island which was all-important to the successful continuation of the struggle in the Mediterranean.[134]

On the other hand, it has been argued critically that it would have been far better to establish a firm grip on Crete and not to intervene at all in Grece.[135] Against this criticism, a variety of arguments have been advanced. Churchill has written that in view of a guarantee given them by Chamberlain as far back as April 13, 1939, the Greeks were pledged support and the British were bound to honor their pledge. Sir Llewellyn Woodward has argued for the intervention on the basis of moral reasons (the guarantee to Greece) and political and military reasons (the threat to British sea communications and to Turkey if the Germans occupied Greece and the surrounding islands). Churchill generally summed up this position in his victory broadcast of May 13, 1945, when he said of the intervention, "We did this for honour."[136]

Whether the intervention in Greece was wise and the risks worth running has produced an affirmative opinion from many of those involved. Wavell to the end of his life believed it right to have fought as far forward as possible in the defense of the Middle East. Eden and Wilson remained similarly convinced that the decision was correct. Certainly the War Cabinet at the time seemed to ratify this position, since it constantly reaffirmed decisions to reinforce the Middle East, and this was in keeping with Churchill's own views.[137] Perhaps the most astute comment on the decision to intervene in Greece is that of Michael Howard: "In this part of the world the jugular veins of the two antagonists ran so close to one another that a struggle for mastery could hardly be avoided."[138]

Churchill's role in this episode has been just as controversial. Was he simply a man swept away with the emotions of combat? Did he run the Middle East on too tight a rein from London? Was he consistently unfair in his judgment of his gifted commander Wavell? John Connell has observed that Churchill's method of running the Middle East from London was a system which did not work well with Wavell and that Churchill had proved incapable of trusting him but was deeply reluctant to sack him. Connell concluded that if a relationship of trust had been established between these two, the course of British campaigns in the Middle East, and thereafter in other theaters of war, would have been profoundly different. Certainly the two men had great difficulty in communicating; and when reports reached Churchill from firsthand participants in the fighting on Crete suggesting that Wavell had not conducted the defense of that island with all possible skill, John Colville observed, "I could almost hear a large nail being driven into Wavell's coffin." In view of the fact that a working measure of confidence was not secured between the Prime Minister and the theater commander, it was inevitable that Wavell would have to go. His form of departure remains one of the worst marks against Churchill's entire conduct in the war, for Churchill's customary humanity and generosity even in adversity failed him on this occasion. By June 1941 not only was the military situation in the Middle East precarious but also the political situation at home. After he was relieved of his command Wavell had asked that he be allowed some time to return to England which he had not seen for years. Churchill, however, ordered Wavell on to India to assume new duties there. Churchill knew of the great admiration with which Wavell was viewed and of his formidable skill as a writer. Evidently he decided to run no risks of a controversy in England. Wavell was not allowed within thousands of miles of London. Perhaps Churchill's conduct on this occasion is understandable, but it remains inexcusable.[139]

Conversely, it is not fair to claim more for Wavell than he accomplished. The judgments he made on critical occasions were clearly mistaken. As late as March 2 he had reassured London, in response to anxious queries and the forwarding of information that the Germans were reinforcing Africa, that there was no significant German force yet on the African coast. Wavell would have done better to take the warning from London more seriously. His judgment of what could be done to relieve the situation in Iraq had been proved erroneous by events. His part in the decision to hold Greece has been stated. He and his associates on that occasion never provided London with the clear, precise military defense of that decision for which London had asked.[140] Indeed, Churchill was badly served by his advisers on the scene. Ismay believed that if Churchill had thought that the forces remaining in Egypt would be inadequate to cope with any attack which could be made from the west, he would have insisted that the idea of sending substantial help to Greece be abandoned.[141] Certainly the advice he received to go on in Greece was overwhelming. This came from Eden, the Foreign Secretary, who was a former Secretary of State for War, a man with military experience, and a man whose judgment was widely respected; from Sir John Dill, the CIGS and most respected of British professional soldiers; and from Wavell himself, the Commander in Chief in the theater who was supported by his naval and air associates. The Australian and New Zealand troop commanders, Blamey and Freyberg, had also voiced their approval, as had General Wilson, the British field commander. Finally, Field Marshal Smuts, one of the most respected judges of what was possible in war, had added his endorsement. It appears that London kept a better perspective than did the men on the scene.

Kennedy relates that later on Dill explained his support of the aid to Greece on the theory that he hoped the Germans would attack in the desert before the British were committed in Greece and thus his advice would not be acted on. Perhaps this was only a passing comment.

One hopes so, for surely, if he did act in this manner, Dill had failed in his first duty as CIGS to give the Prime Minister honest advice even when it disagreed with his wishes. Further, Wavell's remark to Dill regarding court-martials, as the latter departed for London, suggests that Wavell also harbored misgivings. Perhaps he too should have run the risk of the Prime Minister's wrath in making them clearer. In judging Churchill's conduct, it is well to remember Kennedy's words, "The military opinion tendered to the Cabinet by the Chiefs of Staff and by Wavell was proved wrong in every respect."[142]

Tedder has suggested that the Balkan affair was inevitable, that the British had to support Greece and that the real burden of guilt lay on the authorities in London who had not sent adequate reinforcements to the Middle East. Yet in view of the substantial risks Churchill was taking and his record for supplying reinforcements (including the critical convoy sent directly through the Mediterranean in May), it is hard to see what more Churchill could have done. Furthermore, an American comment reveals that, at the time, the services were inclined to place as much blame on each other as on the Prime Minister for the misfortune. On the way to the meeting for drafting the Atlantic Charter, Harry Hopkins sent back a message to General Ismay: "Pound, Dill and Freeman get on as gentlemen should, and there is never a cross word between any of the Services. They know better than to discuss Crete in mixed company."[143]

What then was Churchill's responsibility? He defended his actions in his memoirs when he wrote that the battle of Crete ruined the striking power of the German airborne corps. The Iraq revolt was finally crushed. The occupation and conquest of Syria ended (as it proved forever) the German advance toward the Persian Gulf and India. "If under all the temptations of prudence, the War Cabinet and the Chiefs of Staff had not made every post a winning-post, and imposed their will on all commanders, we should have been left only with the losses sustained in Crete, without gathering the rewards which followed from the hard and glorious fighting there." Churchill went on to justify his general behavior saying, "There is always much to be said for not attempting more than you can do and for making a certainty of what you try. But this principle, like others in life and war, has its exceptions."[144] One can see how A. J. P. Taylor would conclude that the whole episode had revealed Churchill "as the old Churchill of Gallipoli: a gambler for high stakes who tried to do too much with inadequate resources." Taylor has also concluded that Churchill's relentless pressure on his commanders led them to put a more optimistic view on affairs than they should have and to undertake operations which they should not have.[145]

Yet perhaps in the long run Churchill was right and Hitler was wrong. Indeed, in evaluating the strains between Churchill and the British commanders on the scene, it is sometimes possible to obscure rather than to reveal the primary issues at stake. On April 12, 1941, President Roosevelt received a general report on the situation in the

Middle East drawn up by Admiral R. K. Turner, one of the most gifted of all American naval officers. The report shows deep insight. As its first point, it established that the dislocation of Britain from Egypt and the expulsion of the British Fleet from the Mediterranean "is a MUST for the Germans." And this, in spite of everything, the Germans had failed to do. Turner also correctly appraised the situation in the western desert, that while the Germans would have little difficulty in regaining all of Libya, they would not be able to attack the British position in the Nile basin easily. This too proved correct. Turner believed the decision to support Greece was right, that there had been a chance that Yugoslavia could offer effective resistance, that the Turks did need encouragement (as did Russia), and that to abandon Greece to its fate would have been a heavy moral blow to Britain around the world. Turner correctly predicted that if Greece were conquered by the Germans (which he thought likely) their next effort would be against Crete. He then recited the possible consequences and concluded that, because of the critical state of the British government, he did not think the Americans should bother London by stating their opinion of the seriousness of the situation. He believed that the British were adequately aware of its seriousness and that "warning them on this score could only have a bad influence on their morale, and could serve no useful purpose." He went on to urge a public statement by the President praising the courage and the self-sacrificing stand taken by the British. Perhaps in the long run this American view was the most significant of the whole affair.[146]

The arrival of General Auchinleck to the Middle East command in early July 1941 was paralleled by a steady flow of British supplies to the same area. From this time until October, British reinforcements to the Middle East outstripped the flow of German and Italian supplies into Africa. The reason for this was Malta, which lay across the Axis supply routes and from which British forces were able to impose intolerable losses on Axis shipping. This pattern of loss finally became so severe that the German military decided a major effort would have to be made to neutralize Malta, and both German air power and U-boats were transferred to the Mediterranean in significant numbers. The consequences of this decision were very serious for the British. By December 1941 a large number of U-boats were operating in the Mediterranean, and their effect was not hard to see. By November 13 the aircraft carrier *Ark Royal* had been sunk, and on November 25 the battleship *Barham*. The approaches to Malta were soon mined and the port there rendered almost useless to British naval vessels.

As the strategic pattern in the Mediterranean was shifting against Britain, Auchinleck launched his offensive in the desert at the end of November. Very messy fighting followed, in the course of which the initiative was maintained by the British; by January 5, 1942, Auchinleck held the bulge of Libya all the way down to El Agheila. The strange situation existed in the Mediterranean that the strategic initiative had passed into Axis hands as a result of the neutralization of Malta, while the tactical initiative seemed to lie with the British. In the long run, however, control of the Mediterranean would determine control of North Africa. Malta was the key to the Mediterranean, and after 1941 naval power alone clearly was not adequate to secure that island. The assistance of air power was also required, but to operate tactical air power to assist convoys into Malta required control of the bulge of Libya and the important air bases there. This in turn meant the army had to capture and hold this vital region, and the strength of the two armies in Africa depended on their ability to be supplied.

Thus all three elements of war were intricately connected in the struggle for the Mediterranean, a point very clear to the authorities in London.[147] The proof of this vital relationship was not long in coming. On January 21, 1942, Rommel went back on the offensive in the desert, and by February 7 he had reached El Gazala, only a few miles west of Tobruk. This meant the Germans now held the bulge of Libya and air support for Malta would be difficult if not impossible. The situation again was very critical, and the decision was made in London to attempt sometime in April to pass a convoy into Malta to sustain the base there. It was thought essential in London that Auchinleck risk a counteroffensive against Rommel in an attempt to support this effort at sea.

The view from Cairo was quite different; there it was seen not as a question of helping the island, but whether the effort to save Malta might not jeopardize the whole position in the Middle East if the British armor were destroyed in a premature offensive. This was the deadlock between Auchinleck and London which on March 8 Churchill attempted to resolve by inviting Auchinleck home to reexamine the whole issue. This the general declined to do, having had sufficient warnings of the great power of the Prime Minister's rhetoric in a face-to-face confrontation. Churchill, deeply upset at the general's refusal, considered replacing him, but the new CIGS (Brooke) argued that there was really only one alternative to Auchinleck and that was to take back Wavell. This Churchill said he could not do.

In early May the commanders in the Middle East pointed to the danger of the Japanese advance toward India and suggested that perhaps all land forces should stand on the defensive in the Middle East, abandoning any thought of a Libyan offensive in 1942. Churchill's response to this was even greater dismay. Accordingly, Auchlinleck was told that it was the unanimous opinion of the COS, the Defence Committee, and the War Cabinet that he should attack Rommel and fight a major battle if possible during May. The London authorities were prepared to take full responsibility but stopped short of ordering Auchinleck to fight, although it seems that the Prime Minister may have contemplated even this extreme step. This brought a reply from Cairo that the fall of Malta, while a serious blow, would not necessarily be fatal to the position in Egypt but that if the British armor were completely defeated in the western desert, nothing could save Egypt. Unfortunately this message concluded by suggesting perhaps it would be best to let Rommel attack the British and thus provide an opportunity for a counteroffensive. This report was too much for London. The Cabinet believed that Malta was of supreme importance and that a battle should be fought to save it, and Auchinleck was informed that he was to fight in the desert at the time of an attempt to pass a convoy into Malta in June. Auchinleck accepted with regret this determination from London but received an encouraging message from Churchill indicating he recognized the risks Auchinleck was running and concluding, "There are no safe battles." Churchill also urged Auchinleck to take personal command of the forces as he had done briefly in the preceding year. Auchinleck declined to do this, arguing that he had too many other responsibilities. This long series of exchanges between the Prime Minister and his theater commander tended to repeat to some degree the pattern which had occurred between Churchill and Wavell. Yet in this case it was largely a difference of strategic interpretation regarding the relative significance of Malta and the army in the desert to the total position in the Mediterranean and Middle East. Directly connected to this consideration were, of course, the relative strengths of the British desert army and Rommel. The risks involved simply were judged differently in London and in Cairo. Accordingly, serious doubts existed in London about the Middle East commander when the whole subject was removed from their control on the night of May 26, 1942, when Rommel attacked.[148]

The attack by Rommel should have come as no surprise to anyone. This German general had already demonstrated his aggressiveness and tactical competence. He now reached the pinnacle of his career. The British armor in the desert was badly handled, and on June 21 Rommel captured the position at Tobruk. Hardly pausing, he drove on east toward the Nile valley. Yet even at this bleakest point of the entire Middle Eastern campaign, forces were rallying which would ultimately bring about the downfall of the Axis position in Africa. The British had risked the convoys into Malta from both ends of the Mediterranean in June. At very high expense, Malta was resupplied—barely enough to keep the garrison going but, as time would prove, just enough.

Churchill was in Washington when the blow of the capture of Tobruk reached him. His American allies responded to this misfortune immediately and substantially and proposed to take the newest tanks away from their units which had just received them and rush these powerful reinforcements to Egypt. Churchill himself, although deeply chagrined by having to accept the news of a serious British defeat in the midst of negotiations with his ally, rallied strongly too. A message of great power was dispatched to the Middle East:

Everybody in uniform must fight exactly as they would if Kent or Sussex were invaded. Tank-hunting parties with sticky bombs and bombards, defence to the death of every fortified area or strong building, making every post a winning-post and every ditch a last ditch. This is the spirit you have got to incu[illegible] No general evacuation, no playing for safety. Egypt must be held at all costs.

Again Auchinleck took tactical control as Rommel's forces reached the point of exhaustion and the absolute limits of their supply lines. By early July it was clear that stability had arrived in the desert with Rommel still sixty miles short of the great naval base at Alexandria.[149]

A good bit of slogging fighting around the new desert positions followed, but the line achieved was to mark the high tide of German success in the desert. But since this fact could not be known for certain, there was little satisfaction in London. There was a strong feeling among military as well as political elements that a better job could have been expected from the British desert army; that it still had not been welded into a cohesive force; and that it did not yet have an effective doctrine regarding the tactical use and coordination of armor, artillery, and infantry. Churchill decided that after two years of unhappy conclusions in the desert there was only one thing to do. He would go personally to the scene. On August 2, 1942, the Prime Minister and the CIGS arrived at Cairo. The two figures from London met with Smuts, who had come up from South Africa, and several important decisions were made. The Middle East command was split and a new command facing the threat of a German intervention from the north into the general area of Iraq was established. Palestine and Syria were left part of the old command under the control of Cairo. Churchill wanted to move Auchinleck to the new command based in Iraq, but the general declined. General Sir Harold Alexander was summoned to Auchinleck's place in Cairo; and General Bernard Montgomery was called to command the army in the desert after General Gott (preferred for this assignment by the Prime Minister) was killed. General Wilson was given command of the army in Iraq and Iran.[150] These decisions constituted an important early chapter in the working of the Churchill-Brooke team which for all its strains was to prove so important in the total war effort. The reassignments brought two soldiers of substantial abilities to Cairo just when the strategic tide began to flow in the Allied direction.

FORGOTTEN THEATER: THE FAR EAST

WHEN CHURCHILL BECAME Prime Minister in May 1940, he inherited a nation whose preparations for war were still significantly short of the development reached by its German and Italian foes. The loss of all the equipment of the BEF at Dunkirk was an additional serious blow. The Battle of Britain and the Battle of the Atlantic both placed heavy strains on British resources. In spite of the risks involved, Churchill had extended every effort to support the British position in the Middle East, where for two years the battle swayed to and fro in the face of everything the Prime Minister could do to buttress the British position in

Cairo. With British resources at home and in the Middle East stretched to absolute limits, nothing could be spared to guard the rest of the British Empire, particularly in the Far East where there was another nation with growing ambitions. This became evident shortly after the fall of France when the Japanese government determined that the collapse of the European hegemony offered them a unique opportunity to secure for Japan a great position in the East. As early as June 19, 1940, the British ambassador in Japan was informed by that government that Britain should close the Burma Road along which supplies were reaching the Chinese who were engaged in a five-year-old struggle with Japan.

The British position was painfully clear. There was little Britain could do but pursue a policy of appeasement. The War Cabinet yielded to Japanese pressure to the extent that they agreed to close the road from July 18 to October 18, 1940. Events would determine what decision would be made at the end of that time. Events did not flow in Britain's favor. The Japanese government was now looking forward to nothing less than a complete recasting of its position. It wished to become the center of a new structure of power in the East that would terminate Japanese dependence on American and British foreign trade which constituted about 75 percent of Japanese import-export activity. In early September the Vichy government granted passage of Japanese troops through Indo-China. This had serious effects on the Chinese position to the south. Worse followed. On September 27 the conclusion of a Tripartite Pact between Germany, Italy, and Japan was announced for the creation of a new order in Europe and Asia. While the specific terms of the pact as released were directed more against the United States than any other power, the consequences for Britain were serious.[151]

Since Japan's new policies and the Tripartite Pact threatened British and American interests jointly, one may inquire what these two powers were doing jointly. In fact, they were doing rather little together in spite of the Prime Minister's efforts to achieve some harmony of policy. As early as May 15, 1940, in his first official message as Prime Minister to Roosevelt, Churchill had proposed that the Americans might want to center their naval forces in the Pacific on the British base at Singapore. Not surprisingly, the American military declined any such arrangement. The center for American naval power remained the great naval base at Pearl Harbor in the Hawaiian Islands. Meanwhile, this left Singapore as little more than a symbol of power rather than one in reality.

In late December 1940 Churchill admitted to R. G. Menzies, the Prime Minister of Australia, that because of the naval strains in the Atlantic and Mediterranean, there was simply nothing to spare for Singapore. Churchill told Menzies that for all practical purposes the British imperial position in the East depended on what the United States could do. Even with the American fleet based at Pearl Harbor, the British were not without hopes. Churchill particularly seemed to believe that the Japanese would never attempt a serious attack on either base as long as there was a powerful American fleet in the Pacific. No one at that point fully realized the audacity and striking power of the Japanese naval air arm.[152] At the Atlantic Charter meeting Churchill pressed the Americans for a strong stand against Japan, since up to this point the main line of Japanese expansion seemed to be south toward British positions rather than east across the Pacific toward the United States. It is not hard to surmise that at the time of the Atlantic Charter meeting Churchill feared a Japanese attack that would not directly involve the United States. He must have come away from the meeting badly discouraged, for he received little practical support from the Americans.[153]

On December 7, 1941, the Japanese government disposed of Churchill's fears. The Americans were indeed in the war. While the long-term consequences of this event could not be other than greatly beneficial to Britain, the immediate consequences of the attack on Pearl Harbor were devastating to the Allied position in the far Pacific. There was now no powerful American fleet to operate on the flank of any Japanese thrust south toward British positions. Indeed, the best the Allies could do was to patch together a combined theater of operations known as the American-British-Dutch-Australian (ABDA) Theater. General Wavell was invested with command of this hopeless cause. He was told to hold the "Malay Barrier" which was defined as the Malay Peninsula, Sumatra, Java, and North Australia. He was also to hold Burma as a western flank and to establish communication through the Dutch East Indies with the Philippines and the American garrison there as an eastern flank. The ABDA Theater was to be anchored on the American naval base in Manila Bay and the British naval base at Singapore. It was well that Wavell was so accustomed to adversity. To call the Allied position in the Malay Peninsula, the Dutch East Indies, and North Australia a barrier is surely a semantic rather than a military exercise. The two anchors rested on the finest of sand. Neither the American position at Manila nor the British position at Singapore had adequate strength to sustain them. The crippling of the American fleet at Pearl Harbor, the sinking of the *Repulse* and the *Prince of Wales,* and the general absence of adequate air power anywhere guaranteed that Japan would be able to divide the theater in two; Australia would be largely isolated from the rest of the British Empire and would have to depend on a long supply line running through the South Pacific from the United States. On the other flank of the dissolving theater would be the British imperial position in Burma, if it could be held; if not, the Indian frontier.[154]

Unfortunately, the fullness of these realities was not clear to the Prime Minister. He continued to view Singapore as a "fortress," something it most certainly was not. As early as mid-January Wavell was insisting that the position on Singapore Island was most vulnerable and indicated he doubted that the position could be held if the Malay Peninsula was lost, an all too likely eventuality. In late January the London authorities evaluated their decisions in light of this information. Churchill advised the COS on January 21 that the fall of Singapore would be a terrible shock to India, but if it could hold only a few weeks, it was hardly worth the investment in reinforcements. Churchill indicated it would be better to throw reinforcements into Burma. The heart of his argument was that it would be better to save Burma by abandoning Singapore than to lose both by dividing reinforcements. This was a wise message, but unfortunately the government did not act on it, allowing these additional reinforcements to flow into Singapore to join in the general doom there.

Heavy pressures had been exerted on the British government by Australia, which had indicated it would view as base betrayal failure of the British to make every effort at Singapore. The upshot was that having failed to save Singapore, the British proceeded to lose Burma. The naval base fell on February 15, 1942, after a brief defense which brought world esteem for British arms to an all-time nadir. The ABDA headquarters dissolved on February 25. Wavell returned to his former appointment as Commander in Chief in India, which now included responsibility for Burma. The Japanese acted swiftly and attacked the British forces in Burma. A skillful retreat was carried out by General Alexander and General Slim, and a position was finally anchored on the Indian frontier by late May. The Burma Road of course was hopelessly cut.

The Prime Minister reacted to these misfortunes with decision; in early March he appointed a special commander for the island of Ceylon to strengthen its position so that it could hold against further Japanese attacks. This was a wise decision which reaped its reward when Japanese carrier forces penetrated the Indian Ocean. Thus by mid-1942 a precarious barrier had been erected against the Japanese advance toward India, just as a similarly precarious barrier was being erected in the western desert against a German advance toward the Nile.[155] Although no one could know it at the time, the period of the offensive by the signatories to the Tripartite Pact had come to its high tide in late summer of 1942. The position of Germany, Italy, and Japan would henceforth steadily ebb.

Certainly the position in the Far East had operated for Britain largely on bluff. Two battleships and hard words were not enough to deter aggressive Japanese leadership. British resources were simply stretched farther than they could go, which meant that the British imperial position at the outbreak of World War II already rested on tradition more than on the realities of power. That empire would vanish rapidly at the conclusion of the war. The loss of Singapore was a lasting contribution to the fall of European prestige in the Far East and was decisive in ushering in the new age of nationalism in that part of the world. The unwisdom of the exposed position of the *Prince of Wales* and the *Repulse* again becomes clear in this light.

If the Prime Minister attempted to do too much with too little in the Far East, it must be said that he had little alternative. As he defended his position in the House of Commons, he stressed that his only choice with the resources at hand was to continue the struggle in the Middle East in the hope of success while bluffing in the Far East, or risk the loss of both positions. It may further be said that the Prime Minister was not well served either by Admiral Phillips, who commanded the ships, or by his local generals on the scene in the Malay Peninsula and at Singapore. The extent of British misfortune in the Far East rests in significant measure on sheer tactical incompetence on the part of the responsible military officers, and this should not be washed away amid denunciations of the Prime Minister's general policy there. Churchill concluded his defense to the House of Commons saying, "We had not the resources to meet all the perils and pressures that came upon us."[156]

CONCLUSIONS

The Period of Independent Military Operations

THE EARLIEST CAREER of Winston Churchill had been that of professional soldier. He had been educated at Sandhurst, had taken up a commission, and had served bravely in India. This career had been displaced early by his desire to enter politics, and perhaps even his early military service was intended to provide the name he thought necessary to lay the foundations of a political career.

Churchill never approached military matters with what could be described as a professional viewpoint. He was rather, in Ismay's words, "A child of nature. He venerated tradition, but ridiculed convention." Certainly a man who in earliest youth would defy the military conventions of Lord Kitchener and impose on that great man in his Sudan expedition was the man who in later years would have the capacity of straining the professional attitudes of the military. Yet as Ismay has also said, "No commander who engaged the enemy need ever fear that he would not be supported." Accordingly, Churchill always pressed offensive-mindedness upon his generals. His messages were often irritating, but Churchill too bore heavy burdens. He was responsible for the entire war effort and for seeing that the resources which he rallied so strenuously were employed to maximum benefit. His whole life had been the life of the politician, accustomed to seizing the opportunity for achieving what was within the realm of possibility but also pushing possibilities to the limit. He was long experienced in the cut and thrust of debate where differing viewpoints were hammered out, not always with a maximum of tact. The language of the politician could fall harshly upon military ears accustomed to a more disciplined approach to organization. The early experiences of the professional politician and the professional soldier are necessarily broadly different. That there were strains between Churchill and the military is not surprising. More remarkable is the measure of mutual regard, cooperation, and achievement which was their joint accomplishment.[157]

Churchill brought well-formed views to the conduct of World War II and his relations with his generals. As a young man he had seen aspects of the old British army at its worst, and the conduct of war in 1914–18 had done nothing on the whole to raise Churchill's esteem for the intelligence of the British general staff officer. In early 1941 he asked the Secretary of State for War if it were true that a seven-mile cross-country run was being carried out by all ranks of a division, including generals. Churchill observed that a colonel or a general ought not to exhaust himself in trying to compete with young boys in cross-country running and added,

> Who is the general of this division, and does he run the seven miles himself? If so, he may be more useful for football than war. Could Napoleon have run seven miles across country at Austerlitz? Perhaps it was the other fellow he made run. In my experience, based on many years observation, officers of high athletic qualifications are not usually successful in the higher ranks.[158]

Another characteristic of Churchill's which aggravated his professional advisers was his habit of ignoring the chain of command. Sir Alan Brooke repeatedly complained about Churchill's inclinations to operate a military establishment on an ad hoc basis.[159] Churchill could view the pronouncements of his generals with a measure of certainty which is surprising in a politician of his experience. Montgomery had explained to Churchill how he would defeat Rommel, down to the number of days the battle would take; when the appointed days were up, Churchill became very much disturbed, Brooke recorded, to find that the battle was not yet clearly won. Even allowing for Montgomery's infectious assuredness, Churchill's willingness to accept his word down to the number of days required to fight a battle seems a measure of excessive faith.[160]

Above all, Churchill approached his generals and the conduct of war with a firm conviction that willpower and thrusting audacity constituted the only sound line of approach. He wrote of the early war period that it was very rare for commanders on the spot to press for bold courses. Usually the pressure to run risks came from home.[161] Churchill was always ready to press his views on the professional soldiers. In October 1941 he had circulated a memorandum in which he had declared, "Guns should be fought to the muzzle." While there is a certain spirit of holding the lines at Waterloo in this pronouncement, he made some shrewd observations on what had been learned from the German operations in France. He pointed out, for example, the German habit of carrying highly mobile yet powerful artillery with their most advanced columns and interspersing this artillery with their armor. The British generals in the desert in 1941 and 1942 would have done well to have paid attention to this point. The tactic was used by Rommel with repeated success in the desert, and the British were notoriously slow to recognize and deal with it.[162]

The men who worked with Churchill have commented on the need to sift out his shrewd observations from his mass of memoranda. While Churchill pressed his professional servants hard, he was steadfast in his behavior toward them in adversity. He never went to the House of Commons to blame specific officers for military misfortunes; when things went badly in the field, Churchill's response was to send encouragement and all possible assistance to the struggling field commanders. Churchill told the Commons on one occasion that he liked to feel that the government would stand as a strong bulkhead between the commanders and public criticism. Churchill believed generals would not run risks unless they felt they had a strong government behind them.[163] He was usually true to this statement, but it did not solve all his generals' problems. If they could count on the government to defend them, they also had to count on the Prime Minister to prod them. If there was disagreement between the Prime Minister and the generals, it was their burden to convince him of the validity of their position. Brooke has graphically described how difficult this could be. When in France for a second time in 1940, he was attempting over a bad telephone connection to explain to the Prime Minister that there was no hope of attempting to hold a front in southern France. Brooke found himself stretched to the point of anger in attempting to make his case with the Prime Minister: "At last, when I was in an exhausted condition, he said: 'All right, I agree with you.' "[164] In the end, almost without exception, Churchill would yield to his professional advisers, but often only as they were pushed to the point of exhaustion. Yet Churchill's position is understandable. He had seen too many bad generals as a young man, and he had too full a knowledge of the element of accident and chance in human existence to be prepared to accept a casual explanation, particularly when the ultimate responsibility for the entire war effort rested on his shoulders. If he pressed his generals hard for full and clear explanations of their opinions, he did so not merely out of stubbornness (although that could be present) but also out of a deep sense of the responsibilities he bore. Indeed, at times Churchill would be anxious to postpone decisions until he had been able to examine enough military opinion to reach what he hoped was the best decision.[165]

Because Churchill's experience of war had been largely formed at an early date, he remained rather slow to grasp how fully modern warfare had come to depend upon technical development. He and Brooke argued about the number of spare parts and reserves necessary to maintain armored formations on the desert. On one occasion Menzies went so far as to criticize this attitude in Churchill by telling him, "We are not living in the age of Omdurman."[166] Churchill admitted in his war memoirs that he had a lack of familiarity with how sweeping the effects of technological change were on the conduct of warfare.[167]

The Prime Minister was particularly annoyed by the large number of troops on ration strength which seemed required to maintain a far smaller number of actual front-line combatants. He grumbled unhappily to the CIGS on one occasion, "The army is like a peacock, nearly all tail." This brought a sharp rejoinder from Brooke, "The peacock would be a very badly balanced bird without its tail." (Brooke was a dedicated ornithologist.)[168] Yet Churchill's complaint was legitimate. It was perfectly proper to examine the relative numbers on ration strength and combat strength. The difficulty was in getting any adequate measures of evaluation. Churchill was running a world war on narrow resources; he had no room for luxury.[169] The number of vehicles involved in modern warfare always appalled him. Told by General Montgomery that he would be operating about 200,000 vehicles for an army force which Churchill estimated at about 600,000 men, the general prior to Normandy received a message from the Prime Minister which concluded, "As each vehicle takes at least a man and a half to drive and look after, here are 300,000 men already absorbed. One hopes there will be enough infantry with rifles and bayonets to protect this great mass of vehicles from falling into the hands of the enemy."[170] Many similar memoranda could be cited.

The conduct of the British military authorities themselves in adjusting to the demands of modern warfare was not an unblemished record. One of the most serious problems in sustaining the Middle East turned out to be the utterly inadequate arrangements in the ports there. An investigation of port facilities by a London expert revealed that the military authorities responsible were operating with methods described as "totally inadequate." At one point the disorder in the port of Suez had reached the level where there were 117 ships waiting to use the port when only about one-half a shipload was going through the port in a day, so utterly chaotic had procedures become. The investigator described it as "the most appalling muddle I have ever seen in any port." Great as the burdens were on the military and naval commanders in the Middle East, an expert from London should hardly have been necessary to bring some order out of the chaos. The quality of the staff work in the Middle East was a source of fully legitimate complaint both from Churchill in London and from Tedder on the scene.[171]

Churchill's complaints about the proportions of the army tail often had good grounds. It was found, for example, that the army in the Middle East by mid-1943 had a stock of rifles sufficient for fourteen years of hard fighting and a stock of load-carrying vehicles for four years. Considering the vast effort required to transport the vehicles to the Middle East, the displeasure of the Prime Minister seems fully justified.[172] Finally, it may be said with regard to Churchill's grappling with the technology of modern warfare that at times he was far more imaginative than anyone else. A notable case is the development of the artificial harbors so important to the success of the Normandy landing, the use of which Churchill supported so completely.[173]

Standing at the center of the war effort, Churchill believed that viewing it in its fullness was important. His strategic vision was usually broad, although it contained the risk of becoming dispersed as Churchill lost himself in the details of a range of particular operations. Yet usually he maintained a good sense of priorities. This, strengthened by his courage, had been central in the decision to reinforce the Middle East substantially at a time when Britain's own defenses seemed hardly adequate to meet a German attack.[174]

Churchill's capacity to view the strategic scene as a whole was perhaps its weakest when he tended to move from the realm of the possible into the area of the impossible. Yet the very enthusiasm which led him to attempt more than could be accomplished was part of the same spirit that sustained the whole nation when survival seemed impossible. Churchill always believed that the conclusion of events determined whether they were indeed within the realm of possibility or not. If he undertook operations of doubtful success, like the expedition against Dakar or pressing upon Wavell a premature battle in the desert in the summer of 1941, it must be said on the other hand that at times his judgment proved right, as in the expedition against Iraq. At other times it was the judgment of the professional soldiers which proved overly optimistic, as in the case of Greece.

Churchill's emphasis on the offensive led Britain and later the Allies to face at an early date the need for developing techniques of warfare which would permit a successful offensive strategy. The great amphibious operations which culminated the Allied offensives of World War II owed much to Churchill's early probing enthusiasms.[175] It cannot be said of Churchill, however, that he pushed his offensive-mindedness to the point of folly. In October 1941 he informed his ambassador in Moscow that he was right in rejecting the Soviet proposal that twenty-five to thirty divisions be sent by England to fight on the Russian front. He observed that it took eight months to build up ten divisions in France, just across the English Channel, in the earliest stages of the war when shipping was plentiful and U-boats were rare. At this point in the war all shipping was fully engaged, and any savings could come only at the expense of vital convoys to the Middle East and in Russian supplies. He observed, "The margin by which we live and make munitions of war has only narrowly been maintained."[176] This was the central truth of the whole period when Britain stood alone and is the standard against which Churchill's accomplishment deserves to be measured.

The Prime Minister always made clear that ultimate responsibility was his and that of his colleagues who had to answer to the Parliament, which in turn represented the people.[177] This too was a reality of the war, although one the military sometimes found hard to accept. Kennedy noted one of his colleagues observing, "I don't see how we can win the war without Winston, but, on the other hand, I don't see how we can win it with him."[178] And Kennedy observed that there were times when the military longed for "a leader with more balance and less brilliance."[179] Balance and brilliance are both virtues, but perhaps the former is more easily found than the latter.

There are worse ways to run a war than the way Churchill did. In

Japan politicians became the servants of the military and entered a war which they lost. The German military became the servants of Adolf Hitler, willingly or otherwise, and fought a war they lost. Churchill's sense of priorities was often well worth his occasional lapses. Early in the battle for the Atlantic he recognized the critical importance of dominating the outlets from the Mersey and the Clyde, and to this effort he ordered all energies exerted. He had dispatched convoys both to the Middle East and to Russia against naval advice and had been sustained by events. The island of Madagascar had been secured largely because of his initiative.[180] The initiative of the Prime Minister reached its utter limits when he directed Auchinleck to fight a battle in the desert in mid-1942.[181] It is well to remember that a great American politician, Abraham Lincoln, faced similar hard decisions in his day. Both politicians have not lacked their military critics; the reputations of both seem likely to endure.

Birth of the Peripheral Strategy

By the time Churchill had been Prime Minister for a year, an outline of the principles upon which his grand strategy rested could be seen. First was the all-important principle that the United States must be brought into the war, through every stage short of actual belligerency but finally that too. Second, Churchill believed that France must be recovered and that after June 1941 Russia must be supported against the German attack. He believed further that the attack on Germany must be carried out from the air in the west and on the land and sea in the Middle East and the Mediterranean area by assaulting what Churchill believed to be the weak point in the Axis, that part which rested on Rome. To achieve this he was prepared to accept the risks of standing defenseless in the Far East. The security and centricity of the United Kingdom as critical to the entire war effort was another primary principle.

From the fall of France until Pearl Harbor, Churchill seemed to hold steadily to the view that the vast armies of World War I would never be seen again and that the modern army should be built on small, heavily armored, highly mobile forces such as Churchill was laboriously constructing in the western desert. Perhaps to some degree Churchill retained this attitude even when American entry into the war and the vast battles being waged on the Russian front suggested that circumstances had changed. The return to the Continent as Churchill contemplated it in 1940 and 1941 seemed to depend on creating the conditions in western Europe for widespread popular revolt against German occupation. This attractive vision seems to have underestimated the German capacity to maintain order in occupied countries and to have overestimated the organization of which underground forces were capable.[182] This necessarily dictated a certain approach to warfare, however. Reliance on a small, specialized army and the hope of massive European defection from German rule meant that direct military confrontation in overwhelming force was to be avoided. The war in the west should be so conducted as to create conditions which would leave the German Reich ripe for internal collapse after a brief, sudden, decisive intervention of the specialized army.

Churchill pursued this policy when Britain stood alone, always with a certain element of the politician's reserve and understanding that circumstances change and new opportunities must be seized and exploited. Accordingly, while a great effort was made to develop the bombing of Germany, while the struggle for the Atlantic raged, and while the specialized armored forces fought out a series of engagements in the western desert, Churchill at home pressed the development of what was for Britain a large army—thirty-five purely British divisions and twenty more mixed imperial divisions—and a large production of munitions to support this.[183] Churchill believed at the time (and cautioned in his memoirs) that "he is an unwise man who thinks there is any *certain* method of winning this war. . . ."[184] This encouraged a sense of strategic flexibility which Churchill described in the following terms: "The best method of acquiring flexibility is to have three or four plans for all the probable contingencies, all worked out with the utmost detail. Then it is much easier to switch from one to the other as and where the cat jumps."[185] Added to these attitudes was a further ingredient: "In war armies must fight."[186] All these factors linked together in a significant strategic chain: emphasis on the small, highly mobile, highly armored military force; emphasis on flexibility; determination that armies must fight. There remained only to select a target. There was no doubt in Churchill's mind, "Should Italy become hostile, our first battlefield must be the Mediterranean."[187] The logic of this is easy to see: the strategic importance of the Mediterranean and the correct belief that Italy was the weak link in the Axis. These two elements combined to make the Mediterranean the focus of Churchill's strategic inclinations.

The significance of the Mediterranean to Britain was understood also by the German naval staff, which pointed out to Hitler that control of this region would mean a supply of vital raw materials—particularly petroleum supplies—critical to Britain and Germany alike. Hitler was urged to seize Gibraltar at one end of the Mediterranean and to assault the British position in Egypt at the other.[188] In recognizing all this, Churchill was wiser than Hitler, but to all these reasons was added a certain excessive enthusiasm. Churchill long believed that the Balkans and Turkey constituted a significant military presence. The events of 1941 proved this to be unreal.[189] Even allowing for this particular point of excessive optimism, the summary of the British military position in the period of independent military operations is succinctly stated by A. J. P. Taylor: "The British were in the Mediterranean because they were there."[190] Thus necessity and convenience, the harsh realities of what was possible and the fond desires of what was wished, flowed together in the Mediterranean basin to make it the geographic center of British strategy.

But what was a geographic center when viewed in light of the

British Commonwealth and Empire seemed to stand on the periphery when viewed from the central position of Washington after December 7, 1941. World War II from Washington had two obvious axes of operations. One ran from the West Coast through Pearl Harbor directly across the central Pacific to Japan. This axis possessed a southern loop running through New Caledonia, New Zealand, and Australia and thence north through the Philippines to link up with the more direct axis centered on the Japanese home islands. Throughout World War II these two lines in the Pacific were to maintain their own friction, but it was for all practical purposes an internal American issue, for the United States directed and American commanders operated both lines. The situation was rather different when the planners in Washington looked out toward Europe. There the straight line ran from Washington through London to Berlin by way of northern France, but again there was a deviant southern loop which ran from London through the Mediterranean and possessed any number of spurs which could turn off toward Turkey or the Balkan Peninsula through Greece, or through Sicily into Italy, or through Sardinia and thence into southern France. When the Americans entered the war, the southern line was far better established than the more direct route. The friction between these two lines in the west was not a private national affair, for there the Grand Alliance was truly an alliance and operations were joint British-American efforts. The legacy of the period of independent military operations to the period of Alliance warfare was a strategic approach which commanded strong favor with the Prime Minister but which, as events would show, seemed much less attractive to his new American allies.[191] But the ultimate course of that warfare rested first on the establishment of the alliance.

5 / BUILDING THE GRAND ALLIANCE

THE WORLD VIEW from London in late summer of 1940 was gloomy indeed. Churchill could see seven, perhaps eight, nations who were significantly more powerful than the others. Of these, Great Britain now stood alone. Directly aligned against her were Germany and Italy, and drawing increasingly closer to them was Japan, soon to be joined in a tripartite pact and already making menacing gestures toward the British Empire in the Far East. The nation of questionable strength was China who, engaged in war with Japan, was inclined to be friendly toward Britain. The British Prime Minister correctly appraised the resources and energies available to the government of Nationalist China and concluded that no help could be expected from there other than the limited contribution of absorbing Japanese energies. This being so, there remained only three other great powers. Of these, France, Britain's ally, had just been crushed in defeat, was partly occupied by Germans, and was not free to pursue its own national destiny. There was, however, the French Empire, particularly possessions in Africa and the Middle East. The remaining powers were Russia and the United States. The first leaned toward Germany as a result of the Molotov-Ribbentrop pact; the other's sympathies were with Great Britain. The overriding fact was Britain's isolation in this world arrangement, and from the outset of his ministry Churchill was determined to remedy that situation.

FRANCE

CHURCHILL'S FIRST EFFORT was to reclaim something from the ruins of the French disaster, which had cast upon the shores of England in June 1940 a two-star general of forty-nine, Charles de Gaulle. The government in France had accepted an armistice which was deeply distressing to its former British ally, and there was considerable sentiment in London that General de Gaulle should be supported in his efforts to rally about him all Frenchmen who were prepared to carry on a struggle inside and outside France. On June 22 the British placed facilities at de Gaulle's disposal so that he could broadcast to the French people. The following night he explained that since the political institutions of France could not function freely, he intended to form a committee which would represent French interests until such time as a free government could again exist. The British government then broadcast its decision to take formal notice of the new provisional French National Committee of General de Gaulle, which Britain would recognize and deal with in all matters concerning the prosecution of the war as long as it represented all French elements resolved to fight the enemy.[1]

This was, however, a very slender beginning. There was little immediate sign of a great rally around a relatively obscure French general. The French colonies in particular showed no sign of abandoning the government at Vichy in France. Nevertheless, on June 28 the British government announced its official recognition of General de Gaulle as "the leader of all Free Frenchmen, wherever they may be, who rally to him in support of the Allied cause."[2] This formula gave de Gaulle something less than the status of head of an independent government, but it at least gave him an official position from which to work. An operating arrangement was worked out between de Gaulle's associates and the British government in August against a background of strain, which was to be the continuing thread of Churchill's relations with Charles de Gaulle throughout the duration of his war ministry.

At the beginning of July the British had carried out their attack on the French naval forces lying in the harbor of Oran, while a series of steps were taken elsewhere to control or neutralize the capabilities of the French fleet which might otherwise be employed against them. The concern of the British government and Admiralty was very real. The armistice, while it provided that the French fleet would not be used against Britain, was viewed by the British as a provision ultimately dependent upon German power and thus no real guarantee at all. The British government clearly understood that ultimate survival depended on its ability to keep sea routes open. The action against French forces was understandable but was taken very badly by de Gaulle, who described it as giving off the stale reek of an old naval rivalry, arising from the resentments that had accumulated from the beginning of the battle of France and terminated in the dismal armistice, and showing the violence of the Anglo-Saxon character.[3]

This stress was overcome on both sides by common necessity; the arrangement of August 7, 1940, between Churchill and de Gaulle established a Free French organization and laid down terms for the employment of French volunteers for military service. This memorandum and a covering letter from the Prime Minister became the first working basis between Britain and the Free French. In the letter Churchill expressed determination to secure full restoration of the independence and greatness of France but also made clear that he could not guarantee precise territorial frontiers; he concluded, "Of course, we shall do our best."[4]

The first joint effort fired by this arrangement was a naval operation against the important port of Dakar in late September 1940, an operation which for a variety of reasons ended in failure. It was also a well-publicized failure and did much to get the new relationship off to a bad start. On the plus side the Chad territory and the Cameroons passed under General de Gaulle's administration. All this produced a firm and loud complaint from Vichy. Already two separate French streams were becoming defined. The Free French under de Gaulle repudiated the armistice and regarded the Vichy government as having no true constitutional power based on the will of the people as freely determined. On the other hand, there was the undeniable presence of that regime and the fact that Vichy evidently commanded at least the ostensible allegiance of the great mass of Frenchmen inside France proper and throughout the greater part of the French Empire. The Vichy presence, however repugnant to the British (and it was particularly repellent to the taste of the Prime Minister), was an unpleasant reality which had to be faced.[5]

Churchill clearly preferred de Gaulle to Vichy, but he was by no means an easy associate. In 1941 difficulties erupted between the Free French and the British over the direction of affairs in Syria and Lebanon. The British wanted assurances that these countries ultimately would achieve some form of independence, as had been promised them. General de Gaulle, while agreeing to this ultimate conclusion, wanted a French occupation, which the British believed would long postpone any such day and would only increase the reluctance with which the Arab world supported the cause of Britain and Free France against that of Germany and Italy. In particular, the British asked for an announcement from the Free French setting a firm date for elections. By late 1941 General de Gaulle, resisting what he viewed as British demands for the stronger position, came close to breaking off relations with the British government on which he still depended. Added to this was the problem of Madagascar. In May 1941 this island had been seized by the British without the Free French being involved. Again de Gaulle was outraged, and in 1942 he added to his intransigence over a resolution of policy in Syria and Lebanon his demands that the administration of Madagascar be turned over to him. Not until October was an arrangement achieved whereby the French would agree to a declaration before the end of the year that elections would be held in Syria and Lebanon by the following spring. The British in turn agreed to a French commander to act as high commissioner for Madagascar. At this point a further blow was struck at the de Gaulle-Churchill relationship by the landings in French North Africa in November 1942 of a large, joint American-British assault force which was carried out without the participation of General de Gaulle's forces. Immediately a new strain emerged, the course of which belongs to the description of the period of Alliance warfare.[6]

While the Prime Minister had been backing General de Gaulle, a rather different attitude was held by the American republic. The United

States, neutral, was inclined to maintain friendly relations with the Vichy government and had little faith in what the Free French might be able to accomplish. Churchill was quite ready to permit this American window to exist at Vichy and believed it could be helpful to him, although he put little hope in what might come out of that government. In spite of this Churchill apparently did receive an unofficial representative of Vichy, and some imprecise exchanges took place. Churchill indicated he had little hope in such an arrangement, however; and although he was prepared to have contact with Vichy, he believed that ultimately either German force or the ability of the Allies to impose their will would be most significant to the government in France. The course of the war seemed to bear this out. When the British did well in the desert toward the end of 1940, the French government was more cooperative; when the tide turned against Britain in the western desert, French attitudes stiffened.[7]

The immediate prize on which the Prime Minister's eye was fastened was the large French territory in northwest Africa. This formed an important flank of the British imperial route through the Mediterranean. Accordingly, cooperation from the French authorities there and their eventual linking up with the Allies were of direct concern to Churchill. The Americans had already established contacts in French North Africa, which might prove useful to Churchill in producing a victory there. However, neither British nor American diplomatic efforts were successful.[8] The American government continued to take a more optimistic view of what could be accomplished than did Churchill, and both nations used a variety of diplomatic tools and strategic supplies to encourage their ends. Of the two approaches, that of Britain seemed to be more deeply rooted in the realities of the French situation. American attitudes tended to be colored by the view that the United States and France were nations born of revolution so there was a natural affinity between them which did not exist with imperial Britain. Accordingly, highly placed figures in the American government were inclined to view de Gaulle's autocratic tendencies and his peremptory nature as masking the sinister presence of a new Louis XIV or Napoleon, or worse. The government of Vichy was somehow viewed as retaining a certain aura of the revolutionary past of liberty, equality, and fraternity. This required quite an effort to apply to the sort of men who ran the government of unoccupied France.[9]

These differing British and American attitudes became critical in December 1941, at which point the Prime Minister obtained what might be described as a plethora of allies. Hardly had Churchill arrived in the United States following Pearl Harbor than he was confronted by an immediate crisis of Allied relations. Off the coast of Newfoundland lay the islands of St. Pierre and Miquelon. These islands, under Vichy control, contained a powerful wireless station which could be used to guide German submarines. The British government had suggested that the Free French be allowed to take control of the islands. The American government had refused this request for a variety of reasons, including a desire to give as little offense as possible to Vichy. They further felt that the most sacred of American principles of foreign policy, the Monroe Doctrine, was in some way involved. The British government accepted the American refusal. General de Gaulle ignored it and seized the islands. Churchill was thus presented with a weak ally who had acted in a manner Churchill viewed with instinctive sympathy and a new strong ally which was outraged by de Gaulle's actions. The American Secretary of State, Cordell Hull, was prepared to go so far as to threaten to turn out the Free French by force. A compromise solution was eventually reached, but Churchill made his attitude clear. On December 30, 1941, speaking at Ottawa, Churchill excoriated the Vichy regime and paid glowing tribute to the followers of de Gaulle. This pushed the rage of the American Secretary of State to yet new proportions; and though the anger of the State Department eventually subsided, the tension remained throughout the war.[10]

The Americans, however, had their own interest in dealing with de Gaulle, particularly the fact that they wanted bases in French Oceania which were critically important to American routes to the South Pacific. As these episodes were taking place, the council of de Gaulle named their movement Fighting France, as a symbol of the role they hoped to play as the Alliance grew in strength. That role too belongs to the period of Alliance warfare. At this point it may be said that Churchill had shown from the start his preference for a man prepared to fight and had demonstrated his willingness to deal with the temperamental and often tempestuous de Gaulle. In the unpleasant exchanges which followed the Dakar fiasco, de Gaulle nonetheless acknowledged that Churchill had not disowned him any more than he had disowned Churchill. But it was hardly a relationship between equals.[11]

Churchill continued to back de Gaulle in the face of substantial American hostility and at the same time urged him to take a less unbending attitude toward the Americans who were so important to the success of the Alliance. Yet what Churchill would do for de Gaulle always had its limits, particularly after December 1941 when the sheer realities of power within the Grand Alliance determined the priorities in Churchill's scale of values. For all their storms, it may be said that between the fall of France and the entry of the United States into the war, Churchill had found and supported a French leader around whom it had been possible to rally a significant amount of French force. A symbol of French freedom had been maintained, and Churchill's role in this de Gaulle generously acknowledged when he wrote of the Prime Minister at the time of his loss of the 1945 election:

> His nature, identified with magnificent enterprises, his countenance, etched by the fires and frosts of great events, had become inappropriate in this era of mediocrity. . . . In spite of everything, the essential and ineffaceable fact

remained that without him my efforts would have been futile from the start, and that by lending me a strong and willing hand when he did, Churchill had vitally aided the cause of France.[12]

RUSSIA

WHEN CHURCHILL viewed the world at the beginning of his ministry and his eye fell on Soviet Russia, it could hardly have settled on a less promising ally. The Socialist successor regime to the empire of the Romanovs had emerged from the troubled time of 1917–22 to pursue a policy which would have commanded the approval of the most autocratic and imperially minded of the Tsars. Faced with the hostility of the rest of the powers and in no small measure the intense personal hostility of Churchill in its early years, the Soviet government had learned in the interwar period to place ruthless self-interest above the demands of international ideology. Yet for all his previous hostility to Russia which had flared as acutely at times in 1939 and 1940 as it had in 1917 and 1918, Churchill was prepared always to find friends wherever they might be. He had indicated this attitude in October 1939 when he had described Russia: "It is a riddle wrapped in a mystery inside an enigma; but perhaps there is a key. That key is Russian national interest."[13] Surely Churchill described this key correctly; however, the occupants of the Kremlin viewed Russian self-interest as best served by maintaining cordial terms with Hitler. The stunning success of Hitler's attack on the west in the spring of 1940 probably came as a distinct blow to the Soviet rulers. Now rather than sitting back and viewing Western Europeans locked in a prolonged struggle which weakened them all, the Soviet leadership had to face the predominant power of Hitler. It could hardly have given them much comfort. Churchill also recognized this and was determined to establish a contact with the Russian government and to keep open a line of communication which might at some point become profitable. Accordingly, on June 12, 1940, the new British ambassador, Sir Stafford Cripps, arrived in Moscow. In British domestic politics Cripps had occupied a Socialist position which was receptive to direct cooperation with Communists, a point which had earned him expulsion from tht British Labour Party. Churchill had selected him hoping the Soviets would view him with greater trust than they commonly extended to Western diplomats. However, there is no reason to believe that they did; Sir Stafford Cripps's character and personality would hardly have encouraged them.

Further strain between Britain and Russia erupted at once when the Russians seized the opportunity of Hitler's commitment in the west to compel Lithuania, Latvia, and Estonia to allow the entry of Soviet troops. In late July 1940 new governments emerged in the three Baltic states with the support of a popular vote secured by the usual Russian methods. The British liked these actions no more than the Germans did, but they had to accept them even if not officially and formally.[14] Cripps's ambassadorship was off to a rocky start. Churchill had sent with Cripps a warning to Stalin pointing out the danger that Hitler might turn eventually to the east; Stalin acknowledged to Cripps the reasonableness of the British case but made it clear that the Soviet government had no intention of provoking trouble. The Soviets clearly believed that they could deal satisfactorily with Hitler and his allies. As a result, Cripps became more and more disillusioned about what might be accomplished by his mission; when new economic agreements were concluded between Russia and Germany in January 1941, Cripps viewed this as further evidence of the Kremlin's determination to maintain the relationship with Germany as long as possible.[15]

Yet by this very date a new tide was running through affairs. Already Hitler had made the decision to turn against Russia. On April 3, 1941, Churchill sent an urgent message through Cripps to Stalin, strongly suggesting that German troop movement pointed toward a sudden assault upon Russia. Cripps did not at once deliver this message, because he believed it would interfere with his own negotiations—an ambassadorial attitude which did not win him friends in London. The moment had passed in any case. The German assault on the Balkans and Greece was accomplished before Churchill could have constructed a Soviet intervention. Since that intervention was highly doubtful under any circumstances, it cannot be said that Cripps had frustrated a great opportunity.[16] The information Churchill conveyed could surely have come as no surprise to the Russian leadership. Their own espionage network, particularly an effective agent in Japan, would have provided them warning of Hitler's plans. If this were not sufficient, in March 1941 the American government had warned the Soviets of clear evidence they possessed of an impending German attack. Yet the Soviet government apparently chose not to respond to the clear and pressing warnings, so that when the blow fell on June 22, 1941, Russian armed forces were poorly placed and in the early fighting sustained massive casualties.[17] The Soviet government had pursued to the bitter end its own policy of appeasement and had paid the customary price.

Upon the German invasion of Russia the Prime Minister did not hesitate for a moment to declare his position: Any foe of Germany was a friend of Britain. Churchill broadcast on the night of the 22nd, announcing an offer of British assistance to Russia. Yet even at this time any working agreement between Britain and Russia undoubtedly would be based more on a common hostility to Germany than on any common unity of beliefs and commitments. From the beginning the Soviet leadership was hardly less concerned in maintaining a position separate from its Western allies than in sustaining its position against the attack of Hitler. Nor could any realistic Western statesmen bring much in the way of hopes to dealings with the Soviet Union. There was nothing to encourage the belief that dealing with the Russian leadership would be easy or that much cooperation would be forthcoming. But Churchill and President Franklin D. Roosevelt alike were prepared to do what could be done to establish a working relationship with Russia, and both countries extended early offers of supplies to meet the most pressing Russian needs.

From the very beginning the Soviet government indicated its desire for some sort of political arrangement. On July 8, 1941, Stalin told Cripps that effective cooperation between the Soviet Union and Britain required such terms as reciprocal promises not to engage in separate peace negotiations with Hitler. Churchill responded favorably to this as long as territorial issues were not brought into the discussion. A basic declaration of joint persistence in the war against Hitler to the end was thus signed in Moscow on July 12, 1941. But this was only the first of the political and military demands of the Soviet government on its allies. The Soviets, either deliberately or otherwise, seemed not to realize how bitter and desperate the struggle was in the Battle of the Atlantic, how narrow were Britain's shipping margins, and how precarious was Britain's position in the Middle East. This led to Soviet demands on its ally which strained to the utmost British willingness and ability to cooperate.[18] Yet the British position toward Russia was haunted by the fear of a separate peace, a theme which recurred in Churchill's messages to Roosevelt. A second theme that was to run through the entire Alliance swiftly emerged —the demand of the Russians for a second front somewhere in the Balkans or France, capable of drawing away from the Russian front at least thirty to forty German divisions. This was utterly beyond Britain's capabilities at that stage in the war.[19]

Churchill not only had to meet these unremitting demands (usually presented in blunt language which suggested that the British would not find the fighting too bad once they began) but he also had to stave off constant Soviet pressures for a political negotiation which would bind the West to a territorial settlement repugnant to Western sentiment.[20] Yet, so heavy were the Russian pressures on the British government, and so desperate the position on the Russian front, and hence so great the possibility (it seemed to Britain) of either a Soviet collapse or armistice that in late 1941 Anthony Eden was sent to Moscow in an effort to work out a stronger arrangement which would be acceptable to both sides. Churchill informed Stalin that Eden would be able to discuss every question relating to the war but his primary aim would be to talk over immediate goals and perhaps discuss a future peace settlement. The arrival of Eden in Moscow followed the American entry into the war, which strengthened the Allies but complicated the negotiations since the British government was understandably anxious not to reach any agreement with Stalin that might be unacceptable to the new ally from whom Churchill hoped for so much. In any case, Stalin's demands were specific and large. He asked for British recognition of Soviet boundaries as they had stood roughly before the German attack in June 1941. This meant of course the absorbed Baltic states, the part of Finland secured from that war, and the territory absorbed from Rumania. The Soviet boundary with Poland was to be recognized on the basis of the so-called Curzon line, which was roughly parallel to that part of Poland Russia had occupied in 1939. Stalin indicated that recognition of these boundaries would do as a starter but the price might go up later.

This presented the British government with a substantial problem, since its American ally had already indicated concern that Russia and Britain would be carving up the Continent between them. The State Department stressed to the Foreign Office its belief that it was unwise for any of the three governments to enter specific commitments regarding postwar settlements. Churchill was firm in his response to the Soviet proposal and maintained that frontier questions could be resolved only at the peace conference when the war was won.[21] Thus at the time the Grand Alliance took full shape at the end of 1941, Britain already faced in its relations with its Russian ally those questions which would continue throughout the war. Yet the Eden mission and the results which sprang from it indicated that whatever the Russian demands were, the Soviet government was prepared to settle for less. Perhaps this was a point the Western governments would have done better to recall later in the war.

It is sometimes suggested that Churchill neglected to play "the Russian card." This is hardly justifiable criticism. In fact, Churchill never held that card in his hand until Hitler thrust it there on June 22, 1941. Certainly he had been willing if only he could have grasped it sooner, but even his warnings to the Kremlin in the spring of 1941 had been met with a response of Siberian frigidity. Once he was able to play the Russian card, Churchill did so with all his customary enthusiasm, determination, and perseverance. And all this was required. Brooke records Churchill, at one point of great frustration with Russia, observing, "Trying to maintain good relations with a Communist is like wooing a crocodile. You do not know whether to tickle it under the chin or to beat it over the head. When it opens its mouth, you cannot tell whether it is trying to smile or preparing to eat you up!"[22] In this attitude perhaps Churchill was more realistic than others around him. Lord Cherwell and Lord Beaverbrook urged a superhuman production effort in Russia's behalf, rather ignoring the problems of transportation and the essentially short-term nature of such an effort. Churchill was sensitive to the fact that his most effective diplomatic weapon—his imposing skill with the English langugage—was of little use in his dealings with the Russians.[23] There always remained grave geographic problems to assisting Russia, problems which could not easily be overcome either by the enthusiasm of Russian supporters in London or the somber demands of the Soviet government in Moscow. Relations with Moscow always remained close to a status which Churchill, when he had to bear tidings to Moscow that there would be no second front in 1942, described: "It was like carrying a large lump of ice to the North Pole."[24]

THE UNITED STATES

IN THE SUMMER OF 1940 Churchill assessed the pattern of world power and inevitably looked across the Atlantic to where the hermit republic of the United States lay between the broad barriers of two great oceans. Churchill addressed himself to two questions: How would Britain survive? How would Britain win? The most certain answer to both, Churchill believed, could be provided by the decisive intervention of the United States into the war. Over a year earlier Churchill had warned the House of Commons that, having so far failed to create a grand alliance against aggression, there was the most pressing need to do so.[25] That need was more pressing than ever as Churchill assumed the burdens of Prime Minister. As the last British troops returned to ports from the beaches of Dunkirk on June 4, 1940, Churchill delivered his great address to the British people stating, "We shall fight . . . ; we shall never surrender . . . until, in God's good time, the New World, with all its power and might, steps forth to the rescue and liberation of the Old."[26] The central direction of this affirmation of hope cannot be mistaken, and it constituted an appeal to the New World to hasten God's good time and step forward to the rescue. From the outset Churchill appears to have believed that it would be Hitler who would provide the ultimate impetus for pushing the United States into war. De Gaulle recalled Churchill shaking his fist toward the sky late that summer, calling for the German bombers to arrive. When asked if he were in such a hurry to see his towns smashed to bits, Churchill replied that he counted on the bombing of Oxford, Coventry, and Canterbury to create a wave of indignation which would propel the United States into war.[27]

But the Prime Minister wisely did not depend on such a wave to ripple suddenly across the Atlantic. He determined with patience and tenacity to use every method available to him to get ultimate American intervention on Britain's side. Central in importance was the correspondence he carried on with President Roosevelt. This had been initiated at the President's invitation when Churchill returned to the Admiralty. It was carried on by Churchill over the signature of Naval Person, which was changed to Former Naval Person when he became Prime Minister. Churchill had swiftly accepted Roosevelt's invitation, with the approval of Prime Minister Chamberlain. There followed a correspondence which would terminate only at the President's death, by which time nearly 1,000 telegrams had flowed from Churchill to Roosevelt and nearly 800 (mostly replies) had come back across the Atlantic. This semiofficial channel was particularly useful to Churchill because it permitted him to say things personally, directly, and bluntly which would have been awkward to phrase through the traditional channels of diplomacy. But Churchill was always careful to coordinate this correspondence with the policy of the British government; it was a potent political instrument indeed. Fortunately it was one which Churchill could wield with great effec-

London. February, 1940. Churchill as First Lord of the Admiralty joins the King and Queen, at right, and Prime Minister Chamberlain, at left, in meeting relatives of men killed in the naval action with the *Graf Spee*. *(Radio Times Hulton Picture Library)*

London. 1941. The War Cabinet. Seated, left to right: Sir John Anderson, Churchill, Clement Attlee, Anthony Eden. Standing: Arthur Greenwood, Ernest Bevin, Lord Beaverbrook, Sir Kingsley Wood. (The Times, *London)*

LONDON, 1941. The Defence Committee (Operations). Seated, left to right: Beaverbrook, Attlee, Churchill, Eden, A. V. Alexander. Standing: Sir Charles Portal, Sir Dudley Pound, Sir Archibald Sinclair, David Margesson, Sir John Dill, Sir Hastings Ismay, Colonel Leslie Hollis. (The Times, *London*)

CASABLANCA, 1943. The Casablanca handshake between General Henri Giraud, at left, and General Charles de Gaulle. Seated are President Franklin D. Roosevelt, at left, and Churchill. *(Imperial War Museum, London)*

ALGIERS, 1943. Churchill plans with Allied military leaders. Around Churchill, from left, are: Eden, Sir Alan Brooke, Sir Arthur Tedder, Sir Andrew Cunningham, Sir Harold Alexander, General George C. Marshall, General Dwight D. Eisenhower, Sir Bernard Montgomery. *(Imperial War Museum, London)*

ALGIERS, 1943. Churchill in his dragon dressing gown poses with Mediterranean commanders and their staffs. Sir John Cunningham is standing between Tedder and Alexander. Sir Henry Maitland Wilson is at the right, front, and General Walter Bedell Smith is behind him at the extreme right. *(Imperial War Museum, London)*

QUEBEC, 1944. The British Chiefs of Staff. From the left: Sir John Dill, Sir Andrew Cunningham, Sir Alan Brooke (chairman), Sir Charles Portal, Sir Hastings Ismay. *(Imperial War Museum, London)*

ATHENS, DECEMBER, 1944. Eden (extreme left), Churchill, Archbishop Damaskinos, Sir Harold Alexander, and Harold Macmillan await ELAS representatives. Coats are worn in the unheated building, and hurricane lamps light the table. *(Imperial War Museum, London)*

YALTA, 1945. Churchill, Roosevelt, and Joseph Stalin with their foreign secretaries: Eden, Edward Stettinius, and Vyacheslav Molotov. Averell Harriman is at the far right. *(Imperial War Museum, London)*

THE WAR CABINET ROOMS, LONDON. Known as the "Map Room," this was one of a warren of 150 rooms in the subbasements of Whitehall from which Churchill conducted the British war effort. The smallest room is a tiny soundproof one from which Churchill spoke on the transatlantic line to the White House. *(Imperial War Museum, London)*

LONDON, 1945. Churchill flashes V sign to crowd on V-E Day. Bevin is at the far right. *(Imperial War Museum, London)*

tiveness, for there was much to be done if the United States were to come to Britain's side.[28]

The world view from Washington in the summer of 1940 was somewhat different from that prevailing in London. In Washington the immediate fear was that the British government would seek Munich-type terms from a victorious Hitler, leaving totalitarianism triumphant on the European continent, denuding Britain of any real strength, and leaving the United States as the last significant repository of human liberties anywhere in the world. The sudden collapse of the Allied front in the west had been as heavy a blow to Washington as to London, for many had hoped that the pattern of the western front in World War I would be repeated in World War II. Thus there was stunned shock at the extent of the disaster which had befallen the cause of liberty, and politicians in Washington who looked anxiously across the Atlantic had also to keep a constant eye turned in the other direction for fear Japanese ambition would be greatly stimulated by totalitarian successes in the west. Certainly Roosevelt's ambassadors in Paris and London were not encouraging. In his zeal for the French the Paris ambassador, William Bullitt, heaped criticisms upon British action at the time of crisis. The ambassador in London, Joseph Kennedy, thought there was little hope that Britain alone could stave off the German attack which would now surely fall on her shores. Kennedy did not want the United States to come to the rescue of a hopeless cause only to be left to face Hitler's wrath alone.[29] Churchill's correspondence with the President would have to offset these unhappy counsels which flowed back to Washington. Fortunately, Roosevelt was more impressed by Churchill's messages and the conduct of Churchill's government than he was by the reports of his ambassadors, and his mind inclined in the Prime Minister's direction.

Roosevelt's service chiefs warned him that military supplies were so limited that sending much to Britain would involve the risk of leaving America vulnerable to enemy attack if Britain did not survive. The question of whether Britain would survive was fought out in Washington through late summer and autumn of 1940. Ambassador Kennedy poured reports back from London tinged with gloom and defeatism, but American military observers in Britain were less pessimistic. As one day succeeded another with Churchill maintaining his firm and determined leadership, Washington's pessimism steadily gave way to cautious hope. The American service chiefs, Admiral Stark (a good friend of the British) and General Marshall, were more inclined to run risks to assist Britain as the likelihood of her survival increased. They had already formulated a basic military strategy if war should come to the United States, and it had received the approval of the President. This assumed that the main theater of war would be Europe and the defeat of Germany would take first priority. Dealing with Japan would come second, allowing for sufficient security to communications to the Far East, including Australia and New Zealand. This basic American strategy was thus sympathetic in the long run to Britain's struggle, although it involved no commitment to war at any point.[30]

While maintaining determined resolution at home, Churchill did not hesitate to tell the President bluntly how serious matters were; in a message of May 15 he warned Roosevelt that United States influence might count for little if it were not exerted soon. Churchill raised the specter that he might be swept from office and a government might take his place which would be determined to reach an agreement with Hitler involving the transfer of the British fleet to German control. Ten days later Roosevelt discussed with the British ambassador to Washington, Lord Lothian, the importance to the United States that the Royal Navy never fall under enemy control.

The Americans, now much concerned about their Atlantic naval frontier, were seriously considering the desirability of securing strategic bases on the many islands under British control—particularly Trinidad, Bermuda, and Newfoundland.[31] The British in turn were anxious to secure from the United States a number of World War I destroyers not then on active duty in the American fleet. Toward the end of May Lord Lothian suggested to the British government the desirability of an offer of British bases to the United States. He renewed the point in late June. Both the Foreign Office and the Chiefs of Staff (COS) were sympathetic to the British ambassador's proposal. Churchill had meantime been angling for destroyers, and the American government was sympathetic to this request if a way could be found to carry out the transfer without stirring the American isolationists in Congress to the point of seriously impeding all Roosevelt's efforts to assist Britain. The American government felt it needed an assurance if destroyers were sent to Britain that the British fleet would never fall into German hands. After a long series of exchanges it was decided that the Prime Minister would reaffirm to the President his pledge of June 4 and this would represent adequate assurance to the United States.

On August 14 Roosevelt told Churchill he thought it would be possible to provide fifty destroyers. The United States in turn would hope to receive ninety-nine–year leases to construct bases on British-held territory. The British authorities were reluctant to turn this into a clear *quid pro quo*. They felt the facilities offered were worth much more than fifty old destroyers and believed British public opinion would be unhappy with such an arrangement. The American government feared that American public opinion would be unhappy with anything less than such an arrangement. The result was that the Prime Minister made a free gift of the facilities to the United States without strings attached—an act both skillful and generous, for it achieved a technical separation of the bases from the destroyers. The final terms of agreement actually required long negotiations, but the Prime Minister had given the British the initiative. In August the American government was able to release the destroyers as no longer necessary to defense. The ships, however, passed slowly into British service since they required significant renovation before they were fit for active duty. Only nine of the fifty were in service at the end of December.[32]

Exactly what value Churchill placed on this arrangement is uncertain. He reputedly told de Gaulle late in the war that the fifty destroyers were of no interest to the British and that the object of the bargain was to link the United States to the march of events; thus the British made great concessions with regard to bases. But if this was the Prime Minister's view in late 1944, his attitude had changed from January 1941 when he indicated to Roosevelt that the Royal Navy could use thirty more American destroyers. This would suggest that the ships were not without immediate value. The Americans replied that no more destroyers could be spared but ten American Coast Guard cutters would be transferred to British control. In some respects these were more useful convoy and antisubmarine vessels than the older destroyers were. Certainly the whole arrangement brought the United States further into a commitment to preserve Britain against German attack.[33]

By late autumn of 1940 it was apparent that no German attack would come across the Channel for at least six months. This pause in the pace of events allowed both the British and the Americans to take stock and look toward the future. On both sides of the Atlantic it was recognized that Britain's chances of survival were much better than they had appeared in midsummer. Continued support of Britain seemed all the more justified to the American government. But what should be the extent and the limits of that support? This had to be determined by the United States both in light of its own needs and capabilities and in light of its judgment of those of Britain. Furthermore, the American government had yet to decide to what extent national security was dependent not only on Britain's survival but on the ultimate defeat of the Axis. A constant domestic backdrop to government examination of these issues was the impending election due in November 1940, a concern to which President Roosevelt was acutely sensitive. A misjudgment of public sentiment by the administration could produce a violent isolationist reaction at the polls.

In late summer of 1940 the government received from the War Department a comprehensive statement of the world strategic situation and its implications for the United States. This document, known as the Strong memorandum, bluntly warned that U.S. strategic planning must consider not only Britain's continued survival but also the possibility of her defeat, a prospect that brought no cheer to Washington. The memorandum further asserted that the military forces of the United States were inadequate to the scale of danger they now faced. It recommended immediate increase in war production by methods such as longer working hours and additional work shifts—in short, an end to business as usual and clear recognition of the existence of a state of national emergency. The Strong memorandum was served on President Roosevelt six weeks before the November elections and was so unpalatable that he was reluctant even to read the document much less act upon its recommendations. He continued to believe there was sufficient slack in the American economy in the aftermath of the Great Depression so that increased war production could be achieved without resort to emergency measures. Certainly domestic political considerations reinforced such an attitude on his part.[34]

But the critical nature of Britain's problems could not wait upon the date of American elections. In October 1940 Sir Walter Layton arrived in Washington bearing a full statement of Britain's economic condition—a most discouraging thing to view—and a request for much greater U.S. aid, including no less than the equipment for ten divisions. Not surprisingly, the American government was shaken by the grim combination of the dire warnings in the Strong memorandum, the frightening economic evidence Layton presented, and the vast scale of British requests for material aid. On October 29 Secretary of the Treasury Henry Morgenthau, a firm advocate of all-out support to Britain, convened in his office several of the most powerful men in Washington to meet Layton and Arthur Purvis of the British Purchasing Commission. Present were Secretary of War Henry Stimson and Secretary of the Navy Frank Knox; their service advisers, General Marshall and Admiral Stark; and several important American economic and production chiefs. Before the British arrived Knox bluntly stated, "I can't escape saying that the English are not going to win this war without our help, I mean our military help." This probably was the judgment of every man present, however impolitic it was to make such a statement aloud. Morgenthau was also rather blunt, declaring that he "would never be part or parcel of lending them money again, and if it got to the place that they couldn't pay, I would recommend that we give it to them."[35]

But the most powerful man in Washington gave no clear sign of embracing the sentiments of his chief advisers. His preelection speeches were limited to economic aid to Britain on a cash-and-carry basis. Accordingly, Roosevelt's concerned advisers told Churchill that he must make a direct appeal to the President, tell him all, and hope for the best. This produced a powerful document from Churchill. On December 7, 1940, one year to the day before Pearl Harbor, Roosevelt received the Prime Minister's message. Churchill forcefully described the war situation, sparing no words. He warned of disastrous consequences if shipping losses in the Atlantic continued at their present rate. He warned that Britain soon would not be able to pay for American goods. He asked for immediate U.S. shipping aid direct to the British Isles and for American supplies even after Britain could no longer pay. Churchill concluded:

> If, as I believe, you are convinced, Mr. President, that the defeat of the Nazi and Fascist tyranny is a matter of high consequence to the people of the United States and to the Western Hemisphere, you will regard this letter not as an

appeal for aid, but as a statement of the minimum action necessary to achieve our common purpose.[36]

Churchill's message to Roosevelt was the catalytic agent in a pattern which had been emerging for some time. The President responded on December 17 in a press conference suggesting the idea of leasing material to Britain. On December 29, in one of his fireside chats to the American people, Roosevelt further proposed to remove the dollar sign from Anglo-Saxon production agreements. On this occasion he used his famous parable of lending your neighbor your garden hose when his house is on fire and worrying about payment after the fire has been put out. The American government took the initiative over the isolationists in Congress when the Lend-Lease Bill went before the lawmakers on January 10, 1941. With the full forces of the administration mobilized behind it, the bill became law on March 11, 1941, after bitter controversy. The passage of the bill had been aided by a skillful British combination of silence at the right time and the providing of evidence to Americans who needed to be convinced that lend-lease was the only road left.

As the bill was being steered through Congress, Roosevelt's close personal adviser Harry Hopkins was in London. Hopkins returned convinced of the strength of Churchill's leadership and of the importance of the United States supporting him to the hilt. Churchill had won an influential friend who would perform great service to the Allied cause.[37] To speed the Lend-Lease Bill along its way, Churchill had pitched in with his famous speech of February 9, 1941: "Give us the tools, and we will finish the job," upon which text Hopkins had been consulted. This had helped to relieve isolationist fears that lend-lease was only a step toward direct American intervention. The passage of the bill enabled the President to sell or transfer title or exchange or lease or lend or otherwise dispose of any defense article to any nation whose defense the President deemed vital to that of the United States. The first appropriation bill under lend-lease called for $7 billion worth of goods. While a great boost had been given to Britain's chances of survival, it would require time for the actual production and transfer of materials to occur.[38]

After the passage of the Lend-Lease Bill there followed a lull in the pace of Anglo-American relations which had a depressing effect on the Prime Minister. The summer of 1941 was as dismal as the summer of 1940: British forces were hurled out of Greece, smashed on Crete, and defeated in the western desert; and the German battleship *Bismarck* sank the British warship *Hood* within minutes. The later sinking of the *Bismarck* itself helped to ease the pain of this sequence of events. In early May Churchill was at the point of calling for immediate U.S. intervention in the war before it was too late. Many highly placed Americans agreed that if Britain were to be saved, this was required.

The most important member of the administration, the President, was the least anxious to commit America to direct military intervention.

In the summer of 1941 Roosevelt would go no further than considering escort for American shipping as far as Iceland and for shadowing German forces in the Atlantic and reporting their position. It was doubtful if this would be enough, and in July an important group led by Harry Hopkins arrived in London to take another look at the whole situation.[39] On July 24, 1941, the Prime Minister hosted Hopkins, Harriman, and three high-ranking American officers at Number 10 Downing Street. The COS were also present. Hopkins led off by stating the American position, which was essentially a belief that the British were overextended in the Middle East and, by attempting to maintain their position based on Egypt, were risking losing everything. The American officers believed that the priorities should be: first, security of the United Kingdom and the Atlantic sea-lanes; second, the defense of Singapore and the trade routes to Australia and New Zealand; third, all other trade routes; and last, the defense of the Middle East. Churchill had a relatively easy time convincing the Americans that the security of Great Britain was adequate and that allocations to the Middle East did not jeopardize security in the Atlantic. But it was also implicit in the British position that the campaign in the Middle East rank above security in the Far East. The British pointed out that it was too late to cut losses in the Middle East and to do so could lead to a German smash through Spain, past Gibraltar, and into northwest Africa, which could create a serious situation if the United States should later have to undertake military operations. The British case was persuasive, but as Hopkins told Churchill, "We in the United States just simply do not understand your problems in the Middle East . . . and the interrelationship of your problems in Egypt and India." Because of this, Hopkins decided to urge the President that when he met with Churchill the following month he bring his army and air chiefs, General Marshall and General Arnold. Hopkins was sensitive to a point which was to place some strain on the Anglo-American alliance throughout the war. The British on the whole were far more conversant with the complexities of worldwide military and political problems.[40] Furthermore, in late 1941 the British were much more ready to do business and to attack matters on a practical basis than were the Americans, who had not yet really resolved their degree of commitment. There was no question on that subject as far as the British were concerned; that had been decided in September 1939. These divergencies were to become apparent at the famous Atlantic Charter meeting between the two heads of government.

Churchill held high hopes for this direct meeting with the President in August 1941. The Dominion chiefs of government had all received messages from Churchill indicating that the Prime Minister hoped for important developments, although Hopkins had candidly warned him not to expect too much. Probably Churchill hoped most for a strong American stand in the Pacific to warn off aggressive Japanese tendencies which were becoming more and more evident. Churchill also brought with him a draft of what became the Atlantic Charter. Roosevelt wanted a statement of high principles, and the Prime Minister desired on his part to demonstrate to the Americans that he was not an Old World reactionary imperialist but shared the same spirit of American democracy from which his mother had sprung.

The announcement of the charter constituted most of Churchill's accomplishment. Whatever ambitions he held in the Far East were disappointed, and the military talks tended to be cursory. The Americans had arrived at Newfoundland on August 7, some forty-eight hours before the Prime Minister was due, and apparently only then did the delegation sit down and start thinking about why they were there. The President had evidently provided his military advisers with no political guidelines. Yet some benefit derived simply from the meeting of American and British military opposites, including the beginning of a friendship between General Marshall and Sir John Dill which was to ripen with important consequences for the favorable conduct of the Alliance later in the war. The political discussions centered on a warning to Japan which was to be issued jointly by the two nations. But the language of the declaration remained unsettled, and the American version finally released after the Atlantic Charter meeting was less forceful than Churchill had hoped for. Churchill did get, however, an American commitment to escort British as well as American merchant ships as far as Iceland, and this system was put into operation on August 20.

The Anglo-American military meeting reaffirmed the basic principle that Europe took precedence over the Far East in the event of American entry into the war. In these discussions the British repeated their theme that the war would not involve mass armies but would depend upon smaller, highly mobile, heavily armored forces which would intervene decisively on the Continent only when the German position there was weakened and ripe for collapse. From the beginning the American military doubted the realism of this view, but it was not an issue which could then be put to the test. In military as in political discussions, the main barrier that lay across Anglo-American agreement was the fact that one member of the meeting was a belligerent and the other was not. Until this basic issue was resolved, any ultimate agreement on policy would continue to escape settlement.[41]

Churchill's broadcast to the British nation on August 24 following the Atlantic Charter meeting gave some measure of his disappointment with its conclusion. He had to admit that the meeting was chiefly symbolic.[42] Churchill was left with words more than forces.[43] Thus the overall result was perhaps more discouragement than hope in England, and Churchill's preparedness to assure the Americans that a Japanese assault on them would be followed by an immediate British declaration of war had produced no similar promise from the President.[44]

Churchill's determination to persevere, however, did not flag in the face of his setback in the Atlantic Charter meeting. On September 4

Canadian Prime Minister Mackenzie King spoke at the Mansion House in London and called for the intervention of the United States into the war. Churchill followed him with a strong but still indirect appeal for American intervention.[45] On September 30, speaking in the House of Commons, Churchill prodded the American government yet more directly, observing that nothing is more dangerous in wartime than to live in the atmosphere of a Gallup Poll, "always feeling one's pulse and taking one's temperature. . . ." If Churchill was trying to prod Roosevelt to a decision, he was unsuccessful.[46] By this time there had been clashes between American escort vessels and German U-boats in the Atlantic. But American public opinion and that of the President alike remained unresolved. Obviously, American military power was seriously inadequate for the tasks it might be asked to face very soon; as anxiety mounted in the United States, so it seems also did perplexity and vacillation.[47] This lasted until the dawn of December 7, 1941, when once again Britain's enemies delivered allies into Churchill's arms. As Hitler had given him Russia, the Japanese now gave him the United States.

Churchill has recorded for posterity his feelings on that day.

> No American will think it wrong of me if I proclaim that to have the United States at our side was to me the greatest joy. . . . So we had won after all! Yes, after Dunkirk; after the fall of France . . . after seventeen months of lonely fighting and nineteen months of my responsibility in dire stress, we had won the war. England would live. . . .[48]

Churchill went on to write, "Being saturated and satiated with emotion and sensation, I went to bed and slept the sleep of the saved and thankful."[49] It must also have been a most restoring sleep to the Prime Minister's energies, for he was shortly off to Washington, almost to the astonishment of his new American allies, to work out strategic plans. With U.S. entry into the war precipitated by the Japanese attack, there was every reason for the Prime Minister to make certain that the prior agreement that Germany was the most serious antagonist and thus the first target of an Allied effort should be retained. All the frustrations of the Atlantic Charter meeting must now be brushed away and firm lines of policy swiftly laid down. Churchill took with him to the United States Sir John Dill, whom he had just replaced as Chief of the Imperial General Staff with Sir Alan Brooke. Given Dill's success with the Americans at the Atlantic Charter meeting, the decision to take him to the United States (made at Brooke's urging) was one of the most important steps toward securing an effective Alliance military policy. But Churchill was also there. He, better than any other British politician, could touch the American spirit and could claim a kinship rising from his mother's American origin.[50]

In retrospect, Churchill's hopes of what he could expect from the United States seem to have outstripped the march of American public opinion. In a June 1941 speech in Rochester, N.Y., the birthplace of his mother, Churchill professed to be able to see the American people girding with determination to join the conflict.[51] Perhaps this stands better as a statement of Churchill's wishes than of the actual condition of sentiment at that time. Later that month when Hitler attacked Russia, Churchill returned to this theme in his address accepting Russia as an ally. He observed that Hitler hoped for a quick victory in Russia before winter arrived and hoped that he could overwhelm Great Britain before the fleet and air power of the United States could intervene. Churchill went on to describe Hitler's program of destroying his enemies one by one in preparation for the final act without which all else would be futile—conquest of the Western Hemisphere.[52] All the techniques of Churchill's forensic armory were thus deployed upon the course of American public opinion. In one speech fear was rejected, in the next possible fear was raised. But Churchill could exert only peripheral influence on the situation. The centrally placed politician was not the British Prime Minister but the American President.

Churchill once described the Soviet government as an enigma, but he might better have employed the term with respect to Franklin Roosevelt; compared to the political mind of the President, the policies of the Kremlin leaders seemed crude and self-evident. What policies, what thoughts, what plans moved through the mind of Franklin Roosevelt are hard to capture. Harry Hopkins, who knew him so well, could guess and predict but was seldom prepared to say that he knew for certain what Roosevelt would do. The Cabinet and the responsible military officers had no more certainty than Hopkins.[53] However the President read the American national interest in the summer of 1941, however he read his own political interest, and however those interests were related, a Japanese attack on Pearl Harbor was required to push America into alliance with Britain. American entry was delayed much longer than Churchill had at one time expected and at all times hoped, and part of that delay was probably due to Churchill's own success in rallying the British people to resist Hitler. Yet throughout the long months that Britain stood alone, the very hope of the ultimate arrival of Americans—as they had ultimately arrived in the First World War—served as another force to sustain the spirit of the British people during their finest hour. When material resources are slight, men must be fed on visions and aspirations, and Churchill's persistent desire to achieve a grand alliance played its role in keeping alive his own and the British national spirit in dark days.[54] When the Grand Alliance was finally achieved, much useful preparation had already been accomplished to make it successful in the prosecution of the war; and much of the credit belongs to Churchill. The Grand Alliance was indeed what Churchill called it—"what I have dreamed of, aimed at and worked for, and now it has come to pass."[55] Not the least of Churchill's contributions to the course of man's destiny in the middle years of the 20th century was that he painstakingly educated the American republic in the problems of world power and prepared the way for passing on to the United States the chief burden of responsibility for protecting the rights of men and the freedoms of peoples as they had come to be understood in the Western tradition.[56]

ALLIANCE STRATEGY

THE PROLONGED PERIOD of coalition building which began on the ruins of the first British alliance with France and went forward to its culmination in December 1941 reveals certain guiding principles in Churchill's conduct. First of these was the clear recognition that an enemy of the Axis was a friend of Britain. Grim military necessity dictated alliance policy, and Churchill was prepared to embrace Russia even with enthusiasm if the situation demanded.[57] The United States, hardly so desperately pressed in the summer of 1941 as Britain, was also prepared to accept this arrangement and to rush supplies to the Soviet Union, that is, to give aid by all means short of war.[58] Beside this principle stands its corollary that Churchill was furnished his allies by his enemies.

In retrospect, it seems that Hitler never stood closer to success than in midsummer of 1941. British shipping in the Atlantic staggered on the edge of disaster. The British position in the Middle East tottered on the verge of collapse. America was still unprepared and unwilling to come into the war. Japan posed an ominous threat in the east. Yet Hitler turned against Russia—leaving the battle for the Atlantic, the struggle for the Mediterranean and Middle East, the route to petroleum supplies of the Persian Gulf, and the fortress of Britain all unconquered.[59] Few men served the British Prime Minister as well as the German dictator unless it would be the men who had come to dominate the government of Japan, for they completed the folly of the German government. At the end of 1941 they dragged Japan into a program of military conflict against a power which vastly outstripped her in industrial capacity and natural resources as well as in population and techniques of organization. Compared to the great blunders of the Axis powers in World War II, the mistakes of the Allies seem trivial.

The second principle in Churchill's program of strategy was that the United States was the center and the key to operating the Alliance successfully. Churchill demonstrated this when he departed for Washington almost immediately following the attack on Pearl Harbor.[60] He adhered steadfastly to this principle when the Russians placed heavy demands on Eden, who was in Moscow at the time of Churchill's trip to Washington. The Prime Minister resisted Russian demands for explicit recognition of the 1941 frontiers, not so much because he was unwilling to yield to these demands but because the Americans would not do so. Even hints from Molotov in mid-1942 that the Soviet government would entertain a separate peace with Hitler did not bring Churchill to act against the wishes of his American ally.[61]

If Churchill would not yield the central position of the Anglo-American alliance to the Russians, it is not surprising that he would not do so to the French. No small part of his difficulties with Charles de Gaulle throughout the war arose from the fact that Churchill was forever being thrust into the breach between de Gaulle and Roosevelt. In a tempestuous scene between Churchill and de Gaulle on the eve of D day, the Prime Minister repeated, in the presence of Eden and Bevin (who did not much like it), that if he had to choose he would always choose the United States.[62] This principle, however, was a lonely one, for the American President did not fully reciprocate the special importance Churchill placed upon the Anglo-American alliance. What was to Churchill a first principle of conduct was to Franklin Roosevelt only one political and strategic alternative, albeit an important one, among many. This situation too would have its consequences in the period of Alliance warfare.[63]

A third principle which would govern the conduct of Alliance warfare was one dictated not by Churchill or any other politician but by the intractable circumstances of geography. Churchill grasped the essence of this when he had to reply to a letter from Cripps in Moscow asking for an allotment of resources to Russia which outstripped British capabilities. Churchill told Cripps, "When you speak . . . of 'a super-human effort,' you mean I presume, an effort rising superior to space, time and geography. Unfortunately, such attributes are denied us."[64] Geography dictated much of the pattern of the Alliance: Russia would fight essentially a private land war against Germany, while the Western Allies—Britain and the United States—conducted a world war.

General Ismay summed up Churchill's contribution to the construction of the Alliance when he said that while history may acclaim the year 1940 as Churchill's finest hour, he regarded the fourteen months between the German attack on Russia and the Battle of Alamein as the period of his greatest achievement. In the first case he steeled Britain to defy defeat; in the other he laid the foundation of Allied victory.[65]

As the year 1942 opened, it was possible to see the beginning of the third stage in Churchill's wartime career. In the first stage—from the crisis of summer 1940 until Pearl Harbor—he had sustained the spirit of the British people. The events of June and December of 1941 left no serious doubt that Britain now was part of an Alliance which possessed the manpower and resources to achieve ultimate victory. They also marked the conclusion of the second and almost simultaneous aspect of Churchill's wartime career—his unceasing labors to build a coalition that would be equal to the challenge of overcoming Britain's adversaries. There now opened the third stage—the development of a strategy for Britain and the United States jointly which was matched to the Alliance's emerging capabilities. The question of a Russian strategy did not emerge. Geography dictated that Russia would fight a long single-front war against the masses of German armed might. Neither Churchill nor Stalin nor Hitler had any option in that matter after June of 1941. But options were the very essence of the strategic situation which confronted Britain and the United States. The skill with which a strategy was evolved that made most effective use of the developing potential of the Western part of the Grand Alliance would in turn have great consequence on how long the war would last and what the shape of the postwar world would be. Churchill assumed this vital task when he left England to spend Christmas across the Atlantic in 1941.

6 / ARCADIA TO CASABLANCA, *December 1941 to January 1943*

THE GRAND ALLIANCE completed in December 1941 possessed the potential in human and material resources to gain decisive victory over the European Axis and their Japanese ally. But the Alliance had come into being in such a way and the interests and attitudes of its three main members were such that much remained to be done to weld the members into an effective coalition. Because Roosevelt's infirmity and certain aspects of the American constitutional system of government limited his mobility, and because the critical nature of the Russian front and the form of Soviet government made it unwise for Stalin to travel, it fell upon Churchill to carry the burden of unifying the Alliance war effort, and he took it up with determination.[1] His role was often a demanding one, both in its physical strains and in the tensions involved in harmonizing divergent national interests. Churchill once commented that there was "only one thing worse than fighting with allies, and that is fighting without them."[2]

The tasks of strategic planning were difficult, and Sir John Kennedy speculated on what future historians would make of the records of the Alliance conferences. "When they read the minutes of the discussions they will not get a true idea of what took place, because they do not reproduce the arguments."[3] Fortunately, Kennedy and many others, including Churchill, have reduced that problem with their postwar memoirs. The more serious problem has been to get behind the arguments to those issues of national interest which governed (or which statesmen believed should govern) the war policies. Within the Alliance there was substantial room for conflict. Herbert Feis has noted that while the fighting went on, the field of action was left open to suspicion and maneuver within the coalition, for it provided a temptation for each member to pursue his own political aims through military strategy.[4] If the Alliance should degenerate into a competition of national interests, Churchill's two partners were both more powerful than he. It is a measure of Churchill's ability that he constructed an effective policy for prosecuting the war and upheld Great Britain as an equal partner in that policy until nearly the end of the war.

STRATEGIC VIEWS

As Churchill sailed for the United States to the first great conference, Arcadia, he drafted on December 16, 1941, what constituted a major state paper presenting his views on the war. It argued that Hitler's failure and losses in Russia were the prime factors at that time. He correctly grasped the significance of the Russian front in devouring Hitler's resources and observed that neither Great Britain nor the United States would be able to intervene directly in this giant land struggle except to make sure to send all possible material aid. Churchill was already at work creating in his mind a unity of Allied effort. He observed that Russian containment of Hitler provided a large measure of safety against a German thrust into the area of Iran, Iraq, and Syria. He also correctly assumed that the sweeping changes in the balance of power in 1941 would encourage Spain to resist German demands for a passage through Spanish territory to attack Gibraltar or invade North Africa. Thus the shifting balance of power assured Churchill that both ends of his long-strained Mediterranean Theater were safely anchored. This being so, Churchill believed the initiative was his to exercise toward what he viewed as the most tempting of available prizes—France, particularly the French Empire. First by political maneuver but ultimately if necessary by force, the territories of Morocco, Algeria, and Tunisia should be secured. Then there would again be free passage through the Mediterranean with all the advantages of tightened lines of communication this would bring. This was the operational program Churchill carried with him to Washington.[5]

Churchill's views were shared by his Chief of the Imperial General Staff (CIGS). Brooke wrote, "It was plain to me that we must clear North Africa to open the Mediterranean, and until we had done so we should never have enough shipping to stage major operations."[6] The approach of the Prime Minister and the CIGS was consistent with the views they had developed earlier in the war that the British must make maximum use of their naval superiority to isolate the German position. Their Mediterranean plans involved skillful use of the mobility of sea power to improve the overall strategic position of the Alliance against the central continental position of Hitler. Yet both views also contained hints of a preparedness to abandon the earlier British position that World War II would not be a war of mass armies, for Brooke had mentioned in his observations on securing North Africa that this would reopen the Mediterranean to permit offensive operations against Italy. Churchill also had stated that the Northwest African Theater might also develop into a battle of attrition, suggesting that the Axis would have to reinforce their position in Tunisia and this would ultimately prove to be an expensive operation.[7] A certain note of ambivalence was creeping into British strategic thinking. It would grow in time into an inconsistency which would render the British strategic argument weak compared to the more simply designed and consistently phrased strategic position of the United States. But none of this was clear in December 1941. To the British themselves, and certainly to the Americans whom they were about to meet, the interest of the Prime Minister and the CIGS in the Mediterranean seemed to be the very epitome of traditional British strategic thinking.

The British carried into the twentieth century the traditions of a maritime and trading community which depended on its commerce, flung over a worldwide empire and reaching into every major society in the world, as the foundation of national well-being. Such a structure of economic enterprise was always most vulnerable. There was virtually no part of the world where British interests were not affected in some way by local decisions and power shifts. Accordingly, the British were accustomed to pursuing their interests with caution, examining their policy from every angle, exercising patience, wrestling with events, and if necessary accepting compromise. They understood from long experience that tenacity in the face of adversity and flexibility in the face of opposition could produce an ultimate achievement that seemed unlikely at first sight.

Churchill, with his long political experience and extensive historical knowledge, was the logical inheritor of this British emphasis on perseverance and flexibility. His capacity to cling tenaciously to a position and his skillful political instincts for examining all possible doors to find the one which would yield most swiftly to his pressure linked his character to the political and historical tradition which he served. Consequently, the British commitment to the Mediterranean and Churchill's eighteen-month investment in sustaining the British position there exercised a powerful attraction on the Prime Minister when he set down a strategic plan for the Western Alliance.[8] Churchill could deploy the further convincing argument that opening the Mediterranean would provide a great saving in shipping to the Alliance, and shipping was one of the most vulnerable and critical elements in the successful prosecution of the war. Shortening the trade route around the Cape meant regaining flexibility, but there then followed a certain lack of specificity about how that flexibility would be employed. One alternative was the ability to make a greater effort to hold the Indian Ocean against the Japanese—an argument that would bear a certain weight of persuasiveness upon the Americans, who were acutely concerned with the limits of Japanese expansion. The flaw in Churchill's strategic program rested, however, on the fact that geography presented to those sitting in Washington quite a different perspective from that of the men working in London. To Washington the critical line toward winning the war ran not through the Indian Ocean but across the Atlantic. Those in Washington were apt to be far less attracted to a strategy which wound its way through the Mediterranean and thence through a series of hooks (Who knew quite where?) into Europe than one involving a direct line across the Atlantic from Washington through London to Berlin.[9] Churchill would have to be most persuasive if he was to secure the adoption of his strategic concept.

To Churchill nothing was certain in war. The experience of World War I had convinced him that defeat, misfortune, terrible losses, and frightful dangers were the essence of prolonged military conflict between great powers and that all the struggles to find a way to win ultimately had meant rather little in the outcome. The formulations of the Easterners and Westerners may have exhausted each other in strategic planning, but it was the terrible exhaustion of the battlefield that dictated the end of the war—not any particular plan.[10] Thus Churchill placed a rather low value on an overall master strategic plan, since he rated such plans low in potential for success. He greatly preferred to be prepared for all eventualities and believed more in seizing opportunities than in creating them. Churchill had always kept a certain degree of reservation when he listened to the visions of the Royal Air Force (RAF) about bombing Germany into submission. He was prepared to allow his view that the war would be concluded by the use of small, highly mobile, armored units to be modified by changing circumstances. Among these was the fact that he now had a Western ally with vast manpower and great industrial potential.[11] Added to his proclivity toward a high measure of flexibility and a readiness to seize opportunities was the fact that Churchill was always prepared to run risks.[12] Thus flexibility and audacity were valued by the Prime Minister over rigid adherence to careful planning. Both the strengths and the weaknesses of this view were demonstrated classically by the Gallipoli operation in World War I.

This is not to say that Churchill discarded the importance of strategic planning.

> War is a constant struggle and must be waged from day to day. It is only with some difficulty and within limits that provision can be made for the future. Experience shows that forecasts are usually falsified and preparations always in arrear. Nevertheless, there must be a design and theme for bringing war to a victorious end in a reasonable period. All the more is this necessary when under modern conditions no large-scale offensive operation can be launched without the preparation of elaborate technical apparatus.[13]

This succinctly states the relationship Churchill saw between opportunism and planning in war.

To this attitude must be added the great breadth of Churchill's mind when he surveyed a strategic problem. To Churchill the western front stretched from the North Cape of Norway down the entire Atlantic coast, through the straits of Gibraltar, and across the Mediterranean until it was anchored where the Western Allies met Russia on the northern border of Iran. This provided a long German front open at virtually every point to sea attack and conferred upon the Western Allies the great potential of flexibility to maneuver which command of the seas grants.[14] To Churchill's mind the German defenses could be pinned to this long front at every point by the constant threat of Allied flexibility in operation, while the Allies retained the advantage of being able to decide at what point they would deploy decisive and overwhelming force. He saw perhaps less clearly that these strategies led to diminishing returns. As Churchill himself once observed, in war armies must fight. Sooner or later the Allies had to attack the frontier Hitler held at some point. With Churchill's emphasis on flexibility as a virtue in itself, there was some tendency to underrate the significance of choosing your point.

The inherent risk in a strategy of maximum flexibility is dispersion of effort. Churchill and Brooke tended to see it as a dispersal of German effort, since German lines of communication into southern Europe were far inferior to lines running east and west. They were less prepared to consider that just as the Germans would have to fight down those weak communication lines, the Allies might ultimately have to fight up those same lines.[15] As long as Germany deployed superior military force, there was something to be said for this approach. But once the Allies possessed superiority in numbers and training of troops, in size and power of armor and artillery, and in supporting air power, much more could be said for a strategic program which would deploy superior force where it could be exercised most decisively. This emphasis was apt to be much clearer to the Americans, who began their strategic thinking on the assumption of a superiority of power, than it was to the British, who had been fighting a war for two years without being able to enjoy that luxury.

The Americans quite understood that a conflict of views was apt to develop at Arcadia. Harry Hopkins had warned his friend Churchill against bringing a fully developed plan with him, cautioning him that the Americans might think he came to harness them to his own programs. Churchill chose to ignore this advice. Perhaps he really had no alternative, but certainly the American Joint Chiefs of Staff (JCS) were reluctant to discuss strategy except in the most general terms.[16] There were many reasons for this attitude. The JCS had substantial reservations about British military competence. The record of land operations in World War II up to that point—Norway, Greece, and repeated setbacks in Libya—had certainly not impressed the Americans with British strategic ability. The Americans, however, tended to underestimate the magnitude of British military problems. But there the record stood; it was certain to exercise its influence on American attitudes.[17] Further, the Americans were products of an industrial society built on mechanical pragmatism to an extent hardly approached by other industrialized countries. This encouraged an attitude which approached a problem by stating the most direct solution possible and then simply mobilizing whatever was required to achieve it. That resources might not be adequate was a question which barely entered American thinking.[18] What this meant in practice is perhaps best represented by the fact that the JCS were prepared even before American entry into the war to expand the United

States Army to 200 large divisions. This was mobilization of resources on a mass scale, particularly when one considers that at the end of World War II the United States had only organized and equipped something over 90 divisions.[19] This was the classic Napoleonic doctrine of the decisive deployment of mass.

Like its British alternative this strategic approach had both strengths and weaknesses. In World War I this strategic design was not supported adequately by tactics or weapons. Mass was not decisive on a concentrated front, when faced by the technology of the machine gun and barbed wire, until the accumulated attrition of four years had taken its toll. A breach in a front could usually be repaired before a decisive breakthrough was achieved. But during and after World War I a great deal of thought went into these problems. The rapid pace of technology enabled the Germans to demonstrate early in World War II that they could break through a front beyond any danger of its being closed against them. The Polish and French campaigns were classic examples of this, although it failed on the Russian front because the depth of territory available for Russian retreat was so vast and their available resources so extensive that even the German assets of speed and technology were inadequate to force a decision before the winter of 1941. But even on this vast front it had been a close thing, and what the Germans could do in terms of technology and tactics of armor and air power, the Americans were confident they could do better.

As events would demonstrate, the Americans were quite right. American reliance on overwhelming strength and a straightforward strategic approach to problems was coupled with great tactical boldness which also was part of the American historical tradition. Tedder, who observed both British and American commanders of high ability, firmly believed that the American commanders were always prepared to show greater tactical initiative. Of course they always had greater resources upon which to run the risk. This tactical approach was exercised with great imagination by American commanders, land and sea alike, in the Pacific theaters of operations and will receive slight note here since the British were so little concerned in that primarily American combat area.[20]

This American approach of concentrating decisive power at a specific point carries its own corollary—that dispersion of effort is to be avoided at all costs.[21] This created a conflict in thinking between the two Western Allies. What to the Americans was dispersion of force appeared to the British the skillful use of flexibility to seize tactical and possibly strategic opportunities. The Americans felt these opportunities were not worth having, for they wasted both time and effort. American historical experience had raised efficiency in the use of time and effort to the level of virtues. This was fueled by an impatient desire for decisive results. Accordingly, a straight-line approach exercised as powerful an appeal to the American strategic mind as did the use of flexibility to the British.[22] It also made the Middle East one of the lowest of American priorities.[23]

A senior American military adviser described British views on operations there as more persuasive than rational and motivated more by political purposes than by sound strategic ones. To his mind, North Africa did not offer great advantage as a point from which to attack Europe; Britain itself was better.[24] Further, the Americans viewed the risks in the Mediterranean Theater as being greater than did Churchill. In retrospect, Churchill appears to have been right about the risks of German incursions at either end of the theater, and the Americans apparently were overconcerned.

The Americans always tended to be suspicious of politics, which to them meant imperialism—a term usually left undefined and meaning particularly a certain fear of Churchill himself. Churchill's World War I record and the impetuosity of his character were as well known to the American military as to Britain's. To the Americans Churchill tended to be an imperial politician who with consummate skill would lead them the Lord knew where.[25] As General Marshall freely admitted after the war, Americans could carry this view to excess.[26] This was not a decisive factor in the strategic planning between the two countries but was certainly one which did not make it any easier. In fact, in many ways Churchill was closer to the point of view of the Americans than they ever recognized. In spite of all his love of seizing opportunities and keeping open as many alternatives as possible, Churchill himself did not operate in circumstances of chaos. Just as Churchill the administrator gave the impression of surface disorder, while beneath that surface the operation of principles rolled forward steadily, so Churchill the strategic thinker kept ultimate goals in mind. He summed up the case when he said,

> American military thought had coined the expression "Over-all Strategic Objective." When our officers first heard this, they laughed; but later on its wisdom became apparent and accepted. Evidently this should be the rule, and other great business be set in subordinate relationship to it. Failure to adhere to this simple principle produces confusion and futility of action, and nearly always makes things much worse later on.[27]

Churchill's own position was perhaps more vulnerable to American persuasion than the American position was to Churchill's. Yet, the outcome of Arcadia seemed a denial of this fact. To understand why this was so, it is necessary to understand the short-term factors operating at the time of Arcadia in Churchill's favor and against the American strategic view. It is important to recognize that they were indeed short-term factors and that early British gains in strategic discussions were vulnerable to the very shifting circumstances which British thought treasured so highly. There was a certain irony in this.

Churchill held two aces when he arrived in Washington, and one was the most powerful card in the deck—the attitude of the American President. The attitudes of Franklin Roosevelt, a politician of subtle and complex character, are always difficult to assess with any degree of certainty. Roosevelt's relations with his military advisers were less formal and more casual than those in Britain, but he always possessed the power of the constitutional position which made him Commander in Chief of the Armed Forces of the United States. This carried great weight with Roosevelt's advisers. Added to this was the fact that Roosevelt had his own strategic proclivities. His military associations had been primarily naval, and he was sensitive to what could be accomplished by sea power. Before American entry into the war, the President had glanced occasionally with concern toward North Africa, which he had long viewed as a German stepping-stone to penetration into the Western Hemisphere, a point on which he was always most sensitive. In the summer of 1941 the potentiality of a North African operation had been explored, largely it seems at the President's request. This was done by the reluctant American military, who reported that such an operation would require 150,000 men and tie up an immense amount of shipping. Such an operation was seen as peripheral to a direct line across the Atlantic to London. But the thought evidently lingered on with the President, and when Churchill arrived in Washington, he found a natural sympathy for his proposals in the attitude of Roosevelt.[28]

The second ace Churchill held was the relative strength of the military forces of Britain and the United States. For if British power was well extended, at least it was developed to a point the United States could not yet equal, particularly in terms of trained divisions. Much of the initial American effort had to go into securing lines of communication, and the long line that ran through the Pacific to Australia and New Zealand proved most expensive of manpower. Accordingly, any operations undertaken early in the period of Alliance warfare would clearly involve a substantial and probably predominant British military presence.[29] This too proved to be a trump card in Churchill's hand at Arcadia, for it became apparent that the President had a certain time deadline for involving American forces in offensive operations. These two factors, plus the fact that Churchill had a plan for 1942 which fit the combined British-American capabilities for that year, gave him from the beginning a strong hand, and he believed in playing every card for its full value and—if played well enough—perhaps even picking up an overtrick. Well might the American military harbor a certain measure of concern upon learning that the British Prime Minister was descending on them. It was the most serious British invasion of the American continent since Washington was burned in the War of 1812.

ARCADIA

THE PRIME MINISTER carried with him to Washington a relatively small but important staff: Lord Beaverbrook, then Minister of Supply; Admiral Pound; Air Chief Marshal Portal; and Sir John Dill. The CIGS, Brooke, remained in London to mind the shop. This revealed that

Churchill's priorities for Arcadia were supply and strategy; both were certain to bring problems.

Now that the United States was in the war, domestic demands would make huge claims on the military supplies flowing out of American industry. Churchill would have to safeguard Britain's share. The Americans were more worried about the strategic proposals Churchill would be bringing with him.[30] While on the Atlantic crossing, Churchill had determined he would make no effort to block a natural American response to the Japanese attack so long as it remained secondary to the effort in Europe. The Prime Minister was more concerned that the United States might build a huge army and, until it had reached full development, postpone direct intervention in European Theater affairs.[31] This was why he wanted a program of action for 1942 to fit the joint capabilities of the two countries as they stood at that time. This meant something less than a direct reentry on the European continent. How much less remained to be determined.

In Washington, Churchill wove his spell along those lines, stressing the attractiveness of available opportunities while referring generally to a mass invasion of the Continent as a goal for 1943. He was also prepared to see American divisions arrive in Britain. This would gain American sympathy since that was the direct road to Berlin, but it also possessed the advantage of freeing British troops who could be transferred elsewhere. Either way, Churchill won. He had greater success at Arcadia than he might have anticipated, for the resistance of the American military to his views was slight in proportion to their concern. Significant in this was the intervention of President Roosevelt, who indicated that he was anxious that American land forces should enter into fighting as early as possible; thus North Africa was attractive to him. Churchill could point to North Africa as a feasible operation considering the strength of the two powers in the West by late 1942. The American military could not offer any significant alternative. An invasion of the Continent simply remained beyond the combined resources in the first year of Alliance warfare.[32]

Churchill was not the only man at Arcadia prepared to pursue proposals of his own. So was the American Army Chief of Staff, General George C. Marshall. Before he considered entering into programs of theater operations, he wanted a decision on the nature of Allied command in the various combat theaters. Marshall believed there should be a single supreme Allied commander in each theater. He felt that human frailties were too great to allow a pattern of successful coordination among equals and that if the Allies accepted the principle of unified command at the outset, it would solve nine-tenths of their troubles. This conviction had grown out of Marshall's World War I experience and perhaps also out of his rueful experience of attempting to cooperate with the United States Navy, a task which could be at least as trying to the United States Army as it was to the British.

Roosevelt accepted his Chief of Staff's proposal, but Churchill was much less sure. The British were accustomed to running their theater operations through a team of commanders representing the three services. Beaverbrook and Hopkins arranged for Marshall and Churchill to meet together privately in Churchill's bedroom in the White House on the morning of December 28. It was evidently a classic meeting. The Prime Minister had followed his usual pattern of staying up late, sleeping late, and then remaining in bed until lunchtime while he dictated letters and did other business. When Marshall arrived, he found the Prime Minister propped up in bed and ready for action. Marshall's memory is that the conversation became colorful; in the middle of the whole encounter the Prime Minister departed to take a bath, emerging later with a towel wrapped around him to declare to the American general that he would have to take the worst with the best. Marshall departed under the impression that he had failed to persuade the Prime Minister, but in fact the general had won his fight. The British accepted Marshall's proposal, and it was put into effect first in the Pacific where the most immediate Allied crisis existed; the American-British-Dutch-Australian (ABDA) Theater was created with General Wavell as its commander. Some of the British were as reluctant about this specific case as they were about the general plan, believing that Wavell would become a scapegoat for commanding a hopeless cause. Churchill firmly rejected this line of thinking and insisted that the proposal be accepted at face value—American regard for Wavell's abilities and determination to show their willingness to serve under a British commander. The course of the war would amply justify Marshall's proposal and Churchill's wisdom in accepting it in its broad and most generous spirit.[33]

The establishment of the ABDA Theater with a supreme Allied theater commander raised the further question: From whom was this commander to receive his orders? For the highest political direction of the war there was the steady flow of correspondence between the President and the Prime Minister and the series of conferences of which Arcadia was the model. But there was an obvious need for some continual supervision of the strategy of the war in its purely military aspect. One possibility would be to carve up the world into spheres of influence and assign to British or American military chiefs the responsibility for their particular sphere. But this first Allied theater discouraged such an arrangement, for in the ABDA Theater the interests of both the Western powers overlapped. Churchill quickly saw that what was evident there was no less true elsewhere, and the only workable solution in the long run would be to have an overall body which represented the military of both countries. The group that eventually developed to coordinate the military strategy of the Western Alliance was the Combined Chiefs of Staff (CCOS)—a standing committee composed of the American and British Chiefs of Staff. Its permanent seat was Washington, where the British COS were represented by deputy. The decision to seat the CCOS in Washington was determined by the ABDA area, which could be more directly supported from the United States. The British also shrewdly noted that the American JCS were less likely to delegate sufficient responsibility to representatives in London.

It was arranged, therefore, that the JCS would meet with the British members of the joint staff mission headed by Sir John Dill at weekly intervals, or more often if necessary. When major conferences were held, the British COS would sit in their own right. The CCOS were given the responsibilities of planning the strategic conduct of the war and determining a broad program of requirements based on the approved policy. This would involve allocation of munition resources on the basis of strategic needs and availability of transport. The transport of fighting services would also fall under their overall assignment of priorities. This definition of duties was never full achieved in practice, but the CCOS came close enough to stand as a model of strategic coordination.[34]

The establishment of the CCOS required a modification of the JCS. The Americans, unlike the British, had only two military departments—the Department of War and the Department of the Navy. The Air Force was under the direction of the United States Army; and the Air Force commander, General H. H. Arnold, was subordinate to General Marshall. Marshall gracefully resolved this problem by having Arnold's name included among the JCS. This provided an American opposite for Portal, although an independent American Air Force was not established until after the conclusion of World War II.

The only member of the CCOS who did not participate in its birth rites was the British CIGS, Sir Alan Brooke. Brooke had some early reservations about it but came to acknowledge by the end of the war that it was a most efficient organization for coordinating the war strategy and effort of two allies. This was a judgment ratified by all its participants.[35] A major part of the success was directly attributable to Brooke's predecessor as CIGS, Sir John Dill, now residing in Washington as the permanent head of the British joint staff there. He and General Marshall understood each other and came swiftly to like each other. This close personal friendship of two able and patriotic soldiers smoothed away many differences born of national distinction and varying outlooks.[36]

Arcadia also gave the British Prime Minister an opportunity to see and work closely with the American JCS. From his long experience with the British COS Churchill was certain to appreciate the importance of his ability to work with their American counterparts. The chairman of the American joint chiefs was Admiral Leahy, whose presence on the JCS balanced the two generals. Leahy's role, however, was more that of a chief of staff to the President; he explained rather than formulated policy. He was a man of limited sympathy toward British views and concerns. General Arnold held less firmly developed national conceptions than did Leahy; but like Leahy, his role was somewhat secondary on the JCS. The two most influential men were the Chief of Naval Operations, Admiral Ernest King, and the U.S. Army Chief of Staff, General George C. Marshall. The appointment of King to replace Admiral Stark upon American entry into the war was a blow to the British. Stark had a long sympathy for Britain from his service on Admiral Sims's staff during World War I, but Admiral King would generally take the lead in any opposition to the British viewpoint which might develop in conference. A man of formidable strength and powerful strategic grasp, King could be a powerful adversary when not in agreement, as the British would discover.

The strongest member of the JCS was General Marshall, both in breadth of vision and in fair-mindedness. Churchill has recorded in his war memoirs that he first appreciated the stature of General Marshall in the summer of 1943. When the two men were flying the Atlantic, Churchill turned over to Marshall the task of improving a communication to Stalin that he and the President had been writing. Marshall's capacity to resolve it into a clear and forceful document within two hours elicited the Prime Minister's admiration.[37] Perhaps it was not until then that the Prime Minister recognized the statesman in Marshall. But surely he appreciated at Arcadia the power with which Marshall could organize a strategic position. The circumstances of the Arcadia meeting and its aftermath suggest that the Prime Minister recognized that Marshall was the key member of the American team. When the Prime Minister flew down to Florida in early January for a short vacation, he asked Roosevelt to send General Marshall along with him.[38]

It is unlikely that Churchill missed the crucial point that in case of a conflict of opinion which could not be resolved, the highest court of appeal would be the American President. He probably also realized that he and Marshall would be the ones to present their cases to Roosevelt. This had been clearly foreshadowed in the Arcadia discussions concerning North Africa. Marshall had stressed that failure in any first adventure on the part of American armed forces overseas would have the most serious effect on public morale. But Roosevelt had placed a rather different emphasis on morale—the need to give the American people the feeling that they were in the war. The Prime Minister thus noted that he had a friend in court, in the best of all possible positions—the man vested with ultimate decision-making authority.[39] While the CCOS could sit together with their full membership only at the major wartime conferences, of their 200 formal meetings no fewer than 89 took place at such conferences. Surely it is significant that under these circumstances the Prime Minister was always on the scene where he could ultimately present his own case to the American President.

The purpose of the CCOS was to fill the constitutional gap between the higher and lower orders of responsibility in the prosecution of the war. They translated the priorities of the President and the Prime Minister into operations in the specific theaters. At the same time, they provided to the President and the Prime Minister the plans and proposals which they recommended as best suited to the prosecution of the war; at times the Prime Minister provided them with a plan initially.

Churchill's energies were to fuel the military planning of the period of Alliance warfare nearly as much as they had fueled the British military effort when that country stood alone.[40] The day would come when the President would be at his home in Hyde Park while the Prime Minister in the White House would convene a meeting and preside over military discussions with the American JCS and the President's political advisers along with the British joint staff in Washington. It is doubtful if a parallel to this occasion can be found in the history of any other two sovereign nations.[41]

Thus the basic political and military relationships which would endure throughout the period of Alliance warfare were clearly discernible at Arcadia. Two steps of organization of lasting significance developed there—the CCOS and single Allied theater commanders. But Churchill had come to the conference with two priorities—strategy and supply. He seemed to be well launched on the road to achieving a victory for his strategic concept of an invasion of French North Africa in 1942. Less successful was the resolution of the problems of joint supply. The allocation of supply was placed under the CCOS; later two boards were established, one in Washington and one in London, to report directly to the President and Prime Minister. This seemed incompatible with the Arcadia arrangement of placing responsibility for supply under the combined chiefs. Again it was Marshall who intervened, and while munitions assignment boards were set up in Washington and London, the priority of direction from the combined chiefs was upheld. The gears of military and civilian cooperation and of joint national cooperation did not always mesh smoothly in the realm of supply. Much of the difficulty existed at the American end for a variety of reasons belonging more to domestic U.S. history, perhaps, than to the problems of the wartime Alliance. The problem of supply was a matter always kept within the Anglo-American family. Neither the Russians nor the French nor anyone else participated in the actual assignments of strategic allocation, although the British Dominions, particularly Canada, had a somewhat anomalous relationship here.[42]

As Churchill departed from the Arcadia conference, he carried with him a strategic victory half secured. The President was clearly sympathetic to Churchill's strategic proposal for 1942, the North African landing; the American Chiefs of Staff were clearly unsympathetic. But where Churchill and his staff had presented their case fully, the American chiefs had been much more reserved. They had tended to go along rather than participate in the decision to begin planning for a North African operation; at the same time the buildup of American forces in the British Isles would be pressed forward.[43] As subsequent developments would demonstrate, the Prime Minister had far from nailed down his proposal firmly. In the realm of strategy Arcadia revealed that no firm agreement existed between the two Western Allies on this difficult subject. In a sense, there was not to be agreement until the end of the war, which in itself is a remarkable commentary on the character of the Western Alliance. That the Alliance did not swiftly become unworkable or reach strategic deadlock owes much to the people charged with the responsibilities of making it function. Perhaps highest consideration should go to the two men who became the protagonists of their strategic viewpoints, Churchill and Marshall. Fortunately for the Alliance, the character of both men was cast in the same giant mold as their abilities, and their integrity was such that they could each present the most forceful of arguments while standing ready ultimately to compromise in reaching a mutually agreeable operating program. Ultimately the cooperation between the two men was the measure of the principles for which they stood and the common cause which they defended, which was greater than the strategic differences between them. The Western Alliance in World War II was a triumph of the institutions of political democracy and the sort of men these institutions nourished—politicians and soldiers alike—far more than it was a tribute to any strategic master plan or mastermind.

STRATEGIC DEBATE

By March 1942 American military judgment had hardened against Churchill's North African operation as one which would be wasteful of combat resources and represented the most negative of strategic values—that is, dispersion of the concentration they believed should take place in the British Isles for a cross-Channel assault. The American case was presented in Washington most firmly by General Dwight D. Eisenhower, who submitted that since lines of communication to Britain had to be kept open, the transport of American troops there involved no diversion. This was the shortest direct Atlantic route and thus made for most efficient use of shipping. In addition the geography of the Continent provided the best route to Germany across northern France, an area generally ideal for the deployment of highly mobile, heavily armored forces such as the Americans were developing. And Britain provided a highly developed base from which to launch major operations and substantial air power which could be employed without endangering British home defenses. All these arguments were pressed upon President Roosevelt in a meeting on March 25. The President decided that any shift away from the North African operation and to an assault across the English Channel based on an American military buildup in Britain would have to be presented to the British Prime Minister.

Roosevelt assigned Marshall and Hopkins to present the American case. This was a skillful choice of personnel since it combined the chief exponent of the American military viewpoint and an experienced politician who was on close terms with both the President and Prime Minister. The plan Marshall carried to London called for an Allied landing in France on about April 1, 1943. To this effort the United States would furnish about thirty divisions and the British, eighteen. There was a further provision that should circumstances on the Continent make it possible, a smaller assault could be launched earlier in the fall of 1942 in the face of either of two contingencies—the need to rescue the Russians from the verge of collapse or to exploit an opportunity created by a sudden German weakness.[44]

On April 14, 1942, Hopkins and Marshall presented their case to the Defense Committee (Operations). Churchill had marshaled his full forces and had Attlee and Eden with him as well as his Minister of Supply and service ministers. The COS and Ismay and Mountbatten were also there. Churchill opened the session with his usual skill. He accepted the Marshall proposal as being in accord with classic principles of war but spun out behind his acceptance a string of subordinate considerations. He suggested the ominous possibility of a junction between the Germans advancing through the Middle East and the Japanese advancing through India and noted that this threat made it impossible for Britain to ignore her sizable commitment in the Middle East. He then spoke of the difficulties involved in the enormous preparation for trans-Channel operations. Brooke also cautioned about the significance of the Middle Eastern position, particularly the oil supplies in the region and the importance of denying such supplies to the Axis. Marshall, less skilled in forensic play than Churchill, seemed to place all his attention on Churchill's immediate acceptance of his proposal and paid insufficient attention to the qualifiers which followed. For a second time, in London as in Washington a few months earlier, one gets the impression that the representatives of the two strategic positions were speaking past each other. Hopkins evidently came closest to seeing this. He stated very positively that once the decision was made to go ahead with a cross-Channel operation, it could not be reversed, for the United States would view this as its major war effort. But Hopkins's cable to Roosevelt the following day made clear that he no less than Marshall believed they had nailed down the American strategy in the meeting.

But in fact the American strategy was no more firmly secured in London on April 14 than the British strategy in Washington in the preceding December meeting. If there were any real British enthusiasm for the Marshall plan, it must have faded almost immediately upon the departure of the Americans for Washington. Every time the British glanced across the English Channel, the risks of landing there seemed to grow in proportion.[45] Churchill has set down in his memoirs that he was prepared to give the American plan "a fair run with other suggestions before the planning committees." This was not the impression Marshall and Hopkins carried away from the meeting. They would most certainly have been shocked by the next sentence of Churchill's memoirs: "I was almost certain that the more it was looked at the less it would be liked." Apparently the Prime Minister was prepared to indicate agreement to a plan he believed would fall of its own weight. "But I had to work by influence and diplomacy in order to secure agreed and harmonious action with our cherished Ally, without whose aid nothing but ruin faced the world." For this reason, Churchill wrote, he did not press alternatives upon Marshall and Hopkins.[46] Perhaps he would have been wiser to have fought out the potentialities of varying plans at the time. Certainly his attitude in the meeting gave the Americans a false impression, and when the Marshall plan came to be challenged by the British, the Americans were left nourishing a certain sense of foul play on Churchill's part.[47]

The process of strategic planning by alternative acquiescence—first American in a British proposal and then British in an American one—tended to postpone the sort of head-knocking examination of military potential measured against strategic plans which would have to take place sometime before any operation could be organized along sound lines. One of the most notable consequences of this was that the construction of landing craft seemed to escape from strategic control. There would be no successful landing of any sort anywhere unless there were adequate landing craft to support such an operation. Yet in March 1942 landing craft stood tenth on the President's list of shipbuilding priorities. Not until October, one month before a major operation, were they placed second on the priority list.[48] This was the beginning of what would prove to be a persistent problem to the Alliance strategy—the difficulty of getting the United States Navy to participate. Postponing a clear-cut adoption of a strategic plan had the effect of postponing the day when all its organizational complications would have to be faced and mastered. The members of the Alliance were still learning their way.

While strategic planning between the Western Allies thus existed in a sort of never-never land, the third member of the Grand Alliance was heard from, and Russian pressure was to have significant effect on mobilizing the Western Allies to action. Eden's trip to Moscow at the end of December 1941 had left the Anglo-Russian relations indefinite. The British had been unable to meet Russian demands and had therefore postponed a full reply until the Foreign Minister had returned from Moscow and the Prime Minister from Washington so that the War Cabinet might hammer out a position which would harmonize Anglo-Russian and Anglo-American policies. This proved to be hard going; Stalin provided a prod in late February 1942 when a Russian order of the day left the British with the impression that he was not ruling out a separate peace with Germany. Accordingly, in early March Churchill was inclined to grant Russia recognition of her frontiers at the time Germany attacked her. The Americans continued their resistance. But in late March the War Cabinet decided that Britain had to live with Russia in Europe and negotiated a treaty with the Soviet government which did not recognize the Soviet frontier claims but implied that they would be accepted. The Americans did not associate themselves with this decision.[49]

With this victory secured, the Kremlin was prepared to launch its next demand upon the partners in the Alliance—the demand for a second front. In late May Molotov arrived in London to present this. He wanted to learn how the British government proposed to draw off at least 40 German divisions from the Soviet front in 1942. Churchill responded by describing the difficulties involved in a landing on the Continent but indicated that the RAF would engage a large proportion of German air strength in the West. Molotov had to depart for Washington without a categorical assurance from the Prime Minister regarding a front other than in the air. However, meeting with President Roosevelt on May 30, Molotov received the assurance that the Western Allies intended to form a second front in 1942. A public statement was issued jointly from Washington and London on June 11 which stated that in the course of the conversations full understanding was reached with regard to the urgent tasks of creating a second front in Europe in 1942. Marshall had held out for the exclusion of the 1942 date but had been overruled.[50]

When Molotov returned to London on his way back to Moscow, Churchill, more experienced in dealing with the Russians than the Americans were, took the precaution of delivering a specific document to Molotov clarifying the British position that an invasion of the Continent in 1942 could not be assured.[51] Not surprisingly, upon Molotov's return to Moscow the official communique with the date 1942 received attention in the Russian publicity, while the private note from the British government remained unmentioned. The Russians now argued that the test of the Anglo-Russian treaty would be the opening of a second front. The result of the Molotov visit was to create strong pressure for a joint military operation by the Western Allies in 1942.[52] In a sense the Russians were attempting to force the hand of their Alliance partners. They could not be expected to understand that the Western Allies had not yet placed all their cards in one hand and that each partner was playing a strategic card of his own. The question was which card the Russian pressure would produce first. The establishment of a definite time limit for an amphibious operation would all but require that the Western Allies choose to play the British card. The Russian intervention thus turned out to be in Churchill's favor.

SECOND FRONT VERSUS NORTH AFRICAN OPERATION

When Molotov arrived in Washington in May, Admiral Lord Louis Mountbatten arrived right behind him. In charge of combined operations, Mountbatten was particularly well placed to argue the drawbacks of a 1942 cross-Channel attack. President Roosevelt quickly indicated his sympathy for Mountbatten's arguments, to the considerable distress of his military advisers.[53] In the meantime the British War Cabinet had concluded that the cross-Channel operation could be risked only if there were a notable decline in German power. The Marshall plan now seemed suddenly aborted, and Churchill decided that affairs were pushing so rapidly toward a crisis that he, accompanied by Brooke and Ismay, would risk flying the Atlantic (still a novel and uncertain affair in those days) to work out a solution. The Prime Minister departed immediately with the President for a weekend in Hyde Park, leaving the American military in Washington with their thoughts, which were probably not flattering to politicians.[54] On June 21 the military men faced the two back in Washington. Churchill argued from a position of strength. He bluntly asserted he was not able to find a single responsible member of his staff who would support a landing in Europe as feasible.[55] This forced Marshall back to his second best line—that it was necessary to continue preparations in 1942 in Great Britain in order to make a landing in northern Europe possible in 1943. This argument of course was fatally weak after Roosevelt's conversation with Molotov.[56] Churchill needed only to stress that it was intolerable for Anglo-American forces to stand idle for the whole year 1942; something must be done. The upshot of the meeting was provision that the American buildup in the British Isles would go forward, but that unless German strength were to decline suddenly on the Continent, planning should also go forward for the North African operation. The forces to be employed would in the main come from American units assigned to the British Isles but not yet shipped there.[57] In other words, for the third time in seven months, a nondecision had been made. There was not yet a clear strategic priority for a single offensive operation, and the year was half gone.

Against this background the Prime Minister was informed of the loss of Tobruk to the assault of General Rommel. It was a staggering blow to the Prime Minister and deeply humiliating to sustain this military setback while at the White House as the guest of his ally. Yet if adversity often showed Churchill at his best, it also showed his American allies at theirs, and help was immediately forthcoming. The Americans were prepared to take their most modern tanks from the units that had just received them and ship them directly to the Middle East to support the British position there.

The North African operation became more attractive than ever. It would offer a way of cleaning up what was becoming a running sore in the Allied military effort, and it hardened the Prime Minister's determination to thrust the Germans and their Italian allies out of Africa and into the Mediterranean. In addition, it sharply increased Churchill's need for a victory somewhere—anywhere. He had just survived politically a run of disaster in the Far East, culminating in the loss of Singapore. This had convulsed British politics for the first two months of the year. Tobruk was certain to touch off a new crisis. Faced with the need for a certain victory, Churchill was less prepared than ever to risk a Continental landing. The Washington conference closed on this note. While no operation for 1942 yet had the green light, assuredly any European operation would secure a certain British veto. In short, it would have to be a North African operation or none at all.[58]

STRATEGY FOR 1942

In late June 1942 the American generals, Eisenhower and Clark, arrived in London to start preparations for what they believed was the agreed cross-Channel attack. They learned immediately that the British had no such plan in mind. The Prime Minister had decided that the time had come to bury that operation, which in his opinion had been dead for some time anyway. On July 8 he informed Roosevelt that no British general, admiral, or air marshal was prepared to recommend the Channel operation as practical for 1942. He skillfully added that he was sure French North Africa was the best chance by far for effective relief to the Russian front in 1942 and this should be the true second front. This was certain to be persuasive with the President. The JCS responded violently to the British statement, and General Marshall on July 10 proposed that a Pacific alternative to the North African operation be offered the President. This was a proposal much to the liking of Admiral King, but on Marshall's part it apparently was a reaction to the disappointment he felt at having secured what he thought was British agreement to his plan in mid-April, only to see that plan dashed to the ground in early July. Roosevelt was not much impressed but on July 12 asked the JCS for a statement of any Pacific alternative, including full details. The JCS had no detailed plan to submit and admitted that their proposed alternative to the North African operation would not improve the strategic situation. Roosevelt bluntly told his military advisers that their Pacific alternative smacked of "taking up your dishes and going away." On July 14 he continued his initiative, sending Hopkins, Marshall, and King to London to get the opinion of Eisenhower and the other American planners there and to come to some final decision with the British. He gave his military advisers a clear indication of his thinking when he noted that he did not believe they could wait until 1943 to strike at Germany, and he reminded them of three cardinal principles: decision on plans, unity of plan, and attack combined with defense but not defense alone. He continued: "I hope for total agreement within one week of your arrival."[59]

Before the three Americans arrived, Churchill received a warning from Sir John Dill regarding their mood. Dill pointed out that General Marshall had been studying Sir William Robertson's *Soldiers and Statesmen* and that the American general had sent him a copy of Volume I in which Chapter 3 was marked. The chapter referred to the importance of concentration upon the decisive point; the World War I British CIGS went on to express his opinion that the Gallipoli operation was an unjustifiable diversion of effort. This of course was the most controversial episode in Churchill's long and turbulent career. In the same chapter Robertson stressed the responsibility of military advisers to state their opinions to the politicians fully and clearly. Marshall indicated to Dill that Admiral King had also been reading the work. This was probably the price Churchill had to pay for the impression he had left with

Marshall in the mid-April meeting when the general thought he had secured British agreement to his plan. If Marshall was still annoyed about the results of that meeting, he had succeeded certainly in annoying Churchill with his reference to the Gallipoli campaign. Sir John Kennedy recalled that after the Dill message it was impossible to find a copy of Robertson's book in any London library; everyone in Whitehall was working his way through it awaiting the American arrival. Churchill immediately responded to Dill: "I am glad our friends are coming. . . . Soldiers and statesmen here are in complete agreement."[60] The Prime Minister and the COS were also examining the North African operation once more. They believed it should include landing not only at Casablanca but also at Algiers and Oran at least. The operational plan was growing bolder.[61]

The combined Anglo-American strategy sessions began in London on July 20 with the Americans once more arguing for a French landing. The British countered by stating the minimal requirements for carrying out such a landing successfully; these exceeded what the Allies could muster in 1942. After three days of fruitless discussion the Americans reported to the President that they had reached a stalemate. The President ordered them to reach agreement with the British on one of five alternatives which he listed in order of preference, the attack on French North Africa being first. Marshall and King agreed that if they could not have the European operation, the North African one was best. But Marshall also warned the British War Cabinet that to abandon the European plan for 1942 and substitute the North African operation meant abandoning a return to the Continent in 1943. The British War Cabinet was reluctant to accept this conclusion, and it was necessary to work out compromise wording in the final agreement. The North African operation on July 25 was assigned the code name Torch, and the CCOS agreed to the appointment of an American commander with overall responsibility. Still the American JCS hedged and wanted that commander to be in charge of a planning group but not to have an operational command until a final decision was actually made to mount Torch. This left Churchill uneasy; he feared that for a fourth time a decision to carry out an operation in 1942 would fall apart. He urged Hopkins to intervene with the President and get a clear decision once and for all. Roosevelt cooperated, sending a message to his military that he expected a firm date of October 30, 1942, to become the basis for Torch planning. Thus it was the American President who decided for the North African operation in the face of the reluctance of his military advisers.[62]

The decision was at least as much political as military. Roosevelt had his Russian pledge in mind, and he was determined that the American public must become committed to the European Theater of Operations coming before the Pacific Theater. He believed this required that U.S. and German ground forces should be fighting sometime in 1942.

These desires of the President meshed with Churchill's political need for a victory. The political interests of the two statesmen met in French North Africa. Thus, in A. J. P. Taylor's words, "Political needs came ahead of strategy and determined it, as so often happens in war."[63]

From a military viewpoint the North African expedition was the best that could be mounted in 1942. Any military alternative involved the delay of nearly a year. The Americans firmly believed it meant a delay of more than this and that no cross-Channel operation would be mounted in 1943. Churchill was reluctant to admit this point, but the Americans were quite right. Churchill later believed that this was just as well and came to view a 1944 date for the Channel operation as strategically wise. This too is a respectable military judgment.[64] Perhaps, after all, the politicians were wiser than their military advisers. Even the North African operation meant running substantial risks for Great Britain in 1942. The shipping required to mount the operation would strip Britain bare and actually force a reduction in the planned scale of imports for that year. What would have happened to Britain had the shipping in the North African operation sustained heavy losses is a grim consideration.[65] Military operations, like politics, are the art of the possible, and North Africa was the best possibility.

By the end of July the two Western Allies were at last agreed on the strategy for the end of 1942. This left the reaction of the third member of the Grand Alliance to be faced. Would the Russians view North Africa as an acceptable second front? Churchill, with his usual fortitude, determined that the issue was of such importance that he himself should break the news to Stalin. Churchill had much bad news to carry to the Russian dictator, for British efforts to supply Russia through the port of Murmansk had been overtaken by disaster and convoys had been suspended. To mount the operation against North Africa would also require all possible shipping, so the suspension would last for some time. Churchill set out to do the best he could by facing the Russian bear in his den. Stalin understood little English and this neutralized the most powerful weapon in Churchill's armory—his magnificent capacity for persuasiveness in his native tongue. Yet Churchill believed that personal contact, even across a language barrier, was superior to what he called the "dead blank walls" of correspondence.[66]

Churchill departed for Moscow with an American friend, Averell Harriman. Harriman in London had feared that if Churchill had to bear the full brunt of explaining the Western decision to Stalin, the Russian leader might well believe that he was receiving only a British position. Roosevelt somewhat reluctantly agreed to Harriman's presence in the Churchill-Stalin discussions. It was well that Harriman was there, for inevitably, when Churchill's explanations were met by harsh words from Stalin, anger mounted in the Prime Minister; thus a temperate influence was desirable. The conversations began on August 12, and Churchill recalled them as "bleak and sombre." Stalin presented the situation on his long front, emphasizing that it was a grim affair indeed. Stalin's portrait of the dark situation did not make Churchill's task easier. But he told Stalin bluntly that the British and American governments did not believe they could undertake a major operation until late in 1942, which ruled out the Channel. He eloquently painted the disasters that would come with a premature offensive. Stalin retorted that losses were inevitable in war. But Churchill responded that war is not folly, and it would be folly to invite disaster. Evidently an oppressive silence followed, whereupon Churchill launched into what the Western Allies could do. He described the mounting strategic air offensive against Germany; his rhetoric reached such a pitch of enthusiasm that Harriman later reported to the President that Churchill and Stalin between them had soon destroyed most of the industrial cities of Germany. Having paved the way, Churchill then hauled out his prize offering—the expedition against North Africa. He developed for Stalin where this could lead, including a 1943 operation into southern Europe. He also indicated that he still viewed a cross-Channel operation in 1943 as feasible. Stalin was perceptive to the strategic advantages of the operation. Before Churchill left Moscow, a certain measure of thaw had been achieved in Alliance relations as a result of his fortitude in tackling Stalin directly.[67]

The Prime Minister reported to the War Cabinet and to President Roosevelt that he came away from Moscow encouraged. The Russians knew the worst and having made their protests were now in a more friendly spirit, understanding what could be done for them. Churchill also promised them an Arctic convoy in the autumn. But he also left a hostage to fortune in Moscow when he told Stalin that a cross-Channel operation would be possible in 1943, since American military leaders had already warned Churchill to the contrary. Both Sir Alan Brooke and Sir John Slessor believed that Churchill personally gave Stalin a hard commitment before he left Moscow.[68] If Churchill did so, it is the measure of how heavy he felt the burden of holding together the Grand Alliance; he was the working member. It was he who carried proposals to Washington and promises to Moscow. If on occasion he painted hopes for his two associates which could not be fulfilled, he also painted them for himself, and in mid-1942 the military situation was still sufficiently bleak that hope was a requisite quality for the determined war leader.

1942 OPERATIONS

Murmansk

From the middle of 1941 on, Arctic convoys to Russia were the most direct way that Britain and the United States could demonstrate their support of their Soviet ally. But this was very difficult. It involved a long and dangerous sea route north along the German-occupied coast of

Norway, around the North Cape, to the Russian ports of Murmansk and Archangel. In winter each convoy was an exercise in ultimate horror; if a ship were sunk, instant death awaited the crew in the icy water. In summer only a few minutes exposure in the northern waters produced the same result. The constantly shifting thermal patterns of the waters made submarine detection difficult. Ice was a constant danger, and in late winter and early spring it forced the convoys closer to German air bases. The British Admiralty firmly believed that if they had the responsibility of interdicting the convoys, they would guarantee that not a single ship would get through. That the convoys were run at all is a measure of how desperately the British and American governments believed they must support their Russian ally. Problems on the Murmansk run did not end with the arrival in a Russian port, for the facilities were so inadequate that unloading ships was difficult and prolonged. Nor did Russians in the ports welcome their Allies. Medical facilities for those wounded or exhausted on the voyage were nearly nonexistent.

The 1942 voyages had been conducted against little German opposition, but even these had fallen short of what had been promised Russia (mostly because of supply problems). This had earned the Western Allies a series of hard Russian notes which took no consideration of the problems they faced in maintaining the supply route. In the spring of 1942 the Germans began to attack the northern convoys with aircraft, surface ships, and submarines on an increasingly serious scale, so that each convoy became a major naval operation. The burden fell on the British, although many of the merchant ships were American. The British had to bear a certain amount of American criticism too, for the Americans seemed to believe the number of ships could be increased. Roosevelt was feeling the spur of Stalin's complaints. But Churchill had to reply that what Stalin demanded and Roosevelt requested was beyond British power to fulfill. He told the President the British were "absolutely extended." Indeed, Churchill was running the convoys in the face of the gravest disquiet among the War Cabinet and COS who were firmly convinced that each voyage carried with it the seeds of naval catastrophe. Churchill agreed with his advisers, telling them he shared their misgivings, but felt it to be a matter of duty. Steadily the losses mounted. Of 84 ships dispatched on the Murmansk run in April and May 1942, only 58 got through. In June 1942 the long-predicted disaster occurred. The Germans coordinated a series of attacks on the convoy P.Q. 17, and information reaching the Admiralty created the impression that the naval vessels escorting the convoy were about to be crushed by a powerful German surface force. The Admiralty believed the only hope lay in dispersing the convoy, with the escort retiring toward the British Isles while the ships independently made their way to Russia.

The surface attack did not develop, but the convoy once dispersed left each ship isolated to German submarine and air attack. There followed a terrible harvest of death and destruction in northern waters; 23 of the 34 merchant vessels were sunk, and 130,000 of 200,000 tons of cargo were lost.[69] This shattering blow produced no sympathy from Moscow and little understanding from Washington. Indeed, throughout the war the Arctic run constituted a heavy demand on British naval resources for a return which the British Admiralty consistently believed was not worth the effort involved. The Russians, however, remained insistent in their demands, but after a temporary renewal of convoys in autumn of 1942, the pressures of supplying North Africa and the shortage of escorts required another suspension in the winter of 1942–43.

When the convoys started again in 1943, the measure of Russian callousness toward the effort remained truly shocking. In October 1943 Churchill directed a message to Stalin personally that rotation of British personnel in the Russian ports was essential because of the strain of the climate and conditions on their health. He also requested that Stalin permit a small British medical unit to be sent to Archangel to provide care for Allied personnel since Russian care was grossly inadequate. Even this basic request had been long stalled by the Russians. Churchill complained of a whole series of petty restrictions on the men who were risking their lives on every voyage they took to bring aid to the Russians. Stalin did not even bother to respond to this message for nearly two weeks.[70] The Murmansk operations remained an onerous burden.

Torch

In summer of 1942 plans moved forward for the operation against North Africa. Roosevelt's and Churchill's hopes began to rise, and the American commander for the operation, General Eisenhower, was encouraged to make his plans. These provided that assault forces should sail from Britain to attack the ports of Oran and Algiers on the Mediterranean, while a third force would cross the Atlantic from the United States to land at three points on the coast of Morocco, particularly around the port of Casablanca. Executing these operations required that shipping and escorts be cut to the bone.[71] Six divisions, three British and three American, with full supporting units were to be employed.

The size of this operation was larger than Churchill had at first anticipated, but his advisers and the Americans believed that success must be insured. While the Americans were wise to insist on landing in the largest possible force, they were fearful of conducting operations along the Mediterranean where they believed the landings were particularly vulnerable to attack in the rear from Germans passing through Spain. Here Churchill's judgment was more sure; he believed that the gains to be secured from landing at Algiers and Oran far outweighed the possibility of a German intervention through Spain, a position justified by events. Eisenhower supported Churchill's position, and Washington finally yielded. The British were more worried about the landings on the Atlantic coast of Morocco than along the Mediterranean, for the Atlantic landings would have to face traditionally high and dangerous surf conditions. In the end the Allies were to be uniquely fortunate in the height of the surf when the landings occurred. The pulling and pushing between London and Washington in what Eisenhower described as a transatlantic essay competition was not finally resolved until September 5 when the three main landing areas were finally agreed to. The British yielded in their desire to go even deeper into the Mediterranean.

The Torch operation would require over 600 vessels carrying an initial assault force of 90,000 men with 200,000 more to come with all their supplies and weapons. These had to cross ocean routes 1,500 miles long from Britain and over 3,000 miles from the United States. The only air cover available for the landings would be provided from aircraft carriers and one small overcrowded airstrip at Gibraltar. There was no lack of risk in the operation.[72] It also constituted the first combined operation executed by an Allied planning team and a combined Allied staff. All international problems had to be worked out here for the first time, and a pattern for future cooperation and integration established. Any serious mistake could damage not only the Torch operation but the hopes for any future operation. Fortunately the Allied commander was supremely well suited to the task of achieving cooperation. Indeed, General Eisenhower would become the model commander of World War II in this respect.[73]

On November 8, 1942, the landings took place successfully. But immediately new problems loomed. The Americans had been particularly hopeful that the French garrisons would not resist the landing, but resistance of varying severity was encountered. As the Allies fought their way ashore and established their position, communications were taking place at a frantic pace between the Allied command and various French contacts. The Frenchmen the Americans had counted on failed to obtain support and cooperation for them. But Admiral Darlan was there, and he commanded the obedience of the French officers in North Africa.[74] Eisenhower decided to deal with Darlan, believing what could be gained militarily outweighed what might be lost politically. Eisenhower was right in his military judgment, and Allied forces were swiftly pointed toward Tunisia.

Alamein

The Allied landings in French North Africa occurred against a background of desert victory near the other end of the Mediterranean shore of Africa. When Churchill had set out with Brooke to bear bad tidings to Stalin, he had stopped in Cairo in an effort to resolve the long series of disappointments he had faced in the Middle East. The command there had been reconstructed and new men appointed. Great efforts had been made to supply the revitalized command starting with the tanks so generously provided by Washington on that bleak day when Churchill had learned of the fall of Tobruk. In October 1942 these great efforts were to be put to the test.

The British Eighth Army under the command of Sir Bernard Law

Montgomery had the advantage over Rommel—in men, nearly three to two and in tanks, two to one. Montgomery was to show himself a master in fighting a battle of materiel. On October 9 he opened his set-piece battle against the Germans, and by the 23rd he had smashed the joint German and Italian army to the point of collapse. The battle was a triumph of British arms, for the enemy sustained losses of about 60,000 men killed, wounded, and captured and five-sixths of his armor; British losses were under 15,000 killed, wounded, and missing. The road was open to Montgomery, and on November 13 Tobruk was reoccupied. The port of Tripoli fell to the British on January 23, 1943, an advance of nearly 1,500 miles from the Alamein position.

By this date, affairs in the west had also moved decisively. Darlan had provided a French cease-fire in North Africa, and Eisenhower was moving toward Tunisia from the west as Montgomery drove toward the same goal from the east. In these circumstances Hitler responded with alacrity. Unoccupied France was overrun by German forces, but the vital French fleet in the harbor of Toulon was scuttled on November 27, 1942, and thus denied to the Germans. Eisenhower was running risks to get his men as far east as he could toward the key ports of Bizerte and Tunis. He got within 30 miles of Tunis, but Hitler was flying troops into Tunisia faster than Eisenhower could get troops there by sea and along extremely bad roads. Heavy winter rains now descended, and the Germans possessed the all-weather airfields in Tunisia. A stalemate descended on the front in January and early February. Yet the Axis position was critical indeed. A quarter-million German and Italian troops were pinned in Tunisia. Eisenhower was advancing on a broad front from the west, while Montgomery massed his forces to the southeast preparatory to a break-in attack. Rommel tried to buy time in mid-February by turning away from Montgomery, who was still organizing his assault, and hitting the Americans who were massing on his flank. Rommel fought a spoiling battle through Kasserine Pass on February 20, but his initial success quickly met fierce American opposition, so that by February 23 he was forced to withdraw. Nonetheless, he had temporarily secured his flank when Montgomery finally launched his long-prepared assault on March 20. By March 27 Montgomery had turned the German position and forced Rommel back. Following Montgomery's breakthrough, the Allied forces attacked in strength from the west, and by early May the German position in Tunisia was coming apart. By May 12 it was all over.

The Allies took over a quarter-million German and Italian prisoners. The African coast was clear along its entire length. The campaign had taken longer than had been hoped, for the speed and scale of Hitler's reinforcement of his African position had not been anticipated by the Allies any more than Hitler seems to have anticipated the Torch landings. Yet the prolongation of the African battle brought its own reward. A large enemy force had been destroyed, and the Allies, particularly the Americans, had gained badly needed combat experience which enabled many initial problems of command and coordination to be resolved. The initiative had clearly and decisively passed to the Allies in the Mediterranean, just as the massive battle around Stalingrad in southern Russia had delivered the initiative on that vast front to their Russian ally.

In the summer of 1942 the naval battles of Coral Sea and Midway had also secured Allied initiative in the Pacific, which was being followed up ruthlessly in bitter fighting on the island of Guadalcanal. As the tide of battle flowed decisively for the Allies and church bells rang out for joy in England to celebrate the Battle of Alamein, it was necessary to turn again to strategic planning and political considerations.

THE EMPIRE

On November 10, 1942, with the Torch landings successful and Rommel reeling in defeat on the western desert, the British Prime Minister delivered one of the most memorable of all his wartime speeches. He emphasized that the landings in French North Africa were not intended to usurp French possessions and that the British had no wish but to see France free and strong and with her empire restored to her. He stated that the British did not enter the war for profit or expansion but only for honor and duty. He then proceeded to roar defiance to the world. He said he had not become the King's First Minister to preside over the liquidation of the British Empire. "Here we are, and here we stand, a veritable rock of salvation in this drifting world."[75]

This was not a chance outburst. Churchill had been waiting a long time for the tide of victory to serve as a vehicle on which he could launch the wave of emotion long building inside him. For as the war had proceeded, political burdens had piled upon Churchill. He had struggled with the Dominions, particularly Australia, and he had struggled with his American ally, who viewed the British Empire with little enthusiasm and constitutional monarchy with bare tolerance. American complaints about the British Empire served as goads to Churchill, who had broken with his own political party to defend the imperial position in India. In a rage he had stated that the British had kept their colonies open to the trade of the whole world while the Americans by their high tariff policy had led the world astray.[76]

Churchill was always sensitive to having American revolutionary principles waved in his face. He was deeply devoted to the British Crown and resented criticisms of constitutional monarchy. His support of monarchy extended even further; in 1918 Churchill had fought proposals that the German Kaiser and Crown Prince should be brought to trial. As Beaverbrook once wrote, where Churchill was concerned, all monarchs were safe from the gallows.[77] Churchill deeply valued the British Empire and believed its history was one of the interest of Britain marching forward with the progress and well-being of mankind.[78] Yet Churchill understood—just as he deeply resented—American attitudes toward the Empire, and in attempting to safeguard the British imperial position, he knew he would have to face a lack of cooperation from his Western ally.[79]

India in particular strained the Alliance, especially the personal relationship between Churchill and Roosevelt. The situation in India was difficult. The Congress party there viewed Britain's problems as a time of opportunity to ask Britain to abandon her hold on India. Part of the Congress leadership followed Mohandas K. Gandhi in adopting a position of noncooperation with the British government there. Others, led by Pandit Nehru, believed at first that the Indians must resist the Japanese. In March and April of 1942 British relations with the Congress party were approaching a crisis, and Sir Stafford Cripps had been dispatched by Churchill to work out a satisfactory arrangement which would concede to India promises of substantial self-government following the war. The American government believed that Churchill should be prodded to make the most generous possible offers, and Roosevelt directed a series of unhelpful letters to Churchill, tending to cast the Indian problem in the framework of the American War of Independence. Probably the only line in these messages with which Chuchill ever agreed was Roosevelt's admission that it was "none of my business."[80] Churchill records in his memoirs that the first time Roosevelt raised the subject of India with him face to face in Washington in December 1941, he reacted so strongly and at such length that Roosevelt never raised it verbally again.[81] This surely is an extraordinary measure of Churchill's passion on this subject. Churchill constantly argued with the President that the divisions of religion and status in India cut so deep that the removal of the British would be an invitation to chaos. In early 1942 when Roosevelt suggested to Churchill that he undertake a settlement in India somewhat along the pattern of the American government under the Articles of Confederation, Churchill observed, "I was thankful that events had already made such an act of madness impossible."[82] The President received a more polite reply than this.[83]

Churchill was deeply sincere in what he felt were British obligations to India—the India he had known as a young officer at the end of the nineteenth century.[84] To him, the Congress party did not represent India but only the Hindu elite, and he argued that British responsibilities extended to the depressed classes or untouchables and the Moslems as well as the Indian princes. He believed this was demonstrated by the lack of effect the Congress party had on the Indian army and officials, and especially on the masses who remained loyal to British authority. To Churchill this was a sign of the nonrepresentative character of the Congress party, and he reaffirmed to Parliament and to his ally that he intended to persevere in his Indian program. But disorders followed in late 1943; by September Gandhi, Nehru, and others were back in prison, enjoying what Churchill referred to as a "commodious internment."[85]

Churchill's defense of the British position in India was to be the last stage in the history of British India; the postwar world would sweep away traditions to which Churchill clung so tenaciously. Once the advancing Japanese tide was checked, Churchill's interest turned to advancing operations close to his heart, such as the invasion of North Africa. This neglect of India was general in the Western Alliance; in the allocation of priorities the Indian Ocean area was usually the stepchild at the dinner table. In the summer of 1943 this brought tragic consequences. Shipping margins were cut so close that there was no capacity to supply foodstuffs to India if harvests failed. A complex pattern of inadequate food imports, insufficient shipping, and internal maldistribution combined with poor harvests to visit starvation upon India. About 1.5 million Indians perished as a consequence, the most grievous loss of life within the British Empire and Commonwealth during World War II. It was an early, tragic note in the swelling death-knell of the British raj.

Even the Dominions were a source of difficulty to Churchill. The governments of Australia, New Zealand, and Canada were all demanding a greater policy role in the war than Churchill was prepared to grant. He insisted that Dominion representatives must work with the British government through goodwill and stated that in no circumstances could their presence in government meetings affect the collective responsibility of the British government to the Crown and Parliament.[86] When Australia and New Zealand complained that this left them with no role in policy planning, Churchill instituted a Pacific War Council so that they might participate in the planning there. Sir John Kennedy recalls that the meetings of this council consisted of Churchill arriving, chatting for a while, shaking hands with everyone, and then departing. Evidently no business was ever conducted at such a meeting.[87]

By the end of the war none of these incidents seems to have made much impression on the Prime Minister. In his victory broadcast of May 13, 1945, Churchill described his government as sustained by the Dominions and the Empire in every quarter of the globe; they stood more united and more effectively powerful than ever.[88] In Churchill's view there was more romance than history. The old imperialist remained incorrigible to the end. His was an attitude which impeded to some degree the working of the Alliance and perhaps interfered with the planning of strategy as the tide of victory swept forward.

EVALUATION

CHURCHILL'S SPEECH of November 10, 1942, conveniently marks the conclusion of a chapter which began and ended with Churchill shouting defiance. A new chapter would have to begin, for somewhere, sometime, the reconquest of the Continent must start, with the first soldier wading ashore. While the North African experience had shown that the Western Alliance could achieve victory, it had also shown how substantial an effort was required. Even greater obstacles must be overcome when striking against the Continent.

Torch had taken place because forces were available for it but were inadequate for a more ambitious undertaking. It had also demonstrated that among allies the nation deploying the greatest force in the field has a way of dictating the use of these forces; in 1942 Great Britain still occupied that position within the Alliance. In retrospect, the strategic wisdom of the operation seems clear, as General Marshall himself admitted.[89] Torch was a valuable step in the development of Allied offensive capabilities. It provided the first large-scale experience of troops with landing craft and developed the techniques of supporting a landing on a hostile shore. It allowed this to be done where risks were far less and the enemy less substantial than would have to be faced later. In short, it produced maximum results for minimum cost. Torch had cost Hitler an army of a quarter-million men and had permitted the Allies to gain combat experience and work out problems of unified command.

Each of these developments played its role in the shifting balance of power which now inclined toward the Allies and against the Axis. More and more of Hitler's forces were tied down to static positions to guard his creaking empire. Torch also gave the Allies the psychological initiative. Victory had followed their first major joint operation, and the Germans had been exposed to the force of an Alliance which achieved a harmony in the field far exceeding anything Hitler had managed with his erstwhile allies.

The price of Torch and the subsequent battle for Tunisia was the clear postponement of a cross-Channel attack until 1944. How much a price this constituted may be argued. An astute student of war, Basil Liddell Hart, has concluded that whether a landing in Normandy could have succeeded in 1943 was doubtful. In light of what we now know about the narrowness of the margin there in 1944, an earlier attack would seem premature, although Liddell Hart concludes that the balance of evidence is not definite enough to rule out a possibility of an earlier success.[90]

Churchill had no doubt. He wrote in his memoirs that even if Torch had been completed in 1942 and the cross-Channel assault launched in 1943, it would have led to a bloody defeat of the first magnitude, with serious consequences for the course of the war.[91] As this conviction grew in Churchill, it was certain to have its effect on Alliance strategy; for if the Channel assault could not be launched in 1943, the question immediately arose of what was to be done in that year. Churchill believed that only by landing in Sicily and Italy could the Allies engage the enemy on a large scale and tear down the weaker of the Axis partners.[92] For Churchill Torch led logically to the strategic operation for 1943 which centered in the Mediterranean Theater, and this was certain to open a new round of dispute. For all through the launching of Torch, Churchill and his COS had never disowned the American strategic plan for the cross-Channel landing. Churchill had argued only that Torch was the best that could be done in 1942; he had always acknowledged that Marshall's plan conformed with proper strategic doctrine. Even when the Americans had expressed their belief that Torch would devour the resources for a cross-Channel operation in 1943, Churchill had refused to accept this.[93]

It was clear by the end of 1942 that the Prime Minister and the President both occupied central places in all aspects of the Alliance's plans and operations. Soldiers may plan and soldiers may fight, but the two politicians were accustomed to making the ultimate decisions themselves.[94] This tended to centralize the direction of the Alliance and to permit a great concentration of effort through close coordination. The establishment of this relationship was largely the result of Churchill's effort, and the success of the Alliance in the field owes much to the success of Churchill's politics in the corridors of power.[95]

Churchill approached the Anglo-American Alliance with all the shrewdness and experience of his long political career but also with a certain integrity which did much to secure its success. Hopkins many times told the story of Roosevelt being wheeled into Churchill's guest room in the White House as the Prime Minister emerged from the bathroom wearing only slippers and cigar. As Roosevelt tried to back out, Churchill protested it was quite all right. "The Prime Minister of Great Britain has nothing to conceal from the President of the United States." Robert Sherwood has written that he asked Churchill if the story were true. Churchill replied firmly that it was nonsense; he never received the President without at least a bath towel wrapped around him. He said he could not possibly have made such a statement, as the President himself would have been well aware that it was not strictly true.[96] But the story nicely illustrates Churchill's approach to the Americans. Even when he deployed all his skill to press for what he believed was right and wisest for the Alliance, he recognized the proper limits of his efforts; the Americans, even those who suspected the ancient imperialist lurking beneath the democratic politician, gave Churchill their respect, and many gave him their admiration and affection. His relations with Russia were never as cordial as with America, although here too he had labored manfully to establish good terms.[97]

The tremendous proportions of the tasks Churchill embraced in this period and the results he achieved in spite of all difficulties should not be obscured by the disputes and failures which were part of the Alliance experience. Brooke has described a scene in which the Prime Minister exclaimed that the machine of war with Russia at one end and America at the other was too cumbersome to operate. It was so much easier to do nothing or to sit and wait for work to come to him; nothing was harder than to do things, and everybody did nothing but produce difficulties for him.[98] Churchill had these moments; the wonder is that he did not have them more often. Brooke witnessed what Roosevelt and Stalin seldom saw—a strong spirit wrestling with the circumstances of an age in which events threatened to undo the centuries of labors for Western society. The labor of the British statesman in the heat of events was no less than the labor of the philosopher in the quiet of his study—that of civilized man struggling to bring meaning out of his existence.

7 / CASABLANCA TO NORMANDY, *January 1943 to June 1944*

THE SUCCESSFUL INVASION of North Africa raised again the question of Alliance strategy. Only with some difficulty had the two Western Allies been able to agree on going as far as North Africa. With that operation successfully under way, the two partners must turn again to the question of joint strategy.

The North African operation had taken place largely because of Churchill's support. He had offered it as the only feasible joint operation of 1942, always acknowledging that the cross-Channel operation held first place in Western strategic planning, provided the resources were available. In late summer of 1942 Churchill had continued to recognize the primacy of this operation. He suggested that General Marshall, the prime advocate of this plan, should come to Europe to direct it and that, until such time as major preparations could go forward, General Eisenhower would act as Marshall's European deputy.[1] Churchill had protested in late 1942 against the American insistence that the Channel operation could not take place in 1943. Such a postponement, he suggested in late November 1942, would be a most grievous decision.[2] Many political forces played on Churchill's mind as he insisted on the possibility of Overlord in 1943: constant Soviet pressure for the operation and the additional fear that the Americans might decide to give priority to the Pacific rather than Europe. Thus the differing pressures of his two allies served as spurs to bolster Churchill's determination for the cross-Channel operation in 1943.[3]

But Churchill's enthusiasm for Overlord suddenly flagged. On November 18, 1942, ten days after the landings in North Africa, Churchill was telling the President that the priorities for the Western Allies should be: first, to complete the conquest of North Africa and open the Mediterranean to military traffic; second, to use the position gained in Africa "to strike at the underbelly of the Axis." The Prime Minister went on to extol the advantages of seizing either Sardinia or Sicily as air bases from which to strike Italy. This he now called the supreme effort for 1943. He also included the possibility of bringing Turkey into the war.[4]

This was a very different emphasis from the stress on the cross-Channel operation which Churchill had maintained in the months preceding the North African invasion. Was it always the Prime Minister's intention to allow a Mediterranean strategy to unfold step by step, or did he undergo a significant change of mind in early November 1942? If he did change his mind, what factors brought it about? Was it a new strategic vision evoked by initial successes in North Africa or an increasing fear of the dangers associated with the cross-Channel operation? Pursuing a Mediterranean strategy in 1943 had the advantage of avoiding the Scylla of American withdrawal to the Pacific and Russian cries of betrayal by operating an offensive strategy against Europe from the south as well as avoiding the Charybdis of a cross-Channel disaster.

The problems associated with carrying out Overlord were growing in intensity. General Eisenhower had doubled the number of divisions he now believed essential to a 1943 cross-Channel operation—from six to twelve. There was a shortage of landing craft and a shortage of American divisions in Britain at the end of 1942 which would have to be overcome (and perhaps could not) in order to carry out the operation.[5] The success of the North African landings opened glittering prospects to the Prime Minister. He saw Europe as opened to attack from a variety of angles, and certainly Italy looked less formidable than its German ally. Churchill was always willing to push his opportunities, and in his enthusiasm to do so he perhaps lost sight of the fact that to his allies this might appear as abandonment of what they believed to be agreed strategic priorities.[6]

CASABLANCA

WHEN THE CASABLANCA CONFERENCE opened on January 14, 1943, Churchill was prepared to deploy all his skillful political resources to establish a program of operations centered in the Mediterranean. In this he had the support of his Chief of the Imperial General Staff (CIGS) who argued that the Atlantic submarine crisis and consequent shortage of shipping would result in an insufficient number of divisions in Britain to support a cross-Channel operation in 1943. Brooke thus advocated a battle of attrition in Italy. This argument was not necessarily Churchill's. He tended to view Italy as an opportunity; Brooke tended to see it as another area in which to absorb and grind up German field resources. Churchill wanted to push up the Italian leg; Brooke favored pulling the Germans down.[7]

The Americans did not particularly dispute the British 1943 Mediterranean proposals, but they urged an increased boldness of British planning. Where the British Chiefs of Staff (COS) had preferred Sardinia to Sicily as the next step from the African shore, the Joint Chiefs of Staff (JCS) argued that Sicily offered greater rewards and secured the support of Churchill whose eye also looked in that direction.[8] This is not unduly surprising; the American military leadership had long had doubts about the feasibility of mounting Overlord in 1943, and they too realized that some operation was necessary for that year. American unhappiness at Casablanca resulted more from a feeling that they had been outtalked by the Prime Minister in the preceding year and a fear that he would find a way out of Overlord in 1944 than from any intention to dispute a Mediterranean strategy for 1943. The result was agreement at Casablanca that the Battle of the Atlantic and the struggle to secure sea communications remain the primary obligation on the resources of the Western Allies.

The American buildup in Europe was to proceed as fast as other commitments would allow. Among these was full preparation for taking Sicily, for which planning was to go forward at once with a view to the earliest possible date of attack. Eisenhower was to be Supreme Allied Commander for the Sicily operation with a British team handling army, navy, and air duties. Given this determination of priorities, surely it was optimistic of the Casablanca planners to retain a date of August 1, 1943, for reentry to the Continent. Clearly, neither the British nor the Americans had any real faith in that date.[9]

In retrospect, the great failing of Casablanca seems not so much the continued vagueness about strategic priorities in northern Europe as a failure to implement the first priority of the conference—the security of sea communications. Until the U-boat menace had been broken and there was sufficient shipping and landing craft to support offensive operations, any strategic planning labored under crippling limitations. Yet the fact remains that construction priorities, particularly for landing craft and antisubmarine warfare vessels, remained low, particularly in the United States where the Navy tended to determine shipbuilding priorities on the basis of its Pacific strategy. In both countries the allocation of resources to the strategic air offensive devoured material which would otherwise have been available for shipbuilding. The failure to implement effectively the first strategic priority at Casablanca had in the long run far more serious consequences on the subsequent course of the war than any differences between the two Allies regarding priorities in launching offensives against Hitler's Europe.[10]

Any fears the Americans retained that the British would find a way to back out of Overlord had been met with a categorical assertion by General Brooke that "we should definitely count on reentering the Continent in 1944 on a large scale."[11] The Americans took this pledge far more seriously than Brooke, and this was later to become a source of friction. The Allies came away from Casablanca committed to what should properly be described as a strategy of opportunism. Any real master plan for the overall strategy of the war had been seriously diverted by the hard realities of inadequate resources to mount the primary operation against Germany. There were not enough troops or landing craft in Britain to make Overlord possible, but there were enough in the Mediterranean to make the less serious undertakings against Sicily and Italy entirely feasible. These circumstances, not any high principle of strategy, dictated the campaign of 1943, which was essential since the Russians could not be left to bear the whole burden. The campaigns of 1943 were conceived to aid the Russians and not to forestall them.[12] Thus, both militarily and politically, the decisions at Casablanca were based on what could be done rather than what ought to be done. Perhaps there would be less controversy about the Casablanca strategy if this point were better understood.

The political aspects of the war were far more troublesome at Casablanca than the military ones. Notably, neither the American Secretary of State nor the British Foreign Secretary was present. Roosevelt had determined to leave Hull at home and requested Churchill not to bring Eden. Churchill reluctantly agreed with the President's request; this possibly contributed to the political problems which surrounded Casablanca. Among these was the assertion of the policy of unconditional surrender announced to the press on January 24, 1943. This was a presidential initiative that Churchill supported with varying degrees of enthusiasm throughout the remainder of the war. The declaration removed the problem that had haunted the conclusion of World War I (the question of terms, particularly the binding nature of Wilson's Fourteen Points) which created controversies to plague the interwar period. However, it raised the specter that fanatical resistance on the part of the Axis might ensue. When warned by a member of the Commons to avoid the mistakes of the First World War, Churchill replied that the Allies could be relied on to make a new set of mistakes.[13] The evidence for judging the wiseness of the policy of unconditional surrender is particularly hard to submit to evaluation.

This is much less true of the evidence available regarding Allied policies toward the French, another burning issue at Casablanca. The wisdom or unwisdom of Allied conduct toward the French was put to the hard test when troops landed in French North Africa on November 8, 1942. The pained message from Eisenhower to Roosevelt constitutes its own judgment on American attitudes prior to operation Torch; he stated that existing French sentiment in North Africa did not even remotely resemble prior calculations. Eisenhower also observed that the choice he faced was either to deal with Admiral Darlan or to face serious consequences: at least passive and perhaps active French resistance in North Africa, the loss of the hope of gaining support from French military and naval units, and opposition from the French in Tunisia to a rapid Allied advance.[14] Prior to Torch the Americans had been betting on General Giraud and various liberal elements within French North Africa in the expectation that authoritative cooperation could be gained. The British had doubted this and preferred to back General de Gaulle, but at American insistence de Gaulle had not been permitted to play any role in Torch. The upshot of this was that de Gaulle was not available, the conservative General Henri Giraud proved ineffectual, and either the authority of the highly distasteful Nazi collaborator Admiral Darlan had to be acknowledged or a high military price paid. Eisenhower, acting on military considerations, dealt with Darlan and secured the advantages of the rapid progress and control of French North Africa that followed. The politicians were left to face the outbursts in the United States and Great Britain from elements appalled at a deal with one of the most unpopular members of the Vichy government. The remaining political questions involved the sort of relationship that should exist between the Allied governments and Darlan and later, following Darlan's assassination on December 24, 1942, between General de Gaulle and General Giraud and the French authorities in North Africa or any combination thereof. This situation alone would have been sufficient to test the diplomatic capacities of the most gifted statesmen; it was further rendered difficult by the fact that the Americans approached General de Gaulle with strong antagonism, viewing him as a future French dictator. Churchill had held the day against public storms in Britain only by taking refuge in a secret session in December 1942, defending Eisenhower's arrangements on military grounds. But the whole episode served to convince the Prime Minister that General de Gaulle was the most promising Frenchman to support. The difficulty was selling the Americans on this. Worse yet, General de Gaulle was not particularly anxious to cooperate with the Prime Minister to make himself marketable to the American leadership.[15]

At Casablanca Roosevelt continued to support General Giraud as the man whom the Allies should back, while Churchill held out for General de Gaulle. Such men as Harry Hopkins and Harold Macmillan worked for a compromise between the Allies. They wanted to bring the two French generals together, hoping to fuse them into a French organization which would command the support of the entire Alliance. These efforts encountered two frustrating points of interference. The President proceeded to deal with General Giraud about the reequipment of French forces in North Africa and recognized him as having "the right and duty of preserving all French interests" until the French people were able "to designate their regular Government." This was a rude slap in the face to General de Gaulle, to the Fighting French, and incidentally to the British Prime Minister.

Indeed, the Prime Minister was receiving hard treatment from both his feuding allies. De Gaulle stubbornly refused to meet Giraud on French territory in North Africa occupied by "foreign powers"—the United States and Great Britain, his erstwhile allies. But until the Prime Minister had de Gaulle on the scene, he had little hope of being able to modify the program Roosevelt was pushing. It required Eden's most strenuous efforts in London to finally get de Gaulle to Casablanca. Once there, de Gaulle was maneuvered into a handshake with General Giraud, and the French were left to work out what arrangements they could. Since General Giraud proved to have no political aptitude, it was inevitable that de Gaulle would triumph in the French arrangements even in the face of (or perhaps because of) the opposition of Roosevelt.[16] The position of the Prime Minister resembled that of the long-suffering referee in an amateur boxing match who becomes more the target of the two adversaries than they of each other.

The Casablanca handshake was as close as the two French generals got to each other for several months. Affairs continued to simmer until August 1943 when the French proposed a new committee of national liberation, which the Americans did not want to support. Churchill prevailed upon them to issue a lukewarm recognition of the new committee, which Washington viewed as too much the tool of de Gaulle. Churchill steadfastly believed it was better to support de Gaulle and risk his political pretensions than to leave the French cause in the hands of the inept Giraud. In this judgment Churchill appears wiser than his American ally.[17] Yet Churchill also had to bear a great deal from de Gaulle. The particular point of difficulty continued to be the political status of Syria and Lebanon. Nationalist forces in these countries believed there was no reason by 1943 to postpone the transfer of political power to themselves, and in July and August elections were held in Syria and Lebanon. In each state the Nationalists won a large majority. Fearing French imperial ambitions at the conclusion of the war, the Nationalists wanted to strengthen their position by independence at once, and this brought opposition from de Gaulle. Lack of willingness to compromise on either side led to disorders. Under a British threat to intervene, the Fighting French government worked out negotiations leading to the ultimate independence of the two nations. The whole episode, however, was viewed by de Gaulle as a British attempt to replace French predominance in that part of the world. The subject would flare up between de Gaulle and Churchill again.[18]

Difficulties between Churchill and de Gaulle would reach their peak on the eve of the Normandy landing. As in the case of the Torch operation, the American government would not hear of direct participation by de Gaulle in the landing. Churchill was unhappy with this but accepted it since he was always prepared to place the interests of his alliance with the United States above his relations with the French in exile. He wanted, however, to do what he could to smooth the way for a rapid French return to their own nation. In early June Churchill and Eden took de Gaulle to see General Eisenhower to work out some sort of military arrangement whereby resistance groups in France would take their instructions from Eisenhower through an officer designated by de Gaulle. Beyond this point de Gaulle's attitude toward cooperation hardened, and in the afternoon of June 5 he proposed to withdraw French liaison officers attached to Allied forces since there was no agreement regarding their duties. The British argued with de Gaulle that his best hope for securing a satisfactory settlement in France was to cooperate with the Allied command on this point. Although angry about the failure of the Western Allies to recognize his Committee of National Liberation as possessing the powers of even a provisional government of France, in the end de Gaulle yielded to the need for military cooperation, but not before a thoroughly exasperated Churchill had staged a titanic scene on the very eve of D day.

Considering the great pressures the Prime Minister was under while troops were actually in the process of embarking and moving across the Channel, perhaps his annoyance is understandable. Filled with passion, the Prime Minister told de Gaulle that he must recognize that every time the British must choose between Europe and America, they would choose America. Eden and Bevin, both present, indicated their unhappiness with Churchill's pronouncement. Churchill's own recollection of the scene is only that the general was ungracious. The exhaustion brought on by dealing with his difficult allies surely was an extra burden for the Prime Minister at a time when those he bore were heavy enough without additional difficulties imposed by the temperaments of Roosevelt and de Gaulle.[19] But of necessity, the French situation remained secondary to the strategic situation until military potentialities brought the Allies to the doorstep of France itself. As 1943 proceeded, the strategic situation was becoming in many respects as acrimonious as the realm of French politics.

TRIDENT

IT WAS APPROPRIATE that a conference named Trident should be the one which finally grappled directly with the Allied shipping problem. By spring of 1943 the British government was convinced that something had to be done swiftly or United Kingdom imports would fall below the tolerable level. It had been calculated in 1942 that the British would need enough American help for about 7 million tons of imports beyond what the British could provide with their own shipping in 1943. Yet by February the British had been allocated shipping for only about 1.5 million tons in the first half of 1943. Accordingly, Churchill dispatched Eden to Washington to achieve some sort of a settlement. He carried with him a strong message reminding the Americans that under their terms of agreement, the British were concentrating on the construction of naval craft, particularly antisubmarine type ships, at the expense of the construction of merchant vessels. The message concluded that the British had undertaken arduous and essential operations encouraged by the belief that they could rely on American shipbuilding to get them through. But from the United States they had only promises limited by provisos. Unless they could get a satisfactory long-term settlement, British ships would have to be withdrawn from their present military service even though some operations would be crippled.[20]

The shipping problem must be resolved if offensive operations were to be prosecuted successfully by the Western Alliance. The President acknowledged American responsibility to meet the terms of the 1942 agreement and assured the British that the minimum import figures for 1943 would be met. By April of that year, therefore, one of the most intractable aspects of assuming the offensive had at least been confronted. But when Trident convened in Washington on May 12, 1943, it was faced with the problem of reconciling the minimal import demands of the United Kingdom with the operational needs of the Alliance in all theaters. It was quickly apparent that both the British and the Americans would not have enough shipping to carry out their 1943 plans.[21] The total operational shipping deficit revealed at Trident exceeded 3 million tons for the second half of 1943. The greater part by far was based on American calculations of their operational needs. The British suspected (and it seems correctly) this was largely a paper deficit that could be resolved by more careful planning and more effective central control on the prodigal habits of theater commanders. Britain for her part tightened her shipping belt, particularly in the Indian Ocean area, and turned to her American ally to do the same. For example, while the British found that their troops received between 0.6 and 0.7 measurement tons per man per month in theater operations, the American troops received an average of 1.3 measurement tons per man per month, roughly double. The Americans in turn carried out a belt-tightening of their own, and when Trident adjourned it was agreed that shipping resources would be adequate for all operations planned for 1943 and probably for 1944. This was to some extent a paper agreement and was achieved more by merely asserting that the shipping was there than by actually producing the ships. Yet the optimism of Trident appears justified, and while shipping remained a strain upon Alliance capabilities to the very end of the war, it cannot be said that it actually blocked the carrying out of any operation assigned high priority by the Combined Chiefs of Staff (CCOS). It did, however, seem to be an important factor limiting operational capabilities in the less favored theaters, particularly the Southeast Asia Command (SEAC).[22]

The status shipping commanded in the operational planning of the Western Alliance, in spite of its critical nature, is best revealed by the fact that it was not taken up first at Trident but last, after operations had been assigned priority. This seems to reveal a certain insensitivity on the part of the two great maritime nations with regard to the essential base of the flexible strategy they were attempting to employ. Operational strategy rather than its support received the greatest attention and caused the most debate.

The Americans had held a series of meetings with President Roosevelt in early May to prepare for the conference. The JCS had received a warning from Eisenhower that he feared an adequate buildup for the cross-Channel operation would not be achieved if Mediterranean operations continued at their present pace. He further indicated he believed original estimates for the strength of the cross-Channel assault had been too low and a greater buildup would have to take place in Britain. Eisenhower also informed the JCS that planning for the attack on Sicily was going forward, and there remained the question of what to do then. Four possibilities were outlined: operations could be conducted against Sardinia, Corsica, and the heel of the Italian boot; there could be an all-out commitment to invade Italy rather than simply a limited landing at the southern tip; or operations could be shifted to the eastern end of the Mediterranean with the aim of capturing Crete and the Dodecanese. This had the auxiliary objective of bringing Turkey into the war. The last alternative, which to some degree overlapped the others, was the transfer of forces out of the Mediterranean to the United Kingdom preparatory to the cross-Channel invasion. It seemed to the JCS that whatever operations were pursued in the Mediterranean, there would have to be this sort of transfer if Overlord were to go forward in mid-1944. General Marshall's views were that the decisive effort against the Continent from the United Kingdom must be made sooner or later, and he increasingly believed it should be sooner.[23]

On May 8 the JCS presented this view to President Roosevelt at the White House and secured his agreement that Overlord had operational priority. This seems to have concluded the period which began in December of 1941 when the President was reluctant to make a firm and unyielding commitment to the direct-line strategy against Germany. The President and his military advisers believed in the summer of 1943 that American military power would at last be adequate to make Overlord feasible. This ended justification for continuing a Mediterranean strategy which had always been seen from Washington as peripheral to the central task of ending the war as swiftly as possible. The JCS were determined not to be caught up again by their British allies in operations which would render Overlord impossible in 1944. This then was the basic American attitude on the eve of Trident.[24]

The British also brought to Trident a prepared strategic position. Churchill summed this up later when he said that compelling or inducing Italy to quit the war was the only objective in the Mediterranean worthy of the campaign already begun and for which available Allied forces were adequate. He mentioned the capture of Rome as an obvious step but did not specify whether it was a final one. Churchill still justified the Mediterranean program on the basis of the support it would provide for the cross-Channel operation.[25] His commitment to his Mediterranean program for 1943 had reached a degree of intensity which surely had its effect in obscuring for him the role of the Channel operation. He wrote later that he very passionately wanted to see Italy out of the way and Rome in Allied possession. He was even prepared to ask the British people to cut their rations again rather than throw away a campaign which he believed had possibilities of great success. "I was willing to take almost desperate steps in order to prevent such a calamity" as the Mediterranean campaign stalling short of Rome.[26] This is a remarkably strong statement even for Churchill. Why was his feeling so intense? He wrote in his memoirs that what he feared was not destruction but stalemate.[27]

Churchill believed the initiative in Mediterranean operations needed to be sustained to avoid this. Thus as Trident approached, each of the Allies prepared to present a strategic program which inevitably would demand priority of resources. Trident would have as its central task the assignment of a clear strategic priority, but this had already proved one of the most elusive of objectives for the Western Alliance.

On May 12 the conference opened with the heartening news from Eisenhower that all resistance in Tunisia was at an end. Churchill used this victory as a springboard from which to launch a powerful plea for further Mediterranean operations. He argued that it would reduce the central reserve of German forces and pull Italian troops out of the Balkans, forcing the Germans either to give up control of that region or invest a large number of troops there. In particular the surrender of the Italian fleet would release British naval strength for the Indian and Pacific oceans. Finally, he argued, the Western powers had the responsibility of keeping as much weight of combat off Russia as possible and some operation must be pursued between the conquest of Sicily and the launching of Overlord. This last argument was particularly influential, and Roosevelt agreed. But Roosevelt was afraid to go into the Italian peninsula, fearing that any campaign begun there would of its own momentum devour resources needed to make the cross-Channel operation possible. Churchill believed it possible to conduct the Italian campaign in such a way as to leave the Allies free to transfer resources to Britain for the 1944 operation. He again emphasized that he was committed to a full-scale invasion of the Continent from Great Britain as soon as possible. There was full agreement that the war against the U-boat and the strategic bombing of Germany were both to continue at full force. The presentation of the British case concluded with Sir Alan Brooke reaffirming for the third time in three successive conferences that it was the "firm intention" of the British COS to execute Overlord as soon as conditions made the operation feasible.[28]

The Americans feared that the developing Mediterranean campaign would block Overlord. Marshall in particular believed a firm commitment was essential on the number of divisions to be in Britain by a given date and that the beginning of the cross-Channel operation itself should be assigned a firm date. He also thought the British were too optimistic in their expectations of what could be gained in Italy and at what expense. Marshall summed up the differences of opinion when he said the Americans believed the Mediterranean operations were highly speculative as far as ending the war was concerned, but the British felt that Mediterranean operations would result in demoralization and breakup of the Axis. Subsequent events would seem to justify Marshall's opinion.[29]

With the British and Americans so far apart on strategic priorities, Trident concluded without any clear assignment but simply stated four objectives: first, secure control of the Atlantic; second, pursue the strategic air offensive against Germany; third, mount a cross-Channel operation with a target date of May 1, 1944, with twenty-nine operational divisions available in the United Kingdom; fourth, continue operations in the Mediterranean after the capture of Sicily with the aim of eliminating Italy from the war and containing the maximum number of German forces. The imprecision of these objectives is obvious. No specific Mediterranean operations were spelled out beyond the capture of Sicily, and the possibility of Mediterranean operations conflicting with the minimal requirements for Overlord was allowed to pass by default. The only stipulation was that Eisenhower must provide seven divisions from the Mediterranean for Overlord after November 1, 1943. Even this was to cause future difficulties between the Allies. Another continuing subject of friction was what constituted evidence that Overlord was actually feasible. The British in particular viewed the May 1 date as tentative, stating that until German air power in the west was more clearly reduced the operation was questionable. The Americans insisted the date be treated as firm and came away from Trident believing they had achieved this. Subsequent events were to show them mistaken. The offensive against Japan necessarily took last place, and while Admiral King always found resources to support his operations in the Pacific, the SEAC Theater was less fortunate and its future operations remained largely plans.[30]

It was necessary now to inform Russia of the Trident decisions. Because of lack of clear priority and inherent contradictions, the conclusions proved very difficult to formulate in a message to Stalin. Churchill and Roosevelt labored at a joint message but were unable to achieve a satisfactory text, and Churchill turned it over to General Marshall with whom he was flying to Algiers to see Eisenhower and the field commanders. Marshall provided a text acceptable to both parties; however, it was not acceptable to Stalin. A firm reply arrived from Moscow indicating that while Stalin approved the effort to act swiftly against Italy, he was deeply dissatisfied with the postponement of the cross-Channel operation until 1944. So vehement was Stalin's message that Churchill replied swiftly and in a similarly hard tone.

There followed throughout June an exchange of messages between Churchill and Stalin which neutral observers described as "scorching" and "superheated."[31] Apparently Churchill was particularly sensitive about the failure to open the second front in 1943 because his 1942 pledge to Stalin on that point extended beyond what the official record would suggest. Yet even allowing for this strained relationship, there was much cause for the Grand Alliance to view the future with optimism at the end of May 1943. Whatever its internal difficulties, the whole tone of the Trident conference had been one of planning future victories over Germany. It was conducted in the confident assurance that the initiative belonged to the Alliance and ultimate victory was certain.

Meanwhile, the first of the United Nations conferences, specifically dealing with food, was assembling at Hot Springs, Virginia—a hopeful sign for the postwar world. The U.S. and British governments had also announced abandonment of claims to extraterritorial rights in China, and the Soviet government had announced the dissolution of the Comintern. Finally, on the last day of May the French in Africa had managed to agree on a joint committee with de Gaulle and Giraud both represented.[32] Yet this was to be a false spring and the end of the war was still far away; many of the hopes of May 1943, both for the war and the postwar world, were to be unfulfilled.

Churchill as always did not meditate on such long-range matters; he was more concerned with achieving the next step in his strategic program —the need to nail down some sort of specific program in the Mediterranean beyond the conquest of Sicily. To do this, Churchill flew to Algiers to meet with Eisenhower. He had persuaded Roosevelt to send General Marshall along so he could not be accused of pressuring Eisenhower into a program the American general did not approve of. But Churchill already knew what he wanted. As he later told Field Marshal Smuts, nothing less than Rome could satisfy the requirements of the year's campaign.[33] From May 29 until June 3, the Prime Minister and Marshall met with Eisenhower and his subordinates in Algiers. Eisenhower expressed the opinion that if Italy were to be knocked out of the war, bold and swift steps should follow the seizure of Sicily; the wisest move would be to go directly into Italy. In response Churchill indicated again to the Americans that he had no desire to interfere with the cross-Channel attack projected for 1944 but wished only to seize maximum advantage of the opportunities offered in the Mediterranean. Marshall said only that operations in the Mediterranean should be pushed as hard as possible as long as they did not interfere with the 1944 cross-Channel operation. The Algiers conference ended the same as Trident, without a clear-cut decision on operations after Sicily. The conferees simply agreed that General Eisenhower should act as best he could. Marshall and Churchill seem to have left the conference each believing he had secured what was important to him.[34]

Events smiled on the Prime Minister; losses of equipment, particularly landing craft, proved low in the Sicily operation, so resources for amphibious operations directly against Italy seemed available. By mid-July 1943 there was plentiful evidence that Italian morale was in full collapse. These circumstances led Marshall to the conclusion that bold action directly into the Italian peninsula was justified, with Naples being a prime target for an amphibious operation. Churchill, informed of American opinion on July 16, was clearly delighted. Secretary of War Henry Stimson, a strong supporter of the Marshall strategy, was in London when Churchill received Marshall's message. Stimson immediately reported to Washington that Churchill was interpreting the American approval of a bold move against Naples as a sweeping endorsement of his entire Italian policy. The Americans had never heard Churchill's entire Italian policy, for he had never fully unfolded it to them. But Stimson realized that Rome was the very minimum of the Prime Minister's ambitions. Stimson and Marshall were assailed with the fear that Churchill would commit them to a combat of attrition in the Italian peninsula, slogging slowly up the leg under the most unfavorable geographic circumstances. Accordingly, the Americans reaffirmed to the Prime Minister that their approval of the Naples strategy meant merely securing a strategic position in southern Italy, particularly the Foggia airfields. This American warning probably made little impression on the Prime Minister.[35] By July 18 Eisenhower was prepared to assault Naples, although this involved operating at the extreme limits of his air cover. But the American general decided to run this risk, which the operation fully justified.

Eisenhower's superiors were increasingly concerned as to where the Naples operation would lead. They questioned how far to go in Italy and feared that the Prime Minister's ambitions were growing by the day. Stimson reported to Washington that Eden in particular was talking about opportunities in Greece and the Balkans; the official American military historian observed that whether the Prime Minister was actually prepared to go so far was a moot point. Washington feared that the Prime Minister shared his Foreign Secretary's interest. The Washington planners became increasingly concerned in August when Churchill again raised doubts about the dangers of the cross-Channel operation. By this time Churchill was quite convinced that the Mediterranean was a theater of opportunities where rich prizes were to be gained at low cost. In contrast, the cross-Channel operation increasingly appeared to Churchill as being very expensive. The moment of truth would come when operations in the Mediterranean reached a point of diminishing returns and the question must be reiterated, Should not the strategic priority remain with Overlord once German resistance in the Mediterranean hardened?[36] The rapid pace of events and the rising uncertainties about priorities made another Allied conference essential.

QUADRANT

Quadrant assembled at Quebec in mid-August 1943. As it convened, the strategic air offensive was continuing across Europe and the battle in the Atlantic was improving. Priorities must be sorted out for offensive land operations. On the eve of Quadrant Churchill was thinking boldly. He expressed his Mediterranean ambitions in terms of taking Rome and marching as far north as possible in Italy. In addition he told Smuts that the Balkan partisans must be supported by the Allies or, if necessary, by the British alone.[37] This last ambition was sweeping indeed and in any event impossible. Churchill attacked the Overlord proposal with a strong statement of the risks involved. He painted a picture of the appalling casualties that might be suffered and stressed the communication advantages the Germans possessed in northwest Europe. But even as he argued, the Allies were developing the potential to overcome these obstacles. The growth of Allied air power rendered it possible to disrupt the German lines of communication, and the improvement in the battle for the Atlantic promised a great easing of the shipping problem.

Sir Alan Brooke repeated his regular promise that the British were in complete agreement with the JCS that Overlord should be the major Allied offensive for 1944. But he stated his conditions: German fighter strength in the west must be reduced, the abilities of the Germans to reinforce their garrison in the west must be limited, and problems of beach maintenance must be resolved. While these conditions were being met, Brooke urged a continued vigorous offensive in the Mediterranean. In particular, the British questioned the use of the seven divisions which it had been agreed would be withdrawn from the Mediterranean to support Overlord; they wanted these divisions to remain in the Mediterranean. Not surprisingly, the Americans objected, insisting that the overriding priority of Overlord could be assured only if the Allies were willing to keep their commitments. This meant seven divisions must go to the United Kingdom at the beginning of November.

Churchill affirmed on August 19 that he strongly favored Overlord as the main 1944 operation. He also suggested that the Allies keep as a second string to their bow another operation, the invasion of Norway, long a favorite idea of his. These statements surely weakened the British front at Quadrant and undercut Brooke's arguments. If Churchill agreed to assign priority to Overlord in 1944, it was hard for his CIGS to argue for keeping the seven divisions in the Mediterranean. Churchill's Norwegian proposal was one certain to send shivers down Brooke's spine. It is hard to say why the Prime Minister made such statements; they surely strengthened the American hand in the strategic debate.[38]

The Americans agreed with the British that Eisenhower should launch two amphibious assaults against Italy early in September—one across the narrow Straits of Messina and the other, a bolder operation, into Salerno Bay near Naples. The Prime Minister suggested that the farthest line to be occupied in Italy, if possible, was from Ancona to Pisa. This seemed to be acceptable to everyone present, and the discussion moved on to further diversions to distract German troops from Overlord. Among these was a landing in southern France to be made up mostly of French divisions. Churchill raised some doubts as to whether the French would be ready for such an undertaking. The seven divisions were to go back to Overlord unless held in the Mediterranean by a later decision of the CCOS. This protected Overlord's priority in the American view.[39]

But the tide of events was now running swiftly, and on the evening of September 8 the Italian government's agreement to an armistice was announced. Italian resistance ended as the first landing ships were discharging men on the beaches around Salerno. Churchill seized the moment. He was in Washington following Quadrant and on September 9 presented his ideas for future action to the President and the CCOS. His proposals called for a rush north from Naples until the main German defense line was encountered, which he believed would be well north of Rome. He called for assistance to Balkan partisans and suggested this might involve Allied troops. He hoped there could be rapid exploitation of developments in Greece and Yugoslavia and perhaps beyond. The island of Rhodes was cited as a desirable objective. Churchill concluded that he believed a firm line in the north of Italy could be developed by the end of 1943 and the prime operation of 1944 would remain the cross-Channel one. He wanted it understood that "there can be no question about whittling down 'Overlord'" and reaffirmed the propriety of the decision to stage the seven divisions out of the Mediterranean beginning in November.[40]

The Americans agreed to exploit the Italian situation as far as circumstances would permit but viewed the Prime Minister's interest in the Balkans with less enthusiasm. They believed any operations against Rhodes or other objectives in the Aegean would have to be carried out with the resources available in that region; there were none to spare from other theaters. The Americans remained uneasy about the Prime Minister, for while he talked about thrusting forward either to the left or to the right, it seemed that his eye always drifted to the right where he saw glittering prizes in the eastern Mediterranean; when he turned to the left, in Admiral King's words, he saw in the west only Sardinia and Corsica.[41] In his memoirs Churchill took pains to point out that he did not at that time want to abandon Overlord or deprive it of vital forces and that he did not then contemplate a campaign by armies operating in the Balkan peninsula. "These are legends. Never had such a wish entered my mind."[42] This is consistent with his statements at Quadrant, informing Marshall with respect to Overlord that "we should use every opportunity to further that operation."[43] But while Churchill acknowledged the primacy of Overlord repeatedly, all his energies flowed into the Mediterranean. At the time of Quadrant the American military staffs believed that this was deliberate on Churchill's part; that he was looking toward the end of the war, and it appeared that Russia's postwar position in Europe would be a dominant one which the Prime Minister hoped to balance to some extent by developing a powerful British position in the Mediterranean.[44] If Churchill entertained such thoughts at the time, he did not make them explicit.

The main impression of Churchill's conduct in Quebec and, subsequently, in Washington is that his approach to strategy was largely opportunistic; he was bent on grabbing prizes cheaply and quickly as Italy fell and the Axis position in the Mediterranean collapsed. How much further he was looking belongs to the realm of speculation. Given the Prime Minister's capacity for carrying a wide range of military plans and political goals in his mind—operating more or less simultaneously and sometimes in collision—speculation on Churchill's thoughts seems to be risky.

The strategic situation was shifting rapidly in late summer and early autumn of 1943. The improved position in the Atlantic and the developing air strength of the Alliance made major operations against Hitler's continental position increasingly feasible. A thrust into southern France had appeared among strategic plans for the first time, while the demands of the European area again reduced SEAC to the position of strategic stepdaughter.[45] The degree to which these ambitions could be achieved now depended on the course of events in the field and the rapidity with which the Allies could seize the opportunities offered them by the Italian collapse.

MEDITERRANEAN OPERATIONS

On July 10, 1943, the invasion of Sicily began, and operations went forward rapidly to capture the entire island. These were complete by August 16, and although the capture of the island with its difficult terrain was relatively rapid, the Germans managed to pull their most important units back into Italy before the island fell. The fall of Sicily was too much for the demoralized Italian government, and Mussolini's power in Italy ended. A new government was formed around Marshal Badoglio, who entered into secret negotiations with the Allies for an armistice. This was arranged to coincide with Allied landings on the Italian peninsula. Confused negotiations followed which ended with the Allied landing at Salerno at dawn on September 9 and the announcement of the Italian armistice as they approached the shore. British forces had already crossed the Straits of Messina and had carried out a particularly bold landing at Taranto some days earlier.

The prolonged negotiations, however, had given the suspicious Germans ample warning that they could no longer rely on the Italians; so when the armistice was announced, German troops were already occupying important positions throughout the peninsula, particularly in and around Rome, which made a proposed airborne assault on the Roman airfields impossible. Although the Germans held Rome, the Allied landing at Salerno proved successful in the face of some stubborn German resistance. By October 1 the Allies occupied Naples and had taken the important Foggia airfields.[46] If they had not done as well from the collapse of Italy as Churchill had hoped, they had nonetheless done well indeed. The Allies had a firm position in southern Italy and soon forced the Germans back to a defensive line anchored in the west by the Garigliano River and in the east by the Sangro River. To hold their position in Italy, the Germans had to commit a large reinforcement to that area. And since the armistice had terminated Italian usefulness in holding down the Balkans, the Germans had to inject large forces into this region too. The Italian armistice and Allied landings accomplished what had been the strategic purpose of the Mediterranean campaign: to pin down and extend Hitler's army reserve to such an extent that the

Normandy landing had a high probability of success. The strategy was a complete success, and the Allies picked up the additional prizes of Sardinia and Corsica with relatively slight effort.

The Mediterranean situation, however, created its own anxiety. The German buildup in Italy reached substantial proportions, so there was some fear that the Allied forces in the peninsula were inadequate. The question was, Inadequate to accomplish what? If they were only to pin down German forces, this could reasonably be accomplished. If more was to be done at this point, a new strategic look would have to be taken by someone in authority.[47] That person was of course the Prime Minister. On September 25 he urged Eisenhower to act in several directions, suggesting that Allied resources in the Mediterranean be allotted on the basis of 80 percent to Italy, 10 percent to deal with Corsica and the Adriatic, and the remaining 10 percent to be concentrated on capturing the island of Rhodes in the eastern Mediterranean.[48] This was in keeping with his statement to the House of Commons four days earlier that the best method of acquiring flexibility was to have plans for all contingencies, all worked out in detail. Then it would be easy to switch from one to the other as advantage offered.[49] But now Churchill began to feel the pull of Overlord. The swift German reaction in Italy and the Balkans quickly made it clear that Hitler was prepared to contest these areas with great vigor. Although the strategic objective of the Mediterranean Theater had been fully met, Churchill wanted to respond equally to Hitler's resistance. From this point on, it may be said that the Mediterranean Theater acquired a strategic life of its own in the mind of the Prime Minister. He railed against the Overlord priority, believing that it would continue to hamper and enfeeble the Mediterranean campaign, that affairs would deteriorate in the Balkans, and that the Aegean would remain firmly in German hands. All this had to be accepted for the sake of an operation based on hypotheses that he thought would not be realized by the date set, and certainly not if the Mediterranean pressure was relaxed.[50] To the Prime Minister the opportunities of the Mediterranean continued to glitter more than the distant plan for Overlord in which he appears to have had limited faith, in spite of his assurances to the Americans at Quadrant.

The Prime Minister was particularly reluctant to recognize that the strength of the German response in the Mediterranean Theater had brought to a close the period of quick and cheap victories. Any further gains in that theater would be expensive and would require substantial effort. They must be evaluated in terms of their consequences and in answer to the question of whether an increased effort in that theater could produce results comparable to what might be achieved in northern Europe by conducting Overlord. The Prime Minister believed there was more to be gained in the south than in the west and feared that serious mistakes in the campaign of 1944 might give Hitler the chance to stage a comeback. Thus in his memorandum of October 23, 1943, Churchill revealed his fears of what might happen on the great west European plain where the Germans had demonstrated their military proficiency so convincingly in spring and summer of 1940. The strategic position in the Mediterranean had suddenly become much less opportune, for geography prodigiously favored the defense in that region. Yet Churchill was prepared to fight on there and hoped once again to be able to retain the seven divisions earmarked for withdrawal to Britain.

He also was unwilling to cease looking for quick victories, and his eyes fell on the Balkans. He wrote Roosevelt on October 7 that he believed the Italian and Balkan peninsulas were militarily and politically one theater and it might not be possible to conduct a successful Italian campaign ignoring what happened in the Aegean.[51] The Prime Minister perhaps was seeking not just cheap victories in the Mediterranean but also particularly British ones. In his memoirs he wrote, "We had a preponderance of troops over the Americans in the Mediterranean. There were two or three times more British troops than American there. That was why I was anxious that the armies in the Mediterranean should not be hamstrung if it could be avoided."[52] This was not the best principle on which to attempt to coordinate an Allied strategy. Some Americans had harbored suspicions of this attitude in Churchill for some time. Churchill's best friends in the United States, particularly Harry Hopkins, did not exercise the influence they once had.[53] There was a tendency in the United States to place rather the worst construction on Churchill's proposals. Success in the Mediterranean thus brought a new period of strain to the Western Alliance.

The Americans were so concerned that they seriously considered opposing the appointment of a British commander in the Mediterranean Theater when Eisenhower transferred to Britain to prepare for Overlord —not because of any lack of respect for the competence of the British commanders but for fear of the influence the Prime Minister could exercise upon these men.[54] While the Americans put aside this unhappy consideration, their misgivings concerning the Prime Minister's Mediterranean ambitions remained and indeed reached peak intensity as he was pushing forward most boldly. He had told General Wilson, the Middle East commander, "This is the time to play high. Improvise and dare." In particular, this meant a landing on Rhodes by a small British force in the hope that the Italians there would cooperate in holding it against the Germans.[55] Such hopes were swiftly dashed. The Italians were either unfit or unwilling to fight the Germans, who for their part reacted violently. The British position on Rhodes and some adjacent islands was dangerously overextended and vulnerable to German air attack. Churchill quickly found himself in such a position that the only way out was to pull in greater resources than the Middle East had available. This meant turning to the Americans. For the men in Washington the Rhodes episode was the last straw as far as the Prime Minister's all-embracing Mediterranean activities were concerned, and they steadfastly refused to divert forces committed to other areas. The result was the loss of the British position there, a particularly stinging humiliation to the Prime Minister at a time when the Allies were securing victories elsewhere. The Hopkins papers suggest that the communications between Washington and Churchill during this period were particularly vehement.[56]

Brooke was just as worried about the Prime Minister at this point as the Americans were. His diary reveals:

> I can now control him no more. He has worked himself into a frenzy of excitement about the Rhodes attack, has magnified its importance so that he can no longer see anything else and has set his heart on capturing this one island even at the expense of endangering his relations with the President and the Americans and the future of the Italian campaign. He refused to listen to any arguments or to see any dangers.[57]

The American resistance to the diversion of forces to Rhodes had a perfectly sound basis. As Brooke noted, the alternative was supporting the Italian campaign, since this was the only area close enough from which forces could be quickly drawn. The Americans, like Brooke, believed that the Italian campaign was more important. The forces were needed on the peninsula if an operation was to be carried out from the sea behind the line the Germans had established across Italy, thus hopefully turning the entire German position and opening the road to Rome.[58] The benefits that would flow from the seizure of the Aegean Islands seemed less, and British and American strategists alike viewed the whole operation with some suspicion. Captain Roskill has written of the Rhodes operation, "It is certainly the case that every diversionary or peripheral undertaking always absorbs more resources than are at first envisaged; and the Aegean venture proved no exception in that respect."[59] The Rhodes affair left its impact on the Alliance at the very time when it was necessary once again to review strategic goals and political problems.

At this point of maximum strain upon the Western Alliance, Italian politics flared up to further complicate affairs. The government of Marshal Badoglio had just barely made its escape from Rome as the Germans arrived and took refuge in southern Italy behind the Allied lines. This government clearly retained something of a Fascist quality and thus did not find particularly great favor in the United States, which tended to be sensitive on the subject of political democracy. The Prime Minister, on the other hand, told the President he was prepared to deal with any Italian authority that could deliver the goods. Churchill was not in the least afraid of seeming to recognize the House of Savoy or Badoglio, provided they could make the Italians do what the Allies wished. Instead, the Prime Minister feared the onset of chaos, bolshevism, or civil war.[60] These concerns were more important to him than the democratic character of the government. This was something that could be determined in a country which had passed two decades under Fascist rule only by wide popular elections, and those could not occur until all Italy had been liberated. He therefore was prepared to make the best of the situation.

Yet in terms of Italian treatment on the whole, the British were inclined more toward severity in the final terms than the Americans. The British had a much longer memory of difficulties with the Italians and had not forgotten Mussolini's stab in the back in the summer of 1940. American contact with Italian Fascism was of much briefer, almost passing, duration, and American public opinion tended to view the Italian change of side as sufficient penitence for their earlier alliance in the Axis. The Americans seemed prepared not even to hold the Italians to all the armistice terms, much less the full conditions implied in the concept of unconditional surrender. Not until mid-October was a joint statement worked out announcing Italian entry into the war against Germany in a status of "co-belligerency." This was taken to mean that the Allies were not about to embrace as one of their own a country so recently an enemy, but that Italy would be permitted to work her way toward a full democratic society.[61]

The Italian issue next flared around the subject of broadening the Badoglio government. By March 1944 a variety of politicians of the pre-Fascist period had formed a six-party program and had pressed themselves upon the government into which they were eventually incorporated in the face of some opposition from Churchill, who was doubtful about just how democratic these men were.[62] Churchill's reluctance to admit the six-party group was viewed by the Americans as another sign of his inclination to support monarchies. The Prime Minister had not been helped by an unfortunate Italian broadcast late in 1943, which had described the king of Italy as also king of Albania and emperor of Ethiopia. The slip had incurred Churchill's wrath toward his representative in the Mediterranean, Harold Macmillan, who was told that "any repetition of follies like that will bring our whole policy into discredit here. How would the King like to be sent back to his Empire in Ethiopia to be crowned?"[63] Not surprisingly, Macmillan protested the note, pointing out that in the confusion of reorganizing the government, an old broadcast form had obviously been used in some radio station; he observed that in spite of all difficulties he tried to do his best.

American-British difficulties with regard to Italy resolved themselves in the spring of 1944. Churchill was able to report to the House of Commons in May that the government had been successfully broadened in its character and that the king had indicated he would retire into private life upon the capture of Rome, then only days away. Churchill reaffirmed his unity with the United States to see a democratic government established in Italy, either monarchial or republican as the Italians themselves decided.[64] This issue then passed from the agenda of Allied dispute.

CHAPTER 7

CAIRO AND TEHERAN

IN LATE 1943 strategic disputes were even more pressing than political ones, and against this tense background Churchill and Roosevelt prepared to undertake two of the more important conferences of the war. The Western Allies would met in Cairo to deal with their own problems and those of the Asian area and subsequently go on to Teheran where they would meet with Stalin and coordinate policy. These conferences fell at such a time that the decisions made would have a prime effect on the major direction of Allied strategy for the remainder of the war.

The Western Allies arrived in Cairo in late November 1943. President Roosevelt led into the discussions by indicating the growing predominance of American military strength in theaters of operations. The presentation of these figures was a clear hint to the Prime Minister that the Americans were going to become more insistent on stressing the place of their strategy in the Alliance than heretofore. Thoroughly aroused by what they viewed as the Prime Minister's reckless behavior in the Mediterranean, the Americans were prepared for plain talk and hard decisions.[65]

Churchill was unhappy also, particularly concerning the presence of the Chinese leader, Chiang Kai-shek, at Cairo. The Prime Minister did not believe the contribution of the Chinese to the war was such that effective planning could be done with them, and he believed that their presence would interfere with the two Western Allies settling their own outstanding differences.[66] Thus he did his best to ignore the Chinese and to fight out the issue of relative priorities for the Mediterranean and Overlord with his American ally. In particular, the Prime Minister hoped to hold sufficient forces and landing craft in the Mediterranean to allow a flanking movement around the German defense line in Italy. He continued to acknowledge Overlord's primacy but argued that some flexibility should be allowed in holding back landing craft and troops. He particularly advocated an amphibious operation which would enable Rome to be seized in January and still hoped for a second operation against Rhodes in February.[67]

These ambitions of Churchill ran directly counter to Chinese hopes for extended operations in the SEAC Theater. Roosevelt had promised Chiang that there would be an amphibious operation across the Bay of Bengal in the spring of 1944.[68] Sir Alan Brooke pointed out that the Allies would not have enough landing craft to carry out the Bay of Bengal operation and the amphibious operations against Rome and Rhodes as well as Overlord on its scheduled date. Something would have to give somewhere. The Americans insisted on Overlord and wanted to support their Chinese ally, but they were also sympathetic to the Rome operation, although not to Rhodes. The Prime Miniser acknowledged the primacy of Overlord, wanted both the Rome and Rhodes operations, and was opposed to the Bay of Bengal operation.

There the strategic situation rested as the Western Allies left Cairo for Teheran and the crucial conference of the war.[69] For the first time the influence of the third member of the Grand Alliance would be thrown directly into the strategic debate.

When the three Alliance partners met at Teheran, Churchill seized the initiative to present a full statement of his view of the choices available. He urged that they carry the campaign in Italy through the capture of Rome and beyond to a line extending roughly through the cities of Pisa and Rimini. He again sought an effort to persuade Turkey to enter the war. With this he associated renewed efforts to gain the islands of the Aegean, which he believed would open the straits of the Dardanelles—the best supply route into Russia. He also urged support of Balkan partisans. Then, after a line was stabilized in northern Italy, he was prepared to entertain either a landing in southern France or a thrust at the top of the Adriatic and through the Ljubljana gap into Austria and Hungary.[70]

Churchill's position evidently became the basis for the Teheran strategic discussions; Roosevelt and Stalin merely offered comments. The President suggested that operations in Italy might be shut down before reaching Rome and that the southern France landings should be coordinated with Overlord. Or, conversely, he was willing to entertain a thrust through the top of the Adriatic. Stalin did not encourage the opening of the Dardanelles and believed there was no hope of dragging Turkey into the war. As the discussions continued, Roosevelt turned away from the Adriatic and Stalin began to press for the attack on southern France, an interest on his part which had not been anticipated by the Western planners. The strategic discussions then began to run more swiftly in a western channel, with the Americans and the Russians joining together in their growing enthusiasm for Overlord on May 1 supplemented by a landing in southern France, perhaps somewhat prior to the Overlord landing itself. This enthusiasm on the part of his two huge allies swept away Churchill's Mediterranean position. Any last reservations Churchill may have entertained about the wisdom of Overlord were confronted by Stalin, who challenged him directly, Did the British Prime Minister really believe in Overlord? Churchill responded by pledging that Britain would hurl every ounce of her strength across the Channel at the Germans.[71]

Brooke was receiving a similar challenge from Marshal Voroshilov, who asked the CIGS point-blank if he attached the same importance to Overlord as General Marshall did. Brooke replied that he did but with qualifications of the circumstances necessary for the operation's success. Voroshilov replied that Stalin and the entire Russian general staff attached the greatest importance to Overlord and that any other operation was viewed by the Russians as only auxiliary. Voroshilov said that Stalin did not insist on the operation against southern France but he did insist that Overlord take place in the manner and on the date already set.[72] The simultaneous direct Soviet challenges to the Prime Minister and the

CIGS convey the impression that this was premeditated and that there was a determination to secure an inflexible pledge from the British on support of Overlord.

Certainly Teheran was decisive in according at long last unquestioned priority to Overlord in the strategic planning of the Grand Alliance. This did not, however, mean the abandonment of all Mediterranean operations. The planners at Teheran agreed that the advance in Italy should be continued to the Pisa-Rimini line which Churchill advocated and that assault shipping would be retained in the Mediterranean as late as January 15, 1944, to make this advance possible. The Teheran decisions also included an operation against southern France on as large a scale as landing craft would permit. For planning purposes it was assigned the same date as Overlord—May 1. Efforts to drag Turkey into the war were largely abandoned as were operations in the Aegean. The combined air effort against Germany was to be prosecuted with continuing vigor. The Teheran conclusions also reorganized the command in the Mediterranean, bringing the Middle East area directly under the Mediterranean Theater commander—a British officer. The northern European command which would be responsible for Overlord was to be assigned to an American. Each of these commanders would be responsible to the CCOS on the pattern which had been used since Arcadia.[73]

Churchill has been accused of dragging his feet on Overlord at Teheran, but his affirmation to Stalin was consistent with his repeated declarations from the time of his meeting with Marshall in April 1942. While he may have come to fear its cost, Churchill had never denied its primacy. His introduction of the theme of an assault at the head of the Adriatic and thence north into Austria has also been described as a politically motivated proposal to block Russian movement into that area. If Churchill had such political thoughts, he does not seem to have made them explicit to any Westerner who has recorded them. The emphasis at Teheran seems to have been a genuine effort on the part of the Allies to cooperate in the swift conclusion of the war against Hitler.[74]

Churchill had done rather well in the Teheran negotiations. He had achieved a command structure for the Western Alliance which the British preferred—separate theaters for the Mediterranean and northern Europe rather than one master theater with a sort of super theater commander (an American) over both. Ultimately chosen to command in northern Europe was General Eisenhower, a man with whom the British had considerable experience and who had established a reputation for fairness in dealing with subordinates of all nationalities.[75] In addition, at Teheran and in the rump session at Cairo, the British secured their position by convincing Roosevelt to tell his Chinese ally that the proposed 1944 offensive in the Bay of Bengal was off—the assault shipping for that operation would be needed in the European Theater. This would allow a new thrust against the Italian peninsula where Churchill was particularly anxious to push the offensive.[76] The Teheran decisions had ratified what Churchill had been professing for a year and a half with regard to Overlord.

Stalin also had cause for satisfaction after Teheran. He had secured, he believed, a firm Western commitment finally to launch an offensive against northern France, which he thought was the surest relief to his front.[77] The Americans also were pleased. As they always wished, Overlord had a primacy in Allied strategic planning and a firm date. Thus their primary goal in the west had been achieved. Stalin had suggested strongly that Russian aid against Japan would be forthcoming once Hitler was defeated, and this promised substantial relief to the Americans in the east where they were finding Japanese resistance particularly tenacious. It is not surprising then that the conference at Teheran saw a high tide of Alliance good feeling.

Yet there were a few themes which contained the possibilities of some disharmony. Roosevelt's brief reference to an interest in an operation at the head of the Adriatic had not escaped either Churchill's attention or that of the President's military advisers, who were horrified by the suggestion. Churchill would take it up later to the considerable dismay of the Americans.[78] But Churchill had some cause for unhappiness too, for in the discussions at Teheran some reference had been made to the postwar world, in the course of which Roosevelt had indicated that American armed forces would not remain long in Europe after the war. With his historical sense of balance-of-power politics, Churchill would now have to consider a European continent which might well be dominated by the presence of the Russian army. Churchill would subsequently endeavor to work out political agreements with the Russians; there was as yet no belief that this could not be achieved.[79] American-British relations at Teheran did not show the same warmth as they had earlier in the war. Roosevelt showed some signs of tiring during the Prime Minister's often lengthy presentations. Thus, even at the pinnacle of harmony among the Grand Alliance partners, there were observable elements of future discord.

ANZIO TO NORMANDY

As Churchill departed from Teheran, he appears to have been determined to exploit the decisions on the Mediterranean to the utmost. In late December 1943 he met with the Mediterranean commanders to press for a seaborne assault which would break the deadlock in Italy. The chosen target was the coastal town of Anzio, which lay along the road to Rome behind the German front. In order to have this, Churchill was prepared to abandon further efforts against Rhodes. But even the Anzio operation was threatened with failure by the shortage of LSTs (landing ship, tank) which were essential to the operation and in critically short supply. Churchill believed there must be a delay in the withdrawal of some of these vessels from the Mediterranean if the Anzio operation were to be accomplished, and this in turn meant another approach to the Americans. This was successful and indicates that the Americans were prepared to cooperate with the progress of Mediterranean operations so long as those operations did not interfere with Overlord's priority. On December 28 Roosevelt wired Churchill that 56 LSTs could be held in the Mediterranean until the Anzio operation was carried out.[80]

On January 20, 1944, the amphibious landing at Anzio was mounted on a two-division lift. Unfortunately, the Germans were able to seal in the beachhead so that the strategic goal of the Anzio operation—breaking the Italian deadlock—was defeated. Churchill summed up the situation when he ruefully noted, "I had hoped that we were hurling a wildcat on the shore, but all we got was a stranded whale." Once more the Prime Minister's ambitions to restore mobility to the Italian campaign were frustrated; before that was achieved in late May 1944, the Anzio beachhead had consumed nearly six Allied divisions. The war in Italy remained primarily a war of attrition, not surprising in a land so geographically well suited to defense.[81]

Even as the Anzio operation went forward, attention was turning more and more to the preparation for Overlord. In the interval between Marshall's proposals in April 1942 and the strategic plan which was developing in the spring of 1944 the Western Allies had learned a great deal about amphibious operations and had gained a large body of experience. There had also been a vast development in Western air power and a consequent erosion in German air strength which would contribute vitally to establishing the conditions necessary for a successful landing in western France. The shifting balance of air power would allow the Allies to impede the German rate of reinforcement so that the beachhead could be protected in its early critical days. American troops, who had seen no combat in the west by mid-1942, now had experience, as did both Allies in coordinating their command structure. That unified command had at its head in General Eisenhower the most successful practitioner of cooperation during the war. Finally, it had been possible to thoroughly appraise enemy capabilities, and a large underground movement had developed in France, supplementing Allied intelligence and impeding German response to an Allied invasion.[82] In the spring of 1944 then, the Western Allies possessed the strategic situation and the tactical tools to bring off the greatest of World War II operations.

Because of the obvious importance air power would have in making the landing secure, the British officer chosen as deputy supreme commander was Sir Arthur Tedder, who had demonstrated convincingly in the Mediterranean Theater his ability to cooperate with army forces. Churchill had proposed Tedder, and subsequent events would justify Churchill's decision as one of his best. Tedder was perhaps the only Allied air officer other than the Chief of the Air Staff who would be able to impose his will on the British and American strategic bombing commanders to secure the coordinated air offensive essential for the success of

Overlord. Although the strategic air commanders objected strenuously at having to shift so much attention to attacking communications, the importance of this decision to Overlord's ultimate success was substantial.[83]

Perhaps less happy was the choice of Sir Bernard Law Montgomery as Allied field commander for the early stages of Overlord. The selection of Montgomery was largely the result of the effort of Sir Alan Brooke, who pushed the claims of his protégé against the inclination of both the Prime Minister and Eisenhower for Sir Harold Alexander. Eisenhower found Alexander easier to deal with. Montgomery possessed a more difficult personality for the Americans to work with. On the other hand, his prestige as a fighting commander was very great, and he had a legitimate claim to the position. An excellent trainer of men, Montgomery was certainly effective in preparing the Allied landing forces to face the assault with confidence and enthusiasm.[84] Whether inter-Allied difficulties which developed during the European campaign might have been avoided with the more diplomatic Alexander in Montgomery's place necessarily remains a speculation.

Both Eisenhower and Montgomery, immediately upon reviewing the plans for Overlord, insisted that the size of the initial landings be significantly expanded. This of course meant that more assault shipping must be found. This required bringing great pressure to bear on Admiral King to part with more landing craft, which had a way of vanishing into the vast reaches of the Pacific. King finally promised a full month's American production of landing craft for Overlord. Further, the operation in southern France would have to be at least postponed, and the British were beginning to think that abandonment would be best. Finally, the date of Overlord would have to be postponed one month; the very end of May or the first few days of June now became the accepted target date. These adjustments secured a sufficient sea lift to make the initial landings on a five-division front with three airborne divisions being employed simultaneously.[85] The immense naval preparations under the skilled direction of Sir Bertram Ramsay were coordinated with that gifted officer's usual capacity.

As the spring days passed, the Prime Minister's enthusiasm for the operation mounted until, as May ended, it was necessary for the King himself to intervene to restrain the Prime Minister from departing with the assault troops for the beaches of Normandy. Only one man remained torn with "doubts and misgivings." This was Brooke, who confided to his diary on May 27, "I never want again to go through a time like the present one. The cross-Channel operation is just eating into my heart. I wish to God we could start and have done with it."[86]

In the end, the operation was remarkably successful. In the early hours of June 6, 1944, the assault began. Although there were some difficulties on one American beach and the air drops were not entirely successful, a secure landing was achieved and the buildup of Allied forces in Normandy went forward rapidly.[87] The last chapter of the European war had opened, and it was appropriate that the Allied field commander directing the landing forces at Normandy was a British soldier who had withdrawn through the port of Dunkirk in the summer of 1940.

ALLIANCE STRATEGIST

THE PERIOD BETWEEN the conference at Casablanca and the successful landings in Normandy in June 1944 saw the Prime Minister engaged in a series of strategic proposals and plans which created controversy at the time and some criticism since the war. In particular, the Prime Minister's support for Overlord has been challenged, but he always saw it as the central operation of the Western Alliance. From the fall of 1942, he had constantly struggled for a continuing buildup of American forces in Britain toward the ultimate goal of reentry to the Continent; however some American officers believed this was only to stop the American troops from going to the Pacific.[88] But this suspicion hardly accords with Churchill's firm message to Field Marshal Smuts on September 11, 1943, in which Churchill had no reason to disguise his true feelings. He told Smuts that there could be no question of breaking arrangements made with the United States for Overlord and that British loyalty to the operation was the keystone of Anglo-American cooperation. "Personally I think enough forces exist for both hands to be played, and I believe this to be the right strategy."[89]

This was the true basis of the Prime Minister's strategic thinking in the period between Casablanca and the Normandy landings, with emphasis on flexibility and opportunism. He never intended to betray his Western ally whom he regarded so warmly. When Rommel had mauled inexperienced Americans at Kasserine Pass, Churchill observed that the troops were not yet seasoned but possessed the quality to mature rapidly. He was sorry that the incident had occurred under a British field commander (although General Eisenhower had the ultimate command) and had sent General Alexander a firm letter sharply criticizing the exposed position of the American troops.[90] Churchill was determined to work with his American ally with scrupulous fairness and consideration. He specifically told the House of Commons on September 21, 1943, that he regarded the African operation not as a substitute for a direct attack across the Channel but rather as an essential preliminary to Overlord.[91] In this spirit he was willing to entertain the proposal for a landing in southern France, which emerged rather late in the strategic planning of the Alliance.[92]

The growth of an increasing sentiment (perhaps deeper than he wished to admit) that the Overlord operation was fraught with grave risks became a problem for Churchill by mid-1943. While he never disowned Overlord, he continually sought to postpone it until all the circumstances would be right. This was almost a return to British strategic thinking before December 1941, when a reentry to the Continent was seen as a swift concluding chapter to a struggle in which German powers of resistance would be worn to the point of complete collapse. The degree to which this attitude prevailed is revealed in a long minute the Prime Minister drafted upon the fall of Mussolini in mid-1943, in which he stated that everything must be concentrated on the destruction of Hitler's Germany. Yet almost astonishingly, after reaffirming this central goal, Churchill continued without including any direct action against Germany itself except from the air. In a document of twelve paragraphs (repeated in full in his memoirs) nowhere does Churchill find it desirable to mention a direct assault against the central German position![93] This attitude seems to arise from a variety of reasons. On July 19, 1943, Churchill had told the COS he did not believe sufficient divisions were yet built up for Overlord in view of the fighting efficiency of the German army and the large forces they could bring to bear against the landings.[94] Added to this fear was the constant fascination the eastern Mediterranean had on Churchill. His interest at Teheran in opening the Dardanelles reveals he still dreamed of concluding that old operation he had conceived and launched in 1915.[95] He could not resist what appeared to be cheap prizes in the Mediterranean, even after it became clear that these could no longer be secured without substantial effort.[96]

Some observers have discerned in the Prime Minister's interest in the Mediterranean operations at the expense of Overlord a certain spirit of "sheer chauvinism."[97] Such a theme would seem to emerge hard on the heels of an absolute peak in Churchill's enthusiasm for close Anglo-American association. Churchill obviously took a deep interest in the close ties which existed between the two countries. On June 8, 1943, he told the House of Commons—with considerable pride—that when he had addressed the American Congress, he had not hesitated to touch upon controversial subjects or matters of domestic debate.[98] This is a remarkable statement in view of the rule of self-discipline the British government so carefully observed of avoiding commentary on American domestic matters. The theme of Anglo-American closeness was one which Churchill played on again when he spoke at the Guildhall on June 30, 1943. He saw there a basic harmony in the moral and political conceptions of the English-speaking peoples.[99]

On September 6, 1943, Harvard University conferred an honorary degree upon Churchill, and he in turn delivered a speech of great importance at that time. He told the assembly that in his opinion it would be most unwise for the two governments to dismantle their close association the moment the war was ended. He spoke of the efforts to make the League of Nations work and of the causes of its failure, pointing out that we had learned from hard experience that a stronger effort was required to secure world peace. Churchill said he believed no such effort could be successful without the united effort of the British and American people. But the most striking part of his address came when he said, "This gift of a common tongue is a priceless inheritance, and it may well some day become the foundation of a common citizenship. I like to think of British and Americans moving about freely over each other's wide etstates with hardly a sense of being foreigners to one another."[100] Given the significance of the occasion, this could hardly be simply a passing reference; Robert Sherwood believed Churchill had cleared the statement with President Roosevelt before he made it.[101] It is surely also of retrospective significance that when Churchill set down his account of the Harvard speech in his memoirs, he excluded his reference to the idea of common citizenship.

But that ebb in Churchill's ideals was to come later, for the Harvard speech was followed in five days by yet another flood tide which bore his hopes to a new high. The President had gone to Hyde Park to rest, while Churchill had returned to Washington. Roosevelt had told the Prime Minister to use the White House not only as a residence but for any business Churchill wished to transact. On September 11, Churchill convened not only his British military aides but also the entire American JCS and some of Roosevelt's diplomatic advisers. Churchill wrote that it was a unique historical event for him to preside over a conference of the CCOS and of American and British authorities in the White House.[102] Accordingly, in September 1943, the Prime Minister's vision of an Anglo-American society, perhaps even an Anglo-American nation, had reached its very pinnacle.

Churchill's enthusiasm for British operations in the Mediterranean so soon after these events leaves one reduced to speculation. Given the Prime Minister's capacity to carry in his head simultaneous themes and plans (not always fully coordinated with each other but to be pushed forward as the opportunity permitted), it is always difficult to pronounce judgment on what held the position of primacy. The possibility also exists that some cooling had taken place in the relations between the Prime Minister and the President before Churchill left the United States following the dramatic White House meeting. Churchill in his memoirs conveys the impression that it was an honor to be left in possession of the White House while Roosevelt rested at Hyde Park. But another interpretation of this is possible—that Roosevelt had fled Washington to escape Churchill's stubborn rhetoric. The JCS certainly were not going to follow Churchill's Mediterranean enthusiasms without presidential approval, and the President had removed himself bodily from the arena of debate. Churchill's weakest point as a politician was always that his enthusiasm and determination in pursuit of an objective could obscure the true reactions of others to his project, and he could mistake politeness or silent opposition for acquiescence and approval. Churchill may have exhausted Roosevelt's endurance and perhaps more.

Whatever the explanation of these events, Churchill's commitment to Overlord, with or without enthusiasm, remained. When American military officials in Britain in late April 1944 asked the Prime Minister how he *really* felt about Overlord, they received the response that he had opposed the operation during the past two years but now felt that the time was truly right and thus he was committed to the assault with all his energy and spirit. He indicated he would have liked some further preparations—a commitment of Turkey to the war and an operation in Norway which, it seemed to him, would have completed the encirclement of Hitler's position—before the final thrust was launched. But he concluded that the die was cast and all must vigorously carry Overlord to a successful conclusion.[103] Churchill was even prepared to accept as the commander of Overlord his archantagonist in Anglo-American strategic debate, General Marshall, whom he told, "I do hope to hear of your appointment soon. You know I will back you through thick and thin and make your path here smooth."[104] While American domestic considerations led Roosevelt to retain Marshall in Washington and assign Eisenhower the command of Overlord, nonetheless Churchill's preparedness to support Marshall is the measure of the Prime Minister's magnanimity of spirit and his readiness to see the operation through.

Much had been gained from the Mediterranean, and for those gains, much was owed to the Prime Minister's efforts. German forces were deeply committed in Italy and the Balkans, and the Allies had gained clear communications through the Mediterranean and a strong position in southern Italy to support their air offensive against Germany. What was not achieved in the Mediterranean—particularly the island of Rhodes, the opening of the Dardanelles, or any direct thrusts into the Balkan peninsula—were essentially operations which had developed out of momentary enthusiasms and had never received general Allied or even British sanction.[105] Perhaps by the spring of 1944 the Prime Minister's Mediterranean commitments had reached the point of strategic diminishing returns.

By spring of 1944 the Prime Minister was no longer the one so deeply committed to the Mediterranean. His CIGS, Brooke, confided to his diary in autumn of 1943 that the slowdown in Mediterranean operations at the price of the Overlord buildup was "quite heart-breaking when we see what we might have done this year if our strategy had not been distorted by the Americans. . . ." On November 1 Brooke told his diary, "We should have had the whole Balkans ablaze by now, and the war might have been finished by 1943."[106] One is left with the impression that Brooke was rather tired at this point. Certainly his private reflections did not agree with his formal statements, at one Allied conference after another, of his firm belief in and commitment to Overlord as the prime operation of the Western Allies. In rereading his own diary entries, Brooke felt them rather excessive but reaffirmed his assertion that it would have cost little to gain Crete and Rhodes and these successes might have had happy repercussions in Turkey and the Balkans without committing a single man to the region.[107]

How much could have been gained from these operations continues to produce divided opinion, but a tentative judgment may be advanced that the gains—strategic, economic, and political—which lay in the earliest possible landing in France and in securing the greatest possible area in western Europe outweighed anything the Balkans had to offer. The significance of the Rhineland and the Ruhr compared to the present condition of southeast Europe suggests that the American strategic priority was more soundly based than the Balkan interests of their British ally. Whatever the historical judgment may be upon this strategic dispute, by the time of the Teheran conference it was clearly to be resolved in the Americans' favor. The sheer power of the Americans and their Russian ally overwhelmed any possible British resistance.[108]

The American ascendancy in the West, which may be dated from the Teheran conference, was understandably a hard thing for Europeans, with their strong sense of history, to accept. General de Gaulle said of the growing American presence in Great Britain, "The British, whatever their self-control, did not conceal their gloom at no longer being masters in their own country and at finding themselves dispossessed of the leading role they had played—and so deservingly!—for the last two years." And de Gaulle movingly commented, "It was not without concern that I watched them being taken in tow by the newcomers."[109] And when de Gaulle finally carried out his long postponed visit to Washington, he commented with emotions which many Europeans could well have shared, "During five days in the capital, I observed with admiration the flood of confidence that sustained the American elite and discovered how becoming optimism is to those who can afford it."[110] The proportions of American power had become a dominating consideration for all Europeans, however they may have felt about this historical development.

The dominant note of Churchill's role in this period, regardless of occasional disharmony, was his commitment to making the Grand Alliance work. He suffered many unpleasant barbs from Stalin, and while Churchill rebutted Russian accusations and provocations with firmness and force, he avoided the type of remark which could so easily have been thrown in the face of the Russian dictator, whose record as a humanitarian statesman, to say the least, is subject to certain shortcomings.[111] Churchill's commitment to the Alliance was more than a political tactic. It was founded in the beliefs of a statesman of unparalleled experience and vast historical knowledge. He said in the House of Commons in October 1944 that, even though other countries might be associated, the future of the world depended on the united action of the three most powerful Allies.[112] This occupied the central place in Churchill's wartime diplomacy and is not without its validity in the case of the two superpowers down to the present day.

8 / NORMANDY TO POTSDAM, *June 1944 to July 1945*

THE STRATEGIC OPERATIONS of the Western Alliance had achieved their high tide with the Normandy landings of June 1944. But that operation did not end the many differences of judgment which characterized Alliance planning. Following the Teheran meeting the British Chiefs of Staff (COS) increasingly came to doubt the wisdom of a landing in southern France. The distance between the Mediterranean coast of France and Normandy, the rugged nature of the intervening country, and the tenacious resistance the Germans had shown in defense led the British to believe that the landing would serve the war effort less than an increased offensive in Italy which had demonstrated its ability to attract German resources. By March 1944 an exchange of opinions had begun between the British chiefs and their American opposites that would continue practically to the date of the operation itself in August. In the early stages discussion was characterized by concessions almost exclusively by the Americans, and in the later stages by the British. The earliest argument against the southern France operation by the British on February 21, 1944, concerned the shortage of shipping, particularly landing craft, which threatened to skimp both French operations. Added to this was the failure of Anzio to secure a breakout south of Rome, and the British wanted to continue the pressure in the Italian peninsula. Montgomery summed up the British position to Eisenhower, "Let us have two really good major campaigns–one in Italy and one in Overlord."[1] The Americans were not prepared to cancel the operation in southern France, but on February 24 a compromise was reached between Eisenhower and the COS whereby the campaign in Italy was to have priority over all other operations in the Mediterranean. Plans would go forward for the landing in southern France, but no final decision would be made until the shipping situation was clearer. The President and the Prime Minister accepted this arrangement.[2]

The next stage in the strategic discussion came on March 14 when General Wilson, the British theater commander in the Mediterranean, reported on the failure of the Cassino offensive in Italy. He now believed that Rome could not be secured until the end of May at the earliest. He further calculated that the southern France operation would not be feasible until ten weeks following that, or until sometime in late July. He therefore advised concentration on the Italian campaign, and Eisenhower accepted a recommendation which postponed the southern France landings for some time. This secured additional landing craft for the Overlord operation which by late March he was convinced was necessary.[3]

On March 31 a new chapter in the debate began when the Joint Chiefs of Staff (JCS) suggested that after the Anzio beachhead and the main front were joined in Italy, the offensive in the Mediterranean should shift from Italy to southern France. This in turn was rejected by the British. Churchill entered the lists to deliver a strong message to Marshall on April 16 arguing that the great opportunities in Italy should not be abandoned just as they promised success. He pointed out that the bitter struggle in Italy had succeeded in pulling in more German divisions, thus increasing the prospects for Overlord's success. The American chiefs yielded to Churchill to the point of agreeing that the combat force in Italy should not be reduced or deprived of landing craft essential to its operations and agreed to postpone the southern France operation without any guarantee that it would take place later. At the end of April General Wilson was given a priority for Italy in his theater.

On June 4 the Allies reached Rome.[4] Following its capture the field commander in Italy, General Alexander, presented to the Combined Chiefs of Staff (CCOS) a new proposal which would leave him free to exploit his recent success to the utmost. The CCOS discussed this in mid-June; the Americans believed that if the southern France operation were mounted, Alexander would not have sufficient force to carry out the offensive he anticipated. This time the British chiefs agreed that Alexander should halt on the Pisa-Rimini line which had been viewed as the northern limit of Allied advance in Italy at earlier conferences. Evidently the British chiefs at this June 13 meeting made no particular objection to this halt.[5]

The Americans received this well; they increasingly thought that the southern France operation would contribute to the swift conclusion of the war. They believed this operation would ultimately provide Eisenhower with another ten fighting divisions as he approached entry into Germany. The Americans also believed that this was the only place in Europe where French forces, which they had been vigorously rearming, could be put into the line to earn their way in combat. Also the Americans were not eager to become involved in any long-term European commitments following the war and feared that if their forces became involved by moving from Italy to the east and north into the area of Austria, it might prove very difficult to get them out again. For all these reasons the Americans increasingly urged that plans for the southern France operation proceed and that a target date of August 15 be established. Because of logistic matters the Mediterranean Theater planners were sympathetic to the American proposal.[6]

At this point the Prime Minister again intervened in the strategic discussions. He had been directly in communication with General Alexander and had been swept up by the general's enthusiasm for his Italian plans. This clashed with General Eisenhower's growing belief that he needed the ports in southern France to support his operations and that when he reached the German frontier he would need the heaviest possible concentration of forces to break into the Ruhr. Just as American military opinion hardened around the importance of the southern France operation, British judgment began to harden in the opposite direction. Launching the French operation would require withdrawals from the Italian front which the British chiefs believed was a better investment of Allied resources.

Faced with a deadlock on the subject, Churchill appealed to President Roosevelt on June 28 to examine the two cases. The following day Roosevelt decided for southern France, telling Churchill that American military planners in Washington doubted very much that a right-handed thrust through Italy and over the Ljubljana gap into Slovenia and Hungary could be logistically supported for a force larger than six divisions; this size did not seem sufficient to the American planners. Roosevelt pointed out that the large numbers of French troops now in the Mediterranean Theater would have to be employed in the west rather than the east. He also believed his political position in the United States would become highly vulnerable if there were a setback on the western front at the same time American troops were being used northeast of Italy. Churchill could do nothing but yield to the President, but he did so with deep regret and even with a certain note of abused feelings. Several ferocious messages were evidently composed by the Prime Minister but discarded in early July, and he told the COS, "An intense impression must be made upon the Americans that we have been ill-treated and are furious." He did manage to make his feelings known to the extent of christening the southern France operation with the code name Dragoon. To the very end he struggled against it; as late as August 6 he was still firing off messages to the United States in efforts to stop it.[7] But Churchill typically was on the scene August 15 as the Allied troops went ashore.

Only limited resistance was encountered, and the forces were able to press swiftly north, linking up with the Allied advance in northern France on September 11. The very success of Dragoon merely confirmed each side in its views on the wisdom of the operation. To the Americans it vindicated their arguments in favor of the operation; to the British it proved the operation was unnecessary. Certainly the southern victory did not constitute any immediate contribution to the advance from Normandy, because it did not draw German troops away from Eisenhower's northern front. Its significance would be seen later in the winter of 1944–45 when German resistance in the west stiffened. The British continued to believe that an opportunity had been lost to push swiftly out of Italy toward Hungary and Austria, but this remained an operation with little attraction for the Americans.

By the time Dragoon took place, there was a feeling in Britain, riding on the tide of dramatic success after the breakout from the Normandy peninsula, that the war might be concluded in the winter of 1944. These hopes were based in no small measure on the great weariness the British people naturally felt after so prolonged and desperate a struggle and, at a higher level in London, on an awareness that the British war effort would have passed its peak by the end of 1944 and Britain's role in the Alliance would inevitably decline from that point on. When these hopes for concluding the war in 1944 were unfulfilled, the reaction of the British was to blame what they believed were mistakes in Allied strategy imposed upon them by their American ally. Dragoon (and thus the failure to exploit the opportunity of moving into Austria and Hungary from the southwest) was one of these points of contention. It still remains so.[8]

By the time of the Dragoon operation, political matters were becoming more pressing. On August 30 Field Marshal Smuts warned Churchill to turn his attention closely to matters bearing on the future of Europe—a warning the Prime Minister was fully prepared to consider. By then the Western Allies were taking a less optimistic view of the possibility of cooperating with their Russian ally than they had entertained at Teheran. The second British charge against Dragoon emerged from this and matured in the cold-war period with the belief that a thrust into Hungary and southern Austria would have been significant in holding the Russian advance farther to the east. The military crisis on the western front in the winter of 1944–45 suggests that the price of this might have been rather high and the Western Allies might have found themselves (if the thrust through the Ljubljana gap were logistically supportable) with a position in southern Austria and Hungary but with Russian troops on the banks of the Rhine rather than on the banks of the Elbe. It would seem wiser in retrospect to have made sure of the Elbe line and thus to have secured the great economic and industrial centers of the Ruhr rather than to have possessed hardly comparable territory in southeastern Europe.[9]

A further factor was that of French ambitions and desires. General de Gaulle stated his position that either French forces reenter metropolitan France through the south on a large scale or he would insist on the transfer of French forces from Italy and North Africa through Great Britain and into France through Normandy.[10] This too was a political consideration which could not be ignored any more than Roosevelt's fear that American involvement in southeastern Europe would carry grave political risks for him.[11]

The military feasibility of operating through the Ljubljana gap also raised serious questions. The Chief of the Imperial General Staff (CIGS), Brooke, had his own doubts about the ability to support an advance through the gap and on to Vienna. He warned the Prime Minister that the advance from the Pisa-Rimini line could not start until after September, which meant a campaign through the Alps in winter. Brooke commented that it was hard to make Churchill realize that the season of the year and the topography of the country added two more enemies to the German one.[12] De Gaulle raised a similar consideration and further pointed out that the American and British armies were equipped to function chiefly in level country, heavily reinforced by machinery and accustomed to live without too many privations as the result of their massive logistic support. He too doubted the wisdom of the eastern thrust.[13] Further, the tenacious German resistance in the Biscay ports was creating a serious supply problem for the western front, which greatly increased the importance of having the excellent ports of southern France, particularly Marseilles, opened to Allied supplies.[14] In addition, the terrain of the north European plain was far better suited for the employment of Anglo-American forces than that of either Italy or southeastern Europe. The Italian campaign was one of attrition and slow, slogging progress. Better strategic values could certainly be found elsewhere.[15] All these considerations lent weight to the emphasis on western Europe. Michael Howard summed up the Anglo-American strategic strains and their ultimate outcome:

> The United States had cause to be grateful to British caution and realism during the early years of strategic planning; but it was thanks largely to the stubborn perseverance of the American military leaders that the strategy, for better or worse, was ultimately carried out as had been jointly planned. An effective case has still to be made out, that there could have been any more rapid or economical way of winning the war.[16]

In autumn of 1944 the issue which came increasingly to predominate in British strategic thinking was whether Germany would collapse in that year and if not, what impact this would have on Great Britain in 1945. As a tide of optimism swept over London, the Prime Minister remained distrustful of these hopes. He had watched stubborn German resistance from Tunisia all the way back into Europe; it was with considerable anxiety for the future (he knew well the extent of British war exhaustion) that Churchill embarked for another Allied conference at Quebec.

OCTAGON

IN EARLY SEPTEMBER 1944 the British party arrived for the second Quebec conference, code-named Octagon. Churchill believed such a conference was long overdue.[17] This anxiety was probably heightened by Churchill's growing realization that the time was swiftly passing when Britain could claim to be participating equally in the struggle against Germany. As British power receded beside the vast resources of the United States and Russia, his ability to influence the direction of events was certain to ebb.[18]

Retaining American lend-lease aid to Britain following the conclusion of the German war was most critical to Churchill. This was desperately needed if Britain's war effort were to subside from its intense level and steps were to be taken to rebuild the export trade upon which Britain's economic survival absolutely depended. To secure the continuation of these supplies, Churchill assured Roosevelt that no American goods acquired through lend-lease would be reexported or sold for profit. Roosevelt agreed that after the defeat of Germany the war would enter what was termed Stage II. It was understood that the long and exhausting effort Britain had made would leave her with a minor role in the war against Japan and that American lend-lease would continue. Stage II, it was anticipated at Quebec, would run for perhaps a period of eighteen months. Many British misfortunes stemmed from the fact that it lasted only three months.[19]

Perhaps it was because of this growing dependence on American economic aid that Churchill involved himself at this conference in one of the most controversial chapters of postwar planning. This was the proposal of Henry Morgenthau, the American Secretary of the Treasury, that following the war Germany should be reduced to a predominantly agricultural land with sharp limits placed on the scope of her industry. This extreme suggestion at first received the approval of Roosevelt and Churchill, but on second thought both politicians rapidly drew away from it. Why Churchill embraced this plan even temporarily is subject to many explanations, all listed by Herbert Feis who provided perhaps the best comment, "How many possible ways there are of explaining an action that was unwise in a way that Churchill was so seldom unwise!"[20] Within a month or so of Quebec, both the President and the Prime Minister had returned to the position that they would prefer to await the conclusion of the war in the west before undertaking final decisions regarding the postwar character of Germany.[21]

In the realm of European planning at Quebec, the Americans indicated a willingness to support on a limited basis an offensive by Alexander through northern Italy toward Vienna. They insisted, however, that it must take second place to all of Eisenhower's requirements in the theater they viewed as decisive—western Europe.[22] The CCOS also approved Eisenhower's intentions of striking through the German defenses on the Rhine frontier by two thrusts, one north into the Ruhr and a more southerly one into the Saar. Also approved was his proposal for an attempt to open the ports of Antwerp and Rotterdam to relieve his logistic bottlenecks before poor weather set in.[23] The British chiefs would later revise their attitudes toward Eisenhower's plan.

The second Quebec conference also saw some inter-Allied dispute over zones of occupation in Germany. The Britain wished to occupy the northwest part of Germany in which direction their troops were advancing on Eisenhower's left flank. This would tend to secure the traditional British interest of close association with Holland and the strong desire to make certain the German navy, particularly its U-boats, came fully under British control and was adequately destroyed.

President Roosevelt, however, was most reluctant to take the southwestern occupation zone, largely for political reasons. His long quarrel with General de Gaulle, who was by now clearly emerging as the chosen leader of the French people, made the President unwilling to depend on supply lines through France to support American troops in southwestern Germany. Roosevelt was reluctant to have American troops committed any more deeply into central Europe than absolutely necessary. But he ultimately yielded to the British on this question when they guaranteed the Americans the use of the ports of Bremen and Bremerhaven and lines of communication and supply through their zone. There was no consideration yet of a French occupation zone in Germany, and the Russian zone was left rather roughly defined as running southward from Lübeck on the Baltic some 200 miles west of Berlin toward the southern border. This left to the Soviets about 40 percent of the German territory of 1939 and a somewhat smaller percentage of the population and still less of the productive resources, exclusive of Berlin which would be jointly occupied.[24] European plans at Quebec did not go much beyond these general lines of demarcation.

Octagon marked a shift of emphasis away from Europe and toward the Far East. For the first time in Allied strategic thinking, this theater was beginning to receive major attention. From December 1941, the war against Japan had by mutual agreement been given second place to the war against Germany and Italy. But at this point Allied agreement virtually ceased on consideration of the war against Japan. When Americans looked toward Japan, they saw the Japanese home islands directly across the Pacific, and their gaze was a wrathful one inflamed by the memories of Pearl Harbor. The British view was quite different. It ran from India and their traditional position in the Indian Ocean through Burma and Malaya to the Dominions of Australia and New Zealand and only then turned north to look toward the Japanese home islands. For the British Prime Minister there was also a disaster to be avenged—the loss of Singapore. These considerations focused Churchill's gaze upon safeguarding the Indian frontier as well as supporting the two Dominions. Then the peoples of southeast Asia who had been under British rule could be freed from the Japanese incursion.

The Americans placed great value on their duty to the Philippines, toward which they felt a responsibility somewhat akin to that which Churchill felt toward southeast Asia—with perhaps the notable exception that the Americans were committed to the granting of Philippine independence at the conclusion of the war. The Americans also valued China as an ally far more highly than the British did. Indeed, the Americans insisted on viewing the Chinese government as representing a great world power. Churchill's views were sharply different and unflattering: "Certainly there would be a fagot vote on the side of the United States in any attempt to liquidate the British overseas Empire."[25] This statement neatly summed up two prime views of Churchill's when he contemplated the war in the East: his contempt for the Chungking government and his fear that the Americans would enthusiastically participate in the dismantling of the British Empire. In addition to these differences was the difficulty of the conduct of war against Japan. Supply lines were long, logistics were always difficult to maintain, and the character of the land and climate in which the campaigns had to be fought would discourage the most enterprising soldier. The assignment of second priority completed the grim and discouraging picture. Understandably, after a long session of the British Defence Committee on Far Eastern strategy, Clement Attlee scribbled a note to Eden, "Two hours of wishful thinking."[26] This constitutes perhaps the most profound comment on Churchill's relationship to the war in the Far East. After the collapse of the ill-starred American-British-Dutch-Australian Theater, little was done from the British side other than to secure the eastern frontier of India and to spend the subsequent time in acrimonious debate with the Chinese government and the difficult American general, Joseph Stilwell.

The picture on the Pacific front was much different. The United States Navy regained the initiative in the summer of 1942 and drove forward from that point with the full blessings of Admiral King. The U.S. theater commander in the Central Pacific, Admiral Chester Nimitz, was a shrewd and capable man who directed a naval war of unprecedented proportions with great boldness. He was usually well served by his fleet and task force commanders, the best of whom was probably Admiral Raymond A. Spruance, who twice commanded American naval forces when they inflicted heavy losses on Japanese carrier forces—first at Midway in June 1942 and again off the Marianas in June 1944. In a war dominated by the fast carrier task force, these were lethal blows to Japan's Pacific position. Further, the Allied commander operating from Australia, General Douglas MacArthur, was undeniably a soldier of great abilities and not without political influence in the United States. Despite his unusual temperament his demands for support could not be ignored by the Roosevelt administration. Therefore, British plans and Allied disputes in the Indian Ocean area always followed far behind dramatic gains in the American theaters in the Pacific.

At the time of the Cairo and Teheran conferences, strategic conflicts in the Indian Ocean area revolved around an operation known as Buccaneer, which involved the seizure of the Andaman Islands in the Bay of Bengal. The British, who had predominant responsibility for supplying forces to this operation, were firm in opposition to it, believing that it directly served the interests of the Chinese government only and would produce little Chinese support in return. Roosevelt seemed deeply committed to supporting his Chinese ally and at Cairo had given Chiang a firm promise of the operation. The Russian declaration at Teheran that she would come into the Japanese war at the conclusion of the German war gave Churchill a powerful lever for arguing against Buccaneer. And as the demand for assault shipping in the Mediterranean and cross-Channel operations became pressingly clear, Roosevelt abandoned Buccaneer, told Chiang he could not keep his promise, and overruled the advice of his own JCS. This constituted an impressive victory for Churchill.[27]

Remarkably, the two Western Allies seemed to feel little restraint in postwar planning about the Pacific, in sharp contrast to their usual approach in Europe. At the first Cairo conference they announced their preparedness to strip from Japan all islands in the Pacific which she had seized or occupied since the beginning of World War I as well as all territories she had gained on the Asian continent. The islands of Formosa and the Pescadores were similarly to be denied Japan. Such a pronouncement left in the realm of hopes the condition of China at the end of the war, not to mention the ambitions of Russia. Nor, as Herbert Feis noted, did anyone seem to have considered the plight in which the people of Japan would be left on their four small and rocky islands. Perhaps the wisest of the members of the Grand Alliance on this point was Stalin who stayed away from Cairo and kept Molotov away and preserved a free hand.[28]

The cancellation of Buccaneer did not end the drain which keeping China in the war placed on the Western Alliance. Substantial efforts were made from the time of the Cairo conference to supply China over the Himalayas. This had a very high price, as Henry Stimson noted a year after the Cairo and Teheran decisions. The so-called Hump supply route was consuming transport aircraft which in autumn of 1944 were badly needed in Europe. The American Secretary of War was sufficiently distressed to comment, "This effort over the mountains of Burma bids fair to cost us an extra winter in the main theater of war."[29] The rapid developments on the Pacific front constantly forced revision of the plans which called for approach to Japan across the continent of Asia. This consideration, added to the Prime Minister's political concern, produced the most prolonged dispute on record between Churchill and his military advisers.

Early in 1944 the COS produced their plans for British participation in the final overthrow of Japan. They recommended that as the war in Europe neared conclusion, a self-supporting naval force should be based in Australia to operate across the Pacific under American command. They insisted that base installations must be developed in Australia beginning immediately. Churchill vigorously opposed this. He wanted to come across the Bay of Bengal against Sumatra and from there to strike at Malaya and to recover Singapore. The COS were appalled at the prospect of such a long and involved commitment which they believed would contribute little to the speedy conclusion of the Pacific war, for they believed all the rest would drop as prizes if the Japanese home islands were rendered vulnerable to direct assault. On the eve of Overlord the dispute between the Prime Minister and the COS was so deep that General Ismay observed that a breach between the two would be little short of catastrophic at this juncture.[30]

In the end, the rapid American advances in the Pacific came to exercise so dominating an influence on the strategy of the war against Japan that Churchill yielded to his COS. Thus, when Octagon opened in September, Churchill was prepared to give the Americans direct assurance that the British would bear their share of the burden in the Pacific. This was part of his bargain in exchange for American economic support to Britain in the later stages of the war and was also consistent with his integrity as an ally.[31] This did not prevent him from promoting the recapture of Singapore, but this was put aside.[32] Also firmly set aside by President Roosevelt was the cool reception of the United States Navy to Churchill's generous offer of a British fleet to participate in the main operations against Japan. Admiral King entertained fears that the British fleet, which was not equipped with the elaborate fleet train the Americans used to sustain their combat forces, would be a burden to him. Perhaps added to this was a certain element of naval chauvinism on the American admiral's part. Whatever his reasons, King was overborne, and the Americans accepted the British offer. The British COS assured the Americans that the fleet would be balanced and self-supporting. British strategic bombing assistance against Japan was also offered at the conference and left subject to further examination.[33] To the very end, events in the Pacific outstripped planning. A major British air effort was never required, although a substantial British naval force did operate in the Pacific in the last stages of the war and provided good service. The Octagon conference virtually ended Churchill's direct participation in planning of operations against Japan.

THE SOVIET ALLIANCE

THE MEETING of the Western Allies at Quebec took place against a background of one of the grimmest chapters of World War II—the tragedy of the Warsaw rising. The war had begun because of the guarantees of Britain and France to Poland, and from the outset the British government felt a responsibility for the fate of the Polish nation and people. The attitude of the Russians was very different, and when Hitler seized western Poland in autumn of 1939, the Soviets claimed the eastern part. From the very beginning of the Second World War the centuries-old antagonism between Russia and Poland flared again in all its intensity. Until June 1941 this was not a greatly complicating factor to the British. The Polish exile government was housed in Britain, and the British continued to support Polish fighting forces in the Middle East and later in Italy and to maintain contacts with the Polish underground. Since Russia was an unfriendly neutral as far as Britain was concerned, the occupation of eastern Poland was not critical.

But Hitler's attack on Russia created a dilemma in British relations with the Poles on the one hand and with the Russians on the other. The obvious direction for British statecraft to move was toward a Russo-Polish détente—never, under the best of circumstances, a very hopeful diplomatic undertaking. Events quickly demonstrated this when a crisis arose in Russo-Polish relations over the subject of a large number of Polish officers found in mass graves in the Katyn forest. Polish accusations that the massacres had been carried out by the Russians led to the severance of the precarious diplomatic relations between Moscow and the exile government. There the situation was largely left simmering until the conference at Teheran. By then the Western Allies had reports of Soviet intentions to foster a Communist-dominated Polish government. Since Soviet armies were fast approaching the old Polish frontier, the Russians were well placed to install that government if they chose. Accordingly, the British anxiously sought some sort of a settlement with the Russians on the subject of Poland before any influence they might exercise dwindled.[34] Churchill's thinking on the eve of Teheran seemed to consist of an effort to create a settled Polish state which would exist on friendly terms with Russia but not be politically dominated by that country. He was willing to leave Russia with the lion's share of what it had taken in 1939. And indeed, what had gone to Russia in 1939 was not far off the old Curzon line which had some measure of demographic validity. Churchill was willing to offer the Poles extended territory on their German frontier which would bring them to the Oder. This would leave Poland, of political necessity, inclined to depend on Russian support against any German resentment in the postwar period. This was giving a good bit to the Russian position which was already strong.

The remaining problems were whether the Polish government in London would accept any such arrangements and whether the Russian government would be willing to accept merely this position of advantage. As diplomatic developments painfully revealed in the first half of 1944, neither party was particularly sympathetic to reaching an agreement. The Soviet minimums were the Curzon line and the reconstruction of the Polish government in a way highly favorable to the Soviet Union. The Polish government in exile was not yet prepared to accept the Curzon line and wanted to postpone any reconstruction of their government until they returned to Warsaw. Here the deadlock remained. By summer of 1944 the British were becoming increasingly restless about Soviet policy in the areas the Russians were recovering in eastern Europe. Churchill summed up the situation for Eden when he asked the Foreign Secretary on May 4 for a short paper on the issues between the West and the Soviet government which were developing in Italy, Rumania, Bulgaria, Yugoslavia, and above all Greece.[35] By mid-1944 the whole problem of Poland was becoming part of a much greater one—the postwar relations between the Western powers and their Soviet ally. Against this darkening horizon the Warsaw rising took place.

By the end of July 1944 Russian forces were approaching the outskirts of Warsaw. The Polish exile government and its underground leaders in Poland believed it important to their future independence that their underground army play a decisive role in the liberation of the Polish capital. Accordingly, on August 1 that army of 40,000 armed men in the Warsaw area rose against the German occupiers. The Soviet armies, however, did not continue their forward advance, stopping to regroup and reorganize short of Warsaw. More ominously yet, the Moscow government took a dim view of the rising. Stalin indicated he viewed it as premature, and in communication with Churchill on August 5 said that the whole affair did not "inspire confidence." By August 12 the struggle in Warsaw was at a frenzy of bitter street fighting, and the Polish government in exile appealed to Churchill and Roosevelt to bring pressure on Stalin for help, as well as to do what they could to supply the insurrection from the air. Allied attempts to establish an air shuttle service were firmly rejected by the Soviet government on August 15 when Vyshinsky described the Polish underground army as a group of adventurers.[36] By August 28 the Polish government reported to the British that the situation in Warsaw was almost hopeless. The British warned Moscow that if the Poles were overwhelmed in the face of complete uncooperation from the Soviets, the shock to British opinion would be incalculable. Not until September 9 did the Soviet government agree to cooperate with the air supply of the Warsaw rising.

Churchill was so upset by this time that he was even considering cutting off the convoys to Russia to demonstrate the extent of his concern. The American government, which perhaps harbored greater hopes for the Russian alliance than Churchill did, was also badly shaken. Churchill was bombarding his Soviet ally with strong messages and also resorted to public statements. On September 26 in the House of Commons he paid tribute to the heroism of the Polish army and the population of Warsaw. He remained discreet about the absence of Soviet support but concluded with the hope that the capital's liberation would soon be achieved.[37] Such hopes were crushed as the Germans methodically destroyed the last remnant of Polish resistance in Warsaw, and on October 2 the tragic struggle concluded. From Warsaw came a final message: "This is the stark truth. We were worse treated than Hitler's satellites, worse than Italy, Rumania, Finland. May God, Who is just, pass judgment on this terrible injustice suffered by the Polish nation, and may He punish accordingly all those who are guilty." Warsaw itself was completely destroyed; it is estimated that 200,000 men, women, and children in a population of one million were killed. The shock in the West was profound.[38]

Churchill's statement to the House of Commons on October 5 upon the conclusion of the struggle remained remarkably mild as he paid tribute to the heroic stand of the Poles. He also said that despite all efforts of the Soviet army, the strong German positions on the Vistula could not be taken.[39] This indeed may have been militarily valid, but it placed an emphasis on the whole episode which was hardly in keeping with what the British and American governments knew privately about Soviet attitudes. It indicates that even in the extremity of emotion Churchill was not yet prepared to abandon efforts to bring about a settlement with the Soviet Union. But no other approach was open to Churchill short of a full break with Russia. This action was also an unmistakable warning to the West that they would have to shape all their future plans on the grim consideration that their Soviet ally must be dealt with on the hard basis of power politics and that political issues would have to be debated from military positions of strength. As the European war entered its last phase, in John Ehrman's words, "the shadow of Warsaw lay over British strategic thought."[40]

A deeply concerned Churchill was not yet prepared to abandon the utmost tools of diplomacy, and he decided that he and Eden must go to Moscow. They arrived in the Soviet capital on October 9. Again the Prime Minister attempted a Russo-Polish settlement, and again he failed. He was now faced with Soviet recognition of a Polish national committee in Lublin as the provisional government of Poland. To the British the Lublin Committee, as it became known, was little more than a puppet of the Moscow regime. Churchill believed he did better in dealing with Stalin on the subject of southeastern Europe. There he agreed to allow the Russians great influence in Rumania and Bulgaria. It could hardly be otherwise, given the position of the Soviet army. In addition to this the Soviets claimed a predominant interest in Hungary as well. Yugoslavia was to be a sphere of equal influence between the British and the Soviets, a position of balance which was, remarkably, to work out. Britain was left with a predominant influence in Greece. These terms were little more than a recognition of the realities in the area dictated by the strategic deployment of the forces of the respective powers.[41]

Informed of these rough lines of influence, Roosevelt remained noncommittal in keeping with his general desire to stay uninvolved in the Balkans. This in turn limited the amount of influence which Churchill could bring to bear in the give-and-take with Stalin. Yet Churchill came away from his meeting with the Russian dictator somewhat encouraged. He believed that many possible dangers in Europe had been eased and some degree of understanding had been restored among the Alliance partners. He further speculated that some of Stalin's harshness sprang from internal necessities within the Soviet Communist party. Of Churchill's attitudes at this time, it may perhaps be said that he hoped for the best and continued to work for it.[42] But certainly his relations with his Soviet ally made him increasingly sensitive to the military position in the west and the bearing it could have on politics in the postwar world.

CHAPTER 8
THE WAR IN THE WEST

As CHURCHILL BORE his burdens of increasing concern to Moscow in autumn 1944, there followed him across western Europe the advance of the forces of the Alliance which had gone ashore successfully in Normandy on June 6. The landings had been followed by a prolonged period of small advances characterized by tenacious fighting in the Bocage country of Normandy, which was well suited to defense. By mid-August 1944, however, the German defenses in Normandy had collapsed in a spectacular fashion, and the combat forces of the Western Alliance had thrust into northwest France at a rapid pace. The battle of Normandy had consumed about 200,000 Germans killed, wounded, and captured and over 600 tanks and large quantities of transport and equipment the German army could ill afford to lose. In late August the capital of France was the scene of a partisan rising quickly supported by French troops which joined in freeing the city of Paris.

As the Allies moved north and east across the Seine, the problem of supply became increasingly crucial to the pace of their advance. It seemed to General Montgomery, the Allied field commander, that either operations everywhere on the western front must be reduced to conform to the supplies available or a decisive concentration on one part would have to take place at the expense of progress elsewhere. The proper decision, Montgomery believed, depended on the condition of the enemy; it was his view that the German front might collapse if the current pressure could be maintained continuously. He therefore favored a concentrated offensive in one sector. There were two possible targets—the Rhine on either side of the Ruhr or the Rhine in the area of Frankfurt, farther south. In Montgomery's judgment, the Ruhr axis of approach was better because it struck toward the industrial heart of Germany and pointed to an area beyond the Rhine where Allied armor could best be used. It would also move toward opening the great ports along the Channel, particularly Antwerp, which in turn could help the supply problem.

The Allied supreme commander, General Eisenhower, doubted that the Germans were weak enough for this single thrust to be decisive and also doubted that its momentum could be maintained. If not, it ran the risk of leaving his forces badly placed to meet a German counteroffensive in the winter. Yet the temptation was sufficient that Eisenhower was willing to risk it, so he transferred the U.S. First Army to Montgomery's Twenty-first Army Group and allotted them some increased supplies. However, Eisenhower insisted that the U.S. Third Army continue its advance along a more southern axis, joining up with the Sixth Army Group moving into line from the south. On September 1 Eisenhower assumed direct field command on the western front, and these plans were put into operation. The command discussions were being followed with interest, particularly by the British COS and the Prime Minister, although they did not intervene in the debate at this point.[43]

On September 17 Montgomery launched his offensive, employing a three-division Allied airborne corps. The divisions were dropped to secure river crossings to open the road for an armored thrust through the German ranks. This very bold operation deserved better luck than it had, but the most forward division (the British one), which was to secure the river crossing at Arnhem, had the misfortune to drop in clear view of the German commander, Field Marshal Model. The enemy commander was thus in a perfect position to take personal control of the battle and summon all available resources to stop the Allied thrust. Poor weather and inability to reinforce the advanced units from the air contributed to the Allied failure to hold the Arnhem crossing. On September 26 it was necessary to order the last remnants of the British division to withdraw to the Allied front. This failure made clear to the Western Allies that the Germans would not be beaten before winter of 1944–45, for the supporting thrusts of the U.S. First and Third armies had also been checked at Aachen and in the area of Metz-Nancy respectively. With his front at its limits of supply, the problem of opening ports took first place in Eisenhower's mind; and he ordered Montgomery to turn to Antwerp—the approaches to which proved, like the ports along the Biscay coast of France, most difficult to take.[44]

On October 5 Brooke sat in on an Allied conference led by Eisenhower at Versailles. There Eisenhower explained that his future strategy consisted of capturing Antwerp, followed by an advance to the Rhine in both the north and south, exploiting the Rhine crossing toward Berlin either from the Ruhr or from Frankfurt, depending on which line of thrust proved more promising. Brooke at this time felt that "Monty's strategy for once is at fault. Instead of carrying out the advance on Arnhem, he ought to have made certain of Antwerp in the first place. Ramsey brought this out well in the discussion and criticized Monty freely. Ike nobly took all blame on himself. . . ."[45] The Prime Minister, however, did not share his CIGS's view. The sudden slowing of the dramatic advance in the west coupled with increasing problems the Western Allies were having with their Russian associate had their joint impact on Churchill. And the fighting in the west from October to the beginning of December proved slow and disappointing to the Prime Minister. He wrote to Field Marshal Smuts on December 3 that the Allies had sustained a strategic reverse on the western front. Churchill believed Montgomery should have been more substantially supported and attributed that failure to the declining British influence in the Alliance. Churchill was similarly disillusioned by the slow winter advance in northern Italy (which he attributed to the weakening of the position in Italy to benefit the operations in France), although the CIGS had warned Churchill that winter campaigning in northern Italy would prove slow and difficult.[46]

Churchill's growing concern with lack of progress on the western front led to a conference between the Prime Minister and Eisenhower with the COS present. By this meeting on December 12, Brooke's attitude had changed toward Eisenhower's emphasis on a broad-front advance. In the discussions at Downing Street, Eisenhower was supported only by his deputy, Tedder, and—to Brooke's surprise—by the Prime Minister. But Churchill explained to his CIGS the following day that his support for Eisenhower sprang from a decent reluctance to leave him overwhelmed in debate by the massed British presence.[47] By early December then, the British, led by the Prime Minister, were convinced that Eisenhower's strategic program in the west was faulty. There was a mounting tension inside the Alliance on how to resolve this conflict of views. The resolution was abruptly postponed by the intervention of the enemy, for in mid-December the Germans launched a bold thrust against a thinly held part of the western line in the Ardennes, an action known as the Battle of the Bulge. While initial success followed the surprise attack, the German position from the outset was not hopeful, and Eisenhower quickly realigned his forces to meet the attack. This involved turning over command north of the German salient entirely to Montgomery. In the process of restoring the front, Montgomery held a press conference where some of his comments were interpreted by the Americans as indicating that he had had to come to the rescue of his bungling Allies. This unfortunately heightened the strain already evident in the upper ranks of the Allied command in the west.

By the end of the second week of January, the German salient was largely eliminated at a heavy cost to the Germans. Although U.S. casualties were high and they had lost more tanks than the Germans, the Allies could afford these losses better than the Germans could. The main benefit of the Battle of the Bulge accrued to the Russians; for to mount his offensive in the west, Hitler had scraped the bottom of his barrel in the east. This only increased Churchill's concern, and as he departed for the Yalta conference at the end of January, he had arranged a short meeting (the best he could secure) of the CCOS on the island of Malta.

The British arrived at Malta deeply concerned about what they viewed as Eisenhower's general mismanagement of the western front. They also carried with them the knowledge that Britain's war effort was in decline and that every passing month took an increasingly heavy toll of Britain's military and economic resources. Brooke in particular, a man of high-strung temperament and Montgomery's warmest champion, felt the strain of events. Unfortunately, the JCS arrived bearing similar emotional baggage, for General Marshall, Brooke's counterpart, was the equally warm supporter of General Eisenhower. The

Americans felt that Montgomery had not done well in handling the ground action prior to the Normandy breakout. They also felt he had been given the opportunity to show what he could do at Arnhem and had failed, and they deeply resented what they interpreted as Montgomery's slurs at the time of the Battle of the Bulge. The unfortunate result was that both groups arrived at Malta in distinctly high temper, and the meeting which followed was evidently the most acrimonious of the entire war. So angry were the participants that the last phase of the debate took place in closed session without a detailed record of the exchange.

Yet for all the thunderbolts hurled about the conference room, the two sides were not that widely divided. Eisenhower's Chief of Staff, General Bedell Smith, brought to the meeting Eisenhower's spring plan of operations. It was very close to what the British desired—a major offensive thrust along one line which would have predominant support over other operations. Eisenhower also favored placing that action to the north of the Ruhr area. No small part of the problem at Malta sprang from a certain imprecision in Eisenhower's use of language, a characteristic which would become more notorious in his later political career. He had qualified his commitment to the northern line of advance with a rider, "as soon as the situation in the South allows me to collect the necessary forces and do this without incurring unnecessary risks." By now the British were so disenchanted with Eisenhower that they feared allowing even this to stand. In the end, however, the assurance of General Smith that this was not an evasion was accepted. The spring plan was essentially what the British had argued for—a main thrust in the northern area pushing through the Ruhr and on east. Other lines of advance, particularly in the south, would have to be supported with what remaining forces were available. Thus basic agreement on strategy was reached by the Allies in the spring of 1945.[48]

The subsequent collapse of the German front in the west in the spring of 1945 seems to have satisfied everyone that he was right. Eisenhower viewed his broad-front emphasis, even with his heavy thrust in the north, as being justified by events; Brooke held that it became justified only when the Germans reached a state of collapse and that his (Brooke's) strategic concept was crucial to producing that result.[49] Tedder believed Eisenhower had acted as boldly as was reasonable and always maintained that Eisenhower accepted risks more willingly than his British counterparts.[50] De Gaulle also said of Eisenhower,

> But if he used skill, he was also capable of audacity. . . . Yet it was chiefly by method and perseverance that he dominated the situation. By choosing reasonable plans, by sticking firmly to them, by respecting logistics, General Eisenhower led to victory the complicated and prejudicial machinery of the armies of the free world.[51]

Whether more could have been accomplished sooner in the west remains something of a moot point. The Prime Minister had hoped for more. His burdens were increased at a time when political concerns were pushing for precedence as he had to grapple increasingly with the prospects of the postwar world heavy with the threat of new risks to the security of free men.

This concern to prepare the world for the postwar era plus his traditional emotional attachment to his French ally of two wars brought Churchill to Paris in November 1944 to celebrate with de Gaulle the armistice of World War I and to plan regarding the conclusion of World War II. On November 11, 1944, Churchill and de Gaulle marched through the streets of Paris amid scenes of overwhelming emotion; the Prime Minister, tears flowing down his cheeks, laid a wreath at the tomb of the French Unknown Soldier. He and General de Gaulle then entered discussions which quickly revealed Churchill's growing concern about the shape of the postwar world. Churchill indicated that he would be happy to have a French zone of occupation in Germany, and he would later urge President Roosevelt to support this, arguing that when the American armies were gone the British would have great difficulty maintaining large forces overseas, "so contrary to our mode of life and disproportionate to our resources." The British Foreign Office was prepared to go even further than the Prime Minister and had been urging the formation of a "western group" which would include Britain, France, Belgium, and the Netherlands. Eden favored this as providing a defense in depth in the west (against whom was not too clear—a revived Germany perhaps, but more realistically, an expansive Russia, although it was not yet polite to mention this). The Foreign Office also believed that such a West European coalition would be better able to hold its own against the two emergent superpowers. Closer economic and commercial ties were also seen as beneficial. These views were to gain in substance in the postwar era.

But in late 1944 Churchill doubted whether the western group would be strong enough, fearing that the reorganization of the forces of France, Belgium, and the Netherlands might impose heavy military burdens on the British. He thought the best way for Britain to deal with her own defense was by strengthening air and sea forces. Churchill also believed that the greatest surety to Great Britain was to persuade the United States to act as its guarantor in a dangerous modern world. Yet it was on just this point that Churchill was most jolted by Roosevelt. In response to his urging of increased American supplies to the French army, the President responded that while he was sympathetic to this, he was not sure if his authority extended to rearming what he viewed as a postwar army. The President asserted he must bring American troops home as rapidly as transportation problems would permit. This produced a prompt response from Churchill that a swift American withdrawal and an inadequate French force would threaten the rise of a new European disorder such as followed the First World War: "All would therefore rapidly disintegrate as it did last time."[52] De Gaulle's recollections of the meeting with Churchill seemed to indicate that the Prime Minister was torn between his hopes for dealing successfully with the United States and his fears that in a world of two great superpowers Europeans would have to close ranks to protect their interests. De Gaulle recalls that he warned the British that they would emerge from the war covered with glory, but with their relative power diminished by war losses and expenses, by the centrifugal forces at work within the Commonwealth, and by the rise of America and Russia. To this emphasis on a closer European unity, de Gaulle recalls Churchill's response that in politics as in strategy, it was better to persuade the stronger than to pit yourself against him. That was what he was trying to do with the Americans.[53] It was typical of the Prime Minister's approach to problems of politics and strategy that he would simultaneously attempt to pursue both courses—influencing the two great powers within the Grand Alliance and building up a European position.

The efforts to build an Anglo-French alliance as the foundation of a West European position faced many difficulties, particularly problems regarding Syria and Lebanon which rose again in early 1945.[54] While differences over these countries seem small in retrospect, they were important in terms of prestige to de Gaulle and hampered the natural development of a West European alliance which might have aided the stability of the postwar world.

THE GREEK DRAMA

THE SWEEP of Churchill's historic vision, the depth of his compassionate concern for the values of western civilization, and the greatness of his courage and fortitude were all dramatically demonstrated in the Greek crisis which closed the traumatic year 1944. The historical associations between Britain and Greece had been forged over long centuries and were as important to Churchill as they had been to his predecessors. The events of the Second World War had greatly strengthened this. The British had sustained heavy casualties in attempting to defend Greece against Hitler and had nourished a Greek government in exile toward the day of return to their own country. This had been a difficult task, for Greek politics were extremely fragmented. There was a major cleavage between those who wished for the return of the monarchy to Greece at the end of the war and those who opposed monarchy. Among the antimonarchists there was further fragmentation which ran the spectrum of ideology from out-and-out Communists organized in the political party EAM to moderate conservative politicians of the Republican right. With considerable difficulty the British had been able by mid-1944 to support a government in exile with some claim to breadth of representation under the leadership of M. Georgios Papandreou. The government of Papandreou occupied a difficult and vulnerable position, subject to pressures from the king on the one hand and the threats and ambitions of EAM on the other hand. The collapse of Italy had greatly helped EAM and its military arm, ELAS, which had secured a large supply of Italian arms and was thus in a position to dictate a solution to Greek politics the moment the Germans withdrew. This was clear to Churchill, and in early August 1944 he was already taking steps to meet the threat. He advised Eden to support Papandreou in the face of Communist attack and observed,

> We cannot take a man up as we have done Papandreou and let him be thrown to the wolves at the first snarlings. . . . Difficult as the world is now, we shall not make our course easier by abandoning people whom we have encouraged to take on serious jobs by promises of support. . . . The case seems to me to have reached the following point: either we support Papandreou, if necessary with force as we have agreed, or we disinterest ourselves utterly in Greece.

The latter alternative was clearly unpalatable to the Prime Minister, for the same day that he brought the matter to Eden's attention he also minuted the CIGS that it might be necessary to send forces to Greece.[55] Churchill had cleared the possibilities of such an intervention with Roosevelt and received the President's approval on August 15.

The moment the Germans left Greece, British troops under the command of General Scobie moved into Athens on October 14, followed four days later by the Papandreou government. Recognizing that he was a hostage to the armed forces of ELAS, Papandreou proposed that all guerilla bands be dissolved. The Communist leaders, unprepared to yield without a struggle, attempted an armed revolt in Athens at the beginning of December. The situation in the city swiftly became critical, and on the night of December 4–5 Churchill informed Scobie that reinforcements would come. For a week the situation in the city was perilous, but Scobie's troops held on and Papandreou did not resign. The speed of Churchill's response is indicated by the fact that there was no time for the Cabinet to be called. As he observed later, there was no use doing such things by halves.[56]

Public response to Churchill's moves, in both Britain and the United States, was anything but approving. Skillfully portraying itself as the force of light in Greece, EAM appeared to lead the struggle for democracy against the imposition of a reactionary monarch on the Greek people. This theme went down well with the Western publics, who knew much less about Communist behavior than did their respective governments. But the British government held fast, and in the face of a violent press and parliamentary storm Churchill secured a vote of confidence on December 8. Throughout the struggle in Britain, Ernest Bevin remained Churchill's unflagging ally; he defended this Greek policy at a critical meeting of the Trades Union Congress on December 12. But no such closing of ranks was forthcoming from Washington. The American government and public seemed more sympathetic to EAM than to the

Prime Minister, and Secretary of State Edward Stettinius delivered a public statement regarding liberated countries working out their problems of government "without influence from outside"—obviously and painfully pointed at the British intervention in Greece. An American officer at one point ordered all his American forces in the Mediterranean Theater under no circumstances to participate in any way in support of the action in Greece. Churchill was much aggrieved, and American leaders received some messages of extraordinarily plain speech from the Prime Minister.[57]

Scobie and the British minister Leeper reported to London on December 10 that the Papandreou government was without sufficient authority; the most effective step toward pacifying the Greek crisis would be for the king to appoint the greatly respected Archbishop Damaskinos as regent. This advice was strongly supported by Harold Macmillan and Field Marshal Alexander, both of whom now arrived in Athens. Churchill approved this advice and proposed it to the Greek king, who twice refused to appoint Damaskinos. There followed a period of considerable confusion, from about December 13 to December 23, with the British in Athens reporting one thing and and the king telling Churchill and Eden in London that his information from that city was quite different. Churchill began to doubt the Damaskinos appointment, believing he could not force the king to appoint the Archbishop as sole regent against the advice of his ministers—if indeed he were suited for the post and it were clear at all what the Greek ministers were advising.[58]

Faced with these uncertainties, Churchill responded characteristically. On December 24 the seventy-year-old Prime Minister gave up a well-earned Christmas at home and with Anthony Eden departed for Athens. The situation there was not under control. During Churchill's entire four-day stay he was frequently in danger of capture, wounding, or indeed death—he enjoyed every minute of it. Discussions with Damaskinos quickly convinced Churchill he was the right man and that Communist demands must be resisted. A conference was called at which Damaskinos would preside in an effort to establish peace and pull all elements together; ELAS was invited to attend as were American, French, and Russian observers. Churchill convened the conference in the Greek Ministry of Foreign Affairs in Athens without either heat or electric lights, the conference table lit only by hurricane lamps. The thud of artillery and crackle of sniper fire could be heard as the Greeks and British awaited the appearance of the Communist representatives. When these finally appeared, Churchill made a firm statement of British military power to impress the ELAS representatives. He also carefully observed that such power would not be used to support a reactionary policy and that the British wanted peace and amnesty and continuation of the work of relief and economic rehabilitation of the Greek people. Eden and Alexander followed with helpful remarks. The Archbishop was then left to preside, and the British retired to HMS *Ajax* in the harbor.

On the morning of December 27, Damaskinos reported to the British the results of the conference, which were encouraging. While the Greeks were struggling toward a settlement, Churchill found time to castigate the American ambassador, making clear how deeply offended he was by Washington's attitude. In the afternoon Churchill and Damaskinos met together in the British embassy, with Churchill (by Macmillan's account) delighting "in the broken and patched windows and the marks of the bullets on the far wall."[59] This is substantiated by Churchill's description of his trip from HMS *Ajax* to the embassy:

> I remember that three or four shells from the fighting which was going on a mile away on our left raised spouts of water fairly near the *Ajax* as we were about to go ashore. Here an armoured car and military escort awaited us. I said to my Private Secretary, Jock Colville, "Where is your pistol?" and when he said that he had not got one I scolded him, for I certainly had my own. In a few moments, while we were crowding into our steel box, he said, "I have got a Tommy-gun." "Where did you get it from?" I asked. "I borrowed it from the driver," he replied. "What is *he* going to do?" I asked. "He will be busy driving." "But there will be no trouble unless we are stopped," I answered, "and what is he going to do then?" Jock had no reply. A black mark! We rumbled along the road to the Embassy without any trouble.[60]

Churchill had earned his enjoyment the hard way, but his intervention proved decisive. The king was persuaded to appoint Damaskinos as regent and to promise not to return to Greece unless summoned by a fair expression of the national will. Churchill had even secured Roosevelt's support in bringing pressure on the unwilling king to make this declaration on December 30. The Archbishop was installed as regent on January 1 with the assent of all the parties including EAM, and two days later a strong government under General Plastiras, a vigorous Republican, was appointed. In return for government promises of fair elections, respect for civil rights, and amnesty—this last, a controversial point—the Communists concluded an armistice on January 15, 1945. This was followed by a major conference at Varzika near Athens on February 3 which ratified the terms of the armistice and secured the release of the hostages ELAS had not already murdered.[61] Events had fully justified the Prime Minister's courageous action.

The Greek situation created an intense strain on the Anglo-American Alliance. Only one of Churchill's allies had remained unwavering; Stalin adhered to his October agreement of giving the British predominant influence in Greece. This inevitably made a strong impression on Churchill, particularly when viewed in contrast to the conduct of the American government. Churchill had not flagged in the face of these difficulties; in complaining in Parliament about the abuse being heaped upon Britain from some Americans, he had concluded that at least he knew where he was going.[62] The Greek crisis had shown Churchill at his very best. He told the House of Commons when he summarized the entire affair on January 18, 1945, that he had never been surer in mind and conscience of the rectitude of his motives and the clarity of his principles than in what he had done in Greece.[63] It was also typical of Churchill's capacity for judgment in action that upon meeting Damaskinos he recognized that he was the man to support.[64] The fracas also displayed the seventy-year-old statesman at his most human and attractive best. When he departed from the Crimea after the Yalta conference, he returned directly to Athens to see how his work had endured. There he found order and enthusiasm, and he addressed a huge Greek crowd—few of whom could have understood him—in words expressing his affection for their country, its past, and its future. After a rousing harangue, he concluded: "Greece forever. Greece for all!" The ovation was tumultuous.[65] He had earned it.

During the whole Greek episode, Churchill had continued in the face of all opposition, sustained by only a few men like Eden and Bevin. Misunderstood though he was, he had been struggling for the most basic of principles—the right of a people to determine their own political life. His actions were in the highest tradition of enlightened statesmanship. By mid-1944, associates had noted the strains of age and illness and sustained expenditure of energy which would have exhausted a man half Churchill's age. Yet in the bitter winter of 1944–45, Churchill found in himself the courage and the conviction to fly to an endangered Athens, bereft of any creature comforts of civilization and filled with the potential for death, to wrestle from the most intractable of situations a settlement to secure freedom for the Greek people. It was the tidemark of a new theme in Churchill's career—his increasing struggle to find some political way to bring order to a perilous world which would restrain Communist ambition and protect the liberties of free peoples and yet avoid precipitating the world into an even greater catastrophe than that with which it was presently grappling. This was a cause worthy of the greatest of statesmen, and Churchill was a statesman worthy of the greatest of causes.

YALTA AND AFTER

STALIN'S SILENT LOYALTY in the Greek crisis left its mark on Churchill and encouraged him to believe that it was possible to negotiate settlements with the Soviet government which they would observe.[66] This hope, however, was modified by what Churchill saw happening in Rumania and Bulgaria where Soviet pressures for communization were being supported by Russian armed might. The problem of Poland also hung heavy on the Prime Minister's mind. The combination of his success in negotiating at least one point with Stalin and his forebodings over the course of affairs where the Red Army had marched led Churchill to believe that a new Allied conference was imperative to plan the future of Europe and the postwar world. He thus urged President Roosevelt to allow sufficient time for the Western Allies to work out their problems before meeting with Stalin at the Crimean resort city of Yalta, which the Russian dictator had insisted upon as the site of the first full meeting of the Western Allies since Teheran. Churchill revealed his concern to Roosevelt in a message on January 5, 1945, when he said he thought that the end of this war might well prove to be more disappointing than the last one.[67] This dismal forecast made a limited impression on Roosevelt, and it was only possible for the British to persuade the Americans to meet for a few brief days at Malta before moving on to Yalta on February 4. This conference was also briefer than Churchill wished, largely to accommodate the President's pressing concern that he get back to Washington within a reasonable time, and concluded on February 11.

Military decisions at Yalta were relatively simple. The CCOS reported to the Russians concerning Eisenhower's spring operations, which they acknowledged without much comment and offered little statement on their affairs in return. The Mediterranean Theater would be cut back still further, with several British and Canadian divisions being transferred to Montgomery's command.[68]

Of much greater concern were political affairs, in particular the anxiety of the Western Allies to discover how far the Russians intended to collaborate with them after the war. This was more critical to the British than to the Americans, for Britain had to live in much closer proximity to Russian power in Europe. The Americans thus tended to place considerable emphasis on Russian participation in forming the United Nations Organization (UN); the British were more concerned with specific settlements dealing with Europe. The Americans also negotiated directly with Russia concerning her entry into the Pacific war. The British did not participate in these plans and were only informed of them late in the conference. Churchill was concerned far less with the Pacific than southeast Asia and Europe, and he was not particularly interested in the terms between the United States and Russia for despoiling Japan. To him the problem was "remote and secondary."[69]

Not so was France. Churchill wanted to secure a French zone of occupation in Germany to encourage a strong French army in the postwar world and a French government committed to maintaining stability and order. Roosevelt had been persuaded by Churchill to support this request. While Stalin was prepared to see such a zone carved out of the British and American share, he did not want France to be a member of the control commission; Roosevelt was prepared to agree to this. Churchill and Eden argued tenaciously that this would create more problems than it would solve, and in the end the British secured the assent of both Roosevelt and Stalin. The course of this debate led to some sharp remarks from Stalin regarding French conduct in 1940; he went on, astonishingly enough, to say that the control commission should consist only of those powers who had stood firmly against Germany from the beginning. Churchill's self-control on this point was magnificent; he replied only that "we had all got into difficulties at the beginning of the war."[70] This was surely British understatement at its extreme and a characteristic for which Churchill was not particularly noted. The British were long experienced with the reluctance of the Washington government to accept France as a great power, but Russian reluctance to do so was more worrisome because the British were less sure of the causes. Accordingly, when Stalin, like Roosevelt, yielded to the British position with regard to a French seat on the control commission, Churchill was again encouraged that it was possible to deal with his difficult Soviet ally.[71]

Discussions on the character of postwar Germany were even more difficult than the role allotted to France. While the Western Allies had moved rapidly away from the Morgenthau plan, the Soviets had a similar one. Such an arrangement was particularly unsatisfactory to the British, for they would occupy that part of Germany which was most highly developed in industry and supporting an industrial population. Without the industry, as the Soviet plan proposed, there would be an acute problem of feeding the population, a burden which the British were reluctant to assume. They were having sufficient problems feeding themselves and were aware that it would require all their industrial and commercial effort to sustain their own position in the postwar world. No clear decision was possible on the level of postwar German economy to be allowed; however, the Yalta report stated that the Allies were determined to eliminate or control all German industry that could be used for military production—a remarkably broad definition. The question of reparations was also raised, a subject the Western Allies, with their unhappy memories of the conclusion of World War I, wanted to avoid. But the Soviets insisted that reparations be demanded, with the lion's share going to Russia. Again it was possible to postpone any firm decision on this point for later consideration.

The next problem in connection with Germany was the question of dismemberment. Again it was Stalin who advocated the most extreme position and Churchill who showed growing hestitation. The concluding report at Yalta said only that the three Allies were prepared to take such steps as they deemed requisite for future peace and security with regard to German disarmament, demilitarization, and dismemberment. Once again Churchill secured the postponement of a decision which might have been more severe than the British would desire.[72] In short, on the subject of Germany, Churchill did as well as could be expected at Yalta. He kept several doors open, allowing a variety of ultimate decisions, depending on the relations within the Grand Alliance as the war moved into its last months. Considering how strong Russian feeling ran against Germany, this was no small accomplishment.

Churchill's success at the conference with regard to France and Germany was not paralleled on the question of Poland. Here his bargaining power was far less, for Poland clearly would come entirely under the domination of the Red Army and the so-called Lublin government. The Western Allies could only hope to save Polish independence by getting that puppet government either replaced or broadened into a wider government based on free elections. Whether free elections could be accomplished was questionable. It was easier to get some general agreement among the Allies about Polish borders. The Curzon line was adopted as the basis of Poland's eastern frontier. The western frontier was more difficult, with Stalin advocating one which absorbed East Prussia and ran west to the Oder. Roosevelt asked how long it had been since these areas had been Polish, producing the response from Molotov that it had been very long ago. Whereupon, Roosevelt laughingly inquired of Churchill if perhaps he would want the United States back. Churchill shrewdly observed that the United States would be as indigestible to Britain as too much German territory might be for the Poles. The Soviets absorbed the point and withdrew this extreme proposal. However, it was accepted that Poland would be large and would embrace substantial areas which had long been under German rule. Thus a measure of imprecision was left in the Polish conclusions at Yalta, revealing again that the Grand Alliance was having great difficulties formulating a postwar settlement.[73]

If the Russians did not get all they wished with regard to frontiers, the Western Allies got much less with regard to the future government of Poland. They reluctantly consented to a formula which stated that the Lublin government should be reorganized on a broader, democratic basis and be known as the Polish provisional government. While this held out hope, it nonetheless left the advantage with the Lublin government as far as recognition was concerned. Churchill and Roosevelt got what they hoped was a clear pledge for the holding of free and unfettered elections as soon as possible on the basis of universal suffrage and the secret ballot. This was the Western Allies' best chance and indeed only hope in Poland. In time they would be bitterly disappointed. Poles in London were not happy with the outcome, and the news which flowed out of Poland after Yalta was steadily discouraging to British hopes. Nonetheless, the government formed in Poland was recognized by the Western powers on July 5, 1945. The exact character of its western frontier was still at that time undecided. The government included some Poles from the exiles in the West, but how limited their role was to be would quickly become evident.[74]

Nevertheless, the problem of Poland was not foremost at Yalta, for the Western Allies had to consider that Poland was intimately tied to Russia's concern about its own frontiers and historic fears about security. The Western Allies were more interested in seeing the degree to which their Russian ally would cooperate in establishing a secure and peaceful world order. It was possible to resolve problems on voting procedures in the UN, a point to which the Americans in particular attached great importance. Moreover, Stalin was at his best at Yalta; his friendliness on informal occasions and the apparent Soviet willingness to deal reasonably in matters of importance to the Western Allies left them with a feeling that there was reasonable hope of bringing Russia into a stable postwar world order. As Churchill later commented in his memoirs: "Our hopeful assumptions were soon to be falsified. Still, they were the only ones possible at the time."[75]

Perhaps more revealing was a lengthy memorandum Churchill had sent to Eden before the Yalta conference, expressing his attitude as he approached the problem of negotiating with the Soviets. He wrote that it was not possible to predict the shape of the postwar world and advised Eden that there was wisdom in not forcing premature decisions upon still fluid situations. One should wait until the flow of events gave a clear idea of what was politically possible.[76] Churchill had clearly followed this procedure in his approach to the problems of Germany and Poland and had broken about even, doing better in Germany than in Poland. The Western Allies had a military position to support them on the German question, but not for the Polish one. This touched the very root of Churchill's approach to diplomacy—the art of the possible.

World affairs in the early part of 1945 were an ebb tide of British power. Churchill later bluntly told the Americans he did not wish to make public a divergence between British and American views, but he might have to state in Parliament that the Yalta agreement had broken down and that "we British have not the necessary strength to carry the matter further."[77] This struck at the heart of the matter. At and following the Yalta meeting, Churchill not only had to struggle with the problem of fitting an expansionist Russia into a secure world order but also had to depend on the United States to exercise its power in establishing that order. Because the Americans tended to view world problems from a very different perspective and were slower than the British to grasp how important a military position in Europe could be toward securing a long-term settlement, a certain note of discouragement and frustration in Churchill's messages to Washington in this period is understandable. Churchill, with his powerful historical grasp and his clear memories of the World War I settlement firmly in mind, was struggling tenaciously against the intractable realities of power to secure the most stable postwar world possible. That this would not be the best of all possible worlds was painfully clear to the Prime Minister. However, his courage did not flag, and he manfully struggled on.

British thinking on the character of postwar Germany in particular had been evolving very rapidly in the last stages of the war. By September 1944 the COS were thinking in terms of the dismemberment of Germany to prevent German rearmament and renewed aggression. They also viewed it as insurance against the possibility of a hostile Soviet Union, since it could guard against a future Russo-German combination such as had existed in 1939–40. The Foreign Office did not agree that this dismemberment was wise. They believed the Germans would try to evade it and that British and American opinion would come to regard it as an injustice. They also considered as dangerous the COS concept of Britain, France, and perhaps a western Germany being able to maintain a military balance against Russia and her allies and an eastern Germany. The Foreign Office also believed this would destroy any hopes of preserving the Anglo-Soviet alliance, a fate they were not yet ready to accept. The COS had replied to the Foreign Office that while that department might hope for a continued successful Anglo-Soviet alliance, they had to think of the worst possible case since they were responsible for military security. The capability of a postwar Germany to support itself was also a serious consideration. Anything short of self-support would impose heavy burdens on the occupying powers, particularly the British who were in the worst position to assume that sort of responsibility.

Fears of German dismemberment working against British interests were increasingly strong in the months after Yalta as Russia's behavior in eastern Europe became clearer. Churchill observed: "I hardly like to consider dismembering Germany until my doubts about Russia's intentions have been cleared away."[78] By April 1945 the Prime Minister was reluctant even to withdraw troops into the zones of occupation agreed upon as early as the Octagon conference until he had a firm commitment from the Russians to share the anticipated food surplus in the eastern zone of Germany with the more highly industrialized western zones, particularly the one occupied by the British.[79] Accordingly, the provision for dividing Germany into several separate states was not pursued.

Following Yalta the attitude of the British government tended steadily to harden and move toward a position of dealing with their Russian ally from a position of strength and aiming at hard conclusions rather than general formulas. This attitude indicated a readiness to use military forces for clear political purposes. While there is nothing surprising in this—indeed, war is but the conduct of diplomacy by other means—it was not a point of view which was popular in the United States at that time. The problems arising from this can be seen in Churchill's efforts to hold a position in the Trieste area against the ambitions of Tito and likely support for him from Moscow. Toward the end of April, as German forces in northern Italy began to give up, Tito's partisans rushed toward Trieste and occupied the Italian province of Venezia Giulia. Churchill was anxious to reach that strategic point first and urged the new American President, Harry S. Truman, to allow American cooperation. As he told Truman, possession is nine points of the law, and he suggested that a final settlement could be postponed once possession was secured. The American response seemed sympathetic to an Allied occupation of the region but specified that it must be on the basis of military necessity, a point which left the British in some confusion as to just how far the Americans were prepared to go in the region.

Churchill continued to argue that there were overriding political reasons for such an operation—the need to check the Communist movement in northern Italy and the need of some counterbalance when Allied armies in the west withdrew and turned an area of central Germany over to the Russians as had been arranged earlier. While Truman was most adverse to seeing Tito get a firm grip on the Trieste region, he was not happy at the thought of a prolonged American involvement in the region, particularly with the Pacific war still ahead. Therefore, Truman told Churchill that Alexander's forces could go as far as possible as long as they did not fight the Yugoslavs. Since the British were still uncertain of American support, Alexander ordered only the British divisions under his command to seize Trieste, the anchorage at Pola, and the lines of communication between Italy and Austria; and on May 1 he informed Tito of his plans. The following day New Zealand troops met with Yugoslav forces in Trieste, and the British were able to take the surrender of the German garrison and occupy the dock area, thus scooping Tito by the narrowest of margins. As the arbitrary behavior of Tito's partisans in the area around Trieste became more flagrant, Truman's support for the British became firmer. This in turn enabled Churchill to hold his position and force the issue to the peace conference without the Communists being able to present an accomplished fact as the Soviets had so successfully done in eastern Europe. The episode emphasized the essential need for the American government to maintain a military presence in Europe, without which the Prime Minister feared it would be increasingly difficult to limit the appetites of the Soviet government and its Communist puppet regimes.[80]

In the post-Yalta period Churchill most wanted to employ the policy of using military forces to secure positions of strength from which to negotiate with the Soviets on the central German front. Here his new inclinations clashed more directly with accepted American doctrine. Both the JCS and General Eisenhower were inclined to halt the western advance along the demarcation line of the future inter-Allied zones of occupation, as had been previously agreed, and thus leave it to the Russians to take Berlin and finish the war in eastern Germany as well as in western Czechoslovakia and most of Austria. Churchill seems as late as the end of March 1945 to have been under the impression that Eisenhower would continue his advance to the east until he met Russian forces in the field. Churchill also believed that Eisenhower's spring plan of operations, which pointed in the direction of Berlin, still held. Accordingly, the copy of a telegram which Eisenhower had dispatched directly to Moscow fell upon London on March 28, 1945, with the force of a new V-weapon. The message stated that the supreme commander now believed his best axis of advance would be toward Dresden, splitting Germany in two and thus preventing a governmental withdrawal into a mountain fortress in southern Germany. He also asked the Soviet government to assist him in establishing liaison between the advancing forces.

The British had evidently not conceived of Eisenhower dealing directly with the Soviet government, especially on military questions, which they believed should go through the CCOS. The British also seemed not to have known about Eisenhower's new plan. The extent of British concern was largely due to the lack of explanation of Eisenhower's reasons, which in fact he did have. He believed encirclement of the Ruhr had ended resistance of the enemy in the north and center and that his main task was to destroy the last organized military resistance in the west, which he saw in southern Germany. He also saw vast Russian armies on the Oder only 40 miles from Berlin, while the Western Allies were still almost 200 miles away across country broken by lakes and waterways. He concluded that a thrust to Berlin was thus much more likely to be completed from the east than from the west. The British were to doubt this judgment, particularly whether the retreat of the German government into the south was real. And they were also to doubt whether the effort toward Berlin should be abandoned without a try, for they placed considerable importance on the significance to morale of capturing that city and believed it would influence the state of German resistance. The COS sent a message to their American colleagues expressing concern about Eisenhower's lack of interest in northern Germany. They were particularly worried that neglect of this area would have an impact on the last German efforts to mount a U-boat offensive. The British were anxious to get to the north German ports, to get troops into Denmark, to free shipping in the Baltic, and then to be able to clean up the prolonged resistance in the Netherlands which was inflicting heavy suffering on the civilian population there.[81]

Churchill's view was rather different and suggests that at this point he had a firmer grip on the realities of the world situation than did his COS. He promptly informed them that he did not entirely approve of their message, reminding them that there was really very little they could say about Eisenhower dealing directly with the Soviets if as supreme commander he chose to do so. He pointed out that Britain deployed only one quarter of the forces the United States had in the field and that Eisenhower had the added prestige of having successfully executed his strategy in the west in the face of British criticism. Churchill therefore believed that the appeal of the COS to the JCS would make no impression. He bluntly told his military advisers that they could hardly argue against the overall strategic concept of the destruction of the main enemy forces and that any determination overriding this was political and not for the military to make. Nor did he believe the anti-U-boat argument held much weight, for the Germans had notably failed to mount their last desperate U-boat offensive with any measure of success. He argued that the British were entitled to press Eisenhower to keep some offensive momentum moving in the north only on the grounds that he was underrating the significance of Berlin in both military and political terms.[82] In this argument Churchill scrupulously avoided mentioning his increasing concern with the implications of the Red Army's advance. He clearly believed it did not belong in an exchange of military views, but it was a point he opened with the White House. He warned the President that the Russians would certainly overrun Austria and enter Vienna, and if they took Berlin as well "would they not become overbearing?" His conclusion was therefore that it was wise from a political standpoint to march as far east into Germany as possible.[83]

Eisenhower immediately responded to British concerns by reassuring Churchill that he intended to push Montgomery across the Elbe and reinforce him if necessary with American troops to enable him to reach "at least a line including Lübeck on the coast." Churchill promptly replied in a cordial tone to Eisenhower and contented himself with repeating the opinion that he believed it important to shake hands with the Russians as far east as possible. The Prime Minister also dispatched an encouraging message to the President.[84] Churchill had been careful to state, with an eye to General Marshall's view, that he reposed complete confidence in Eisenhower.[85] Churchill was fully aware that whatever could be accomplished in central Europe would depend on American support. On April 18, however, he again presented his arguments to Washington, this time to the new President, Harry S. Truman.

The JCS advised Truman to leave the matter to Eisenhower, who decided to stop his advance on the central front along the line of the Elbe and Mulde rivers.[86] Meanwhile the British in the north were pushing forward as rapidly as possible. Montgomery swept past Hamburg to Lübeck and Wismar on the Baltic, reaching this last port mere hours ahead of the Russians, thus cutting off their entry into the Danish peninsula. The Americans suggested quick realignment of the forces in the field into the previously agreed zones of occupation; Churchill believed the Western Allies should hold the line they had reached by force as a counter in negotiations with the Russians.[87] He presented such a proposal to Truman, but the Americans were not impressed. They were not prepared to maintain large armies in Europe with a Pacific war yet unconcluded. They also believed this method of negotiation with the Russians to be, in Herbert Feis's words, "inadvisable, ineffective, and impractical." They saw such a position as more likely to provoke a harsh dispute with the Russian government than to lead to a good settlement. They also saw the Russians as holding some good cards which they could play against the West. In particular they could deny Western authorities access to Berlin and Vienna and greatly impede any operation of control councils for Germany and Austria. The Americans further believed it would be difficult to carry on this sort of a struggle in Europe when American public opinion anticipated a swift transfer of forces from Europe to the war against Japan. The American position was supported by the CIGS who believed that Churchill had found a poor bargaining counter.[88]

Churchill's real problem, of course, was finding a strong bargaining counter. His pressure on the American government to take a strong stand in Germany had shaken the people in Washington substantially. More distant from the immediate problems of Europe than Churchill and with their attention increasingly diverted to the Pacific, the Americans were not as sensitive to what was happening in eastern Europe. Accordingly, they interpreted Churchill's proposal as that of an old power politician of the imperialist school. One American presidential adviser expressed the American attitude by saying he thought Churchill was basically most concerned over preserving England's position in Europe.[89] Given such an attitude, Churchill had little hope of securing his proposed hard line in central Europe. Nor indeed was it likely that such a firm stand would have elicited broad-based British public support. What the proposal most reveals is the degree to which Churchill's concern regarding the shape of the postwar world had risen and the degree to which his confidence in working with the Soviets had declined.

POTSDAM AND THE END OF CHURCHILL'S MINISTRY

CHURCHILL WAS GRANTED one more attempt for a working relationship with Russia—the concluding conference of the war at Potsdam which began on July 17. The immediate issues under discussion were the questions of Poland's share of Germany and the place of Germany and the Soviet Union in Europe. Churchill arrived heavy with forebodings for the future. The progressive takeover of Rumania by Soviet-supported Communists was particularly disturbing to him. He feared that if he pressed Stalin on the matter of Rumania, he would be reminded of his actions in Greece.[90] There remained only a firm determination to adhere to the Western interpretation of the Yalta declaration and to gather what could be salvaged out of the Allied differences at Potsdam—not a very bright prospect.[91] The most difficult issue revolved around Poland's western border, which Stalin wanted to extend along the Oder River and then along the western Neisse. Churchill particularly feared that movement of Germans out of this region into the occupation zones of Germany would create a crushing food problem. He observed that much of Germany's grain came from the very land which the Poles had seized; if this were taken away, the Western Allies would be left with wrecked industrial zones and a starved and swollen population.[92]

Churchill had known for some time that the Americans soon would have atomic bombs. The British government had largely allowed the Americans alone to make decisions on whether or not to use the weapon because of the preponderant role the United States had played in its development. At Potsdam the Prime Minister was not prepared to make any claims to exercise direct operational control over the weapon but would cooperate with American authorities who believed it should be used first as a threat to Japan to accept peace terms or be bombed. If these terms were rejected, he was not prepared to raise any objection to American employment of the bomb.[93] Further, he clearly recognized that this weapon significantly shifted the balance of power and involved the most serious consequences with regard to the future conduct of world affairs. It immediately rendered Russian participation unnecessary in the war against Japan, and Churchill believed that the Americans at Potsdam no longer wished for that. He believed the weapon also constituted a lever which could be employed to encourage Russian good behavior. "We seemed suddenly to have become possessed of a merciful abridgment of the slaughter in the East and of a far happier prospect in Europe."[94] It was thus in these hopeful terms that Churchill saw the new weapon, but he was not given the opportunity to complete the Potsdam negotiations. In the middle of the conference he and Labour leader Clement Attlee returned to London for the counting of the ballots of the British national election of 1945. Upon the conclusion of the count, Attlee returned to Potsdam as Prime Minister.

The terminal stage of Churchill's war ministry is best summed up in his own words: "I moved amid cheering crowds, or sat at a table adorned with congratulations and blessings from every part of the Grand Alliance, with an aching heart and a mind oppressed by forebodings."[95] Churchill presided over an exhausted nation, and the full weight the war had placed upon British shoulders was formally set out by a government statement. For five years of blackout and four years of intermittent blitz, the British at home had been laboring fifty hours a week, men and women alike, while enduring strict food rationing and constant scarcity of goods and services.[96] In addition, Britain had suffered all sorts of physical damage and a general wearing down of resources. Britain's overseas assets by June 1945 had been sold to such an extent that she had an external debt of over 2.8 billion pounds and had reduced her gold and silver reserves by 152 million pounds. She had therefore to pay for her essential imports immediately and into the indefinite future almost entirely by what she could sell; "In sober truth, a matter of national life and death for a nation of 47,000,000 people crowded into an area one-third the size of Texas."[97] Faced with such stark reality, Churchill was under no illusion regarding what he could do with British resources alone. This impelled him to turn to what he viewed as the absolute need to reestablish a balance in Europe and to provide those elements of stability so necessary in a world torn by the chaos of widespread war.[98]

For years, to Churchill the brightest hope amid his trials had been the United States. But this flame of hope had never flickered more dimly than in the spring of 1945. When Churchill had appealed to Roosevelt for support in maintaining American troops in Europe and in supplying European forces, he had received a most discouraging note calling on the Prime Minister not to plead for American forces in France; that they must come home.[99] In view of England's ruinous economic condition and the utter destitution of Western Europe, Churchill must have read such a message with emotions amounting to despair. He renewed his efforts with President Truman who, suddenly thrust into office, tended in foreign affairs to follow the line laid down by his predecessor and to accept the guidance of Roosevelt's advisers. This continuation of American foreign policy led Churchill grimly to minute the Foreign Office on June 18, 1945:

> It is beyond the power of this country to prevent all sorts of things, at the present time. The responsibility lies with the United States and my desire is to give them all the support in our power. If they do not feel able to do anything, then we must let matters take their course—indeed that is what they are doing.[100]

How much could have been done by the American government in this period, and whether a stronger stand against the Soviets at this time would have been significantly productive toward a more secure and peaceful world, remains hard indeed to measure. That some sort of effort should have been made and that the American government should have been more sensitive to Churchill's arguments were at least strongly suggested by so thoughtful and experienced an American diplomat as George Kennan.

> An international organization for the preservation of peace and security cannot take the place of a well-conceived and realistic foreign policy . . . and we are being . . . negligent of the interests of our people if we allow plans for an international organization to be an excuse for failing to occupy ourselves seriously and minutely with the sheer power relationships of the European peoples.[101]

The American government was not lacking in eloquent pleas from their British ally. On May 27, 1945, Churchill had sent a note to President Truman, urging the Western nations to stand together against Soviet ambition.[102] Certainly in this period Churchill was laying the groundwork for what would become the policy of containment in the emergent postwar world, and it is not surprising that his views found support from one of the leading American formulators of that policy for the conduct of foreign affairs.[103]

Churchill never completely abandoned the hope of dealing satisfactorily with Russia as a friend and not as an enemy. He had faith in the future of the UN and was encouraged by Russian participation in that organization. He did not despair of a solution with the Russians so much as he despaired of the reluctance of the American government to pursue policies which he believed would encourage the Russians to come to a settlement of outstanding differences.[104] Throughout the final year of the war, Churchill's moods swung sharply as Russian attitudes and policies seemed to vary. Churchill was always a sensitive barometer of the movement of world affairs in politics as in military matters, and he grappled with each situation as it emerged.[105] After Teheran Churchill had given the House of Commons a hopeful report, particularly toward securing a satisfactory Polish settlement.[106] His conversations with de Gaulle in November 1944 had confirmed in private his statements in public that Russian appetites could be restrained and a satisfactory Polish settlement achieved.[107] After Yalta Churchill's public report to the Commons was positively enthusiastic.[108]

Not until April 1945 did Churchill's note of cautious optimism deepen into an attitude of serious foreboding. On April 29 he told Stalin,

> There is not much comfort in looking into a future where you and the countries you dominate, plus the Communist parties in many other States, are all drawn up on one side, and those who rally to the English-speaking nations and their associates or Dominions are on the other. It is quite obvious that their quarrel would tear the world to pieces and that all of us leading men on either side who had anything to do with that would be shamed before history. . . .[109]

In May he was dispatching grim warnings to the Foreign Secretary and to the American government.[110]

Not until he passed into the opposition and was no longer responsible for the policy of the government did he feel free to speak publicly much of what he had been saying privately in the summer months of 1945. In his first address to the Commons as the Leader of the Opposition on August 16, 1945, he dwelt on reports reaching the West of Germans expelled from the new Poland. In addition to those moving toward the West and the problems of famine they brought with them, Churchill was also moved to inquire, "But enormous numbers are utterly unaccounted for. Where are they gone, and what has been their fate?" He continued on, discussing eastern Europe, "Sparse and guarded accounts of what has happened and is happening have filtered through, but it is not impossible that tragedy on a prodigious scale is unfolding itself behind the iron curtain which at the moment divides Europe in twain." He said he would welcome any statement Prime Minister Attlee could make which would throw light upon "this very anxious and grievous matter."[111]

Churchill's wartime ministry thus ended much as World War II had begun for him, with the great statesman tormented by the harsh evidence of a world power showing doubtful willingness to live peacefully within the world community. Time would show, however, that Russia's methods were not as reckless as Hitler's, provided the Soviet government were faced with a cohesive, consistent Western foreign policy. At the conclusion of his ministry Churchill had labored to lay the foundations of such a policy. In 1945, as in 1940, Churchill stood rather lonely as the advocate for a suffering mankind against the unrestrained appetites of the forces of tyranny. His methods and his tactics varied with the situation throughout his war ministry, and flexibility toward military and diplomatic problems was the hallmark of Churchill's political approach to the world. But the principles for which he labored and the values which fired his energies and sustained his convictions were firm and consistent. He was the most humane of statesmen, and it was in behalf of humanity that he steadily toiled in those years.

9 / STATESMAN IN BEHALF OF MANKIND

On May 8, 1945, Winston Churchill delivered his victory message to the House of Commons. He concluded:

> I recollect well at the end of the last war, more than a quarter of a century ago, that the House, when it heard the long list of the surrender terms, the armistice terms, which had been imposed upon the Germans, did not feel inclined for debate or business, but desired to offer thanks to Almighty God, to the Great Power which seems to shape and design the fortunes of nations and the destiny of man; and I therefore beg, Sir, with your permission to move:
>
> "That this House do now attend at the church of St. Margaret, Westminster, to give humble and reverent thanks to Almighty God for our deliverance from the threat of German domination."
>
> This is the identical Motion which was moved in former times.[1]

Harold Nicolson described the scene that followed. The motion was carried, and the Speaker and the Sergeant at Arms, bearing the mace on his shoulder, led the members of the House of Commons through the central lobby and St. Stephen's Chapel into Parliament Square. There in the spring sunlight a large cheering crowd parted to allow the members to file across to St. Margaret's, the parish church of the members of Parliament. Inside, a short and simple service of thanksgiving concluded with the reading of the names of those members of the House who had given their lives in the conflict.[2]

It was altogether fitting that this moving scene in St. Margaret's should conclude the major part of Churchill's war ministry, for the scene played out on that May day was to Churchill the heart and spirit of man's organized existence. Historical memory and customary traditions were to Churchill the guides essential to man as he grappled with his present existence and sought his future fortune. He had demonstrated his commitment to this proposition at the close of the long session of 1944 when he expressed his gladness that the closing scene should show all the respect for the traditional and ceremonial occasions which Churchill so valued.[3] He had quoted Disraeli in a speech in December, 1944:

In a progressive country change is constant; and the great question is, not whether you should resist change, which is inevitable, but whether the change should be carried out in deference to the manners, the customs, the laws, the traditions of the people, or in deference to abstract principles and arbitrary and general doctrines.[4]

Churchill believed that customs and laws and traditions, the entire body of historical memory for a people, were a living guide which man badly needed as he attempted to chart the course of his life amid the disorder of the modern world. In October 1943 Churchill had told the Commons: "Logic is a poor guide compared with custom."[5] Churchill valued custom as a guide in its broadest sense as a formula of human experience which alone can bring man maturity to grapple with himself and his environment. Churchill would have ratified the words of George Santayana: "When experience is not retained, as among savages, infancy is perpetual."

To Churchill the historical continuity of man was a living process to which each generation contributed its part. In 1939 he had said that Britain's greatness in that time of peril was based not on its strength relative to the power of the European dictatorships but rather on the principles it upheld and to which its history bore testimony in the Magna Carta, habeas corpus, trial by jury, the common law, and parliamentary democracy.[6] This historical consciousness fired Churchill, sustained him in adversity, and guided him in times of confusion. His knowledge of the English historical tradition of parliamentary democracy always checked in Churchill any leanings toward unbridled power which can so easily creep unnoticed upon the man long accustomed to the exercise of authority. In 1940 he acknowledged, "The right to guide the course of world history is the noblest prize of victory. . . . I hope—indeed, I pray—that we shall not be found unworthy of our victory if after toil and tribulation it is granted to us."[7] Thus he spoke at the beginning of the war, and he was true to his profession at its conclusion. When he addressed the House of Commons on August 16, 1945, with the world reeling from the devastation of Hiroshima and Nagasaki, Churchill told the assembled House that while the bomb brought peace, men alone could keep that peace, and henceforward they would keep it under penalties which would test the wisdom of governments and demand the best in statesmen.[8]

Man's history was always alive to Churchill and man's destiny his compassionate concern. His historical understanding impelled his efforts to secure a better future and was not a bed of memories for comfortable repose. Churchill saw meaning in life only within a historical setting cast on a grand scale and running down the tides of time from generation to generation. From his historical vision Churchill drew his values of life. At their root he saw man's institutions, his society, and the states of the world as organized to serve the people; it was his most serious statement that he was the servant of the Crown, of the House, and of the British people. In the same speech of August 16, 1945, he quoted the President of the United States that the Allied triumph in Europe was the victory of an ideal founded on the rights of the common man, on the dignity of the human being, and on the conception of the state as the servant, not the master, of its people. Churchill said of President Truman's words: "This is what in our heart and conscience, in foreign affairs and world issues, we desire."[9] Churchill did not believe that man lived only by the bread of wealth and power but also by conscience and the spirit.[10]

Politics is a hard living and one which can leave its disciple cynical from the experience of man's failings. But a career in political life of over four decades left no such mark on Churchill. His faith in man sustained him, just as he in turn found the energy to sustain the people he led when they needed his leadership. He said in 1944, "You must look very deep into the heart of man, and then you will not find the answer unless you look with the eye of the spirit. Then it is that you will learn that human beings are not dominated by material things but by ideas for which they are willing to give their lives or their life's work."[11] From these assumptions followed his views on the organization and bases of man's society.

He explained in a broadcast to the United States in April 1939 that the system of compulsory service then introduced into Britain in peacetime was a sacrifice of a deeply rooted tradition but that it was an act of faith and a symbol of Britain's resolve "not to fail in her part of the conflict which is now opening for individual liberty and public law."[12] Individual liberty and public law were to Churchill the twin pillars of society around which man's life in the state should be organized. He understood what was necessary to the quality of justice, and in 1944 he had told the House of Commons that the reign of law must uphold the principles of justice and fair play and protect the weak against the strong.[13] Churchill was most certainly, by the standards of the mid-twentieth-century West, a social conservative, but one whose roots were set in libertarian concepts of man's rights and basic dignity.[14]

Churchill did not confuse the living value of historical tradition with the obscurities of empty rituals or meaningless words. Slogans had no appeal to this master of language.

> The foundation of all democracy is that the people have the right to vote. To deprive them of that right is to make a mockery of all the high-sounding phrases which are so often used. At the bottom of all the tributes paid to democracy is the little man, walking into the little booth, with a little pencil, making a little cross on a little bit of paper—no amount of rhetoric or voluminous discussion can possibly diminish the overwhelming importance of that point.[15]

Churchill's approach to politics was simple and straightforward. It was rooted in a faith in parliamentary democracy. One is inevitably struck by the lack of complexity or sophistication in Churchill's political views after a career which spanned nearly half a century. He was to the end as Adlai Stevenson described him, "a man of simple faith." Speaking as Leader of the Opposition for the first time in August 1945, Churchill took the occasion to reaffirm his faith in the traditional aspects of parliamentary democracy: the secret ballot, universal suffrage, the rule of the majority, and the protection of the law for minorities and for individuals. He summed up by calling on British foreign policy to affirm these principles throughout the world.[16]

It would seem that Churchill's convictions were forged out of his own experience rather than hypothesized out of theoretical reflection. He said to the House of Assembly of Bermuda in 1942 concerning parliamentary representation that democratic governments with all their weaknesses and strengths, with all their faults and virtues, with all the criticisms that may be made against them—lack of foresight, lack of continuity of purpose, or guided by only superficial purpose—they nevertheless assert "the right of the common people—the broad masses of the people—to take a conscious and effective share in the government of their country."[17] This simple faith ran in many respects in a direct line from his father, Lord Randolph Churchill, who had taken up the cause of Tory democracy where Disraeli had left off. Perhaps Winston Churchill was the last of the Tory democrats. To him the will of the people was the sanction for government, which in turn owed to the people the security of their freedoms.

In a message to the Italian people in August 1944, Churchill spelled out what freedom meant to him. He set out a series of questions as tests by which men could judge the character of a government by free men. He asked if there is the right to free expression of opinion and of opposition and criticism of the government of the day. He wished to know if the people have the right to turn out a government of which they disapprove, and have constitutional means provided by which they can make their will apparent. He called for courts of justice free from violence by the executive and from threats, courts which will administer open and well-established laws which are associated in the public mind with basic principles of decency and justice. He asked if there will be fair play for the poor as well as the rich, and for private persons as well as government officials, and if the rights of the individual will be maintained and secured from public abuse.[18] It is easy to expand this list by the standards of modern social democracy, but it is hard to compact it except at the expense of basic principles of human rights.

Churchill was sensitive to the restrictions which were placed on the authority of public servants in a system of parliamentary democracy. He wrote in his memoirs of the powers of the American President, his fixed term of office, and his explicit powers under the Constitution, notably his position as Commander in Chief. He noted the vast, arbitrary power of Stalin in Russia. He said that his two allies could thus order, while he had to convince and persuade, but that he was glad this was so. For while the process was laborious, he had no reason to complain of the way it worked.[19] The whole of Churchill's political views rested on his view of man to which he had adhered tenaciously throughout the turmoil of his long political life. "Let us have no fear of the future. We are a decent lot, all of us, the whole nation. Wherever you go you need have no fear. I was brought up never to fear the English democracy, to trust the people."[20]

Churchill was the most faithful of public servants, and even under the burden of his wartime illnesses he labored to discharge the responsibilities of office meticulously. When he was passing through one of his bouts of pneumonia he noted that the flow of paper work reaching him was declining. He complained bitterly that he had his duties to discharge; whereupon the doctor informed him that pneumonia was known as the old man's friend, and Churchill asked why. The doctor told him because it takes them off so quietly. To this, Churchill observed, "I made a suitable reply." He admitted, however, that there was a gap in his flow of minutes for six whole days in February of 1943.[21] It would not do for a man of sixty-nine who was busy to waste more than six days on pneumonia.

His remarkable dedication to public service was fueled by that sublime spirit stimulated by grappling with the events whirling about him. He recorded on the eve of the general election of 1945 that he awoke from his sleep with "a sharp stab of almost physical pain. A hitherto subconscious conviction that we were beaten broke forth and dominated my mind. All the pressure of great events, on and against which I had mentally so long maintained my 'flying speed,' would cease and I should fall. The power to shape the future would be denied me."[22] Churchill derived his energy from the constant conflict of his will with the intractable forces of his environment. In a man of Churchill's proportions this was a monumental engagement.[23]

In his titanic contest with events, Churchill could become careless and insensitive to people around him. This sprang from the proportions of his burdens and the vastness of his vision and the activity of his imagination rather than from a lack of sympathy and humanity. Another Prime Minister has told of his occasions of exasperation with the old statesman but has also recalled Churchill's ability to call the young Harold Macmillan to his bedroom to discuss affairs and seek out the rising young politician's views. Macmillan said of this, "I was deeply touched, and my love and affection for him came flowing back. His amazing power of recovery, as well as his devotion to work and duty, were beyond belief."[24] Anthony Eden has also recorded a scene typical of Churchill. In the summer of 1944 the Foreign Secretary and Churchill dined together; Eden's son Nicholas, on his public school vacation, was with them. Churchill found time to regale Nicholas with tales of his own youth at Harrow. Eden recalled that, upon departing, "I got into the car [and] I found Nicholas bubbling with excitement and he confessed that £2 had been thrust into his hand with injunctions not to tell 'him.' "[25]

Churchill did not permit the press of events to overrule the primacy of place which human compassion occupied in his personality. When Harry Hopkins, who had served the cause of the Grand Alliance so well and so unselfishly, lay desperately ill in the Mayo Clinic with his influence on affairs nearly at an end, he sustained the loss of his son Stephen in Pacific combat. Hopkins received from Churchill a beautifully lettered scroll inscribed:

STEPHEN PETER HOPKINS.
AGE 18
Your son, my Lord, has paid a soldier's debt:
He only liv'd but 'till he was a man;
The which no sooner had his prowess confirm'd
In the unshrinking station where he fought,
But like a man he died.

—SHAKESPEARE

To Harry Hopkins from Winston S. Churchill
13, February, 1944.[26]

Sir Alan Brooke, who labored with Churchill for so many strenuous years, was led to wonder "whether any historian . . . will be able to paint Winston in his true colours. . . . He is quite the most difficult man to work with that I have ever struck, but I would not have missed the chance of working with him for anything on earth."[27] Any historian may share Brooke's wonder. The full colors of that man whom Beaverbrook described as a glittering bird of paradise may well elude the most sensitive historical palette. Ismay thought Churchill could be described as a man born into the world not without some special Providence.[28] I have tried to paint him by the standard Cromwell demanded in the portraiture of statesmen—warts and all. Perhaps it is Miss Behrens who in her remarkable book in the official histories has set the proper stage upon which to see Churchill:

It follows in consequence that the achievements of British shipping were not those of the Merchant Navy and the Ministry of War Transport alone, but, in proportions impossible to assess, of an enormous number of different authorities, and indeed of the whole British people and Commonwealth. They were enacted on a stage as large and by actors as many and diverse as Tolstoy liked to portray. The actions, however, were not unplanned, directed by chance and wholly inexplicable, as in *War and Peace,* but in a large degree disciplined and coordinated, and often demonstrably inspired not only by a great cause but by a great leader.[29]

In capturing the character of that leader, the sensitive language of Harold Nicolson comes close. Nicolson had heard Churchill's address to the Italian people early in the war. He wrote that he had been bothered during the preceding afternoon by people who urged him to press upon the Prime Minister the exercise of tact. Nicolson refused to intervene, saying that he had confidence in Churchill's conception of great events. He then listened "with some trepidation. As a message to Italy, and to the Italians here and in the U.S.A., it was magnificent. But even as a message to our own people it shows that he was not a war-monger but a heroic pacifist."[30]

When time has set her hand upon the historian's canvas of this man and his era, future generations will see, I hope, in the career of Sir Winston Churchill the story of a man who never ceased to labor to create a world safe from the worst of those terrors which afflict mankind. To the degree that Churchill failed he shares a commonality with all other men; in that he never ceased trying he stands as an inspiration to every man. In Sir John Kennedy's words: "His glory remains."[31]

LIST OF SHORTENED TITLES

Attlee	C. R. Attlee, *As It Happened*. Viking, New York, 1954.
Beaverbrook	Lord Bridges in Sir John Wheeler-Bennett, chon Books, New London, Conn., 1968.
Behrens	C. B. A. Behrens, *Merchant Shipping and the Demands of War*. H.M.S.O., London, 1955.
Birkenhead	Lord Birkenhead, *The Professor and the Prime Minister*. Houghton Mifflin, Boston, 1961.
Bridges	Lord Bridges in Sir John Wheeler-Bennett, ed., *Action This Day*. Macmillan, London, 1969.
Bryant, I	Sir Arthur Bryant. *The Turn of the Tide* (The Alanbrooke Diaries, I). Doubleday, New York, 1957.
Bryant, II	Sir Arthur Bryant, *Triumph in the West* (The Alanbrooke Diaries, II). Collins, London, 1959.
Bullock	A. Bullock, *The Life and Times of Ernest Bevin,* II. Heinemann, London, 1967.
Butler, II	J. R. M. Butler, *Grand Strategy,* II. H.M. S.O., London, 1957.
Butler, III (2)	J. R. M. Butler, *Grand Strategy,* III, Part 2. H.M.S.O., London, 1964.
Churchill, I–VI	Winston S. Churchill, *The Second World War*. Houghton Mifflin, Boston, 1948–1953.
Churchill, *Blood, Sweat, and Tears*	Winston S. Churchill, *Blood, Sweat, and Tears* (War Speeches). G. P. Putnam's, New York, 1941.

Churchill, *Dawn of Liberation* — Winston S. Churchill, *The Dawn of Liberation* (War Speeches). Cassell, London, 1945.

Churchill, *End of the Beginning* — Winston S. Churchill, *The End of the Beginning* (War Speeches). Cassell, London, 1943.

Churchill, *Into Battle* — Winston S. Churchill, *Into Battle* (War Speeches). Cassell, London, 1941.

Churchill, *Onwards to Victory* — Winston S. Churchill, *Onwards to Victory* (War Speeches). Cassell, London, 1944.

Churchill, *Secret Session Speeches* — Winston S. Churchill, *Secret Session Speeches*. Simon & Schuster, New York, 1946.

Churchill, *Unrelenting Struggle* — Winston S. Churchill, *The Unrelenting Struggle* (War Speeches). Little, Brown and Co., Boston, 1942.

Churchill, *Victory* — Winston S. Churchill, *Victory* (War Speeches). Cassell, London, 1946.

Colville — John Colville in Sir John Wheeler-Bennett, ed., *Action This Day*. Macmillan, London, 1969.

Connell — John Connell, *Wavell, Soldier and Scholar*. Harcourt, Brace & World, New York, 1964.

De Gaulle, I-III — Charles de Gaulle, *War Memoirs:*
- I. *The Call to Honour*. Collins, London, 1955.
- II. *Unity*. Simon & Schuster, New York, 1959.
- III. *Salvation*. Weidenfeld & Nicolson, London, 1960.

De Gaulle, *Documents,* III — Charles de Gaulle, *Salvation: Documents*. Simon & Schuster, New York, 1960.

Eden — The Earl of Avon, *The Reckoning*. Cassell, London, 1965.

Ehrman, V — John Ehrman, *Grand Strategy,* V. H.M.S.O., London, 1956.

Ehrman, VI — John Ehrman, *Grand Strategy,* VI. H.M.S.O., London, 1956.

Feis — Herbert Feis, *Churchill, Roosevelt, Stalin*. Princeton U. P., Princeton, 1957 (Paperback edition, 1967).

Gretton — Vice-Admiral Sir Peter Gretton, *Former Naval Person*. Cassell, London, 1968.

Grigg — P. J. Grigg, *Prejudice and Judgment*. Cape, London, 1948.

Gwyer, III (1) — J. M. A. Gwyer, *Grand Strategy*, III, Part 1. H.M.S.O., London, 1964.

Hancock and Gowing — W. K. Hancock and M. M. Gowing, *The British War Economy*. H.M.S.O., London, 1949.

Hansard — *Parliamentary Debates, House of Commons*, Fifth Series, Vols. 345–413. London, 1939–1945.

Howard — Michael Howard, *The Mediterranean Strategy*. Weidenfeld and Nicolson, London, 1968.

Ismay — Lord Ismay, *Memoirs*. Heinemann, London, 1960.

Jacob — Sir Ian Jacob in Sir John Wheeler-Bennett, ed., *Action This Day*. Macmillan, London, 1969.

James — Robert Rhodes James in *Churchill Revised*. Dial Press, New York, 1969.

Kennedy — Sir John Kennedy, *The Business of War*. Morrow, New York, 1958.

Langer and Gleason — W. L. Langer and S. E. Gleason, *The Undeclared War*. Harper, New York, 1953.

Liddell Hart — B. H. Liddell Hart in *Churchill Revised*. Dial Press, New York, 1969.

Macmillan — Harold Macmillan, *The Blast of War*. Harper & Row, New York, 1966.

Martin — Sir John Martin in Sir John Wheeler-Bennett, ed., *Action This Day*. Macmillan, London, 1969.

Matloff — Maurice Matloff, *Strategic Planning for Coalition Warfare 1943–1945*. G.P.O., Washington, 1959.

Matloff and Snell — Maurice Matloff and E. M. Snell, *Strategic Planning for Coalition Warfare 1941–1942*. G.P.O., Washington, 1953.

Nicolson — Harold Nicolson, *Diaries and Letters, 1939–1945* (Edited by Nigel Nicolson). Collins, London, 1967.

Normanbrook — Lord Normanbrook in Sir John Wheeler-Bennett, ed., *Action This Day*. Macmillan, London, 1969.

Playfair — I. S. O. Playfair, et al., *The Mediterranean and Middle East*, II. H.M.S.O., London, 1956.

Pogue	F. C. Pogue, *George C. Marshall: Ordeal and Hope.* Viking, New York, 1966.
Roskill, *Strategy*	S. W. Roskill, *The Strategy of Sea Power.* Collins, London, 1962.
Roskill, *War at Sea*	S. W. Roskill, *The War at Sea,* 3 vols. in 4. H.M.S.O., London, 1954–1961.
Rowan	Sir Leslie Rowan in Sir John Wheeler-Bennett, ed., *Action This Day.* Macmillan, London, 1969.
Sherwood	R. E. Sherwood, *Roosevelt and Hopkins.* Harper, New York, 1948. (Published in Britain under the title *The White House Papers of Harry L. Hopkins,* 2 vols., 1948–1949.)
Snell	John Snell, *Illusion and Necessity.* Houghton Mifflin, Boston, 1963.
Storr	Anthony Storr in *Churchill Revised.* Dial Press, New York, 1969.
Taylor	A. J. P. Taylor, *English History 1914–1945.* Oxford U. P., Oxford, 1965.
Taylor in *Churchill Revised*	A. J. P. Taylor in *Churchill Revised.* Dial Press, New York, 1969.
Tedder	Lord Tedder, *With Prejudice.* Cassell, London, 1966.
Webster and Frankland	Sir Charles Webster and Noble Frankland, *The Strategic Air Offensive against Germany,* 4 vols. H.M.S.O., London, 1961.
Woodward	E. L. Woodward, *British Foreign Policy in the Second World War.* H.M.S.O., London, 1962.
Young	Kenneth Young, *Churchill and Beaverbrook.* Eyre & Spottiswoode, London, 1966.

NOTES

CHAPTER 1

1. Butler, III (2), 433; Macmillan, 197; Grigg, 175.
2. Storr, 235–36; Churchill, II, 550.
3. Colville, 81; Butler, II, 2.
4. Beaverbrook, 143.
5. *Hansard,* Mar. 28, 1945; Churchill, II, 264.
6. Beaverbrook, xiv.
7. Jacob, 182–83; Young, 233.
8. Young, 75; Jacob, 191; Normanbrook, 38.
9. Colville, 116; Nicolson, 412; Grigg, 179; Young, 61.
10. Quoted in Young, 38.
11. Quoted in Young, 84; Beaverbrook, 119.
12. Colville, 55.
13. Colville, 55; Churchill, V, 452–53.
14. Churchill, I, 409, 401.
15. Young, 132; Roskill, *Strategy,* 126; Churchill, I, 475–76.
16. Churchill, V, 159–60.
17. Roskill, *Strategy,* 139; Churchill, II, 382.
18. Grigg, 177, 332.
19. Churchill, I, 79–80.
20. Hancock and Gowing, 62.
21. Hancock and Gowing, 67; Churchill, I, iv.
22. Churchill, I, 41, 33, 94.
23. Churchill, I, 93, 148–56, 234; Ismay, 81.
24. Churchill, I, 200.
25. Churchill, I, 257.
26. Young, 120; Churchill, I, 330–31.
27. Nicolson, 35.
28. Nicolson, 34.
29. Nicolson, 36, 50; Taylor, 456; Butler, II, 63.
30. Butler, II, 5, 7; Roskill, *War at Sea,* III (2), 390; Macmillan, 52.
31. Macmillan, 53–57.
32. Attlee, 157; Churchill, I, 659–60; Macmillan, 58–62; Nicolson, 79.
33. Macmillan, 63; Butler, II, 179; Eden, 96–97; Churchill, I, 661–65.
34. Churchill, I, 665.
35. Churchill, I, 666–67; Eden, 98; Taylor, 466–67, 472.
36. Taylor, 473–75. Taylor argues that Churchill "succeeded by calling in the people against the men at the top." This is ultimately true but not complete. Churchill did not have the opportunity to demonstrate his power to Chamberlain and Halifax on May 9 until the House of Commons had done its work on the two preceding days. Honors must be shared equally among Churchill, the Commons, and the people.

CHAPTER 2

1. De Gaulle, I, 63.
2. Nicolson, 115–16; Woodward, xxix.
3. Churchill, *Unrelenting Struggle,* 184; Churchill, I, 328.
4. James, 122, 128.
5. *Hansard,* May 13, 1940.
6. *Hansard,* May 19, 1940.
7. *Hansard,* June 4, 1940
8. Nicolson, 93; Churchill, *Into Battle,* 225.
9. Churchill, *Into Battle,* 251.
10. Nicolson, 102.
11. Churchill, *Into Battle,* 295.
12. Churchill, *Into Battle,* 296–97.
13. Ismay, 180.
14. Nicolson, 20.
15. Churchill, *End of the Beginning,* 100; Tedder, 168.
16. Ismay, 116.
17. Sherwood, 257, 276.
18. Churchill, II, 232; Young, 153; Gretton, 297; Butler, II, 227; Nicolson, 100.
19. Churchill, IV, 61.
20. Nicolson, 238; *Hansard,* Sept. 21, 1943.
21. Sherwood, 836; Taylor in *Churchill Revised,* 41.
22. Nicolson, 347. One is tempted to say: "Winston a politician! Thank God!" Churchill is reputed once to have said: "Democracy is the worst form of government—except for all the others." To that could be added the corollary: "Democracies are worst governed by politicians—except for all the others."
23. Normanbrook, 45.
24. Nicolson, 465.
25. Nicolson, 127–28.
26. *Hansard,* July 6, 1943.
27. Nicolson, 373; *Hansard,* May 24, 1944.
28. Nicolson, 413.
29. *Hansard,* Oct. 13, 1943.
30. *Hansard,* Jan. 20, 1942.
31. Nicolson, 322.
32. Churchill, III, 840.
33. *Hansard,* Oct. 28, 1943.
34. *Hansard,* Nov. 21, 1940.
35. *Hansard,* June 8, 1943.
36. *Hansard,* Aug. 4, 1943; Aug. 31, 1943.
37. *Hansard,* Nov. 29, 1944.
38. *Hansard,* Apr. 4, 1944.
39. *Hansard,* Nov. 29, 1944.
40. Churchill, IV, 917–18.
41. *Hansard,* Mar. 29, 1944.
42. Churchill, V, 168–69.
43. Churchill, *Dawn of Liberation,* 259.
44. Colville, 70.
45. Churchill, III, 370–71.
46. Ismay, 169.
47. Bryant, II, 42–43.
48. Kennedy, 229.
49. De Gaulle, I, 63.
50. Eden, 507.
51. Nicolson, 37.
52. Nicolson, 125.
53. Nicolson, 185.
54. Nicolson, 320–21.
55. Nicolson, 70.
56. Nicolson, 161–62.
57. *Hansard,* Sept. 29, 1942.

58. *Hansard,* Jan. 18, 1944.
59. *Hansard,* Mar. 9, 1944.
60. Nicolson, 280.
61. *Hansard,* Jan. 22, 1942; Oct. 13, 1943.
62. *Hansard,* Oct. 13, 1943.
63. Woodward, xliii; Nicolson, 208.
64. Quoted in Young, 187–88.
65. Churchill, II, 496.
66. *Hansard,* Jan. 27, 1942.
67. Taylor, 477.
68. *Hansard,* Feb. 24, 1942; Churchill, II, 9.
69. Young, 187.
70. Churchill, VI, 595.
71. *Hansard,* Nov. 12, 1941; Jan. 27, 1942.
72. Macmillan, 137; Bullock, 67; *Hansard,* July 29, 1941.
73. Grigg, 393.
74. *Hansard,* June 18, 1940.
75. Bullock, 146.
76. Churchill, II, 11–12.
77. *Hansard,* Oct. 13, 1943.
78. *Hansard,* Oct. 12, 1943.
79. Macmillan, 92.
80. Bullock, 167–68, 256–59.
81. Hancock and Gowing, 476.
82. *Hansard,* Oct. 6, 1944.
83. Churchill, VI, 268.
84. Churchill, II, 13; Taylor in *Churchill Revised,* 43.
85. *Hansard,* Jan. 22, 1941.
86. Butler, III (2), 426.
87. *Hansard,* Feb. 24, 1942.
88. *Hansard,* Feb. 5, 1942.
89. Woodward, 379.
90. Woodward, xxvi; Bullock, 108.
91. Sherwood, 361.
92. Hancock and Gowing, 90; Nicolson, 241; *Hansard,* Mar. 12, 1942; Young, 164.
93. Colville, 50.
94. Bridges, 235.
95. Bullock, 107.
96. Bullock, 112.
97. Grigg, 350.
98. Taylor in *Churchill Revised,* 42; Young, 173.
99. Taylor in *Churchill Revised,* 42; Young, 173; Churchill, II, 569–70.
100. Macmillan, 134–37; Taylor, 558–59.
101. Bullock, 114.
102. Nicolson, 358.
103. Macmillan, 96–99.
104. Young, 240–45, 255.
105. Macmillan, 139–40.
106. Attlee, 162–63; Macmillan, 93; *Hansard,* Mar. 7, 1945.
107. *Hansard,* Apr. 21, 1944; May 1, 1945; July 2, 1942.
108. *Hansard,* July 2, 1942; Macmillan, 94.
109. *Hansard,* Oct. 8, 1940; Grigg, 391; Sherwood, 372.
110. Colville, 76.
111. *Hansard,* Oct. 8, 1940.
112. Nicolson, 164.
113. Quoted in Young, 226.
114. *Hansard,* Dec. 11, 1941; Churchill, III, 623.
115. Nicolson, 205–9; *Hansard,* Jan. 27 and 29, 1942; Butler, III (2), 423.
116. Nicolson, 209, 212; Bullock, 147; Young, 227.
117. Churchill, IV, 86; Bullock, 152–54.
118. *Hansard,* Feb. 24, 1942; Churchill, IV, 91.
119. Nicolson, 226.

120. Churchill, IV, 392; Young, 247.
121. Bullock, 176.
122. Bullock, 177–78.
123. *Hansard,* July 2, 1942; Churchill, IV, 404–7; Macmillan, 126–27.
124. Butler, III (2), 611; Churchill, IV, 408; Kennedy, 249.
125. Eden, 356; Pogue, 422; Macmillan, 164, which dates the secret session of Dec. 10 a day late.
126. Bullock, 225.
127. Bullock, 226–27; Churchill, IV, 958.
128. Churchill, IV, 959–60.
129. Nicolson, 282.
130. Churchill, *Onwards to Victory,* 33–34, 38–40.
131. *Hansard,* June 24, 1943.
132. *Hansard,* Oct. 13, 1943.
133. Nicolson, 402.
134. Macmillan, 500.
135. Macmillan, 501; *Hansard,* Dec. 8, 1944.
136. *Hansard,* Jan. 18, 1945.
137. Nicolson, 103.
138. Attlee, 185.
139. Churchill, *Onwards to Victory,* 266–67.
140. *Hansard,* Oct. 31, 1944.
141. Churchill, VI, 588.
142. Churchill, VI, 588–89.
143. Churchill, VI, 590.
144. Churchill, VI, 597, 742; Bryant, II, 464.
145. Nicolson, 468, 472.
146. Churchill, VI, 675.
147. Sherwood, 793.
148. *Hansard,* July 2, 1942.
149. Churchill, *Onwards to Victory,* 228.
150. Churchill, IV, 917–18; VI, 600.
151. *Hansard,* Oct. 31, 1944.
152. Churchill, V, 679–81.
153. Attlee, 208, 211–12.
154. De Gaulle, I, 167.

CHAPTER 3

1. Roskill, *Strategy,* 139.
2. Colville, 63.
3. *Hansard,* July 29, 1941.
4. Colville, 48.
5. Jacob, 159–61.
6. Bullock, 10.
7. Grigg, 176.
8. Woodward, xliii.
9. Young, 95.
10. Taylor, 482.
11. Churchill, I, 455–56.
12. Churchill, I, 457–58.
13. Churchill, I, 462.
14. Bullock, 100; Roskill, *Strategy,* 55.
15. Ismay, 51–52.
16. Ismay, 89.
17. Ismay, 97–98.
18. Butler, II, 130–31; Ismay, 109–13; Churchill, I, 586–88, 627.
19. Sherwood, 421.
20. Hancock and Gowing, 71, 103, 106, 119.
21. Hancock and Gowing, 88.
22. Churchill, I, 418–19.
23. Sherwood, 243.

24. Churchill, *Secret Session Speeches,* 37 (June 25, 1941).
25. Hancock and Gowing, 94.
26. Young, 139–40; Butler, II, 253.
27. Hancock and Gowing, 302; Tedder, 14–16.
28. Hancock and Gowing, 452.
29. Bridges, 234.
30. Butler, II, 258.
31. Hancock and Gowing, 288–89.
32. Grigg, 360.
33. Ehrman, V, 41, 43; Hancock and Gowing, 445–49.
34. Taylor in *Churchill Revised,* 41.
35. Hancock and Gowing, 216; Ehrman, VI, 323; Ismay, 159–60; *Hansard,* Feb. 24, 1942.
36. Ehrman, VI, xiii–xiv.
37. Bryant, II, 39.
38. Ehrman, VI, 324; Churchill, II, 16; Bryant, I, 255.
39. Ehrman, VI, 325–26.
40. Churchill, II, 17–20; Ismay, 158; Colville, 51.
41. Colville, 52; Jacob, 169–70.
42. Ismay, 113–14; Jacob, 162–65; Rowan, 249–50; Bryant, II, 274.
43. Butler, II, 356–57; Gretton, 286; Ehrman, VI, 330; Ismay, 161.
44. Bullock, 72–73.
45. Churchill, *Blood, Sweat, and Tears,* 117 (Apr. 13, 1939); Birkenhead, 220–21; Churchill, I, 468.
46. Churchill, *Secret Session Speeches,* 27 (June 25, 1941); Birkenhead, 222; Churchill, V, 524–25. The indictment against Churchill can be found in C. P. Snow, *Science and Government* and the defense in Birkenhead, notably pp. 182–249. Churchill, V, 232; Colville, 103; Grigg, 392; Ismay, 173.
47. Churchill, III, 39–41; Ismay, 161; Churchill, V, 586.
48. Churchill, III, 349; Ismay, 192; Woodward, xxii–xxiii.
49. *Hansard,* July 29, 1941.
50. Ismay, 159.
51. Taylor in *Churchill Revised,* 41; Attlee, 161; Ehrman, VI, 321–22; Hancock and Gowing, 217, 220.
52. Ismay, 83; Bullock, 110.
53. Hancock and Gowing, 218; Churchill, III, 115; Churchill, *Secret Session Speeches,* 31 (June 25, 1941); Behrens, 128.
54. Behrens, 129–38. Miss Behrens' work is one of those rare historical studies which may be said to have pushed forward the frontiers of the historian's craft. Her capacity to integrate the evidence of statistics with the humane themes by which men order their lives is an important step in the historian's effort to comprehend the modern, scientific era.
55. Behrens, 139. A concise description of the inland sorting depots issue appears in Appendix XXI, 148–50.
56. Behrens, 200.
57. Hancock and Gowing, 219; Bullock, 148–55; *Hansard,* Feb. 10, 1942; Macmillan, 107–8; Churchill, IV, 85; Butler, III (2), 425.
58. Churchill, *End of the Beginning,* 127; Hancock and Gowing, 146, 333–34; Macmillan, 104; Behrens, 197–99; Churchill, V, 162.
59. Quoted in Ehrman, VI, 315.
60. Ehrman, VI, 320; *Hansard,* Jan. 18, 1944.
61. Churchill, *Onwards to Victory,* 228.
62. Butler, II, 247; Churchill, II, 15.
63. Butler, III (2), 427; Churchill, III, 28; IV, 90–91; Ehrman, VI, 316, 334.
64. Churchill, *Blood, Sweat, and Tears,* 80 (Nov. 17, 1938).
65. Ehrman, VI, 317–19.
66. *Hansard,* July 29, 1941; Churchill, II, 687; Macmillan, 84; Churchill, II, 637.
67. Macmillan, 332.
68. Rowan, 257; Gretton, 286.
69. Churchill, III, 828–29; IV, 844.
70. Sherwood, 527; Roskill, *War at Sea,* III (2), 27.
71. Churchill, *Onwards to Victory,* 41; Churchill, *Blood, Sweat, and Tears,* 103 (Mar. 16, 1939).

72. Churchill, I, 728.
73. Gretton, 260; Churchill, I, 762–63.
74. Kennedy, 156.
75. Kennedy, 146.
76. Bridges, 229.
77. Grigg, 179.
78. Grigg, 391.
79. Churchill, V, 196–97.
80. Colville, 114–15.
81. Bullock, 186.
82. Eden, 452.
83. Bryant, I, 241–42.
84. Kennedy, 93.
85. Kennedy, 60.
86. Kennedy, 61.
87. Ehrman, VI, 332.
88. Ismay, 167.
89. Taylor, 483; Ehrman, VI, 337.
90. Martin, 150; Kennedy, 94; Sherwood, 240.
91. Ismay, 176.
92. Churchill, I, 452.
93. Young, 144.
94. Macmillan, 358.
95. Colville, 53–54; *Hansard,* Nov. 8, 1939.
96. Rowan, 262–63.
97. Ismay, 186–87; *Hansard,* Oct. 8, 1940.
98. Churchill, I, 757–58.
99. Hancock and Gowing, 267.
100. Butler, III (2), 664; Behrens, 440–41.

CHAPTER 4

1. Churchill, V, 624.
2. Churchill, V, 582.
3. *Hansard,* June 8, 1943; Churchill, IV, 75; Liddell Hart, 204.
4. Liddell Hart, 204; Butler, II, 187–89.
5. Churchill, *Secret Session Speeches,* 50 (June 25, 1941). See also Churchill, III, 155.
6. Kennedy, 275.
7. Eden, 182.
8. Taylor in *Churchill Revised,* 50.
9. Churchill, IV, 720.
10. Churchill, IV, 290; III, 338.
11. Churchill, III, 432.
12. Ehrman, V, 17–18; Jacob, 195.
13. Roskill, *Strategy,* 184–85; Churchill, V, 69; Roskill, *War at Sea,* III (2), 404.
14. Colville, 61; *Hansard,* Sept. 28, 1944.
15. Bryant, I, 204; Kennedy, 60, 74; Grigg, 439.
16. Bryant, I, 212, 253.
17. Bryant, II, 95.
18. Kennedy, 108.
19. Grigg, 419.
20. Kennedy, 235.
21. Bryant, I, 499.
22. Bryant, II, 105, 332–33; Liddell Hart, 216.
23. Bryant, I, 419.
24. Bryant, I, 579.
25. Ismay, 318.
26. Churchill, II, 266.
27. Churchill, I, 171, 410–11; Bryant, I, 246–47, 256; Pogue, 270; Churchill, V, 133, 163–64.
28. Gretton, 287.

29. Gretton, 288.
30. Ismay, 318; Pogue, 270–71.
31. Tedder, 532–33.
32. Tedder, 93–94. Portal has not set down his own account. This constitutes the most serious gap in our understanding of the higher direction of the war from the British side. The picture of the personality and intelligence of Portal which emerges from other accounts is such as to suggest that his record of the war would be particularly valuable.
33. Kennedy, 232.
34. *Hansard,* Feb. 24, 1942.
35. Bryant, I, 257–58; Butler, II, 249–50; Normanbrook, 27–28; Bryant, II, 163–64.
36. Kennedy, 62.
37. Butler, II, 308–9.
38. Bryant, II, 168–71; Ismay, 164–65.
39. Liddell Hart, 219.
40. Bryant, II, 457.
41. Taylor in *Churchill Revised,* 17; Gretton, 160.
42. Roskill, *Strategy,* 157; Butler, II, 77.
43. Taylor, 469.
44. Kennedy, 64.
45. Butler, III (2), 650; Bryant, I, 206–9; Churchill, III, 57–59; V, 88.
46. Quoted in Roskill, *War at Sea,* III (2), 415.
47. Gretton, 247–48; *Hansard,* Mar. 16, 1939.
48. Churchill, I, 164; Roskill, *War at Sea,* III (2), 179.
49. Churchill, I, 465, 747; IV, 850.
50. Churchill, I, 160–63.
51. Churchill, I, 159.
52. Churchill, III, 747, 753.
53. Ehrman, V, 477–78.
54. Gretton, 73; Churchill, III, 667.
55. Butler, II, 93.
56. Roskill, *War at Sea,* I, 152; Churchill, I, 562.
57. Roskill, *War at Sea,* I, 296–97. Roskill notes that the COS never recommended withdrawal to the Defence Committee or Cabinet, but Churchill seems to have felt he was "vetoing" a proposed withdrawal "three weeks" prior to his July 15 memorandum to Pound (Churchill, III, 443), or on about June 24. Pound had tentatively proposed such a withdrawal to Cunningham on June 17, Roskill tells us, and Cunningham argued that the fleet stay at Alexandria. Evidently at this time Churchill also expressed a similar opinion to A. V. Alexander (Roskill, I, 297).
58. *Hansard,* Mar. 16, 1939.
59. Churchill, I, 424, 453–54; Gretton, 254–55, 266.
60. *Hansard,* Dec. 15, 1942; Gretton, 293–94; Churchill, *Secret Session Speeches,* 32–35 (June 25, 1941); Churchill, III, 147.
61. Churchill, I, 461; quoted in Roskill, *Strategy,* 105.
62. Gretton, 263–64.
63. Roskill, *War at Sea,* I, 134; Gretton, 265.
64. Gretton, 265; Churchill, V, 8; Ehrman, V, 3–4.
65. Churchill, *Dawn of Liberation,* 38.
66. Gretton, 289.
67. Playfair, 108–9; Roskill, *War at Sea,* I, 431–33; Churchill, III, 242–44; Tedder, 95–96.
68. Roskill, *War at Sea,* I, 554–59.
69. Bryant, I, 219–20; Gretton, 267, 299; Churchill, III, 620.
70. Churchill, I, 428.
71. Nicolson, 59; Churchill, I, 434.
72. Roskill, *War at Sea,* III (2), 388–90, 400.
73. Churchill, III, 149; I, 416, 623; *Hansard,* May 8, 1940.
74. Churchill, I, 158.
75. Taylor, 485, 497; Ismay, 139–40; Churchill, II, 154, 324.
76. Taylor, 500.
77. Butler, III (2), 530; Tedder, 136; Playfair, 287–88.
78. Taylor, 517; Webster and Frankland, I, 46, 64, 268.

79. Webster and Frankland, I, 43, 47.
80. Churchill, II, 458.
81. Young, 154; Sherwood, 239.
82. Taylor, 518; Churchill, II, 643.
83. Gwyer, III (1), 33–34; Webster and Frankland, I, 130.
84. Webster and Frankland, I, 161; Churchill, IV, 279; Gwyer, III (1), 37–38.
85. Kennedy, 87; Bryant, I, 189–90; Taylor, 519.
86. Taylor, 519–20, 552–53; Webster and Frankland, I, 340–43, 402–3.
87. Webster and Frankland, I, 463–64; Birkenhead, 257.
88. Butler, III (2), 528–29; Webster and Frankland, I, 327, 335–36; Churchill, V, 518; Roskill, *Strategy,* 180.
89. Webster and Frankland, II, 5, 10–12; Churchill, V, 519–20.
90. Webster and Frankland, I, 356, 361–62; II, 6, 32, 38–40.
91. Churchill, V, 522–23; Webster and Frankland, II, 61–70.
92. Webster and Frankland, II, 268; III, 5; Ehrman, V, 295–97.
93. Webster and Frankland, III, 34–37; Ehrman, V, 304.
94. Webster and Frankland, III, 63, 77–80.
95. Webster and Frankland, III, 6, 100–103.
96. Webster and Frankland, III, 104–9; Taylor, 591–92.
97. Quoted in Webster and Frankland, III, 112.
98. Webster and Frankland, III, 117–18. See their discussion of the morality of the Strategic Air Offensive, III, 117.
99. Colville, 86.
100. Churchill, VI, 540–41.
101. Taylor, 541, 571; Webster and Frankland, III, 479; Churchill, V, 531.
102. Kennedy, 247; Webster and Frankland, I, 481; Roskill, *Strategy,* 150, 180.
103. *Hansard,* Oct. 8, 1940.
104. Churchill, *End of the Beginning,* 103–4.
105. *Hansard,* Sept. 21, 1943.
106. *Hansard,* Feb. 22, 1944.
107. *Hansard,* Feb. 22, 1944.
108. Sherwood, 617.
109. Churchill, I, 17.
110. Churchill, II, 348–49.
111. Taylor in *Churchill Revised,* 49.
112. Butler, II, 302–3.
113. Eden, 131–33; Churchill, II, 424–25.
114. Connell, 265–66, 276–80.
115. Connell, 281.
116. Churchill, II, 547.
117. Butler, II, 374–75; Connell, 296–97.
118. Langer and Gleason, 392; Sherwood, 239.
119 Tedder, 49; Connell, 310–13.
120. Churchill, III, 19; Langer and Gleason, 393, 396; Tedder, 51; Butler, II, 385.
121. Churchill, III, 65; Kennedy, 75, 85; Butler, II, 440–41; Churchill, III, 70.
122. Butler, II, 442–43; Connell, 336.
123. Butler, II, 444–47; Woodward, 135–36; Connell, 350–54; Ismay, 199; Churchill, III, 104–5.
124. Butler, II, 452; Playfair, 79; Connell, 401, 413–14.
125. Connell, 406; Butler, II, 453.
126. Playfair, 124; Tedder, 74.
127. Connell, 417.
128. Bryant, I, 203; Kennedy, 106–7; Connell, 421–22.
129. Langer and Gleason, 413; Playfair, 201–3; Butler, II, 462–63.
130. Butler, II, 512–14; Playfair, 142.
131. Butler, II, 525–26; Gwyer, III (1), 94; Churchill, III, 343–46.
132. Playfair, 243; Butler, II, 527–28, 555; Tedder, 108.
133. Butler, II, 541; Gwyer, III (1), 72.
134. Playfair, 128; Gwyer, III (1), 172.
135. Roskill, *War at Sea,* III (2), 390.
136. Churchill, II, 533; Woodward, 132; Churchill, *Victory,* 134.
137. Connell, 330–31; Eden, 408; Behrens, 218–20.
138. Howard, 11.

139. Connell, 18, 301; Butler, II, 310–11; Colville, 62; Connell, 507.
140. Butler, II, 451; Churchill, III, 266–67.
141. Ismay, 198.
142. *Hansard*, Apr. 9, 1941; Bryant, I, 198; Kennedy, 87, 133.
143. Tedder, 82, 108.
144. Sherwood, 351; Churchill, III, 332.
145. Taylor, 526–27.
146. Quoted in Langer and Gleason, 415.
147. Langer and Gleason, 781; Tedder, 244.
148. Butler, III (2), 452–61.
149. Butler, III (2), 613.
150. Butler, III (2), 614–15, 652–54.
151. Woodward, 165–68.
152. Matloff and Snell, 35; Butler, II, 493–97.
153. Sherwood, 354–57.
154. Gwyer, III (1), 379–81.
155. Butler, III (2), 413–17; Bryant, I, 248; Butler, III (2), 470, 479–83.
156. Taylor, 541–42; Roskill, *Strategy*, 174–75; *Hansard*, Jan. 27, 1942.
157. Ismay, 209, 270–71.
158. Churchill, III, 730.
159. Bryant, I, 366.
160. Bryant, I, 388.
161. Churchill, II, 484.
162. Churchill, III, 498–500.
163. Grigg, 394; *Hansard*, July 2, 1942.
164. Bryant, I, 136.
165. Tedder, 341.
166. Bryant, I, 187; Kennedy, 114–15.
167. Churchill, II, 43.
168. Tedder, 384.
169. Ehrman, V, 49; Grigg, 362.
170. Churchill, V, 690.
171. Behrens, 210–15.
172. Behrens, 314.
173. Tedder, 13.
174. Churchill, III, 645; Roskill, *War at Sea*, III (2), 391; Bryant, I, 199, 271.
175. Butler, II, 562–63; Bryant, I, 308; Roskill, *Strategy*, 242–43.
176. Churchill, III, 465.
177. *Hansard*, May 7, 1941.
178. Kennedy, 123.
179. Kennedy, 115.
180. Churchill, II, 608; Kennedy, 100, 239.
181. Churchill, IV, 291.
182. Butler, II, 551; Sherwood, 262, 358; Howard, 7.
183. Churchill, *Onwards to Victory*, 94; Churchill, II, 626.
184. Churchill, III, 509.
185. *Hansard*, Sept. 21, 1943.
186. Churchill, III. 5.
187. Churchill, I, 415.
188. Howard, 10; Langer and Gleason, 58.
189. Churchill, *Into Battle*, 95 (Apr. 15, 1939); Woodward, 131; Sherwood, 799.
190. Taylor, 522.
191. Matloff, 244.

CHAPTER 5

1. De Gaulle, I, 89; Woodward, 76.
2. Woodward, 77.
3. De Gaulle, I, 96, 99.
4. Woodward, 93–94.
5. Macmillan, 156.
6. Woodward, 109, 122–23.

7. Langer and Gleason, 75, 92–94, 112, 772.
8. Langer and Gleason, 374–76.
9. Langer and Gleason, 382–83; Macmillan, 160.
10. Woodward, 110–11; Sherwood, 483.
11. Macmillan, 158; De Gaulle, I, 134.
12. De Gaulle, I, 246; Woodward, xiv; De Gaulle, III, 201.
13. Churchill, *Blood, Sweat, and Tears,* 173.
14. Feis, 5; Woodward, 140–43.
15. Langer and Gleason, 122–29, 335.
16. Gwyer, III (1), 80–81.
17. Langer and Gleason, 337, 411, 526.
18. Woodward, 151; Langer and Gleason, 531, 536; Gwyer, III (1), 202–3.
19. Langer and Gleason, 790–91; Woodward, 154.
20. Langer and Gleason, 815.
21. Woodward, 160; Feis, 24–27; Langer and Gleason, 824–26.
22. Butler, II, 544; Bryant, II, 140.
23. Young, 198; Churchill, *End of the Beginning,* 174.
24. Behrens, 253; Churchill, III, 384; IV, 475.
25. Taylor, 445.
26. Churchill, II, 118.
27. Sherwood, 369; De Gaulle, I, 108.
28. Butler, II, 417; *Hansard,* Apr. 17, 1945; Churchill, I, 440–41; II, 23; Woodward, xxiv.
29. Sherwood, 125–26, 150.
30. Pogue, 52, 125–27; Langer and Gleason, 56, 60; Butler, II, 424.
31. Woodward, 78–79; Butler, II, 241–44.
32. Butler, II, 245; Woodward, 82–88; Langer and Gleason, 432–33.
33. De Gaulle, *Documents,* III, 75; Langer and Gleason, 423–24; Churchill, II, 404.
34. Langer and Gleason, 175–84.
35. Langer and Gleason, 187–89.
36. Langer and Gleason, 232–34; Butler, II, 419–20.
37. Woodward, 89–90; Butler, II, 421; Langer and Gleason, 238; Sherwood, 236–37, 259–61.
38. Butler, II, 422; Churchill, *Blood, Sweat, and Tears,* 462.
39. Langer and Gleason, xiv, 456, 579.
40. Langer and Gleason, 591–92; Sherwood, 314–17.
41. Gwyer, III (1), 119; Churchill, III, 434; Sherwood, 350, 355; Pogue, 142–44; Langer and Gleason, 665, 677.
42. Churchill, *Unrelenting Struggle,* 232.
43. Churchill, *Unrelenting Struggle,* 239.
44. Gwyer, III (1), 124; Taylor in *Churchill Revised,* 53.
45. Churchill, *Unrelenting Struggle,* 242–43.
46. Langer and Gleason, 734.
47. Behrens, 195; Langer and Gleason, xiv, 746; Macmillan, 118.
48. Churchill, III, 606–7.
49. Churchill, III, 608.
50. Bryant, I, 227, 237; Sherwood, 444.
51. Churchill, *Unrelenting Struggle,* 166.
52. Churchill, *Unrelenting Struggle,* 174.
53. Pogue, 131.
54. Woodward, xxxiii.
55. Churchill, *End of the Beginning,* 51–52.
56. Butler, II, 239–40.
57. Feis, 3, 8–9.
58. Feis, 6.
59. Langer and Gleason, 494, 514.
60. Churchill, III, 625.
61. Snell, 110.
62. Eden, 453.
63. Langer and Gleason, 456, 735.
64. Gwyer, III (1), 199.
65. Ismay, 282.

CHAPTER 6

1. *Hansard*, Oct. 27, 1944.
2. Snell, 107.
3. Kennedy, 338.
4. Feis, 37.
5. Churchill, III, 646–51.
6. Bryant, I, 222.
7. Matloff and Snell, 55; Howard, 17.
8. Woodward, xxvi.
9. Pogue, 314; Matloff and Snell, 189.
10. Churchill, *Blood, Sweat, and Tears*, 313.
11. Churchill, *Blood, Sweat, and Tears*, 431–32; Langer and Gleason, 740–41.
12. Langer and Gleason, 762.
13. Gwyer, III (1), 335.
14. Churchill, *End of the Beginning*, 224–25; Gwyer, III (1), 336–37.
15. Butler, III (2), 563–64.
16. Gwyer, III (1), 349.
17. Butler, III (2), 617.
18. Howard, 22.
19. Howard, 21.
20. Ehrman, V, 115.
21. Butler, III (2), 577.
22. Pogue, 305–6, 314.
23. Matloff and Snell, 201.
24. Matloff and Snell, 104; Gwyer, III (1), 125–27.
25. Pogue, 132–33.
26. Pogue, 264; Howard, 24.
27. Churchill, I, 225.
28. Matloff and Snell, 32; Langer and Gleason, 777–78.
29. Pogue, 267, 316–17.
30. Hancock and Gowing, 379; Gwyer, III (1), 315, 318–19; Pogue, 263.
31. Gwyer, III (1), 333–34.
32. Matloff and Snell, 100; Pogue, 268; Gwyer, III (1), 354, 358; Feis, 47.
33. Sherwood, 455–57; Pogue, 276, 279–81.
34. Churchill, III, 675; Sherwood, 457; Hancock and Gowing, 402; Gwyer, III (1), 382–83; Ehrman, VI, 339.
35. Pogue, 282–83.
36. Pogue, 272.
37. Ehrman, VI, 344; Churchill, IV, 812–13.
38. Pogue, 287.
39. Gwyer, III (1), 398; Pogue, 288.
40. Churchill, III, 686–87; Bryant, I, 254; Ehrman, VI, 347.
41. Churchill, V, 137.
42. Pogue, 286–87; Ehrman, VI, 338; Hancock and Gowing, 404.
43. Matloff and Snell, 105, 113; Gwyer, III (1), 359–62.
44. Feis, 48–49; Matloff and Snell, 176.
45. Sherwood, 534–38; Pogue, 318; Feis, 50.
46. Churchill, IV, 324.
47. Pogue, 319.
48. Sherwood, 554.
49. Woodward, 192–93.
50. Bryant, I, 301; Butler, III (2), 594–95; Pogue, 326.
51. Butler, III (2), 596–97.
52. Woodward, 197.
53. Pogue, 327
54. Pogue, 328.
55. Feis, 52.
56. Pogue, 329; Matloff and Snell, 239.
57. Butler, III (2), 626–27; Bryant, I, 325–28; Matloff and Snell, 240–44.
58. Bryant, I, 329; Feis, 53; Pogue, 335.

59. Pogue, 340–41; Bryant, I, 340; Feis, 42–43, 54–55; Matloff and Snell, 272.
60. Kennedy, 254; Butler, III (2), 632–33.
61. Churchill, IV, 444.
62. Matloff and Snell, 278–82; Pogue, 345–49; Churchill, IV, 447.
63. Howard, 30–31; Taylor, 556.
64. Howard, 32; Churchill, IV, 659.
65. Behrens, 308.
66. Feis, 57; Butler, III (2), 630–31, 651; Churchill, *Dawn of Liberation,* 259.
67. Feis, 73–75, 78; Butler, III (2), 658–59; Sherwood, 620.
68. Butler, III (2), 663; Webster and Frankland, I, 375 and note 1.
69. Behrens, 254; Sherwood, 545; Bryant, I, 304; Churchill, IV, 259–64.
70. Behrens, 321–22; Churchill, IV, 262-66. For a full account of these operations, see B. B. Schofield, *The Russian Convoys* (Batsford, London, 1964).
71. Butler, III (2), 636; Roskill, *Strategy,* 192–93.
72. Gwyer, III (1), 362; Kennedy, 265–66; Feis, 89; Sherwood, 629; Bryant, I, 400–404.
73. Pogue, 418.
74. Feis, 90; Macmillan, 159–61.
75. Churchill, *End of the Beginning,* 215.
76. Sherwood, 656; Churchill, IV, 928.
77. Sherwood, 743; Beaverbrook, 306.
78. Churchill, *Blood, Sweat, and Tears,* 124.
79. Woodward, xlviii.
80. Sherwood, 512.
81. Churchill, IV, 209.
82. Churchill, IV, 219.
83. Churchill, IV, 220.
84. Churchill, IV, 220.
85. *Hansard,* Sept. 10, 1942; Taylor, 545–46.
86. Butler, III (2), 665; *Hansard,* Jan. 27, 1942.
87. Kennedy, 253.
88. Churchill, *Victory,* 132.
89. Ehrman, V, 2; Matloff and Snell, 14; Roskill, *Strategy,* 191–92; Pogue, 76.
90. Tedder, 395; Grigg, 370; Gwyer, III (1), 338–39; Liddell Hart, 214–15.
91. Churchill, III, 660.
92. Churchill, III, 661.
93. Howard, 29.
94. Woodward, xliii.
95. Butler, III (2), 666.
96. Sherwood, 442–43.
97. Grigg, 393.
98. Bryant, I, 410.

CHAPTER 7

1. Sherwood, 615.
2. Sherwood, 657.
3. Feis, 93–95.
4. Matloff and Snell, 363.
5. Matloff and Snell, 366; Matloff, 24.
6. Howard, 34, 45; Tedder, 389.
7. Macmillan, 210–11; Bryant, I, 450–51.
8. Roskill, *Strategy,* 201.
9. Howard, 35; Churchill, IV, 683; Sherwood, 690.
10. Behrens, 328.
11. Matloff, 26–27.
12. Howard, 36.
13. Feis, 102; Churchill, IV, 686–87.
14. Sherwood, 652.
15. Woodward, 210–12; Feis, 91; Macmillan, 164; De Gaulle, II, 45–46.
16. Woodward, 218–19.
17. Woodward, 222–23; Churchill, V, 182–83; Feis, 314.
18. Woodward, 256; Churchill, V, 185–86; Nicolson, 303.

19. Woodward, 260–61, 267; *Hansard,* May 24, 1944; De Gaulle, II, 253; Churchill, V, 630.
20. Behrens, 363–64.
21. Behrens, 365; Ehrman, V, 30.
22. Ehrman, V, 31; Behrens, 366–73.
23. Matloff, 75.
24. Matloff, 124–25.
25. Churchill, IV, 822.
26. Churchill, IV, 826.
27. Churchill, IV, 831.
28. Feis, 126–27; Matloff, 128–29.
29. Matloff, 130–31.
30. Ehrman, V, 7; Matloff, 134; Feis, 128–30.
31. Feis, 134–35.
32. Sherwood, 733.
33. Matloff, 152.
34. Matloff, 153–55.
35. Matloff, 157–58.
36. Matloff, 158, 163; Churchill, V, 52.
37. Ehrman, V, 8; Feis, 147.
38. Sherwood, 747; Matloff, 220–23.
39. Matloff, 224, 227, 243; Churchill, V, 86; Feis, 150.
40. Feis, 152; Matloff, 250–51; Churchill, V, 135.
41. Matloff, 252; Feis, 153.
42. Churchill, V, 254.
43. Matloff, 222.
44. Sherwood, 748.
45. Sherwood, 747.
46. Roskill, *Strategy,* 202–3; Churchill, V, 112.
47. Churchill, V, 153–54; Ehrman, V, 58–59, 69; VI, 52–53.
48. Churchill, V, 150.
49. Churchill, V, 162.
50. Churchill, V, 332.
51. Churchill, V, 312.
52. Churchill, V, 377.
53. Churchill, V, 82.
54. Matloff, 340.
55. Matloff, 254; Churchill, V, 114.
56. Matloff, 257; Sherwood, 765.
57. Bryant, II, 51.
58. Matloff, 258.
59. Roskill, *Strategy,* 206–7.
60. Churchill, V, 64.
61. Woodward, 232–33.
62. Churchill, V, 504–5.
63. Churchill, V, 195.
64. *Hansard,* May 24, 1944.
65. Matloff, 352, 541–43.
66. Churchill, V, 318.
67. Churchill, V, 330–34.
68. Churchill, V, 328.
69. Matloff, 355–56.
70. Feis, 260.
71. Bryant, II, 89; Matloff, 361; Ehrman, V, 176; Sherwood, 788.
72. Bryant, II, 94; Ehrman, V, 178–79.
73. Ehrman, V, 182; Matloff, 380.
74. Feis, 261–62.
75. Ehrman, V, 200–201.
76. Ehrman, V, 203; Churchill, V, 412.
77. Feis, 263; Woodward, 249.
78. Sherwood, 780.
79. Sherwood, 786; Feis, 272.
80. Churchill, V, 433, 440–41.

81. Roskill, *Strategy,* 210; Tedder, 490; Matloff, 415–26; Feis, 302–3.
82. Matloff, 168.
83. Tedder, 490; Ehrman, V, 286; Bryant, II, 182.
84. Bryant, II, 114–15.
85. Matloff, 132; Bryant, II, 150–51; Ehrman, V, 52.
86. Bryant, II, 196.
87. Kennedy, 309.
88. Matloff and Snell, 325–27.
89. Churchill, V, 131.
90. Churchill, IV, 734–35.
91. *Hansard,* Sept. 21, 1943.
92. Churchill, V, 345.
93. Churchill, V, 56–58.
94. Howard, 45.
95. Ehrman, V, 111–12.
96. Matloff, 263.
97. Howard, 56–57.
98. *Hansard,* June 8, 1943.
99. Churchill, *Onwards to Victory,* 126–27.
100. Churchill, *Onwards to Victory,* 183–86. Compare with Churchill, V, 124–25.
101. Sherwood, 749–50.
102. Churchill, V, 137–38.
103. Matloff, 427–28.
104. Matloff, 278–79.
105. Howard, 49.
106. Howard, 47; Bryant, II, 56, 59.
107. Bryant, II, 59.
108. Pogue, 284.
109. De Gaulle, II, 3–4.
110. De Gaulle, II, 268.
111. Feis, 276.
112. *Hansard,* Oct. 27, 1944.

CHAPTER 8

1. Ehrman, V, 239, 252; Matloff, 414, 420.
2. Matloff, 421.
3. Bryant, II, 172–73; Matloff, 422.
4. Bryant, II, 177; Feis, 306–7.
5. Ehrman, V, 268.
6. Matloff, 425, 470.
7. Macmillan, 419; Churchill, VI, 62–63; Matloff, 472; Ehrman, V, 361; Sherwood, 812.
8. Matloff, 474; Ehrman, V, 392–93; Colville, 94; Bryant, II, 222.
9. Churchill, VI, 100–101; Taylor, 576–77.
10. De Gaulle, II, 295.
11. Matloff, 472.
12. Bryant, II, 223.
13. De Gaulle, II, 291.
14. Roskill, *War at Sea,* III (2), 105.
15. Liddell Hart, 217.
16. Howard, 70–71.
17. Ehrman, V, 402–3; Churchill, *Dawn of Liberation,* 257.
18. Matloff, 518.
19. Matloff, 512; Taylor, 586.
20. Churchill, VI, 156–57; Feis, 371.
21. Feis, 372–73.
22. Matloff, 510.
23. Matloff, 510.
24. Ehrman, V, 515–16; Feis, 361.
25. Ehrman, V, 129; Feis, 211.

26. Ehrman, V, 123; Eden, 462.
27. Sherwood, 800; Matloff, 384.
28. Feis, 252–53.
29. Feis, 251.
30. Ismay, 399–400; Bryant, II, 461.
31. Churchill, VI, 147; Churchill, *Onwards to Victory*, 127.
32. Matloff, 513.
33. Ehrman, V, 523.
34. Woodward, 200–201; Feis, 287.
35. Feis, 288; Woodward, 285, 290–92.
36. Woodward, 300–303.
37. Woodward, 305; Ehrman, V, 374–75; Churchill, VI, 140–43; *Hansard,* Sept. 26, 1944.
38. Ehrman, V, 276.
39. *Hansard,* Oct. 5, 1944.
40. Howard, 65; Ehrman, V, 376.
41. Woodward, 306–8; Feis, 437, 448.
42. Feis, 450–51, 467; Churchill, VI, 237–38.
43. Ehrman, V, 379–81, 527.
44. Ehrman, V, 528.
45. Bryant, II, 291–92.
46. Churchill, VI, 266–67.
47. Bryant, II, 352–53.
48. Ehrman, VI, 89; Bryant, II, 392–95; Ismay, 385.
49. Bryant, II, 436–37.
50. Tedder, 458.
51. De Gaulle, II, 132.
52. Woodward, 270–72; Feis, 472.
53. De Gaulle, III, 54–57.
54. Woodward, 275–77.
55. Churchill, VI, 76, 109.
56. Woodward, 357; Churchill, VI, 288.
57. Woodward, 358.
58. Woodward, 359–60.
59. Woodward, 361–62; Macmillan, 522–25.
60. Churchill, VI, 315.
61. Feis, 542; Woodward, 363.
62. Macmillan, 146–47, 500; Churchill, VI, 292–93; Sherwood, 839.
63. *Hansard,* Jan. 18, 1945.
64. Woodward, xliv.
65. Feis, 543.
66. Feis, 336.
67. Churchill, VI, 331; Woodward, 484–85.
68. Feis, 494–95.
69. Woodward, 485–86; Feis, 515–27.
70. Woodward, 489 and note 2.
71. Woodward, 492; Feis, 532.
72. Feis, 534, 537–39.
73. Woodward, 493–94; Feis, 525.
74. Feis, 528–29; Woodward, 500–501 and note 3, 514.
75. Ehrman, VI, 111; Churchill, VI, 402.
76. Feis, 540; Churchill, VI, 351.
77. Woodward, 505.
78. Woodward, 469–70, 526; Feis, 619; Churchill, VI, 443.
79. Feis, 633.
80. Woodward, 516; Feis, 628–32; Churchill, VI, 554–55.
81. Bryant, II, 448; Ehrman, VI, 132–34.
82. Ehrman, VI, 135–37.
83. Feis, 606–7; Churchill, VI, 465.
84. Feis, 607.
85. Churchill, VI, 464.
86. Feis, 609.

87. Feis, 611, 634–35; Churchill, VI, 502–3.
88. Feis, 636; Bryant, II, 469.
89. Feis, 652.
90. Churchill, VI, 420, 647.
91. Churchill, VI, 432–33.
92. Churchill, VI, 648.
93. Ehrman, VI, 298–99, 305.
94. Churchill, VI, 639, 670.
95. Churchill, VI, 456.
96. Ehrman, VI, 239–40.
97. Ehrman, VI, 240.
98. Churchill, *Dawn of Liberation,* 254.
99. Matloff, 491.
100. Feis, 599; Woodward, 518–19, 523.
101. Quoted in Feis, 436.
102. Churchill, VI, 579.
103. Snell, 140.
104. Ehrman, VI, 150–51.
105. Feis, 468.
106. *Hansard,* Feb. 22, 1944.
107. De Gaulle, *Documents,* III, 74.
108. *Hansard,* Feb. 27, 1945.
109. Woodward, 510; Churchill, VI, 497.
110. Churchill, VI, 73.
111. *Hansard,* Aug. 16, 1945.

CHAPTER 9

1. *Hansard,* May 8, 1945.
2. Nicolson, 457–58.
3. *Hansard,* Nov. 29, 1944.
4. Churchill, *Dawn of Liberation,* 313.
5. *Hansard,* Oct. 28, 1943.
6. Churchill, *Blood, Sweat, and Tears,* 125.
7. Churchill, *Blood, Sweat, and Tears,* 350.
8. *Hansard,* Aug. 16, 1945.
9. *Hansard,* Aug. 16, 1945.
10. Churchill, *Blood, Sweat, and Tears,* 124.
11. *Hansard,* Apr. 21, 1944.
12. Churchill, *Blood, Sweat, and Tears,* 131.
13. *Hansard,* May 24, 1944.
14. Churchill, VI, 694–95.
15. *Hansard,* Oct. 31, 1944.
16. *Hansard,* Aug. 16, 1945.
17. Churchill, *End of the Beginning,* 4.
18. Churchill, *Dawn of Liberation,* 164.
19. Churchill, V, 386.
20. *Hansard,* Nov. 29, 1944.
21. Churchill, IV, 727.
22. Churchill, VI, 674–75.
23. Churchill, VI, 590.
24. Macmillan, 369.
25. Eden, 466–67.
26. Sherwood, 806.
27. Bryant, 592.
28. Ismay, 157.
29. Behrens, 440.
30. Nicolson, 131.
31. Kennedy, 356.

INDEX